Pacific Coast
FLIES & FLY FISHING

Pacific Coast
FLIES & FLY FISHING

A Comprehensive Guide to
Tying and Fishing Over 60 Patterns

Scott Sadil

STACKPOLE
BOOKS

Essex, Connecticut
Blue Ridge Summit, Pennsylvania

This one is for Joe Kelly,

who keeps me going, and then some,

in the face of oblivion.

STACKPOLE BOOKS

An imprint of Globe Pequot, the trade division of
The Rowman & Littlefield Publishing Group, Inc.
4501 Forbes Blvd., Ste. 200
Lanham, MD 20706
www.rowman.com

Distributed by NATIONAL BOOK NETWORK

British Library Cataloguing in Publication Information available

Library of Congress Cataloging-in-Publication Data
Names: Sadil, Scott, author.
Title: Pacific Coast flies & fly fishing : a comprehensive guide to tying and
fishing over 60 patterns / Scott Sadil.
Other titles: Pacific Coast flies and fly fishing
Description: Essex, Connecticut : Stackpole Books, [2023] | Includes index.
   | Summary: "Examines the fly patterns and fly-fishing adventure unique
   to these waters, with over seventy fly patterns, tying instructions, an
   image of the completed fly, and the story of each fly—its development,
   the fishing situations in which it's typically used, angling problems it
   might solve, and its historical antecedents"— Provided by publisher.
Identifiers: LCCN 2022027339 (print) | LCCN 2022027340 (ebook) | ISBN
   9780811770804 (paperback) | ISBN 9780811770811 (epub)
Subjects: LCSH: Fly fishing—Pacific Coast (U.S.)
Classification: LCC SH456 .S225 2023 (print) | LCC SH456 (ebook) | DDC
   688.7/91240979—dc23/eng/20220808
LC record available at https://lccn.loc.gov/2022027339
LC ebook record available at https://lccn.loc.gov/2022027340

♾™ The paper used in this publication meets the minimum requirements of
American National Standard for Information Sciences—Permanence of Paper
for Printed Library Materials, ANSI/NISO Z39.48-1992.

APRIL 2023

CONTENTS

INTRODUCTION

It's been almost ten years now since Richard Anderson, publisher and editorial spirit behind *California Fly Fisher*, invited me to take over the magazine's fly-tying column. For my first "At the Vise" essay, I invented a collective of fictional fly tyers who gathered regularly at a fictional venue, the Tyers' Roost. Near the entryway to this make-believe setting hung a sign that read, oddly enough, "Your fly doesn't matter."

A heretical notion to say the least—more so, perhaps, from someone assigned the task of writing about flies and fly tying. But it was hardly my own. For as long as anglers have thrown themselves at this silly game, there have been those who argued, contrary to popular belief, that success depends on *how* you fish, rather than *what* you fish with.

We all know the story, apocryphal or not, of the famous angler who said he could catch 90 percent of his trout with just two patterns, the Adams dry fly and the Gold-Ribbed Hare's Ear Nymph. "But I don't sell flies to fish," goes the punch line. Knowing anglers, usually of the gray-beard sort, nod their heads sagaciously at this salient point—while just as many or more of us will continue to fret over what to do about the other 10 percent.

My thesis, anyway, serves a writer's rhetorical cant, one that stands in opposition to the belief that success depends on choosing or discovering the Right Fly—that the difference between catching fish and not catching fish is a matter of what you tie to the business end of your line.

Off to the races: giving chase to a tundra creek Alaska king salmon hooked just above tidewater. Rainbow Camp, Bristol Bay Lodge.

Left: Joe Kelly swings his infamous Big Jelly for rainbows and native cutthroat trout on the Stehekin River below Washington State's northern Cascades.

Green Drake, *Drunella grandis*, captured and identified by Dave Hughes and Rick Hafele following years of local misinformation shared on the American Reach of the upper Columbia River, just below the Canadian border

This late in my career, nothing seems farther from the truth.

Still, you do have to knot *something* to your tippet—which may well have prompted the reader to open this book in the first place. And let me be frank: Much as I might like to come off as a keenly focused minimalist, a fellow who gets by on his wily presentation skills and a handful of patterns lined up neatly in a small box tucked into the breast pocket of his faded flannel shirt, that image, too, borders on fiction. I *like* to tie flies; I like to write about flies and the craft of constructing them. I also enjoy exploring the regional and historical development of patterns and how they've come to serve me in the fishing I do from Alaska to the tip of the Baja California peninsula. The outcome, besides this book, is that whatever species I'm fishing for, in whatever water I'm fishing, I carry far too many flies—boxes and boxes of them, a redundancy of insecurities and hope that belie my faith in the myriad other skills asked of the accomplished fly fisher.

It's a character trait I'm not proud of. Why can't I settle, if only metaphorically, on an Adams and a Gold-Ribbed Hare's Ear? If there's a good answer, I suspect it's somewhere in the pages of this book, if not also in the response so many of us share in the face of these uncertain times. I can't quite free myself from the need to carry lots of patterns, lots of flies, because, well, you just never know.

Joe Kelly floats a little dry fly through pocketwater in Herman Creek, one of several Columbia Gorge drainages recovering with vigor following the transformative Eagle Creek Fire.

PART ONE

Trout Flies

I learned to trout fish on the Deschutes. I'd been at it a while, of course, two decades at least, but until I moved to Oregon, trout fishing was a spotty affair, periodic adventures to remote waters far removed from the arid Southern California coast, the blight of suburban sprawl. Yellowstone. The High Sierra. Ruby Marsh. Tiny secret creeks in Baja's Sierra San Pedro Mártir. That sort of thing. I knew a little—and my first tentative passes along the wide, swift waters rumbling at the bottom of the rugged Deschutes canyon revealed to me just how small my game really was.

I recall drifting the first time from Mecca to Trout Creek with Dave McGregor and his father and spotting a fellow pinned to a heavy fish, rod bent double—a tense, touch-and-go moment that ended with a sparkling redside stretching the net, a trout bigger by far than any I had seen yet on the river, the tableau accompanied by the wail of the ecstatic angler.

My heart, need I say, cried *Gimme!*

And then all those painful evenings face-to-face with rising fish, none of which showed interest in my casts until, suddenly, something was tearing line from the reel, a relief more than any sense of accomplishment as it felt, each time, like little more than a chance encounter, as though I had stood there tossing a rock up in the air and, finally, a pigeon flew by and miraculously bonked its head and tumbled from the sky.

I had to get better.

Dave Hughes helped. I had never been a fan of how-to literature, preferring, instead, the cosmic humor of a John Gierach story or the rarefied airs given off by an essay by Tom McGuane. But the more I read by Hughes, the more I understood where he was coming from, both technically and geographically, his game steeped in all the classic elements of the sport yet canted, just so, toward the rough-and-tumble waters of the Pacific coast West, most specifically his own home waters, the very same Deschutes that continued to frustrate me more times than not.

Upon arrival, in 1995, of *Wet Flies*, Hughes's comprehensive celebration of "soft-hackles, winged and wingless wets, and fuzzy nymphs," I discovered a guide to what I was looking for, a style of fishing that suited my temperament, an approach to trouting that relied on presentation skills and impressionistic patterns rather than exact imitations of insects with Latin names that nobody seemed to agree on and most everyone mispronounced anyway, just as often as they stumbled on my own name.

The trout, at least, supported the thesis.

There were other mentors along the way, most notably Bruce Milhiser, a doctor from The Dalles who, along with his wife Linda, fishes the Deschutes regularly, plus remote waters throughout the rest of Oregon and its neighboring states. Bruce is what you might call a bamboo rod junkie; I can't follow the names of rod makers and descriptions of different tapers, but I saw what Bruce could do with cane—tight, pretty loops that delivered the fly at distances most of us cast beyond with our powerful, fast-action graphite.

Tailwater rainbow trout found in northern Nevada, home of the sort of trout fishing you should reveal to no one, not even your mother

Native rainbow from Nevada's Jarbidge Wilderness—a remnant population left behind when multiple dams blocked passage of anadromous fish to this and countless other historically important spawning tributaries in the Columbia River basin

Not surprisingly, Bruce is also a soft-hackle aficionado; when the trout are up and snooty, he quickly turns to sparsely dressed, nondescript smudges of imprecise lineage, subtle offerings fished on the swing or, just as often, exactly like a dry fly even though they are all but invisible once they settle into the film. The trick, says Bruce, is to drop the fly right on the nose of feeding fish. You don't need to see your fly when that hole in the water appears and a trout gulps down something right where your cast just landed.

Add that kind of ruse to your swinging wet flies and some hard-core, short-line, high-stick nymphing, and you can usually get by. If it were a beauty contest, you might not always win. But to paraphrase something Dave Hughes said somewhere, you're more than likely to find yourself with a trout dancing on the end of your line.

Big Yellow May, *Hexagenia limbata*, pays a visit to the author's boat shop after presumably escaping the feeding trout in Lost Lake, below Mount Hood, in the Oregon Cascades.

KAYLEE'S STONE

Kaylee's Stone, designed by Todd Miller

Just inside the door to the Tyers' Roost hangs a sign that grabs the attention of every fly fisher who enters: "Your fly doesn't matter."

Nobody's sure who painted this peculiar piece of art. Nor if the mayflies fluttering about the fairly sophisticated rendering of the front of a pair of Levi's were part of the original watercolor or added later. At some point it became the custom at the Roost to have first-time visitors add their names to the sign and, if so moved, embellish it with the aid of pens and pencils and fine-point Sharpies standing inside the bottom half of a dried gourd hanging from a lanyard affixed to the sign's frame.

That about covers the "Rules of the Roost."

Today the sign serves as a kind of guest book, a record of both regulars at the Roost and fly tyers who drop in now and then or once and never again. Still, there's also the sense a signature acknowledges the sign's unsettling message—and sometimes late at night, after the tying's finished and spirits descend from the shelves, someone will feel moved to address the matter directly, forgoing the usual slippery ironies and rhetorical sleights of hand, an appeal to reason which, if left unchecked, we know from experience can lead to fistfights, backbiting, or, at the very least, censure on somebody's Facebook page.

Your fly doesn't matter. Is it a joke? A sorry shot taken by someone with a sophomore's sense of humor? Or is

it a suggestion for tyers at the Roost not to take themselves too seriously—a reminder to check our egos at the door because, after all, the only thing going on here is fly tying and, say what you will, there's just as much at stake practically everywhere else we turn *besides* our neighborhood rivers and beaches and trout streams?

Or could it possibly be that the statement is essentially . . . *true*: It's *not* the fly that catches fish but, instead, the fly fisher's presentation—the stalk, the cast, the drift, the strike—these and the many other intricate and elegant and subtle skills that anglers of a certain bent will argue outweigh the importance of the fly by about a hundred to one?

Yet if that's the case, who are all these fly tyers?

And what are they doing here at the Tyers' Roost?

Immediately past the sign in the entryway of the Roost you notice the light—a big picture window filled with sky, a snowcapped mountain, the sense of a wide river below the rooftops and trees. In a corner beside the window stands the requisite woodstove; across the room a modest kitchen, the appliances there the only electrical devices in view besides lighting and lamps.

Furniture?

What furniture?

Instead we face a tidy arrangement of half sheets of plywood set atop pairs of sawhorses and surrounded by assorted straight-backed chairs, as though the seating area in a cozy hipster coffee shop—or your parents from the valley have set the stage for their monthly bridge group.

And at the tables this evening, five tyers at work at five vises, a modest crowd at the Roost, the pitch of their work an odd but not inexact reminder of the subtle movements of the nymphing trout that the flies they are tying this very moment are meant to fool.

●———————————●

Here's one way a session at the Roost can work.

This coming weekend, Mr. Kelly is scheduled to spend two days in a frothy sheer-walled river canyon where nymphing with big dark bugs—usually of the stonefly persuasion—is the go-to M.O., at least until something more obvious happens, attracting the trouts' attention and, hopefully, our own.

Everybody has a favorite stone nymph, from young Gabe's simple Woolly Bugger to Fred Trujillo's sparkplug-like rendition of the classic Kaufmann's Stone. But someone else recalls a trip to one of the all-time gnarly canyons in the wide reaches of the West, and following a couple of emails and an internet search, he's got his hands on a recipe for that famed peacock stone, the 20 Incher, a fly he remembers using to such good effect, dipping it along the edges of the brawling canyon runs, where brown trout slipped from under the shadows of rocks, each spotted body as thick as the head of a moray eel.

Only now that he thinks of it, the fly wasn't exactly the 20 Incher. Instead, the fellow he fished with had tweaked the pattern for the usual private reasons, settling on a version he now calls the Kaylee's Stone, an attractor nymph named in honor of his pretty young daughter.

So it begins.

Everyone's got opinions. Everyone's got habits, manners, ways—some proven, some far out as whalebone stays. Some changes made to a well-known pattern like the 20 Incher are simply a matter of materials at hand; more tyers than not pull from their own stashes of hooks, beads, dubbing, wing case material, materials for legs. Not that anyone won't share: At the Roost, what's mine is yours. At the same time, you bring it, you share it—at least while any bit of it lasts.

But tonight what everyone agrees on is the appeal of the long peacock herl abdomen of both the 20 Incher and Kaylee's Stone. Does anything else about these big nymphs really matter?

The discussion heats up. Peacock herl is hardly a new idea. Yet at a time in the sport when so many anglers believe their flies need to replicate what *they* see when they look at an adult insect or the nymph, there's a tendency to reject proven materials simply because the color or some other visual attribute seems wrong. In the rush to fish strict, imitative patterns, anglers often ignore or forget about the alchemy of classic patterns, the way in which traditional materials combine to create patterns that, for no clear reason, simply work. Many anglers understand and readily accept the notion of classic dry-fly attractor patterns—the Royal Coachman, the Trude, the Humpy, even the generic Adams—but they turn away when the same ideas are applied to their patterns for nymphs and emergers.

Finally, someone recalls a week thirty years ago in New Zealand, fishing upstream nymphs two at a time, flies so simple the guide had no name for them but "Copper and Peacock"—an ancient pattern that needed little tweaking to become a Leadwing Coachman, Prince Nymph, My Favorite Terrestrial, or other peacock herl flies that have been rolled out and championed across the decades, one after the other.

But what about the rest of Kaylee's Stone?

We go at it our separate ways. It's not as though anyone *disagrees* on other aspects of the fly or how it should be tied—but only, one suspects, that nobody feels strongly one way or the other once that bottle brush of herl's been wound. For the rest of it you could just say "complete the nymph"—and nine tyers out of ten would know exactly what you mean and how, more or less, to go about doing it.

Which may be what the sign in the entryway of the Tyers' Roost is really trying to say. *Your fly doesn't matter.* By the end of an hour of casual tying, we've got close to two dozen Kaylee's Stones puddled on a table, no more than two of any one of the versions quite the same. Where the hell did that *purple* peacock herl come from? And yet, if we all just closed our eyes and randomly grabbed the same number of flies we just tied, not one of us would hesitate to fish the flies we ended up with.

Your fly doesn't matter. Most of us at the Roost are pretty good at this. Most of us have a lot of experience both at a vise and on the water. Most of us are fairly clever when it comes to mimicking or tweaking somebody else's flies. Yet there comes a point in most tying careers when we recognize that, say what we might, the flies *we* tie don't give us one bit of an advantage over the flies tied by others.

Your fly doesn't matter. That's a good way to think about it—even if none of us believes it.

KAYLEE'S STONE

- **Hook:** #6-8 6X-long nymph/streamer
- **Bead:** Gold tungsten (³⁄₁₆″ or ⁵⁄₃₂″)
- **Weight:** .030 lead wire, 10-15 wraps
- **Thread:** Black, 8/0 UNI-Thread, or similar
- **Tail:** Brown goose biots
- **Rib:** Flat gold tinsel (small)
- **Underbody:** Dark green dubbing material
- **Abdomen:** Peacock herl
- **Wing case:** Turkey tail feather
- **Thorax:** Gray dubbing
- **Legs:** Black or brown rubber, two pairs

Tying Kaylee's Stone

The hardest part about tying a big nymph—or perhaps any big fly—is getting the proportions right. With all that room on the hook, you think it ought to be easy—when in fact what can happen is that you end up making a bigger or more obvious mistake instead of striking the appropriate balance for the fly's forward and aft components.

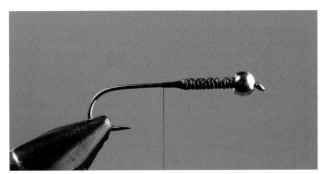

1. Slide the bead onto the hook. Clamp the hook into the vise. Wrap lead wire around the forward third of the hook and jam it into the back side of the bead. Start your thread and build a slight taper between the lead wire and the hook shank, securing the wire tight against the bead. Cover the lead wraps with thread wraps as well.

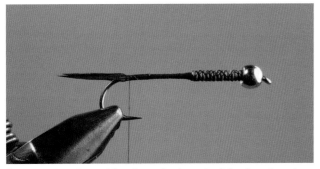

2. Take the thread back to the bend of the hook or just above the barb of the hook and tie in the pair of goose biots. Start the biots about a quarter of turn toward you on the hook shank. As you tighten your thread, they will roll up into place.

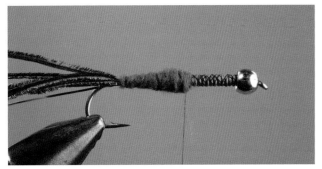

3. Secure a length of tinsel at the root of the tail. At the same point attach four to six strands of peacock herl. Add the dubbing material to the thread and build the underbody of the abdomen, creating an even taper that ends at the back of the wraps of lead wire.

4. Wind the peacock herl forward to create the abdomen. (Normally I would create a dubbing loop for a body tied of peacock herl, but I trust the ribbing to keep things from unraveling, even after a couple of encounters with toothy trout.) Don't worry if small bits of the underbody dubbing material show through. Follow with several turns of tinsel spiraled forward in evenly spaced wraps.

5. For the wing case and legs, first tie in a slip of turkey tail by the tips, dull side up. Wrap your thread back over the turkey slip to just about the midpoint of the fly. Then tie in a length of round rubber leg material. Create a beefy thorax with plenty of dubbing wound forward over the lead wraps. Stop the thorax just short of the bead.

6. Tie in a second set of legs. Add a bit more gray dubbing to your thread and use the noodle wraps to help position the forward pair of legs and fill in up to the bead. Now pull forward the turkey slip wing case and secure it directly behind the bead. Clip the excess material and finish with several wraps of thread and whip-finish directly behind the bead. Tease out some of the gray dubbing on the underside of the fly and around the legs.

BIRD'S BWO EMERGER

Steven Bird's BWO Emerger

I was surprised to learn that Steven Bird, a recent visitor to the Roost, spent his seminal years as a soft-hackle convert just up the road from me in the L.A. basin. I usually don't ask anyone's age, if only to avoid revealing mine, but it seems likely I might have passed Bird's way had I ever taken Highway 39 toward the mountains instead of heading compulsively to the beach. Then again, who's to say Bird didn't swing through In-N-Out Burger the night I lost my leather jacket—the same night Rodney McNeil disgraced our defense with nearly 300 yards rushing, a game against Baldwin Park that haunted me for the next twenty-five years.

Still, before our paths might have crossed, Bird had already found home waters far removed from my own— plus the definitive text to embrace them with the fever of young fly rodders anywhere. While I was studying, as so many others did, the photos in *Surfer* magazine, searching for clues how to imitate Corky Carroll or David Nuuhiwa, Bird—by his teens a regular on the forks of the creek-like San Gabriel River—was reading and rereading *The Art of Tying the Wet Fly & Fishing the Flymph*, the 1971 Crown edition with Pete Hidy's new chapters knotted neatly to his original collaboration

with the Brodhead's wingless wet-fly master, James Leisenring.

That book—especially the pictures of flies and the theories that supported their creation—fired young Steven Bird's imagination. Everything made sense. Everything seemed right. We all know what this is like—or at least we did, when a book or magazine could transform us with a nugget of inspired insight that helped us penetrate a level of sport previously beyond our reach. At the risk, again, of sounding like an old fart, I'll contend that nothing in digital media, linked to an infinite number of information bits, is quite like carrying around a single photo and well-scripted caption of a truly gnarly moment—an explosive fish or exquisite wave—one we return to again and again, unmolested by a battery of replies, comments, or impulse opinions clamoring for our immediate view.

The Art of Tying the Wet Fly & Fishing the Flymph grabbed Bird's attention. It has never let go. Launched into the impressionistic school of soft-hackled flies, he has spent the decades guided by the same principles of fly construction offered up in his copy of that slender book that grew smaller still as it shed both its covers and pages through one reading after another. Movement, obfuscation, the subtle color-blending produced by a weave of natural materials—this triad of soft-hackle notes has steered Bird toward a harmony of design found most often in the frank, unassuming patterns that seem descendants of an older, less complicated style of fly fishing. Armed as a teenager with his very first attempts at tying "in-the-round" nymphs and wingless wets, Bird discovered the perfect pitch for his forays up and down the hardscrabble banks of the forks of the diminutive San Gabriel, an assault on little trout, bright and feisty as June warblers, that he still feels the need to apologize for.

•———————————•

We've both come a long ways.

Bird again lives up the road from me—but it's a much longer road to much bigger water, the American Reach of the Columbia just below the Canadian border, no doubt the biggest trout stream in the West. Bird guides, writes, blogs—a subversive existence common to the sport. Most years he also overwinters in Morro Bay, where he keeps a home-built Tracy O'Brien stitch-and-glue Oregon dory stretched to eighteen feet with wheelhouse, live-bait well, and external motor mount, a boat he uses for casting flies into the Central Coast salt and all points south.

I share all of this not because any of us needs to hear about another somebody who's gone apeshit over fly fishing. Instead, I wish to clarify that despite Bird's northward migration, he remains an all but iconic native son (he actually got started fishing in Massachusetts), an angler with roots that run deeper than most through the fertile turf of California fly fishing.

So we head to the vise.

Pressed to divulge a favorite pattern, a soft hackle that might prove effective on something other than trout as big as steelhead fetched from waters broad and deep as a Swedish fjord, Bird holds up a hand. The trout in the American Reach, he says, feed on the same things trout everywhere feed on. They can be just as finicky, too, sipping Blue-Winged Olives or Little Black Caddis from back eddy foam lines as delicately as spring creek browns.

"But you're right about them being as big as steelhead," he adds.

Then let's take a look at his Blue-Winged Olives? I suggest. It's a hatch we're all familiar with—which doesn't necessarily make it any easier to match. Little flies, squeaky drifts, snooty fish often feeding selectively on a specific stage of the insect's life—all of this makes Blue-Winged Olives an opportunity that most of us have witnessed, only to see our best efforts fail, more than once in our careers.

Many more than once for some of us who have been around a while.

"First mayflies of the year," says Bird.

"Last to go," I add.

Bird ends up tying the half-dozen BWO soft hackles he uses most often: Hare's Ear. Pheasant Tail. Leisenring Black Gnat Variant. Nemes Variant. And so on. None of them is particularly unusual; all of them look right, that quiet blurring of color and line that makes soft hackles so suggestive of real life. I'm encouraged as well that he feels the need to carry the extensive lineup. Apparently I'm not the only one who's found himself pawing through his box in the heat of desperate uncertainty.

Still, is it the fly or the fly fisher? I ask, baiting Bird with the oldest question at the Roost.

Pattern? Or presentation?

Bird pauses, gathering his thoughts. He has a habit of waiting before he speaks, the writer's tendency to want to get the words right. He's also one of those lean, gray-fringed guys who's either entering or leaving middle age, it's difficult to tell which, so that he's already got the listener slightly off-balance. There is, he says finally, no be-all, end-all BWO imitation. Size and silhouette are the place to begin. But the key is . . . *simulation.*

Simulation. I like that. I like it a lot. It gets right to the heart of the soft-hackle school of fly fishing. All six of Bird's BWOs—a combination of traditional ties and his own variants and patterns—offer an impression that, animated in the hands of a skilled angler, will *simulate* the little critter on which trout feed. These are the same flies, essentially, that the good doctor, Bruce Milhiser, uses so effectively on those big, discerning trout that humble or humiliate so many of the rest of us. Bird's BWOs aren't patterns so much as they are a commitment to a style of fly fishing that says the fly's important—but I've got to fish like a wizard if I'm going to make these things work.

Still, you have to wonder: Why don't we see more soft hackles? Why don't we find soft hackles championed in the sporting press? Why don't *guides* favor soft hackles on their clients' lines? I have a range of unfounded opinions for just about everything that goes on in fly fishing—but in this case I might actually be right. Soft hackles are imprecise, unglamorous, a fuzzy splash of fur and feather completely lacking in qualities that inspire fly buyers to reach for their wallets. *That's it?* you think. *How am I supposed to believe in that?*

Believe, says Bird.

Still, there's a lot more to the answer. Bird's BWOs, like most soft hackles, don't look like much—unless you picture them alive in the water. Size, shape, color—all of that, yes, plus the magic of movement imparted through those tender hackles by the myriad manipulations of rod and line and leader, partnered with the current, to simulate the emerging Blue-Winged Olive. It's a complex equation—one founded on a host of variables that fluctuate in direct proportion to an angler's knowledge, insight, and expertise.

The good news is, the trout will tell you when you get it right.

BIRD'S BWO EMERGER

- **Hook:** #14-20 Daiichi 1150
- **Thread:** Camel or olive 8/0 UNI-Thread, or similar
- **Tail:** Bronze mallard, gadwall, or mallard flank fibers
- **Rib:** 6X Maxima Ultragreen or fine copper wire
- **Abdomen:** Mix of ⅓ dark olive, ⅓ medium brown, and ⅓ blue-gray rabbit without guard hairs
- **Thorax:** Natural dark brown hare's ear with guard hairs and pinch of abdomen dubbing
- **Wing case:** Pinch of black rabbit fur
- **Hackle:** Faintly speckled ginger or tan hen or partridge
- **Head:** Thorax dubbing in front of hackle

Tying Bird's BWO Emerger

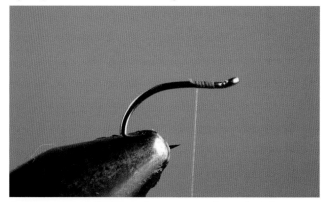

1. Secure your hook and start your thread. Soft-hackle advocates put a lot of stock in different hooks for different applications; the Daiichi 1150, or one like it, is worth tracking down. It's stout, for one, and the wide gap grabs plenty of flesh—a concern when fighting big, hard-running rainbows in big, hard-running water.

2. Prepare your hackle feather and secure it, tip pointed forward, behind the eye of the hook. Unlike some other tyers, I follow this traditional sequence for all of my soft hackles, rather than securing the hackle feather just before winding it in place.

3. Wind your thread toward the bend of the hook. Tie the tail deep in the bend, using the curve of the hook to give your fly the silhouette of a flexed, swimming Blue-Winged Olive nymph.

4. Secure a short length of Maxima Ultragreen directly in front of the root of the tail. Then wax your thread and create a dubbing noodle, using just enough premixed material to cover the thread. Bird, like other traditional soft-hackle tyers, loves to mix dubbing colors. Mixing three different rabbit fur colors seems a wee bit precious—but I'm always happy when I do it. Build the abdomen, aiming to make it as slender as possible. Rib the abdomen with three or four evenly spaced wraps of the wire or Maxima monofilament.

5. Wax your thread again. Create a slim, spiky thorax out of dark dubbing material from an ear of a hare's mask, with a trace of your abdomen dubbing material mixed in.

6. For the wing case, tie in a pinch of black rabbit fur from either a Zonker strip or the very tip of an ear of a hare's mask.

7. Hold the tip of the hackle feather and take two turns *back* to the thread and wing case. Then wind the thread *through* the hackle, locking the stem of the feather in place. Now add a tiny pinch of the thorax dubbing to your thread and make a couple of turns in front of the hackle. Whip-finish and add a drop of lacquer or head cement to the final thread wraps.

IOBO HUMPY

IOBO Humpy: It Ought to Be Outlawed, adapted from design by Jack Turner

I send an email to my friend Fran Noel, the artist and inveterate angler, asking if he might share one of his low-water steelhead patterns that he's been refining each fall since retiring from teaching—with maybe a print of the fly like the one used on the cover of an earlier book of mine.

Fran, it turns out, is whiling away the summer week on Silver Creek—*the* Silver Creek in Idaho. He'd love to help, he says, as soon as he's home—a response, sent from a smartphone, filled with the spelling errors and egregious grammar of a teenager.

Or an ex–art professor whose been at it all day on the water.

No rush, I reply. I imagine that stretch, just below the footbridge, where big rainbows smile and shake their heads as your fly drifts teasingly overhead. By the way, what are they eating?

Fran's answer arrives early the next day. Brown Drakes in the morning, mostly PMDs around noon to two. The occasional beetle and *Callibaetis*. "Fish are fussy," he adds, "but a few can be fooled."

Attached is a blurry image of what appear to be some freshly tied PMD cripples, turkey-flat wing posts and sparse parachute hackles.

"Good looking bugs," I type.

Then, as an afterthought—picturing again those snooty fish sneering below the footbridge—"You ever tried an IOBO?"

Maybe he didn't see the article. A couple years earlier, I wrote a piece about my introduction to the IOBO, a pattern passed along to me by another friend, the great and stylish trout angler and cane rod aficionado Bruce Milhiser. Bruce—along with his wife Linda—lives for opportunities to fish over big wary trout, often turning to delicate nondescript soft hackles fished on the surface exactly as if they were dry flies. Bruce slaughters tough trout. So when he mentioned he'd added a new style of fly to his already deadly lineup of soft hackles, I figured I should pay attention—even if I profess, ad nauseam, that it's *not* about the fly and that an angler like Bruce Milhiser catches more and better fish because he's a more and better fly fisher.

Still, how can *anyone* ignore a fly with a name distilled from the line *It ought to be outlawed*?

Apparently plenty did. To date, Bruce and Linda are the only two anglers I know—besides myself—who faithfully fish this funky pattern.

Which begs one very big question: What are *you* waiting for?

My phone rings just as I'm about to sit down to dinner. I consider ignoring it, only to remind myself that since my last sweetheart vanished, it rarely rings anymore.

"Fran Noel."

An odd greeting. Did I call him?

"I can talk a lot faster than I can type."

Fran, I should add, is old enough that he hasn't been using digital devices his whole life. Unlike me, however, he seems to enjoy them, perhaps because they're so different from the heavy mechanical implements he's used so long as a printmaker. I remind myself that he is also one of those ageless guys who still ends up on the awards podium after a ski race and, afterward, demonstrates a sophisticate's pride in his ability to fashion a martini.

"What's with that fly, anyway?"

"Why?" I ask. "What happened?"

"What happened is I looked it up online and tied a few—and about the third cast I started catching fish."

He likes the name nearly as much as hooking good trout all morning. He's already called his wife, knowing *she'd* get a kick out of it, too.

"Any size?"

"I had two *big* fish to my feet. Lost them both while trying to video."

"Serves you right," I say.

What's with that fly, anyway?

Many favorite patterns, both old and new, raise this question, even though by now we should all be keenly aware that there's an alchemy at work in all good flies, a mysterious balance between a host of different aspects made to look like something *we* think a fish wants to eat. Size, shape, color, movement—these are what most of us see when we gaze at a fly, imagining how it looks to the fish we hope to catch. Yet we nearly all know by now that if someone with the aid, say, of digital imagery and CAD/CAM micro-milling techniques were able to reproduce an exact replica of a *Callibaetis* spinner, it would end up catching as many trout as the imitation of a penny.

Good flies are much more than we see or know or understand. *After* they work, we have all sorts of reasons for their superior performance, and with enough experience, we can, on occasion, predict whether a new fly has a genuine chance to make its mark in the sport. But mostly we're all just guessing. Say what we might, the only proof that exists is the pudding.

There's no good reason, really, why year after year a little Gold-Ribbed Hare's Ear outfishes every nymph this side of a Copper John—another fly with nothing exceptional going for it except that it works whenever and wherever there are nymphing trout. Now that the Copper John—or some variation of it—is the world's most popular nymph, guys can write dissertations on *why* the pattern works so well, although only rarely do you hear anybody talk about how the Copper John's efficacy is linked, to a large degree, with the development of modern tight-line nymph-jigging techniques.

Dry or surface patterns pose their own mysterious appeal to feeding trout. No matter where we are in our careers, most of us are still pretty sure that an Adams, tied how we like to tie them and in the appropriate size, will take care of almost all of our needs for a mayfly dun—especially if, not only in sizes 12 to 22, we tie them in a range of colors.

But then it's not an Adams, someone will claim.

That's sort of the point. If you tie a parachute Adams, or a no-hackle Adams, or a hair-wing Adams, and you fiddle this way and that with colors, you end up covering most all your mayfly dun needs—regardless what you call your flies.

Most—but not all. Time and again, with trout rising, taking bugs on or *in* the surface, we find ourselves frustrated, unable to elicit a take. We're all pretty sure what we need now is some sort of emerger pattern, that the trout are taking something trapped, if only momentarily, by the membrane between water and air. If we've been paying attention, we know that a wide range of simple soft hackles fished right in the film can save the day—as long as we fish them with the finesse of a brain surgeon.

What you might not know—and what Fran Noel, for example, didn't know until he tried a few on Silver Creek—is that this is the time and place for the IOBO, named specifically because it works, more often than not, better than any fly ought to.

Take a look at the picture and you may ask yourself why. What's the deal? *One* feather. Crude profile. Color and texture of a dirty dishrag. It looks about as interesting as a . . . *bug*.

Don't be deceived. The IOBO, specifically the Humpy version shown and described here, doesn't work because of its looks—at least how it looks through *our* eyes when we see it out of or even on the water. Or at least I don't think that's why it works. My thesis in this drifting essay is that *we don't know*—that our reasons why our flies work, however sound, are incomplete, that for all the new ideas and new materials and new techniques and flies, very few patterns, new *or* old, have what it takes to make a genuine difference in anyone's fly box.

Still, the consensus regarding the original IOBO and its several derivatives, including the IOBO Humpy, is that nothing else in the fly tyer's vast array of materials works quite like CDC (cul de canard feathers). European tyers seem to have an especial affinity for the stuff, yet it was Jack Turner in Pennsylvania who first developed the all-CDC fly that he eventually called the IOBO because—well, you know the story. The one thing everyone should also know about CDC feathers is that they grow at the base of a duck's tail, the location of the gland that produces oil to keep the feathers dry. This oil saturates CDC feathers. More important, however, is the structure of the feathers themselves. Tiny barbs cover the plumes extending from the center quill of each feather, dramatically increasing the surface area of each plume and its capacity to trap and hold air. The result: a "hydrophobic" feather rather than a feather that absorbs water. CDC feathers offer a mechanical advantage to flies fished on or in the surface film—but, again, I hesitate to claim that this is the secret to the IOBO or IOBO Humpy.

What we do know is that the fly works—that it catches tough trout in tough situations. I suspect some anglers don't like that it takes but a couple of fish before the fly can look pretty ragged—and the nature of CDC is that you have to *dry* the fly rather than treat it with floatant should it get slimed and soaked by fish. My response to these complaints is that tough fish are generally good fish, and it takes just one to remind you why you enjoy the sport so much. Bruce Milhiser catches oodles of tough trout, and more and more, he says, the IOBO Humpy is his "fly of choice." Simple, quick, no flash, nothing fancy: "It catches trout, not fishermen," he adds.

There's a story waiting to be written about how we learn to tie flies today, especially how so many of us watch online videos to find out how to tie new patterns. The world of fly fishing really has grown small. The sad part of this phenomenon is that the constant and almost immediate cross-pollination of fly patterns and fly-tying techniques often comes at the expense of the regional breeds of patterns that were once such a quirky and vital aspect of the sport.

This is no place to talk about the threat of homogeneity in fly fishing and culture at large, other than to mention the excitement I still sometimes feel when I open the box or wallet of a traveling angler and see patterns I've never seen before—patterns that stir me at some profound liminal level, inviting me to approach challenging fish in new and unexpected ways.

That said, I can't recommend highly enough the IOBO Humpy tying video by Hans Weilenmann (http://www.youtube.com/watch?v=jbUCtVGY6Ok). There's not much to tying this homely fly, but I love listening to Weilenmann's accent, the way the *th* in his *the* and *then* and *those* can sound like a *d*, producing a tone of gravity that gives the IOBO the weight of a device developed by advocates of secret weaponry. "This silly-looking pattern," says Weilenmann, "is just utterly devastating."

IOBO HUMPY

- **Hook:** #14-20 dry fly
- **Thread:** 8/0 UNI-Thread, or similar, color to match CDC feather
- **Body/back/wing:** One CDC feather

Tying the IOBO Humpy

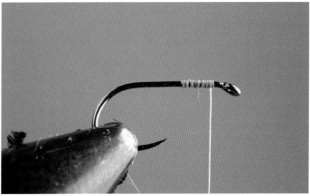

1. Secure your hook. Start your thread near the eye, wind back to the middle of the hook shank, and then return to the starting point.

2. With the tip pointing forward, secure the butt of a single CDC feather directly behind the eye of the hook. The quality of CDC feathers varies greatly, as does the length of the plumes. Don't sweat it. The trick at this stage is to cock the feather so that it ends up more perpendicular than parallel to the hook shank. This angle helps prevent the thick butt of the feather from breaking when you start winding the feather onto the hook.

3. Wrap your thread to the bend of the hook. Holding the tip of the feather in hackle pliers, begin winding the feather toward your thread. As you wind, stroke any loose fibers toward the hook bend; try to trap the fibers under the wraps of the feather itself. At the start of the hook bend, secure the feather with a couple of turns of thread.

5. Create the wing by pulling the fiber clump upward and holding it vertical with thread wraps. Once the wing is in place, simply whip-finish. That's it. Some tyers fuss about loose fibers extending from the body or butt of the fly; others trim the wing tips to a uniform length.

4. Advance the thread in an open spiral to the head of the fly. Take hold of the clump of feather fibers extending from the butt of the fly and pull them forward, creating the "Humpy" profile. Lock these fibers into place with a couple of thread wraps directly behind the eye of the hook.

MAILMAN

Mailman, adapted from design by Curtis Fry

The first time somebody gave me a fly while singing the praises of an attendant ultraviolet material, I placed the fly in a box and, like any right-thinking steelheader, forgot all about it. Later, on a day it seemed nearly every fish had left the river, if not also the entire state, I dug through my box, rediscovered the fly and, reasonable guy that I am, decided I would give it a try.

No surprise to me, the fly failed completely. Worse, on even my longest casts, the alleged UV material woven into the wing could be seen radiating rays of vibrant blue with the same Las Vegas light show intensity now popular with highway patrolmen and their strobescent steed, a kind of rock-and-roll laser fest that surely sent the very last steelhead, be it buck or hen, bolting for distant cover.

Today, with most of us a little savvier about UV materials, I'm certain it was some sort of ultraviolet *fluorescent* material that caused my steelhead fly to glow as though a dollop of radioactive waste swinging on the end of my line. Clearly, I wasn't sold, not any more than the fish were—at least not on a lazy low-water afternoon, a day designed for waking a sparse little muddler, a tactic that had failed earlier to stimulate a single rise. Having never had much faith in flash or bright colors

in the first place, I accepted this brief UV experiment as a momentary lapse in judgment, yet another instance of believing in the possibility of a miracle fly, one that might spin the odds my way.

Which is pretty much the UV buzz today. Only now we're privy to a host of new and allegedly scientific explanations for why we need UV this and UV that, a line of reasoning that makes you wonder how any of us ever caught a fish in the past.

It's hard not to sound skeptical. And lately the naysayers have posted some fairly harsh criticism, weighing in with published findings supported by genuine research, the kind of heady data that will quiet a room full of fly fishers quicker than a mention of Shakespeare. The gist of the current UV claims is that fish see a broader range of light than we do, and since insects and other prey have a number of reasons for reflecting ultraviolet light, we should incorporate fly-tying materials that do the same.

Critics, however, contend that many of the fly-tying feathers we traditionally use already have UV-reflective properties. More significantly, the scientific literature suggests that once trout get past the fingerling stage, they actually *don't* have the optical mechanisms mentioned so frequently since Reed Curry sparked interest in UV materials with publication of his book, *The New Scientific Angling.*

Who do you believe?

I must confess, I'm reluctant to probe the debate too deeply. The whole notion of "scientific angling" smacks of something contrary to my own aims as a fly fisher. If I thought that fish could be sighted, stalked, and fooled by methods gleaned from data gathered in a laboratory, I would have given up the sport long ago and retreated to the monastery with my begging bowl and deck of tarot cards. Like gardening, poetry, and love—to name but a few of my other favorites—fishing remains interesting to me this late in life because it *can't* be reduced to a science. Formulas and recipes are at best suggestions for where to begin. The adventure starts when you run out of answers.

Even the best maps end at the edge of the wilderness.

There's also the notion that we see only what we believe in the first place. Even the scientists come up against this one. If I believe stars travel through the sky, that's what I'll see as I follow the course of Orion's Belt on a sleepless night. If I believe the Buttercup Bruise is effective because the angle of its wing mimics the cant of the wings of the emergent Pale Evening Dun, I'll refuse to fish the flies I tied with wings that didn't turn out just right—and the flies I use that work will prove again how important it is to get those wings cocked precisely so.

Still, we owe a lot to those willing to take the empirical "data" that most of us gather throughout our careers and elucidate it with genuine science. If, after all these years, it turns out that peacock herl is such an effective tying material because of its UV-reflective properties, not just because it's "good shit," we might devise even more reasons to weave it into our favorite patterns.

But the question remains on the table and, for some of us, fuel for debate: Should ultraviolet properties now be considered a significant element of fly design and fly-tying materials? Do we add the UV component to the short list of other essentials—size, profile, color, movement—that we've traditionally attended to in patterns we've fished and tied in the past?

●————————●

Faced with these and other UV questions, I invited Curtis Fry to swing by and pay us a visit at the Roost. Curtis has posted a few blogs about UV materials; he belongs to that new niche of tyers who have created an online presence that allows them to tie flies for an audience and generate support from companies that sell the materials that go into their designs. This is pretty much the business model that Gary LaFontaine developed thirty years ago; the main difference is that Gary relied on books and magazines, as well as sportsmen's shows and other personal appearances, to share his innovative patterns—and, of course, he also sold the materials needed to tie the flies he invented.

The good news for modern tyers—and even old farts such as me—is that today we get to actually watch skilled tyers like Curtis Fry simply by clicking a link to a website. Like tyers from any era, Curtis owns the usual assortment of theories, speculations, and prejudices. He's also a heck of a tyer, creating lovely patterns that you're absolutely certain will catch fish, if only because they look so much better than anything you produce— and your patterns don't do so badly already, thank you. What Fry and his ilk are really demonstrating, of course, is that you too can create handsome, effective flies, and since pretty much everybody agrees that tying flies only enriches the pleasure we derive from the sport, we should be grateful somebody's taking the time to show us how it's done.

But what's his take on the UV buzz?

Is there something here we all need to know?

Thankfully, Curtis is enough of a gentleman—*and* angler—that he refuses to make any far-reaching claims. He's *interested* in this notion of ultraviolet reflectance or reflectiveness or reflectivity, whatever the case may be, and he's taken to employing UVR materials in some of his patterns. But for every time he suggests that these are concepts applicable to flies and fly fishing, he adds something more that reveals his own uncertainty about whether UVR is the game-changer others make it out to be.

The most he's willing to say is *maybe.* A strong maybe, yes, but maybe nonetheless. Or, in Fry's own words, "There's some pretty compelling evidence that it might actually make a difference."

That's a fairly soft endorsement—and this from a guy who could be motivated to pitch these products for personal gain. Like most of us, Fry knows it doesn't really matter what anybody *says* about ultraviolet reflectivity and UVR tying materials. The fish will let us know if we're on the right track.

Which is where Fry's own soft-hackled drake, the Mailman, enters the story. First off, you have to like the name. And I enjoy few things more than seeing traditional designs hold their own despite the hype and hoorah of the next best thing. Of course, I've made it no secret I'm a sucker for soft hackles.

Because so are trout.

Whether the Mailman delivers because of its UVR materials or in spite of them—or maybe even because you've actually happened upon a hatch of Green Drakes, perhaps the most intoxicating hatch of all to both trout and anglers alike—I doubt science will ever provide the definitive answer. Really: Is there any reason anybody anywhere should be getting paid to perform this kind of research? In the face of all that ails the planet and the last of the wild rivers in which trout swim?

It's only a game, friends. If you think ultraviolet is the answer, you're probably asking the wrong question.

- **Hook:** #10 wet fly
- **Thread:** Light olive 70-denier UTC Ultra Thread, or similar
- **Tail:** Wood duck Spirit River UV2 Mallard Flank
- **Body:** Pearl Mylar, coated with Clear Cure Goo Hydro
- **Rib:** Pheasant tail, dyed green
- **Thorax:** Dark olive Spirit River UV2 Seal-X
- **Hackle:** Olive Hungarian partridge

Tying the Mailman

1. Secure the hook and start your thread. Although this is Curtis Fry's pattern, it's a traditional soft hackle, so I suggest tying it the traditional way. Select a partridge feather with fibers about the length of the hook shank. Peel away the fuzz at the bottom of the feather. Now hold the hackle in line with the hook with the concave side toward you and peel away the fibers on the top half of the stem. Then tie the hackle stem to the top of the hook just behind the eye, the concave side still toward you.

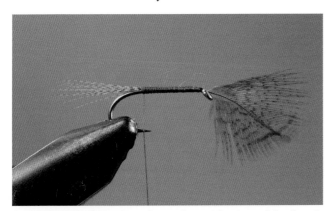

2. With your thread at about the midpoint of the hook shank, tie in eight to ten fibers from the UV-treated mallard flank. The tail should end up about the length of the hook shank. Cover the tail fibers so that your thread hangs just aft of the hook point.

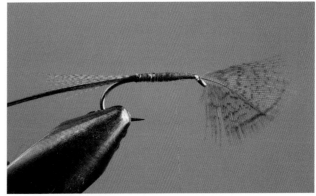

3. At the root of the tail, tie in two pheasant tail fibers. Then tie in a length of pearl Mylar. Advance the thread to the thorax area. Wind the Mylar forward and tie off at the thorax area.

4. Before ribbing the fly, coat the Mylar with Clear Cure Goo Hydro—or head cement or lacquer if that's what you have. Hold the pair of pheasant tail fibers in your hackle pliers and wind directly over the wet coat on the Mylar. By the time you finish winding the rib, the coating material will already be drying, strengthening the ribbing.

5. Load a pinch of dubbing to your thread and create a pronounced thorax. Your thread should still be aft of the hackle stem tie-in point.

6. Now for the hackle. Hold the tip of the feather with your hackle pliers and wind *back* from the hook eye. After two or three winds of hackle, take a turn of your thread and lock the hackle stem to the hook shank. Continue winding your thread forward, working it between the hackle fibers, which will prevent the feather from unraveling the first time a fish bites. Tidy up any errant hackle fibers with a judicious turn or two of your thread. Then create a slender head, whip-finish, and dress with lacquer, your favorite head cement, or UV-activated goo.

DABBLERS

Claret Dabbler, variation on Donald McLarn's original Dabbler

I shake the rain off my jacket and push through glass doors of the county expo center, uncertain what I'll find inside. Behind tables across the foyer stand a group of ticket sellers and smiling greeters, not unlike a lineup of educators ready for parent conference night. What this *isn't*, apparently, is one of your humongous sportsmen's shows—the kind that takes out full-page ads in the newspaper and makes you feel just a wee bit silly as you plunge down yet another aisle promising more fun than you can enjoy in a lifetime. Instead, once inside the exhibit hall, today's event, hosted by a "regional council of fly fishers," looks a lot like lunchtime in the cafeteria of a public elementary school.

A pretty *big* elementary school. Rows of tables as long as bowling alleys, with benches attached along both sides where the ball gutters would be, reach back to the far end of the hall. Staggered along each table, dozens of fly tyers sit working at vises—while around them drifts a crowd of onlookers, in equal measure interested, enlightened, a few perhaps perplexed.

Who are these tyers? It doesn't take long to recognize some of the old guard. There's Jim Schollmeyer, Jim Teeny, John Shewey, Brian Silvey, Dave McNeese. There's Trey Combs, for God's sake. And then there's the rest, who I wouldn't know from a lineup of backgammon stars, every one of them with a fly in a vise, or encircled with flies already tied, that seem capable of fooling any fish that's ever learned to swim.

●———————————●

In all things fly fishing, we are never far from the belief that at the heart of the matter lives the elemental quest for the Right Fly. How else explain 180 tyers, working two-and-a-half-hour shifts, displaying their talents over the course of two weekend spring, if slightly showery, days? Granted, there is a school of tyers, the sprinkling of nineteenth-century salmon fly aficionados, who appear to have transcended the sport of angling altogether, in pursuit of something akin to the ornate finery of model railroading—or shipbuilding inside of antique bottles. But for the rest of the tyers at this or any similar sort of public fly-tying exhibition, it seems unlikely that the motivation for this meticulous and often challenging work is anything but an interest in catching more fish.

Because by and large, on display today are flies you know, without question, will work—beautiful patterns tied as well as flies can possibly be tied. There are Spey flies that would move even the most pestered steelhead, Intruders to give salmon cause to pause rather than venturing farther upstream, deer hair bass poppers with variegated bodies as tight as solid cork. You see mayflies tied upside down, baitfish patterns fashioned from single feathers held upright on edge as if the combs of excited roosterfish, minnows designed to ride inverted like desert fighter pilots flying below radar.

Somebody's tying butterflies. Another guy's got a ghost shrimp bonefish pattern you could serve unnoticed scattered atop a dinner salad. Given the need, a particular hatch or unusual feeding opportunity—brown trout macking on swallowtails?—you can see yourself reaching for any one of these particular flies and thinking to yourself, "Dude, it's over."

Yet at the same time, it's hard not to wonder: *Do I really have to do* all that?

You know my answer. Which is why I'm particularly pleased when I stumble upon Jerry Criss, a regional all-star tying deceptively simple soft hackles that look like flies I'd fish *and* tie, something I just can't say is necessarily so for nine out of ten flies I've watched tied today. There's no point in revisiting, yet again, my sharp bias toward this broad genre of flies that dates back to the earliest recorded dressings and continues to intrigue and inspire anglers, especially trout anglers, today. Still, when Criss finishes the fly he was working on when I joined the small group facing his vise, he holds up a small, scruffy, nondescript bug that makes my heart tremble.

"We use this," says Criss, "for a little summer caddis that shows up out East where the sun shines."

Oh, yeah, I think. *Don't they ever.*

I'm reminded how, for a long time, I thought my attraction to soft hackles had to do with the kind of trout water I often fished. I've never visited Yorkshire, Scotland, or even Ireland, where North Country soft-hackled flies remain standard dressings for "the swift, choppy hill streams" that I nevertheless imagine, to this day, are so similar to the western waters I've fished for the past fifty years.

Across the way I spot Dave Hughes, his great shock of white hair floating amidst a cluster of fans and friends, and I remember the point in my career when I began reading his books and articles with increasing interest as I realized he was writing about the same kind of trout fishing, in the same kinds of rivers and streams, that I usually experienced. Hughes's *Wet Flies*, twenty years old and counting, remains one of the few technical fly-fishing books I've ever owned. Earlier I was glad to hear from him that he's coming out with a new edition; the elegant Schollmeyer color plates in my old copy long ago came unglued.

Meanwhile, Jerry Criss has begun fashioning something new—a different kind of soft hackle. As he ties, he explains that in this style, unlike other soft hackles, you're able to use feathers with longer fibers; only the tips are used, and they're allowed to spin around the entire fly, cloaking the fly rather than winging it. What

he ends up with looks like a cross between a flymph and a bugger—and about as pretty a lake fly as you'd ever want on the end of your line.

He calls it "a dabbler."

Dabbler?

I've heard of spiders, bloas, needle flies. Even Hughes, I don't think, has mentioned dabblers.

But, of course, we live in the modern age. Secrets can't hide. And, oddly enough—and despite its obvious old-school pedigree—the dabbler is a relatively new dressing, yet another instance of an alleged "mistake" becoming a favored pattern in its own right.

The details of the fly's origin, however, seem less important than the insights afforded by its cultural context. Although widely debated, one story has it that the first dabblers were tied for an upcoming competition on Ireland's famous Lough Melvin, home of what some consider four genetically distinct races of native brown trout, including the sonaghan, the gillaroo, and the ferrox. *Lough*, I should add, is the anglicized spelling for both the Irish and Scottish *loch*—pronounced roughly the same to an American's ear—generally water we call a lake, although it can also be used for an estuary or brackish inlet as well.

In the past twenty years, dabblers have become *the* ubiquitous Irish lough fly, perhaps not quite the claim it sounds when you consider that lough fishing is almost always done three flies at a time, your offerings spread out toward the end of an eighteen-foot leader. Dabblers are said to often be most effective when fished "in a wave"—heavy wind chop that causes your flies to bob up and down, conditions that would probably drive most American fly fishers off the water unless they happened to find themselves in a sturdy, seaworthy Irish lough boat.

How does all of this translate into our own fishing? These days, "dabbler" refers more to a style of fly than any specific dressing. Which is another reason Jerry Criss's version grabbed my attention. The very best flies, in my book, are ones that can be easily adapted to the subtle differences in hatches and types of water one finds from one river or lake or stream to the next. Unless I've been someplace before, I'm usually tying an approximation of what I suspect I might find; I'm drawn to patterns, therefore, that offer an impression of different hatches, patterns that hopefully work well enough until I home in, if necessary, on details and begin to revise.

Which is why I've already gone from the Claret Dabbler to versions in various shades of green. There's a nearby lake that opens late, a summer trout fishery that gets you out of the lowlands and is always worth swimming a fly. Eighteen-foot leaders? Three flies at a time? I don't know. But if I can get this new dabbler just right, I ought to be set—to paraphrase John Gierach—for the olive bugger hatch.

CLARET DABBLER

- **Hook:** #8-12 standard wet fly
- **Thread:** Black 8/0 UNI-Thread, or similar
- **Tail:** Golden pheasant tail breast feather, topped with bronze mallard
- **Body:** Peacock herl, dyed red
- **Body hackle:** Badger, dyed red
- **Rib:** Fine copper wire
- **Shoulder hackle:** Badger, dyed red
- **Wing:** Bronze mallard, tied "cloak" style
- **Eyes (optional):** Jungle cock

Tying the Claret Dabbler

You can watch Scotsman Davie McPhail tie a dabbler very similar to this one on YouTube (https://www.you-tube.com/watch?v=v0z5Tc0RifQ), a video in which he demonstrates the technique for tying the cloak-style wing described below.

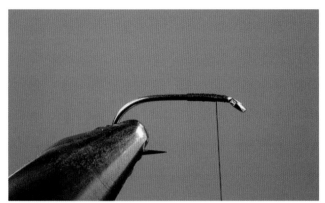

1. Secure the hook and start the thread. Cover the forward half of the shank, then return the thread to a point about $1/16$ inch back from the eye.

2. Align the tips of the wider, darker side of a bronze mallard feather by stroking the fibers perpendicular to the stem. Once the tips are aligned, remove or cut about an inch-wide section of the fibers. With the tips still aligned, roll the fibers into a loose bunch. Hold the fibers so that the tips are pointing forward of the hook eye. At a tip length approximately the length of the hook shank, take a loose wrap of thread just back from the hook eye. As you slowly tighten the thread,

allow the feather tips to spin around the hook shank. Try to end up with a fairly even distribution of fibers all around the shank. Trim the butts of the fibers and cover with thread.

3. At a point directly above the hook point, secure a half-dozen fibers from a golden pheasant breast feather. On top of the breast feather fibers, tie in a small bunch of bronze mallard feather fibers.

4. At the root of the tail, secure a short length of copper wire. Advance your thread to a point just behind the forward-facing wing. Now secure two or three strands of dyed peacock herl. Wind your thread over the strands, down to the root of the tail, and back near the wing. Wrap the peacock herl up the body with turns *toward* instead of away from yourself. Tie off the herl just back from the wing.

5. Just behind the wing, tie in the butt of an appropriately sized saddle hackle. Take a couple of turns directly behind the wing, and then palmer the hackle to the tail. Secure the hackle fiber with a turn of the copper wire. Cut off the excess hackle feather. Continue to wind the copper wire forward, ribbing the fly and protecting the peacock herl with four to six wraps of wire. Secure the copper wire with your thread and clip excess.

6. Position the cloak-style wing by pulling the fibers back over the hook shank. Aim for an even distribution around the entire fly. Hold back the fibers with tight turns of thread, winding up over the folded fiber butts where necessary.

7. If you have the patience, talent, or inclination, tie in jungle cock eyes before whip-finishing and saturating the head of the fly in lacquer or head cement. I'm never sure such eyes are worth the effort.

VANILLA BUGGER

Vanilla Bugger, adapted from design by Mark Boname

Of the countless iterations of fly fishing, none seems older and less refined than the swing of a streamer at the end of taut line. Despite all of the fanfare and high-minded chants, the swinging lure defines the essence of steelheading. We've all seen enough good work done with a Super Duper or Blue Fox Spinner to question deeply what it is we're trying to prove with even our simplest trout flies, and as soon as we fashion our first Mickey Finn or Silver Darter, we're pretty sure the destination traces a route through territory that claims allegiance with its own brand of representational democracy.

A swimming bait, the traditional streamer recalls a time when fish and forage were both infinitely more abundant and, by way of most modern anglers' logic, dumb as dodoes. You could catch them back then on doorknobs, we believe. No wonder a Hornberg worked. There's also the suspicion that the Victorian era, during which the early ethics of the sport evolved, embraced a template of low hems and high necklines, not to mention purple prose, a fanciful denial of subsurface life that fell beneath a class of angler who favored the celestial order of the sonnet over the grubby dog-eat-dog realism of a serialized Dickens novel.

Many of us, anyway, come to streamers with a good deal of skepticism. Or no confidence at all. I'm especially aware of how infrequently a streamer will enliven a challenging day of trout fishing way out here in the Far West. It happens. Of course. Yet, Kelly Galloup notwithstanding, very often knotting a streamer to your tippet feels like a desperate move, one step shy of pulling off your waders and heading for the nearest bar.

It's different elsewhere. We all hear from friends or relatives who swing or strip streamers through shadows and hidden lies, usually in places without the pitch and vigor of the typical Far West stream. Brown trout are often involved, a part of the equation that further distances the sport from many of our home waters, even though we all know that brown trout, like Iowa farm girls, are found in every corner of the world. And I suspect most of us know at least one particular streamer aficionado, often a big-fish angler, someone capable of keeping a long, lascivious fly in the water on the off chance of sticking a genuine pig, while the rest of us go about meeting our hatches as if gentlemen hoping to network our way into the good graces of firm and fortune alike.

Which is sort of the point: Unlike so much else that glitters and glows in the sport, there's something sly, even sinister, about streamer fishing. We read little about streamer fishing because, really, nobody cares to digest a piece that begins "I knock them dead with my five-inch rabbit leech and seven-six Pucker Pole." The whole impetus of streamers and streamer fishing precludes the learned nitpicking and postulates so popular among writers and experts who view fish, especially trout, as proof of their angling prowess.

Or maybe it's the *kind* of fish we hope to catch that degrades the status of streamers. Try as we might to claim the high ground, most trout fishers can't excuse any fish that feeds on trout—and should the predator in question turn out itself to be a trout, indignant anglers can consider the culprit a blight, one that deserves reprimand, if not outright eradication, by any means at hand.

An overstatement? Perhaps. Yet we need only recall the sad fate of, say, the bull trout in California and much of the Pacific Northwest to understand that when we talk about trout and trout fishing, we immediately join a much larger discussion, one that offers its own damning evidence for why so many of our favorite watersheds are in the mess they're in today.

———•———

I mention bull trout with some reluctance. Isn't fishing for them a little far-fetched? Yet if you wander from the beaten path and poke around in waters to the north, you might find yourself in bull trout country, a designation that means you may encounter and can even target these native fish—remembering, of course, that you're required to do everything in your power to return them safely to river or stream.

And bull trout, don't you know, were put on earth to eat swinging streamers.

They make brown trout look like ducks. Someone will argue that northern pike are way gnarlier—but my point here is to talk about traditional fly fishing for trout. I'm not going to include mako sharks and bluefin tuna in the discussion either. I may have to fend off critics who contend that bull trout are actually a char, not a true trout—but unless someone dares to convince members of the Theodore Gordon Flyfishers in New York that Eastern Seaboard brookies don't qualify as native trout, I think I'm safe including bull trout on our own list of natives.

Bull trout, for those who don't know, belong to that list of elite predators that can and will eat anything that shares the habitat in which they live. Think cougars, peregrine falcons, wolves. When I first heard about bull trout and realized that they feed on the very fish I was trying to catch, I immediately had to recalibrate my image of a healthy trout stream, especially one that justified any sorts of claims that labeled it *wild*.

I also decided I should make it a point to meet some of these badasses on their native turf.

Of course, I can't tell you where that might be. This is a fly-tying book, remember? I'm also quite aware that there are no secrets anymore, that these days everyone is capable of tracking down fish anywhere in the West.

But I'm not the guy who's going to make that search any easier than it already is.

What I *can* tell you about is my favorite bull trout fly, the Vanilla Bugger, the first streamer I also tie on when prospecting for any of the other trout typically found on western streams. Tied with the appropriate golden badger or cream-colored saddle hackle, feathers with those dark webby fibers that grow longer and longer toward the base of the quill, the Vanilla Bugger offers an impression of fry and fingerlings that seems as perfect in its lack of specificity as a Hare's Ear's suggestion of virtually any nymph. I fish a range of sizes, from 2s down to 12s—although the one time I really got into bull trout, not just the odd fish here and there, I would have liked to try a 6- or even 8-inch Vanilla Bugger, something on the order of what you might throw at a roosterfish in Baja.

Not that it seemed to matter. I knew I was in a bull trout drainage, but it seemed just as interesting to stir up some action on spunky rainbows with a little red Humpy. I didn't raise anything in the first lie—which seemed odd, considering the stream's usual generosity with small trout. I finally fooled a fish alongside a half-submerged tree that had taken a section of bank with it when it collapsed in high water—and as soon as the hooked trout squirted into the middle of the stream, a massive gray shape flared from the shadows of rocks and just as quickly disappeared.

Hmm.

Minutes later, the same thing happened while I played another small trout. This time I got a better look at what, apparently, was after my hooked fish. I backed out of the stream and switched flies. At the top end of the fallen tree, I made the same cast I would make if I were steelheading. The Vanilla Bugger tightened the line and began to swing over the shadowy midstream rocks. When the bull trout rose, it never had a chance: I pulled the fly right out of its mouth.

After I settled down and began letting fish eat the Vanilla Bugger, I discovered why I didn't raise anything where I started with the red Humpy. Bull trout and little rainbows don't mix. Show a bull trout a Vanilla Bugger and you'll know why.

VANILLA BUGGER

- **Hook:** #2-12 Mustad 79580Head: Black or nickel conehead (medium)
- **Weight (optional):** .010 or .020 lead wire, 20-25 wraps
- **Thread:** Black 6/0 UNI-Thread, or similar
- **Tail:** Tan marabou blood plumes with pearl Krystal Flash
- **Rib:** Copper wire (small)
- **Body:** Strands of cream and tan yarn twisted with cream Antron yarn
- **Hackle:** Golden badger or cream saddle hackle

Tying the Vanilla Bugger

The Vanilla Bugger is a trademark pattern created by Mark Boname of the North Platte River Fly Shop. I heard about the pattern from my old pal Jeff Cottrell while he was giving me some inside dope on Wyoming, specifically the Gray Reef section of the North Platte. Jeff didn't have an actual pattern; I began tying Vanilla Buggers on my own, somewhat differently, it turns out, than Boname ties his. Now, years later, you can watch Mark Boname tie a Vanilla Bugger online. The recipe and directions here are how I tie mine.

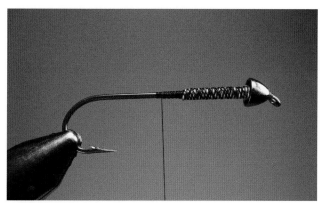

1. Since this could be your bull trout fly, pinch down the barb. Slide the conehead around the bend of the hook and up to the eye. Wrap lead around the front half of the hook and jam the coils tight against the conehead. Start your thread, build a dam at the back of the lead wraps, and spiral the thread back and forth over the lead to keep it from spinning.

2. Clip the straight aligned blood plumes from the center of a marabou feather, including the center stem. Tie in the tail directly above the flattened barb of the hook. You want the tail to be about the same length as the hook shank. Cut the forward excess tail material so that it creates a fair taper from the root of the tail up to the lead wraps.

3. Alongside the root of the tail, tie in a pair of Krystal Flash fibers. Fold the fibers and secure along the far side of tail root as well. Trim the two pairs of fibers about even with the tips of the tail.

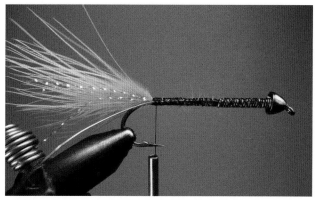

4. Tie in a short length of copper wire at the root of the tail. This will be used later to rib the fly and secure the palmered hackle.

5. For the body of the fly, Mark Boname uses Furry Foam. I've never tried it. Instead, I unravel single strands from both cream- and tan-colored yarns, and I add these to a length of cream-colored Antron yarn. Secure all three of these pieces at the root of the tail, then twist them to form a single variegated cord. Wrap the cord forward to form the body. Tie off directly behind the conehead and clip the excess.

6. For your hackle, you want a feather with a dark center. Strip the base of the stem, leaving some of the dark webby material that you would normally discard. Tie in the feather with the stripped base of the stem directly behind the conehead. Hold the tip of the feather with your hackle pliers. Make two wraps tight to the back of the conehead, then continue wrapping toward the tail, making five or six wraps with a clear space between each turn. Catch the tip of the palmered hackle with a turn in the opposite direction of the copper wire.

7. Continue to wind the copper wire forward, working it between the hackle fibers so that it crosses the hackle stem without smashing the fibers. Your bodkin or dubbing needle works well for this. Bring the copper wire up to the conehead. Tie it off with wraps of thread.

8. Cut the copper wire. Whip-finish directly behind the conehead.

FLYMPHS

Hare's Ear Flymph, Dark, adapted from traditional design shared by Dave Hughes in *Wet Flies*

We reeled in lines at dark. Joe was cold, shivering some—and when we waded the fast water between the island and the cottonwoods, I could see he was stiff and maybe even a little clumsy, hanging on to his wading staff with his legs spread like a guy riding a big wave in 1962.

But I had some Scotch in my bag back at his truck because it was March and I had figured one of us was bound to get chilled. It seemed too early in the year, anyway, to go trout fishing, at least on this stretch of the river, which had always been closed, as long as I could remember, until about the time the Salmonflies grew restless. Yet when the new regs came out, there it was: open year-round for trout all the way up to the dam.

Joe was fine, of course, by the time we climbed through the sage and crossed the railroad tracks and leaned our rods against the juniper alongside his truck. Younger by fifteen years than I am, he could pass for my son—if he didn't tower over me like an NBA power forward. The real problem turned out he had a hole in his waders—the same pair with a hole in them last time we fished.

He got into dry clothes and came around to the tailgate, rubbing his hands.

"What about next week?" he asked.

I pointed to the flask while I tugged at my waders.

"Can't. I'm going to talk to this guy about some new flies to write about."

"*New* flies?"

Joe held the flask up to the light inside the camper shell, checking what was there through the glass above the leather sleeve.

He pulled the cork.

"Or you mean just more about the same ones?"

Maybe he *was* cold.

Or maybe, more than sloshing around in a wet sock all day, Joe had seen trout enough dancing at the end of my line that he had to say *something*.

But that was only part of his point.

True, we hadn't had much of a day. The Blue-Winged Olives never came off, and the only thing we saw resembling a March Brown was in our fly boxes. Yet now and then we did spot this funky little brown stonefly, a winter stone, if you like, no bigger than a 12, maybe even a 14. Not a single rising trout, mind you—just now and again one of these little cinnamon-colored guys fluttering through the air, positioned vertically, like they are, their two pairs of wings beating furiously so that they appear to be spinning, as though a miniature seedpod from a maple tree spiraling toward the water.

Which is why I had tied on a medium-size brown flymph and kept it swinging, most of the day, through likely-looking water.

A few good trout whacked it real hard.

The one fish Joe got, he got the same way.

Soft hackles enjoy a lot of press these days. The attention is well-deserved. The flies are simple, effective, pretty—and they appeal to a school of angler who believes that suggestive flies outfish attempts at precise representation nine times out of ten, placing demands on streamcraft and presentation more than the finery tied to the end of one's line.

The flymph, on the other hand, remains the overlooked cousin of the traditional soft-hackled fly. It's probably not just the silly name; a lack of understanding about the design of the flymph might well be reason for the inferior status. "On any soft-hackle fly it is obvious," wrote soft-hackle guru Sylvester Nemes, "that the hackle is everything. It must do all the work to make the fly so successful." Yet where the soft hackle relies on the movement and coloration of feather fibers for its guile, the flymph makes use of a loosely dubbed fur body to suggest the movements and mottled play of colors so effective in flies fished across stream and down on a well-mended line.

Joe's gripe, of course, was that a fly like a flymph has been described in the literature many times before. Fair enough. Yet on the river I'm surprised how rarely I see anglers fishing subsurface patterns in any manner except dead-drifted under an indicator, which means they can't possibly be fishing a soft hackle—or at least not effectively—and thus the chance they've refined their wet-fly game to include the subtleties of the flymph seems remote at best.

Shame on them.

Still, I want to believe these are matters of ignorance—not a lack of insight. For while the traditional soft hackle has found a place in many modern fly boxes, offering important options to any trout angler intent on entering a river with something approaching a "compleat" game, the flymph, as mentioned, remains an outlier—a style of fly rarely applauded and perhaps less frequently tied as originally designed.

"The main feature of the wingless wet fly, or flymph," wrote Dave Hughes in his definitive text *Wet Flies*, "is the body." Hughes, as most readers probably know, was passing along what he learned from Pete Hidy, who in turn had fished with and chronicled the patterns and tying methods of the famed wet-fly master James Leisenring. Leisenring and Hidy coauthored *The Art of Tying the Wet Fly* in 1941. Thirty years later that same book was republished along with several chapters added by Hidy, titled *The Art of Fishing the Flymph*.

It's through Leisenring, then, that we were introduced to the notion that when it comes to subsurface flies, it's all about the body. Seventy-five years ago that meant natural furs spun onto waxed silk threads.

Today it means exactly the same thing.

Hidy showed Hughes how it's done. To create the bodies of their flies, both Leisenring and Hidy used a spinning block—a simple tool that makes it easy to spin fur onto waxed thread. The spun-fur body is then removed from the spinning block and set aside—Leisenring and Hidy attached their prespun bodies to stiff note cards—where it's ready for use when, later, you actually tie your flymph or other subsurface fly.

If you follow the instructions, what you end up with is a stash of prespun bodies that go a long way in helping you create flies with far more *life* to their bodies than anything you can fashion by starting with the typical twisted dubbing noodle. It's worth the effort. Even flies tied after creating a dubbing loop into which fur is spun have a hard time reaching the same degree of spiky sparseness—or sparse spikiness—that makes the prespun-body flymph such an effective fly.

There's more. In addition to lifelike movement and the air-trapping properties of the traditional prespun body, you also have that core of silk thread spiraled through the center of the fly. The silk thread remains visible because of its oversized gauge, especially in comparison to modern tying threads, and also because of the light touch of fur you're able to use while still attaining the spiky untidiness that gives the flymph its impressionistic suggestions of life. Few things that come out of a vise offer the effect you get from that spiral of silk thread resonating inside your dubbing fur. To my eyes this *internal* patterning suggests a later stage of an insect that so often follows the stage we're trying to replicate; it's as though you can see the makings of that imminent stage taking shape inside the other.

Do the trout see it, too? We may never know. What we can be sure of, however, is that as long as guys like Joe and me fish for them, trout will continue to eat a scruffy flymph that offers the general impression of any insect on the water. And as long as we keep making claims about new and better flies, someone's going to have more to say about an all-but-forgotten pattern that has often saved the day.

How to Make a Spinning Block

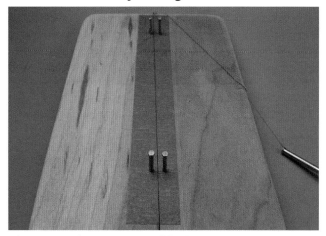

You can make a spinning block in minutes. Mine are 5½ × 3¼ × ½" scraps of hardwood. Orient the block in a portrait layout; round off the top edge. Draw a center line top to bottom. Centered at the top edge, stick a brad or small finish nail; with a razor knife cut a fine slit centered along the bottom edge. Now place a pair of brads side by side straddling the center line about an inch from the bottom edge; place another pair of brads the same distance from the top edge. Because my blocks are dark, I ran a strip of masking tape—blue on one, tan on the other—along the center line before placing my brads so that I have a better background for seeing my thread and dubbing material. Finally, using your razor knife again, cut a slit about halfway down one side of the block—right side, as you face it, for right-handers.

Using a Spinning Block

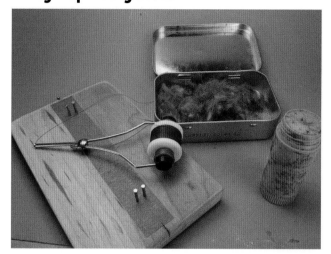

Prespun body outfit

Wax the first 5 or 6 inches of your silk thread. Hook the end in the slit at the bottom of the block. Run the thread between the two pairs of brads and pass it around the brad along the top edge of the block. Hook the thread and bobbin in the slit along the side of the block.

Dap your body material along the waxed thread between the two pairs of brads. The trick, of course, is getting just the right amount of material; plus, you'd like to have longer fibers somewhere forward of the middle, so that your body shows something of a taper when you wrap it to the hook shank. With the dubbing material sprinkled and spread evenly on top of the waxed thread, free the thread and bobbin from the side of the block. Wax this portion. Keeping the thread looped around the brad along the top of the block, lay the thread between the pairs of brads and on top of the dubbing material. Hook the thread into the slit at the bottom of the block with the end of the thread where you started.

Now it's simply a matter of getting hold of the two pieces of thread in the slit at the bottom of the block. Keep tension on both lengths of thread; spin them between your thumb and forefinger. The waxed thread will hold on to plenty of dubbing material; as the twisted thread lengths shorten, the dubbing fibers will draw together to form a spiky fur rope—just what you need for the body of a flymph.

Storing Prespun Flymph Bodies

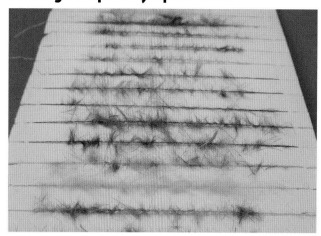

Store these prespun bodies on 7 × 4" pieces of white foam board. Cut short slits ½ inch apart aligned along both sides of the foam board. The opposing slits will hold each end of a prespun body. You can fit eighteen bodies on each piece of foam.

HARE'S EAR FLYMPH, DARK

- **Hook:** #12-16 TMC 3761 or similar 2X stout
- **Thread:** Crimson red Pearsall's Gossamer Silk or Morus Silk or similar
- **Hackle:** Dark dun hen
- **Tail:** Dark dun hackle fibers
- **Rib:** Narrow gold tinsel
- **Body:** Hare's mask

HARE'S EAR FLYMPH, PALE

- **Hook:** #12-16 TMC 3761 or similar 2X stout
- **Thread:** Yellow Pearsall's Gossamer Silk, Morus Silk, or similar
- **Hackle:** Medium dun hen
- **Tail:** Medium dun hackle fibers
- **Rib:** Narrow gold tinsel
- **Body:** Hare's mask

Tying the Hare's Ear Flymph, Pale

1. Secure your hook and start your thread. Because silk thread is so much thicker than modern threads, you need to use a judicious number of thread wraps. Select a hackle feather with fibers about twice the hook gap. Clean the webby fibers from the lower portion of the stem. With the concave side toward you, tie in the feather directly behind the eye of the hook so that the tip of the feather points forward.

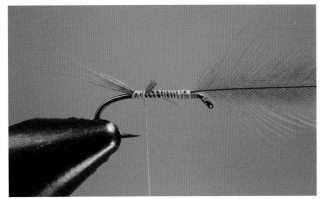

2. Wind your thread to the bend of the hook. Take six to eight fibers from one of the bigger feathers of your hackle neck. Align the tips of the fibers and tie in the tail.

3. Tie in a length of tinsel at the root of the tail. Pull aside for use later.

4. Select a prespun body from your card or foam board. Tie it in at the root of the tail so that your first body wraps are not as heavy or dense as in the middle of the body. Advance your thread to just behind the hackle tie-in point. Wind your prespun body forward. Secure behind the hackle tie-in point.

5. Spiral your tinsel in three or four evenly spaced wraps to the front of the body. As you make your wraps, try to work the tinsel *between* the spiky body fibers rather than matting them flat. Tie off the tinsel at the front of the body and clip excess.

6. Attach hackle pliers to the tip of the hackle feather. Start your first turn of hackle directly behind the eye of the hook, making sure the hackle fibers curve back toward the body. Working front to back, make two complete hackle wraps, side by side. Then make one or two more spiral wraps so that the hackle covers about the front third of the hook shank. Work your thread through the hackle wraps, making sure you don't mat down the hackle fibers. Forward of the hackle, create a tidy head, wax your thread, and whip-finish. Saturate the head with lacquer or head cement.

TOO BIG TO FAIL

Too Big to Fail, adapted from Improved Sofa Pillow and Randall Kaufmann's Stimulator

My buddy Joe Kelly, the fish biologist, likes to point out that the reason so many guys are disappointed by the Salmonfly hatch is that it really isn't a hatch at all.

"They show up thinking they're going to see bugs all over the water—the way they've seen the Mother's Day Caddis or Blue-Winged Olives coming off the river like steam."

We make our way along the railroad tracks, the river a sparkling promise unwinding through rangeland and pampered green fields. Threatening skies collide and recoil above ridgelines to the south. The sharp scent of sage clings to the breeze as though somebody's grandmother is cooking nearby.

Joe pauses to watch an angler casting at the bottom of the riprap thirty feet below the stony bed of the tracks.

"Only this time they think the bugs'll be big as hummingbirds—and that the fish'll feed like teenagers served up Hot Cheetos and Takis."

Below a bright riffle, bent like a comma before entering a long, wide run beyond, three anglers worry the water with a scramble of lazy loops.

"But then the guy shows up, the bugs are in the grass and bushes, and not a single fish is rising. He throws his fly out there and nothing happens. Barely a bug in the air—and even when he sees one on the water, it floats past undisturbed. What the—? he asks himself. Did he miss it somehow?"

Almost on top of us before I notice him, a guy hurries our way, taking the railroad ties two at a time. There's a look guys get during Salmonfly season when, by all rights, they should be crushing fish but they're not. For one, every other angler is the enemy. This deep into our own shift, I have to believe Joe and I look like a couple of lucky gamblers after a second pass, the morning after, through the all-you-can-eat buffet.

Our friendly hellos fail to check the guy's gait. Backlit by tangled gray skies, the fly hung from his rod's stripping guide offers the suggestion of a gaudy bath toy—or something you might share with a pet ocelot.

"'Course, it doesn't help," says Joe, turning back to inspect the river, "when he's fishing with one of those commercially tied abominations—the kind that looks like it's got a rubber *bleep* sticking out of its *bleep*."

Now, now, Joe.

We turn off the tracks, step through the sage, plunge toward the river. Halfway down the steepest of banks we're scrambling for purchase. Yet I can't really fault Joe for his show of attitude, a tone it's easy to adopt when, after so many tries, you find yourself whacking big trout during a Salmonfly hatch that isn't a hatch at all. A third spell of eighty-degree weather since the first of May and, just like the books predict, we're on the river the same time as the bugs. But of course it's an *emergence*, not a hatch, we're fishing, as Joe keeps reminding me—a distinction, I admit, reaching the bottom of the bank, that can make all the difference in the world.

During the next hour we're reminded why. No bugs, as Joe's said, decorate the water, but they're thick as leaves in the riverside vegetation, having emerged, as winged adults, from nymphs that crawled out of the river and up onto rocks and exposed roots and driftwood and low-hanging limbs. In a true hatch, claims Joe, adults abandon their nymphal shells while still in the water, that profound yet laborious transformation which makes them so vulnerable—and desirable—to feeding trout.

What we're doing, instead, is fishing margins of the river next to where adult Salmonflies, already hatched, now live.

What we're really doing, of course, is looking for likely places where trout have taken up sneaky lies, ready to devour clumsy Salmonflies that fall like manna from above.

I get first licks; a sidearm cast bends the leader around a sickly low-slung branch, landing the fly in trembling shade. I have to bend down and lean forward, as if looking up under a fender, to keep track of the cast as it rides in close to the bank. I can barely see the fly—until it vanishes in a swirl of flesh and color, a fabulous spark that fuses the rod to the awful weight of a truck tire swept by heavy current downstream.

"Don't even think about chasing it," says Joe, near me on a patch of bank, no bigger than a bathtub, impossible to leave by any route other than the thirty-foot climb by which we arrived.

We end up calling it the Landing Beach. The fish have congregated upstream below a tangle of brush and half-downed willows and cottonwood saplings. A single step off the bank and even Joe, a head taller than I am, would be swimming. I miss two rises the length of my leader off my rod tip. Joe steps up and immediately shows me how it's done.

"Bounced that last cast right off the tree," he says, making his stand on the Landing Beach as line melts off his whining reel.

—•———•—

All of which proves—what?

In a book dedicated to tying flies, let me remind readers that my thesis here remains unchanged: The last thing that matters is your fly. I don't want to mislead anyone. The secret to a good day of Salmonfly fishing begins with understanding the insects in question and the manner in which trout generally feed on them. Too many descriptions of Salmonfly sport make it seem that the trick is finding yourself in the right place at the right time—a suggestion I've been guilty of myself. Either that, or the claim is made that you just have to show up with the Right Fly.

So I confess to some of that going on here. Joe's derogatory remarks about commercially tied Salmonfly patterns reflect opinions not far from my own. Readers recognize, of course, I'm an old-school tyer, a traditionalist who believes in understated impressionistic patterns rather than attempts at hyperrealism, those flies that hook fly shop customers but turn out, on the water, to look as lifeless as a carefully embalmed corpse ready for viewing in a silk-lined casket.

Which is only to say I do think flies matter—but only after you get everything else right.

Yet on this occasion, stalking the edges of the river for hidden, surface-gazing trout, I felt I had a pattern that gave me a leg up on the competition, a fly that captured the essential *look* of the real bug in the bushes and, more important, the few we saw on the water. A big fly, it still sat low in the water, yet it remained in the surface film even after repeated dunkings by hoodwinked fish. The color, the outline, the *silhouette* all seemed spot on—a conviction that grew stronger each time a trout rose, out of nowhere, and ate the fly just like that.

The *right* fly? Who's to say?

But one thing's certain: It wasn't the wrong one.

TOO BIG TO FAIL

▨ **Hook:** #6 Daiichi 2340 6X-long limerick bend
▨ **Thread:** Black 8/0 UNI-Thread, or similar
▨ **Tail:** Elk mane
▨ **Body:** Orange poly yarn
▨ **Rib:** Brown hackle (undersized)
▨ **Wing:** Moose body hair
▨ **Thorax:** Peacock herl, dyed red
▨ **Hackle:** Brown

Tying the Too Big to Fail

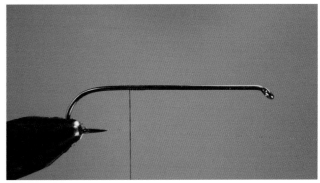

1. Secure your hook and start your thread. Rarely do I call out for a hook style that can't be found on practically every tyer's desk—but in this case I insist on the Daiichi 2340 6X-long streamer hook with the relatively narrow-gap limerick bend. (Oddly, the last pack of size 4 Daiichi 2340 hooks I bought had a classic *round* bend—and the hook shank itself was virtually the same length as the old 5X-long Mustad 79580.) The 6X-long hook shank gives you the room you need to tie a fly as big as we're after here, while at the same time positioning the business end of the hook where it does the most good without adding an anchor's worth of iron off the aft end of your floating fly.

2. Clip, clean, and stack a tuft of elk mane. Create a short flared tail just ahead of the start of the hook bend.

3. Select a hackle feather with fibers no longer than the narrow limerick-bend hook gap. At the root of the tail, tie in the hackle feather by its tip—so that when wound forward, the fibers get longer. For now, move the attached hackle feather out of your way. Secure a length of poly yarn at the same spot you attached the tip of the hackle feather. Depending on the yarn, you may find you first want to unravel a strand for creating a slender, more realistically proportioned body. Advance your thread to a point on the hook shank about one-third of the way back from the hook eye. Wind the yarn forward, creating a smooth, even body. Tie off and clip excess.

4. Palmer the body of the fly with six to eight evenly spaced winds of your hackle feather. Tie off and clip excess at the forward end of the body.

5. For the wing, clip, clean, and stack a substantial tuft of moose body hair. Moose offers the best hair I've found for creating a long wing that remains close to the body even when cinched tight to the hook shank. Position the wing so that it extends to the bend of the hook. Secure the forward portion just ahead of the body, adding more wraps of thread to keep the wing from spinning while at the same time adding to the profile of the fly's thorax.

6. Select another hackle feather, this one with slightly longer fibers than those of the feather for the palmered body hackle. At the root of the wing, tie in this new hackle feather by the lower end of its stem rather than the tip. For the thorax, tie in two lengths of dyed peacock herl just ahead of the root of the wing. Advance the thread to the hook eye. Wrap the peacock herl forward, creating a chunky thorax. Tie off and clip excess.

7. Wind the thorax hackle feather through the peacock herl with a series of closely spaced wraps. Tie off behind the hook eye and clip excess. Create a tidy head with wraps of thread. Whip-finish and saturate with lacquer or head cement.

TROUT CREEK PUPA

Trout Creek Pupa, adapted from design by Joe Kelly

Weekend temperatures promise to crack a hundred. An oil train derails, catches fire, begins belching toxic smoke that drifts overhead as a dirty plume directly downstream. The freeway clogs; winds stutter, bend east. Downtown the Friday-evening crowd doubles in size, the second half, scheduled to be elsewhere, pounding pints as hard as the first—so that come nightfall the mood inside the overfilled brewpub feels strained to the pitch of an Elena Ferrante novel.

"We still on for Trout Creek?"

Joe Kelly, the fish biologist, signals over the heads of a tangle of detoured travelers.

Trout Creek. I glance about, nod, then press a finger to my lips. This deep into it, a career that grows blurry about the edges, a name like Trout Creek still sharpens my imagination, no matter that I live within a four-hour drive of a half-dozen different creeks that go by the same name.

Doesn't everyone, in fact, have at least one Trout Creek within striking range?

Yet it's never that simple anymore. Because if you're paying attention, you can bet that the Trout Creek nearest you, no matter the allure, harbors nothing—or *almost* nothing—like the fishery for which it was named.

This isn't the place to talk about wild fish in our Pacific drainages, other than to point out that every

Trout Creek I've encountered was once, historically, part of a migratory watershed where fish moved freely, upstream and down, in response to severe fluctuations in annual in-stream conditions. Which is nothing more to say than native fish are inevitably part of intricately woven and highly dynamic populations that need every portion of a complex watershed to survive.

Trout Creeks, in fact, were often the critical reach of a watershed—and as such the most severely affected by obstacles to migration, habitat degradation, and the introduction of invasive, nonnative or locally nonindigenous species of fish.

Sadly, many a Trout Creek never had a resident trout in it, but instead was named for extraordinary populations of small, swift, brightly colored parr or smolts—sea-run cutthroat, steelhead, salmon, even bull trout. The creeks got their name because obviously these pretty "trout" weren't anything like the heavy fish encountered lower in the watershed. Nobody much cared about one Trout Creek more than the next. It was a name to identify a particular drainage or reach of water. It wasn't like you were going to go fishing there.

●━━━━━━●

We pull over at the bridge a mile upstream from where the creek spills into the river. Joe wants to show me the site of the old dam, removed nearly a decade ago, a project for which he did preliminary fieldwork while employed by the US Forest Service. Loggers had first used this narrow crease in the bedrock for constructing a small splash dam, a helpful measure for gathering innumerable logs at the bottom of the creek's 225-square-mile drainage before setting them free, all at once—often with dynamite—out of the creek, into the river, and downstream to mills below. In 1935, the Civilian Conservation Corps rebuilt the dam out of concrete—and at the same time one of the earliest fish ladders on any dam in the West.

Ironically, the new dam was built to provide power and irrigation for the Forest Service nursery that grew stock for replanting locally harvested timber. The nursery closed in the mid-1990s. Regional steelhead were listed soon afterward as an endangered species. Despite the fish ladder, both the dam and, behind it, the shallow silt-laden reservoir, subject to dangerous summer temperatures, served as radical impediments to migrating fish, especially steelhead. Given the precarious state of local steelhead populations, it didn't take long for government agencies and environmental groups to begin clamoring for the dam's removal.

Upstream of the old dam site, streambed restoration included moving thousands of cubic yards of sediment, then building and anchoring banks with logs, some from the old splash dam itself, and seeding the bare soil with native plants. Today the old reservoir bed lies beneath the shade of broad stands of alder and cottonwood saplings. Upstream from this recovering habitat, Joe and I begin looking for fish.

At first we don't find them. Above a second bridge we bushwhack our way into a series of pretty pools, wide gentle runs with deep slots tucked beneath riffles and steep cutbanks. I prance a little Humpy through one patch after another of promising shade, up tight to logjams, along root balls of toppled cedar, beneath dangling limbs of hemlock and vine maple.

"Weird," says Joe. "I don't even see any fingerlings or fry."

Which may be the most important part of this Trout Creek tale: Often we *don't* know. Like fishing itself, fish and fish habitat study remains an inexact science. What causes what? How? Why? Joe's fieldwork on Trout Creek included tagging juvenile steelhead to gather information about how they moved through the watershed before vanishing downstream. Today, a complicated grid of streambed conduit housing a system of radio telemetry records the movement of other tagged fish above and below the second bridge. Does the data show where the fish are today? Is there an app I can get for my phone?

All we know, in a healthy watershed, is that the fish are somewhere. If the watershed remains whole, all of its parts connected, that oft-overlooked component of integrity and health, finding fish becomes a big challenge—some would say *the* challenge—of the game.

"But how do you know they're there," we've all asked, "unless you hook one?"

My point—exactly.

Joe and I go searching for different habitat. We find it in the plunging bouldery pocketwater downstream from the second bridge. Pine-colored caddis dance in sunlight atop the stream. Immediately we begin plucking tiny "trout"—in truth, steelhead parr—from every nook and cranny in a tangle of braided pools as complicated as a teenager's life.

Neither of us has need to do much of this kind of thing, in these kinds of precious waters, for very long. Now we *both* know why they call it Trout Creek.

Downstream below the first bridge, in the deep pool alongside the remains of the old fish ladder, I hook and land a fish big enough that it has lost its parr marks.

Or maybe it is a trout.

"Bigger fish, bigger water," I say—knowing it's not always true.

I slide the fish back into the stream.

"What do you say we go check out the river?" says Joe, turning to head for the truck.

TROUT CREEK PUPA

- **Hook:** #6-14 TMC 2457
- **Thread:** Green Pearsall's Gossamer Silk, Morus Silk, or similar
- **Hackle:** English grouse or Hungarian partridge
- **Tag:** Green tying thread
- **Rib:** Copper wire (small)
- **Body:** Peacock herl
- **Thorax:** Dark hare's mask

Tying the Trout Creek Pupa

Joe Kelly, originally from Michigan, fishes this pattern whenever he casts a two-fly nymphing rig. Designed to approximate the Grannom, or *Brachycentrus*, caddis, the pattern fools fish year-round, not only trout but, naturally, steelhead as well. It's always interesting to me to see flies developed elsewhere move into a new regional scene. Anglers seem to forget sometimes that certain patterns work, regardless of the Trout Creek on which you use them.

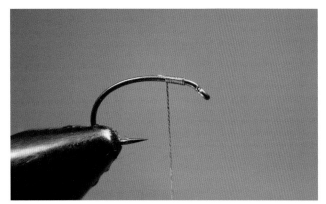

1. Secure your hook and start your thread. Because the TMC 2457 (or the lighter 2487) is such a curved hook, be ready to adjust its forward and aft pitch as you work your way through the fly.

2. Prepare your hackle feather by pointing the tip in the direction of the hook eye, concave side toward you, and stripping the fibers from the lower side. Flatten the stem of the feather and then secure it directly behind the eye of the hook with the remaining fibers aimed upward.

3. Wind your thread deep into the bend of the hook. Then start forward, creating your tag out of a double layer of thread. In front of the tag, secure a length of copper wire to be used later for the rib of the fly. Insert two or three strands of peacock herl into a dubbing loop and spin the loop tight to create a thick herl rope strengthened by the thread. After creating the herl rope, wind it forward, starting ahead of your tag. End the body about one-third the length of the hook shank back from the eye of the hook.

4. Rib the fly with four to six turns of copper wire spiraled forward and secured at the front end of the body.

5. Create another dubbing loop. Wax the thread thoroughly. Use dubbing—including guard hairs—clipped from the darkest part of a hare's mask, usually from either the ears or between the eyes. Dap the dubbing material onto the waxed thread and then spin your dubbing loop, creating a dense weave of spiky material. Wind the dubbing rope two or three wraps forward to create the thorax of the fly. Secure and clip excess.

6. Grab the tip of the hackle feather with a pair of hackle pliers. Take two, at most three, complete turns *back* from the eye of the hook to your thread. Now wind your thread forward through the wound hackle, trying to work your wraps against the stem without matting down the fibers. Create a tidy head, whip-finish, and saturate with lacquer or your favorite head cement.

GOVERNOR

Governor, designed by T. C. Hofland

The most remarkable aspect of Charles Frederick Holder's *Recreations of a Sportsman on the Pacific Coast*, a remarkable read for any angler who has ever called California home, is *not* the fabulous fishing and other outdoor sport it describes. Instead, the perceptive reader glimpses these stories through a lens that tells us as much about the present as it does about the past. The face of the state what it is today, it seems nothing short of a miracle that it could have looked so different barely a hundred years ago.

One hundred years. If you haven't been paying attention, a hundred years is but a blink of an eye; more of us than you might imagine have been fishing at least half that long in our own lives—and if you ask old-timers anywhere, they will tell you it seems like only yesterday that they began their angling journey. Yet in the relatively brief stretch of time since publication of this and Holder's other fishing and hunting books, the changes that have occurred in California and California fisheries give the reader a sense the author describes a world as far-fetched as any Pixar or Hollywood fantasy.

One hundred years. I won't dwell on Holder's tales of catching salmon in boats rowed out into Monterey Bay, when thirty- and forty- and fifty-pound white sea bass were a "nuisance" bycatch while the salmon feasted on schools of anchovies as vast as the summer fog out to sea. Nor do I need to share the details of countless billfish battles engaged in along the shores of Catalina and San Clemente Islands, nor the size and numbers of yellowtail Holder and pals like Gifford Pinchot and Stewart Edward White and the "Baron" fought on tackle as light as anyone had ever dared using on such powerful prey. All of this is telling in its own right, remarkable fisheries that today pale in comparison, if they exist at all. But for this reader, the single most significant chapter in Holder's wide-reaching record of California sportfishing is "The Trout Streams of the Missions," a survey of restful and meditative trout-fishing opportunities with the fly wherever Junipero Serra and his band of Franciscan friars built their famous missions along what ultimately became known as El Camino Real.

If you're reading this in the lower half of the state, anywhere south, say, of Santa Cruz, picture, if you can, the mission nearest you—or one you recall visiting when your friends or family from out of state arrived on vacation and asked about local culture. Or maybe you remember one of the missions from grade school, when the local district still invested in field trips so that all kids might visit historical sites in their communities. Or some of you may even be lucky enough to hold fond memories of building replicas of one of the missions yourself or with a daughter or son, constructing it out of marshmallows or sugar cubes or tongue depressors, back when you or your kids weren't tested on knowing the exact same things as children in Texas, Wisconsin, and West Virginia.

Now, whatever the particular mission you have in mind, listen closely to Holder's thesis: These mission sites were selected, he presumes, because of the beautiful trout streams that ran near them, sites blessed not only by "musical water, but the living rainbows which made joyous every pool to the lover of sport."

One hundred years. Holder's survey takes us from the mission San Diego de Alcala north to San Carlos Borromeo on the Rio Carmelo, which Holder describes as a "rare and radiant little stream, whispering of peace and contentment, and abounding in good and game trout." I can't disclose how this might fit with the feelings of local anglers about the Carmel River today. Holder goes on to describe "lovely and alluring trout streams" near Mission San Juan Capistrano (San Juan River), Mission San Luis Rey de Francia (San Luis Rey River), Mission La Purísima Concepción (Santa Ynez River), the Encino Valley's Mission San Fernando Rey de España (Los Angeles River), and Mission San Gabriel (San Gabriel River). He also mentions the trout (and, in some cases, *steelhead*) streams near San Antonio de Padua, San Antonia de Pala, Santa Clara, San Buenaventura, and San José de Guadalupe—trout streams sprinkled along the first great thoroughfare up the California coast, still resplendent with native and, in many cases, sea-run fish.

One hundred years. Don't get me wrong: My point here is not to bemoan these extraordinary transformations in California fisheries over such a brief period of time. I get it. Things change. Life—in one form or another—goes on. Every angling generation, I suspect, feels a certain envy toward the opportunities enjoyed by those who came before them. But griping or whining about it does exactly nothing to help you stick the next fish to your fly. My own thesis, instead, is that Holder's mission trout streams can be viewed as a blessing, a bright beacon above a rugged shore, a signal by which to navigate challenging waters ahead. Trout streams and native fisheries today are a choice, no longer a given scattered throughout the environment as they were just one hundred years ago along this rare and remarkable coast. Look around you; *we* decide.

Forty-five years ago a single paved road down Baja made it possible for goofy surfers with primitive gear to whack incredible numbers of fish where, in many cases, nobody else had cast flies before. Now, as another new road under construction follows that precious Pacific coast, a road from the oasis at San Ignacio down through once-remote surf breaks at Punta Pequeña and Scorpion Bay, I try to imagine what another future student of the sport might think should he or she stumble upon an obscure book—*Angling Baja*, say—about that *lovely and alluring* and epic coast.

Will it be, "*I can hardly believe it was like that back then*"?

Or, "*Man, I tell you, we sure are lucky to fish here.*"
Forty-five years.
We're almost halfway there.

———•———•———

All of which brings me to the Governor—a fly nearly *two* hundred years old, and one of the few named throughout the astonishing trout-fishing stories included in Holder's book. In fact, it's not Holder who mentions the fly; instead, it appears in a letter to Holder written by California state senator Fred Stratton, from Oakland, who describes the fishing he's enjoyed over the years on southern Oregon's Williamson River, "the greatest trout stream," claims Stratton, "in the world." Stratton includes a list of several other common flies of the era—Silver Doctor, Royal Coachman, March Brown—but the Governor, writes Stratton, "is, to my mind, the best."

Ignoring Stratton's apparent politician's penchant for hyperbole, we can at least allow that the Governor was his *favorite* fly. And it's easy to see why; if you take anything away from this book, it will include how much I value the fish-fooling capacities of peacock herl. Of course, I'm not alone: The list of peacock herl–bodied flies is long, including such traditional favorites as the Leadwing Coachman, Hardy's Favorite, Light Caddis, and the Alder Fly. My own herl-bodied MFT, My Favorite Terrestrial, changed my whole approach to big trout; where I once believed I needed to go smaller and finer in order to fool a stream's best fish, I suddenly found myself using a size 10 dry fly to move big fish when nothing else was on the water. If you don't already have a row or two of peacock herl–bodied flies in your day-to-day trout box, you're missing a reliable producer in your lineup.

The Governor would be a good place to start. First described by T. C. Hofland in *The British Angler's Manual* (1839) and appearing again in Mary Orvis Marbury's *Favorite Flies and Their Histories* (1892), it's a simple tie, with all the elements of the traditional winged wet fly, patterns that go in and out of fashion but, like mid-action rods and long-tapered lines, never disappear. I don't need to explain why. I will say I like the implications of a particular description from New Zealand for the use of the red-tipped Governor, a popular variant of the original: "A great fly as a general beetle-like terrestrial or emerging caddis or something else appealing to trout."

You can go a long way in the game tying flies to your tippet that match *something else appealing to trout*. I wouldn't anticipate catching "in one afternoon forty-two trout, the smallest being one and one half pounds, and the largest eleven pounds," as Senator Stratton recalls from an early visit to the Williamson, just as I wouldn't expect my Governor to fool a brace of feisty rainbows at the confluence of Trabuco and San Juan Creeks, right below the interstate, after surfing the morning glass at Doheny. The Governor can't turn back the hands of time. But it might help you keep in mind what rests unchanged at the heart of the sport—casting flies for pretty fish that live and breed in pretty places.

Those of us with less-than-literal minds might also note the metaphorical cue in a fly called the Governor—especially if we're asked to consider the changes, over the past hundred years, in the fisheries in our own neighborhoods. The Governor is as effective for trout today as it was when first created nearly two hundred years ago—and it may be just what the engines of change need right now if we hope there's reason at all, in another hundred years, to tie this pretty fly.

GOVERNOR

- **Hook:** #12-16 1X fine or 2X stout
- **Thread:** Primrose yellow Pearsall's Gossamer Silk, Morus Silk, or similar
- **Tag:** Flat gold tinsel
- **Butt:** Yellow tying silk
- **Body:** Peacock herl
- **Hackle:** Brown hen hackle
- **Wing:** Pheasant wing quill

Tying the Governor

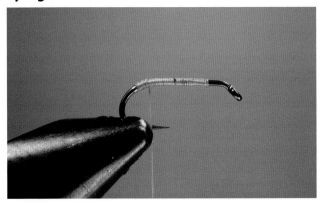

1. Secure the hook and start the thread. When working with gossamer silk, you should try to use the minimum number of thread wraps needed to hold materials to the hook. Attach a short length of gold tinsel and wind the thread down into the bend of the hook. Make the tag of the fly out of a single wrap of tinsel. Secure it with a turn of thread and clip the excess. Advance the thread two or three turns to create the yellow butt of the fly forward the gold tag.

2. Create a dubbing loop. Wax both legs of the loop. Insert a single strand of peacock herl and spin your loop until you have a tight, dense rope of herl spun into the twisted thread.

3. Wind the rope of thread forward, one wrap in front of the other, without overlapping. Don't worry if the thread color shows through the herl. That's part of the effect you're after. Stop the body far short of the eye of the hook, leaving yourself room for both the hackle and wing.

4. From a soft-hackle hen neck, select a feather with fibers slightly longer than the width of the hook gap. Strip the webby fibers from the base of the stem. Secure the feather by the stem so that when you wind it forward, the fibers slant back. Make just two wraps with the hackle feather; tie off with a couple of turns of thread. Clip the excess hackle feather and stem.

5. For the wing of the fly, start with a pair of matched primary feathers from the left and right wings of a pheasant. From the same part of each feather, clip a ⅛- to ³⁄₁₆-inch section. Position the sections so that the concave sides are toward each other, with the tips pointing toward the aft end of the fly. Whether the tips point up or down is your choice and often depends on the shape of the feather tips themselves. The tips should extend almost to the bend of the hook. While holding the wing along the top of the fly, take a loose turn of thread and don't tighten it until you pull directly upward. Repeat two more times, winding forward the first wrap and remembering the loose wrap and upward pull so that the wing rides directly on top of the hook shank. Clip the butts of the wing and create a tidy head. With silk, you should wax the thread before your whip-finish. Saturate the head with lacquer or head cement.

PARALOOP CRANE

Paraloop Crane, adapted from design by Bruce Milhiser

My buddy Jeff Cottrell first told me about crane flies. I was headed to an out-of-state tailwater, a canyon creased by oversized pocketwater churning between boulder-strewn banks and glaring granite walls—the kind of spot you used to hear rumors about but it still took a decade of searching and offhanded questions before somebody finally gave up the goods. Browns. Big ones. Jeff opened a fly box, an old Scientific Angler the color of a Stanley thermos, and he plucked out a dozen flies, his hand hovering over each one, that brief despair we all suffer when our excitement to share comes up, momentarily, against a reluctance to let go.

"Fish these when the water comes up."

With what—a handline? The flies were big, an inch, an inch and a half long, as chunky as a toddler's fingers. And ugly. Today, when I recall those first crane fly larvae Jeff gave me, I keep picturing a pukey olive-green shag carpet that lined the inside of a van I once found myself in while headed to North County looking for surf. Speakers, discharging Led Zeppelin, were covered in the same. Jeff also shared some realistic segmented crane fly larvae—but it was those ugliest ones, fashioned from carpet rags, that he liked best.

"You'll either get thundershowers—or they'll let water out through the dam. Or both. Either way, the river rises, these guys get washed into the current."

Which is pretty much what happened. Three afternoons in a row, thunderheads boiled above the rim of the canyon, eventually blotting out the impossibly blue skies. Hail the size of pea gravel rattled off the rocks; the surface of the river turned to froth. The water rose—and it kept rising, to the point that I would have begun to despair had I not done as I was told and fished Jeff's shaggiest crane fly larva.

The trout, as McGuane once wrote, "liked it real well."

⚫——————⚫

Most crane flies aren't true aquatic insects. The grub-like larvae live in damp soil, burrowing into silt or sand along the margins of rivers and streams, on some occasions into the actual streambed or riverbed itself. Increased flows strong enough to disturb the streambed, however, can dislodge the larvae and wash them downstream. Never available in the numbers of the trout angler's trinity—mayflies, stoneflies, and caddisflies—the chunky crane fly larva still offers a generous wad of protein, a package that big trout rarely refuse.

Which is all well and good, a perfectly satisfying way to lift tight to a bunch of belligerent big-water browns—some of which, once stuck, glanced angrily about in the granite-lined shallows before plunging into heavy current, never to be seen again despite my every effort to put the screws to them or skip like Bambi across the tops of the Volkswagen-size boulders. Still, I don't suspect I would have followed the crane fly thread any further had I not been reintroduced to them, transmogrified as adults, by another good friend on a river I call the Wolf.

Bruce Milhiser and his wife Linda fish the Wolf more than anyone else I know. It's a finicky tailwater, a low-gradient desert stream that meanders along the scree of rust-colored cliffs, its slow, wide pools laced with big brown trout educated by angling pressure. Besides the size of the fish, the best thing about the Wolf is that the trout seem to always be looking up. Even between hatches, the surface of the lazy current is rarely without spent bugs of some sort lying atop or trapped in the film. Still, you had better be ready to fish dainty flies on the Wolf—and not afraid to lengthen and reduce the size of your tippet. Yet given that, and the ability to stalk fish and cast with the accuracy of a military drone, there are few days you can't get your share of trout, with every heart-stopping grab happening right before your eyes.

I've said this before, but nobody does this kind of fishing better than Bruce Milhiser. And nobody I know works harder to find it. Yet despite his talents, his cane rods, and his passion for fooling good trout on surface flies, there is nothing about Bruce that suggests he feels his style of fishing is better than someone else's—nor that he's adverse, on any grounds, to do whatever it takes to catch fish.

Which is how he became such a fan of the adult crane fly. It didn't happen overnight. The details, from the beginning, are now somewhat muddy. Can any of us really remember what it was like the first time? In fact, when I mentioned to Jeff Cottrell that I intended to write about Bruce's adult crane fly, Jeff let on that *he* was the one who told Bruce about crane flies in the first place.

Maybe we're all just getting old. Still, the way Bruce tells it, he was fussing with one of your typical Wolf River browns, a fish on a far bank, tight to windswept willows, that was feeding on what, he couldn't figure out. He tried this, he tried that, each time casting to the fish until it disappeared—only to show itself later, right where Bruce had shown it his last cast. This went on a while; Bruce is the kind of angler who doesn't give up on a fish if it keeps coming back for more. He's patient. If he gives a fish a good look at his fly and the fish doesn't eat, he picks up and tries something else, rather than flogging the water until the fish vanishes for good.

But we all have our limits—and rivers like the Wolf can push you to them as often as not. Bruce was about there, he says, the heat and swirling breeze conspiring against him—when he knotted on the adult crane fly pattern he got either from Jeff Cottrell or, more likely, from inspiration he took from a fly on the Hans Wielenmann Flytier's Page, the Paraloop Daddy posted by Rune André Stokkebekk of Norway.

Now, where the crane fly larva is an ugly, even repulsive grub, a plump package of squishy flesh, the adult crane fly offers up a thin, delicate, ephemeral outline—as light of limb as seeding grass. This difference between larvae and adults holds true for most insects—although I have to say, I think mayfly nymphs, regardless of the species, are about the cutest little critters you'll find anywhere outdoors. What gives adult crane flies their character, however, is that despite their fine lines and lacy texture, they flutter about with little suggestion of grace, like grade-schoolers learning to play lacrosse.

The artificial is a crude cast, too. Yet with his cane rods and gentle left-handed stroke, Bruce delivers flies with the accuracy of a dart thrower. So when he says he didn't make a very good cast with his awkward adult crane fly, I sort of wonder if he's embellishing his story for dramatic effect. His point, of course, is that he had already landed flies *exactly* where they needed to land, gotten casts to drift perfectly over the feeding trout's snout—but this time, when his cast "wasn't very good," the trout swam right over to his big crane fly and ate it.

Really?

"Just like that," Bruce says.

⬤————————⬤

There's a certain chutzpah or braggadocio that comes with tying on a dry fly the size of the Paraloop Crane. Your fly announces, "I am here. Come eat me." Finally, we can stop thinking about all of this as a game of subtle finesse. Throw 'em the chalupa and watch a big dog *boil*.

Last summer while I was fishing with Steven Bird, we matched a mayfly hatch with hair-wing dries that were 2¼ inch long and 1¼ inch tall. I measured. These are opportunities in a fly-fishing career that should not be ignored. Flies this size, and trout big enough and willing to eat them, remind us that the sport is never just about catching fish. What it *is* about, and whether any of it matters, remains anybody's guess. But when a big dry fly like the Paraloop Crane goes on the end of your leader and your cast delivers it to the mark, *all* of the questions, for a moment, can wait.

Bruce Milhiser lists a half-dozen different rivers, and even some lakes, where he's had success with his adult crane fly pattern. He fishes it in frog water and eddies and deep, heavy currents. He uses it as a searching pattern when "nothing is happening" and for sighted fish, whether they are rising or not. Upstream, downstream, stillwater—he'll give the crane fly a try whatever the situation dictates, whatever "bad position," he claims, he's gotten himself into.

I haven't seen many of those. Whenever I fish with Bruce on the Wolf, he seems either to be stalking fish, sending tight crisp loops their way, or, as often as not, leaning into the thrill of a deep bend in the cork of a cane rod.

Unlike some of us, Bruce also goes quietly about the business of landing a good fish. But there's something else I've noticed, too: When he gets one on the crane fly, he always lets you know.

PARALOOP CRANE

- **Hook:** #12-14 standard dry fly
- **Thread:** Camel 8/0 UNI-Thread or similar
- **Abdomen:** Foam cylinder (1/16-3/32"), tan or darkened to brown with permanent marker
- **Legs:** Moose body hair, knotted
- **Wings:** Natural badger hackle tips
- **Hackle:** Natural badger

Tying the Paraloop Crane

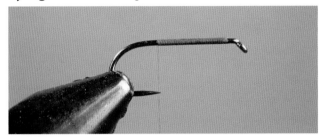

1. Secure your hook and start your thread. Cover the hook shank with thread wraps.

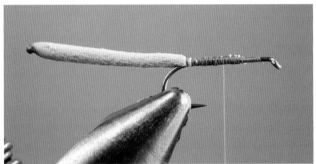

2. At the middle of the hook shank, tie in a piece of foam cylinder about one and a half to two times the length of the hook. Use loose wraps toward the back of the hook; these wraps hold the foam in line with the hook shank rather than cocked skyward. With a match or lighter, carefully heat the butt of the abdomen to give it a slight taper. If you want to darken the abdomen (I'm not sure it matters), use a brown Sharpie or similar permanent marker.

3. Prepare all of the legs. Clip a tuft of hair from a patch of moose body fur. Separate the individual hairs; in each one tie an overhand knot about 3/4 inch from the tip. Tie in the first pair of legs, one on each side, just in front of the abdomen.

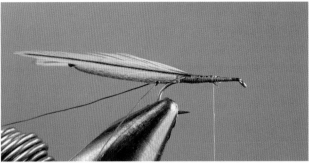

4. For the wings, clip tips from longer saddle hackles so that the wings end up slightly longer than the abdomen. Tie in the wings just ahead of the first pair of legs. Position the wings so that they lie flat at roughly a 20- to 30-degree angle from the midline of the fly. I find it easiest to keep the wings flat if I don't strip the quills from the stem at the tie-in point.

5. Tie in a hackle feather with the base of its stripped stem just ahead of the root of the wings. With the feather held out of the way, tie in two more pairs of legs, leaving space between each pair. Position the legs so that they extend at a sharp angle away from the midline of the fly.

6. Now wind your hackle feather forward. Use your bodkin needle to slip the hackle wraps between the separate pairs of legs. The hackle wraps can also help you reposition any leg that, despite all your efforts, looks like what McGuane once described as the hind leg of a dog next to a fire hydrant. Secure the hackle feather just aft of the hook eye. Whip-finish and saturate the thread with lacquer or head cement. Bruce suggests clipping the bottom hackles so that the fly rests lower in the water. Sometimes I do, sometimes I don't.

PEACOCK CADDIS

Peacock Caddis,adapted from design by Al Troth

This isn't a hunting story. But there's a rifle-shot animal involved, a cow elk felled through a dense tangle of windblown trees, and if that kind of thing bothers you, or pisses you off, you might want to skip to the pattern and tying instructions, glance at the photos, and leave it at that.

I won't hold it against anyone. Yet there's a long history in fly fishing of flies tied from hair and feathers of wild game, and you don't have to go very deep into the psyche of many anglers to find a passion for stalking and ambushing creatures of the wind and water and woods—a passion that nudges up tight to lust, though an easier name for it might be, simply, *fun*.

Some of our time-honored patterns, of course, come directly from remains of the kill. Elk Hair Caddis, Pheasant Tail Nymph, Gold-Ribbed Hare's Ear, nearly all of the traditional soft hackles—these and countless other flies owe their existence to anglers familiar with the taint and texture and fetching beauty of the palette of materials unique to animals brought down by bullet and arrow and shell. There's good reason we don't fish with a Cow's Ear Caddis or Pig Tail Pupa. Traditionally, fly fishers and hunters were often one and the same, and even when not, they usually belonged—at least until recently—to a community of outdoorsmen that extended beyond other anglers.

All of which brings me to the moment relevant to our subject at hand. No, not the moment I looked past the shoulder of my pal and fish biologist Joe Kelly, holding a gun, and through a long tunnel in the chaos of crisscrossed trees spotted a cow elk looking directly our way and thought, *He's got a shot.* Nor was it the instant afterward, just as I completed that thought, when the roar of the rifle filled the woods and the cow elk crumbled to the forest floor. And it wasn't when we gutted her there where she fell, nor during the struggle to drag her out of the woods and load her into the pickup and then drive her to another buddy's place where we could finally hang her and skin her.

Instead, the moment we care about here came the next morning, when Joe and I drove back to the site of the kill, prepared to discard the hide where we had left the viscera, already visited by creatures of the woods happy to discover such unexpected bounty.

An elk hide is a formidable charge. Still wet with skin and fat, it took both Joe and I to lift it from the tailgate and carry it to the edge of the wooded draw. Among the complex emotions I'd been feeling since this stately wild animal dropped to the ground, and especially while we peeled off her heavy hide, transforming a once-live creature into something suddenly resembling simply meat, I was now struck by a sense of waste, a twinge of guilt for discarding what was obviously a wealth of raw material for—what?

Joe suggested I take a knife and slice off a couple of hunks of hide.

●———————●

If you've ever tried to treat and preserve potential fly-tying materials brought home from the field, you're probably familiar with any number of challenges—or disasters. I live alone; that helps. The first thing you're sure of is you have to get things dry; coarse salt seems like the obvious answer. Still, when I found a half-dozen ticks sprinkled about the garage floor, I knew I needed to be careful.

Then, because it was near the end of hunting season, the latter weeks of fall, I set two dinner plates filled with elk hair patches, of various hues, underneath the woodstove to completely dry and even season for a while.

My oldest son, visiting for Thanksgiving, found what we hoped was the last tick.

For Christmas gifts I was able to mail off an assortment of pretty patches of elk hair to unsuspecting but immediately appreciative friends. (They're all married; I didn't mention any ticks.) I tied up a handful of Waking Muddlers with hair ranging from blond to nearly black, all taken from my small swatch of the original hide—but by this late in the season river temperatures had dropped, and I couldn't really expect to move steelhead to the surface, no matter how much I tried.

But as spring approached, and my thoughts turned to trout, I looked again at my gallon baggie labeled "Joe's Elk 11/XX." The obvious place to start was Al Troth's standard Elk Hair Caddis, a pattern for which I nearly always substitute deer hair for the wing, because the elk hair I generally encounter proves too stiff and springy for my tastes and tying skills. Of course, the deer hair wing suggests I'm really tying something more along the lines of the old Bucktail Caddis—but without the tail. Should we even care about these delineations, these names? If you're anything like me, you tie your caddis to work on the waters where you fish them, tweaking them this way and that to match the size and color of the caddisflies you see, as well as in accordance with the speed and temper of the water where you find fish feeding on these ubiquitous summer bugs.

For me that often means the sort of slick, greasy water that good trout move into when feeding in the low light at the end of a hot summer day. The last thing I want in these challenging conditions, when fish push through the surface with the deliberate resolve of turkey vultures picking over a roadkill, is a fly that rides high atop the water—an attitude that suggests an insect about to take flight. In these smooth water situations, I want the body of my caddis pattern to sink into the surface film, a position from which a trout knows a bug can't suddenly lift off and vanish.

As usual, I'm making this all up. To claim a trout *knows* anything is as silly as believing that something I

say or do might jinx the weather or the outcome of the Dodgers' next home game. All I'm really sure of is that a caddis riding low in the water generates more rises for me than the common type with hackle palmered through the length of the body. Needless to say, my sparsely dressed, low-riding caddis are the patterns I tie most often to my tippet, which admittedly invalidates completely any comparisons to other patterns I might try.

So it goes. We catch fish with the flies we fish with. Which is why I hesitate to claim that the Peacock Caddis, tied with elk hair fresh from the hide, can solve all of your problems the next time you find yourself during the evening caddis hour faced with a bunch of good trout nosing through the surface but refusing your perfectly cast flies. I know better; in fly fishing, as in life, there are too many good ways to fail.

●———————●

The Peacock Caddis is not a close imitation of any particular caddisfly. I use it the same way I would use an Adams, except that in the case of the Peacock Caddis, I'm fishing waters rich in caddisflies rather than mayflies. It falls close to the category of flies that Dave Hughes, in his monumental book *Trout Flies*, calls a "searching dry fly"—a nonspecific attractor pattern that floats well, that the angler can see, and that looks *buggy* "in the eyes of the trout."

The fly is only *close* to being a searching dry fly because it's really too specific to be a general, across-the-board attractor pattern. Also, unless you wind a hackle through the herl, palmering the body, the Peacock Caddis won't float as well as Hughes states is necessary for the most successful searching dry. And though the blond wing is easy for the angler to see, the fly sits low enough in the water that it can still test your eyesight as soon as you start to lengthen your casts or the water has much in the way of current or texture or grain.

Probably better to call it a "searching *caddis* fly": Given you've got the right size, you can fish the Peacock Caddis during any caddis hatch and feel like you're in the game. Yet short of an organizing principle for a book—or your fly boxes—naming the *type* of fly you're using seems a little like an exercise in semantics, with not a whole lot to do with fishing.

Still, rather than a searching dry fly, I could call the Peacock Caddis a *hunting* fly—but you might get the wrong idea.

PEACOCK CADDIS

- **Hook:** #12-18 standard dry fly
- **Thread:** Black 8/0 UNI-Thread, or similar
- **Body:** Peacock herl twisted inside a dubbing loop
- **Rib:** Fine copper wire
- **Wing:** Blond (unbleached) elk hair
- **Hackle:** Brown or furnace

Tying the Peacock Caddis

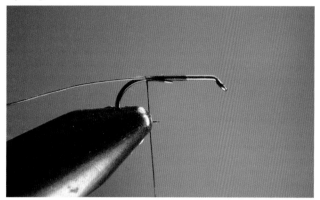

1. Secure the hook and start the thread. Wind the thread back toward the bend of the hook. As you approach the bend, tie in a length of fine copper wire. Continue winding the thread to the start of the hook bend. Position the copper wire out of your way.

2. With the thread still at the hook bend, create a dubbing loop. With the loop held in place by the weight of a dubbing tool, advance the thread to the tie-in point for the wing, approximately one-third of the hook shank back from the eye of the hook. Wax the legs of the dubbing loop and between them slip the ends of two or three strands of herl.

3. Spin your loop, using your other hand to help the thread catch the herl and form a braid-like rope.

4. Wind the braid of herl to the wing tie-in point, catch it under a couple of turns of thread, and clip the excess. As a side note, I feel obliged to encourage, again, the use of a dubbing loop—and some sort of dubbing tool, if only your hackle pliers—for practically any dubbing material, but especially for peacock herl. The fragile herl withstands poorly any touch of a trout's teeth. But spun into a tight rope of thread, and then, in this case, secured further by wraps of copper wire, a peacock herl body becomes virtually indestructible, exactly what you want for a fly destined to get fished in failing light.

5. Advance the copper wire with three or four evenly spaced wraps. Secure the wire ahead of the body with your thread and clip the excess.

6. Clip a tuft of material from your patch of elk hair. Comb out and thoroughly remove any underfur and short fibers. (This is a crucial step; you don't want to tie in any excess material.) Place the hair into a stacker and tap it firmly a few times against your bench top or other hard surface. Carefully remove the hair from the stacker. Hold it by the butts and measure so that the wing reaches the bend of the hook. Position the wing with several light turns of thread, then secure it with increased tension on the thread. Make sure the wing is secure. There's nothing worse than a wing that spins around the hook when you go to wind your hackle.

7. Clip the butts of the wing hair. Unlike with the Troth-style caddis, your aim here is to get several turns of hackle in front of the wing, *plus* finish the fly with a conventional whip-finish directly behind the hook eye. It always feels a little tight. Strip the base of an appropriately sized hackle feather, the fibers about one and a half times the hook gap. Secure the hackle stem directly on top of the thread wraps at the front of the wing. Advance the thread to the hook eye. Take three or four turns of hackle, one tight against the next, until you reach the hook eye. Tie off the excess hackle with a few wraps of thread. Clip the excess hackle.

8. Whip-finish and saturate the wraps with lacquer or head cement.

THE THREE PHASES OF E

Not A Klinkhamer Cripple, adapted from design by Hans van Klinken

The docket is full. And frankly, a little daunting. Who knows, in the middle of winter, if the tyer will even make it to another trout season? Who knows, given the times in which we live, if the trout will still be there?

In winter we tie on faith. Some years are harder than others. We *want* to believe. But for many of us, until we can see it right in front of us, until a trip's been scheduled and we know something about the fish and the fishing, the water and the season and the bugs, it all remains an abstraction, an idea we hold in our minds without the urgency, and dare I say lust, we feel on a visceral level when the time draws near and we head to the vise with purpose.

Tying while we're keen, when emotions are up and the senses sharp, when we can recall immediately the pleasure of hooking good fish and the disappointment of failing to fool others, inspires us to pour into fly tying the same energy and intensity and hopefully creativity we bring to the water. At such times we generally sit down with strong notions as well about what we want our flies to look like, how we want them to behave.

This is one of the reasons I advocate tying flies immediately *after* a trip or any visit to the water. Do it while the memories are fresh, when you know exactly what you wanted to find when you opened your box. Put a dozen of those dogs in there right now, and the next time you encounter the same situation—or something quite like it—you'll open that box again and think, *Dude, you got 'em.*

But it's a lot harder in winter. You know what your life looks like better than I do. Given the demands, the obligations, the quotidian weight, who's got a chance to take a deep breath, much less stop, sit still, and tie? The flies can wait.

Can't they?

I recommend they don't.

For most of us who are amateur tyers, the single biggest obstacle to sitting down and busting out a dozen or two flies is the effort it takes to set up and start. I've written often of the sad angler who hasn't yet claimed the appropriate space in his or her life to create a tying station, however minimal, however small, and leave it there ready for whenever the spirit moves.

Let's be frank about it: That spirit, in whatever guise, will appear more frequently if you can drop into a seat and immediately start tying.

The second biggest obstacle, for many of us, is simply clutter. It's hard to get started if the first step you have to take is to clear a spot amidst a tangle of hooks and spools and materials that have collected like old food in a refrigerator. I'm so bad about tidying up after finishing one pattern and before starting another, that I sometimes just move my vise and tools to a new location—an abdication of efficiency for which there's really no excuse, other than I live alone and I can get away with it. For a while.

Of course, the other kind of clutter that many tyers also have to contend with is stuff that somehow magically appears on any horizontal surface left unattended for any length of time. Since I do live alone, you can imagine my consternation in dealing with this problem. Who the hell put *that* there? For those of you who have chosen a more sociable living arrangement, I suggest either caution tape or a miniature electric fence if someone in your life doesn't respect the boundaries of your tying space.

•————————•

A final problem, for many winter or out-of-season trout tyers, is the question of *where to begin*.

Funny you should ask.

Given a commitment to an established tying station, as well as to maintaining a semblance of order around your vise, let me also propose an organizational strategy for your winter trout tying. Hence the title of this tale. The *E* refers to Ephemeroptera, the order of insects we know as mayflies, favorite fare of our beloved trout. The *three phases*, however, are *not* the well-known stages—nymph, dun, spinner—of a mayfly's life, all of which the fly fisher will find important, to varying degrees, depending on the type of mayfly and where and when it's found. Instead of these stages, my three phases refer to three *types* of flies I tie for any mayfly hatch I hope to encounter during a season.

These three types don't cover the entire scope of a mayfly hatch; nymphs, you'll notice, aren't even included. But these are the mayfly patterns I reach for most often as soon as I see signs of a hatch—either because I know how to fish these patterns or because I like they way they fool fish.

Which may well be the same thing.

HARE'S EAR SOFT HACKLE

- **Hook:** #10-18 Mustad 9671 or similar
- **Thread:** Camel 8/0 UNI-Thread or similar
- **Tail:** Light-tipped deer hair, stacked, tied short
- **Rib:** Flat gold tinsel (small)
- **Abdomen:** Softer, paler hair from face of a hare's mask, spun into dubbing loop
- **Thorax/wing pad:** Dark spiky material from around ears of hare's mask, spun into dubbing loop
- **Hackle:** Hungarian partridge for larger flies, hen hackle for smaller

Notes: Nothing new about tying this pattern. Obviously you can tweak it to cover the mayflies you find on your water. Size is the most important variable, color a distant second. I do like hare's masks that are dyed different colors—but I'm not convinced I ever do better than with patterns tied from the light and dark parts of the natural. Although professionals I know hate using dubbing tools, I find mine indispensable for creating the look I want for both the abdomen and thorax, with its bold impression of wings about to unfold.

Whatever type of hackle material you choose, first tie in the feather by the stem before you tie the rest of the fly. Then, after you've finished the thorax, leaving yourself plenty of room behind the eye of the hook, wind the hackle back toward the thread. Finally, wind the thread forward to the eye, locking the hackle in place.

HAIRWING DUN

- **Hook:** #8-16 TMC 5212 or similar 2X-long dry fly; TMC 100 for smaller sizes
- **Thread:** Camel 8/0 UNI-Thread or similar
- **Wing:** Natural elk hair or coastal deer hair, upright and divided
- **Tail:** Moose body hair
- **Rib:** Pearsall's Gossamer Silk, doubled, shades lighter and contrasting with dubbing
- **Body:** Super Fine Dubbing, dark tan or color to match naturals
- **Hackle:** Dun and brown, mixed

Notes: The Hairwing Dun is an obvious choice once you see mayflies on the water and you're sure that's what the trout are feeding on. This is a generic, impressionistic dun; it's rarely the *only* one I'll have in my box for a hatch I've encountered in the past—but I know it will get me in the game, and it may be the exact fly I need if the water has much pace or texture to it. I wish I got to cast in these situations more often than I do. In fact, this is the phase of *E* I use least, probably because I don't find myself fishing the sort of classic hatch rivers described so often in the literature. If the trout are really up and feeding on duns, this is probably the easiest kind of trout fishing there is. I know dry-fly aficionados who will treat that opinion with scorn. Let's just say if you know how to cast, a fish rising to duns is a pretty straightforward proposition; hit it on the nose, and chances are it will eat.

Everybody probably already ties a generic may-fly dun that works. The Adams is the archetype; this follows more along the lines of the classic Wulff patterns, which float almost as well as a Humpy but offer a more slender, more mayfly-like profile. Anything you haven't seen here? Moose hair makes for a long stout tail, essential for balancing the fly so that it floats in the correct position or attitude, especially important with larger imitations that can end up on their noses because of their oversized wings.

Hairwing flies are never an easy tie; tie in a tuft of stacked hair with the tips pointed forward, then prop up the hair with a dam of thread wraps, divide the wing, and use figure-eight wraps to hold the separated halves in place. But nothing beats a hairwing fly for holding its shape and coming back from a serious dunking. And did I mention these things float? Commercially tied patterns using the latest synthetic materials will always grace the lead-off spots in a so-called cutting-edge lineup. But if you just sit down and get to work on a few dozen Hairwing Duns in about three different sizes, I bet you'll do just fine during the mayfly hatches you encounter during the upcoming trout season.

NOT A KLINKHAMER CRIPPLE

- **Hook:** #10-18 Daiichi 1167 or similar
- **Thread:** Camel 8/0 UNI-Thread or similar
- **Wing:** Dark elk hair, divided and in line with forward curve of hook
- **Thorax:** Butts of wing material
- **Tail:** Tips of marabou barbels used for body
- **Body:** Marabou, tan or color to match naturals
- **Rib:** Pearsall's Gossamer Silk, doubled, color to contrast with body
- **Hackle:** Brown or color to match naturals, a size smaller than for typical dry fly

Notes: Most everybody knows that a crippled may-fly pattern can be just what you need if you find yourself fishing over snooty trout that don't seem willing to break through the surface to grab your floating dun. The beauty of the best cripple patterns is the *attitude* of the fly—the way the body or abdomen hangs beneath the surface, as if the rising nymph is trapped in the film. The curved Klinkhamer hook (or even the old TMC 200 if used correctly) made it easy to create a fly that rides with the bend of the hook beneath the surface of the water. The Not A Klinkhamer takes it one step further, giving you a fly with a body that's perpendicular to the surface—if not even a little *past* vertical.

But it has wings! you might argue. *How can it be a cripple?* Well, I have a lot of answers to this and most every question about why flies I use work. But the only answers that really matter are the ones you get directly from the fish you're after. I suspect there's a real name for the Not A Klinkhamer, and probably a story about who invented it and how it came to exist. I just ran into an old guy (older than *I* am) on a river with big challenging trout feeding each evening on a smattering of big mayflies. The guy was catching fish on this pattern. I tied some up—and the trout I showed 'em to all seemed to say *yes*.

TYING THE NOT A KLINKHAMER CRIPPLE

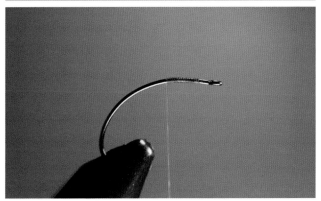

1. Secure your hook. If you're using UNI-Thread, run the first bit of it across your tying or dubbing wax. That gives you a better chance of keeping the wing hair, in the next step, from escaping your control. Start your thread and lay down a base of wraps over the forward third of the hook.

2. Any kind of hair you feel comfortable working with is appropriate for the wing of this pattern. (In smaller sizes, you might consider kip tail or calf body hair, for example.) Clean and stack a tuft of hair; a little is better than too much. Lay the tuft of stacked hair along the top of the hook shank; the tips of the hair should extend forward, past the eye of the hook, about the length of the body of the fly, which is a bit hard to judge because of the shape of the hook. Starting at about the one-third point back from the hook eye, begin securing the hair with light turns of thread, trying to keep the hair above the hook shank as you wind forward. Eventually, your tie-in point should turn into a wide base of thread wraps, over which you'll later wind your hackle. At this point, you can also clip the butts of the wing hair, leaving about ⅛ inch, which, on this cross-phase fly, represents the overdeveloped wing pad.

Now, I wish I had some brilliant advice that could make it easy to create the divided wings, lying in line with the hook, that you're after. Sorry. I know the waxed thread helps, and I go back and forth between figure-eight wraps and a series of wraps around the base of each wing. But mostly I'm just trying to *get it right*,

happy that I'm not also attempting to make money by how many of these things I can tie an hour.

3. Adjust the hook in the vise so you can work deep into the bend. Wind your thread back to where it hangs at an angle at least 45 degrees from the eye of the hook. Cut a short length of silk thread, double it up, and run it over your tying wax. Secure it to the hook, then make several more turns of thread farther back along the hook. From a single marabou feather, clip six to eight barbs; with the tips aligned, twist the feather barbs into a loose rope. Secure the marabou rope, leaving the tips of the barbs extended past the bend of the hook for the tail.

4. Advance your thread to the clipped butts of the wing. Create the body of the fly by winding your rope of twisted marabou to the wing butts. You may find it easier to hold the butt end of the marabou barbs in a pair of hackle pliers, keeping a light twist to the barbs as you wind forward. Secure the marabou aft of the wing butts and clip excess. Now rib the body or abdomen of the fly with the waxed silk thread. It will sort of just disappear in the marabou—but the fish can see the segmented effect, which is where the gills of a mayfly nymph lie, and the thread protects the marabou from unraveling after the first touch of a trout's teeth.

5. Strip the base of the stem of your hackle feather. Secure the stem at the aft end of the thread wraps that hold the wing hairs in place. Advance your thread to the forward end of these same thread wraps. Make five or six turns of hackle, one in front of the other.

6. Secure the hackle with your thread and clip excess. I whip-finish this fly *behind* the base of the wings; I suspect you could do the same between the base of the wings and just aft of the hook eye. Wherever you finish, saturate the thread wraps with lacquer or head cement.

BEETLE BUG

Beetle Bug, adapted by Dave Hughes from design by Bob Borden

I've never fished a Beetle Bug.

Last year, while fleshing out a box of big dry flies for big north country rainbows, I tied up a dozen Beetle Bugs, sizes 10 to 14; at the same time, I was also rereading Dave Hughes's monumental *Trout Flies*, trying to bring some order to my trouting fly boxes, which seemed to be multiplying like box elder beetles in both my vest and my travel bags. Hughes offers a lot of sensible advice on how to go about establishing strategies for organizing our trout flies; his ideas about searching flies can go a long way in helping you maintain a lineup of flies you can take to trout waters anywhere and feel confident you'll be in the game.

Hughes's favorite *searching dry fly*, readers may recall, is the Beetle Bug. Inspired by his clear thinking and pragmatic approach to this business of trout flies, I cleared a space in my box of big Humpys, hoppers, muddlers, crane flies, Trudes, and the like, and I proudly filled it, one by one, with a neat and tidy row of Beetle Bugs.

I remember opening that box and removing a big Green Humpy, size 10—*my* favorite searching dry fly. There was a good fish nudging the surface next to a tangle of slender roots flexing in current that was eating away the bank beneath me. That fish, and a few others, needed nothing more, in the way of coaxing, than was

offered by the big Humpy. Now that I think about it, I also pulled a couple of different hopper patterns out of my box of searching dries during the course of the day, flies that I swung waking across the current as though fishing for steelhead, a presentation that initiated several spectacular rises and even a few heart-jolting takes. Yet for some reason, I never tied on and fished one of my spanking new Beetle Bugs.

Or maybe I did—and I just don't remember it.

What I do know is that when I got home, I couldn't find that box of flies.

•————————•

For many of us, the searching dry fly is what turned us into fly anglers. It certainly wasn't a weighted nymph dangling beneath a strike-indicating bobber. The visual delight of a trout, whatever size, suddenly breaking the surface and snatching the fly became a visceral longing and anticipation that nothing else in life could quite equal. The high-floating dry, often fished in swift, foam-flecked waters, offered a point of focus that eliminated all of the other worries and distractions that otherwise shadowed our days. Finally, one had an answer to the troubling question of the purpose or point of our brief moment here amidst the shitstorms whirling all around us.

Hughes characterizes the searching dry fly as "bold in three aspects: flotation, visibility to the angler, and bugginess in the eyes of the trout." Everyone has his or her own biases in the formula. Rubber floats like a cork—but, really, how buggy can you make it look? Subtle wing colors or materials look more like the real thing—but how do you see the fly in ruffled water or at the end of a cast over twenty-five feet? Trout will nearly always prefer a fly that settles into the surface film rather than standing up on its hackle tips like a cocklebur on the leg of your Levi's—but, again, after a dozen casts, or a single fish, can you keep your low-riding bug from penetrating the surface and sinking completely out of sight?

You favor what you think matters most. The white wing of a Royal Wulff stands out like a spotlight as it rides merrily down the stream. The hollow hair of a Humpy seems capable of returning the fly to the surface like a bath toy despite repeated dunkings. And nothing looks buggier than an Adams—even if they never float as long or as well as you wish they did, or they seem to disappear on the water the moment the sun drops behind the treetops or the lip of the ridgeline or canyon wall.

In *Trout Flies*, Hughes describes how he came to the Beetle Bug through a sequence of changes or accommodations that speak to what this book argues, one fly after the next. The most effective flies in our boxes, goes the thesis, will nearly always be regional or personal iterations of traditional, more widely fished forms. Like many anglers of his era, Hughes's first go-to searching fly was the standard Royal Coachman. (On early trips to the west side of the Sierras, as we called them, I remember my father claiming the Royal Coachman his favorite as well.) The problem with the Royal Coachman was that it never floated well for long, and its duck quill wing was quickly trashed by trout.

Then Hughes's father came upon a Coachman-like pattern that was easier to tie and equally effective—although it still didn't hold up well to grabby little trout. This new pattern, explains Hughes, was the earliest Beetle Bug, tied by Audrey Joy, "the famous northwest tyer" who worked in the 1950s for Meier & Frank, the big-deal Portland department store. Can anyone even imagine such a job today? With its all-red floss body, the original Beetle Bug eliminated the fussy peacock herl segmenting of the Royal Coachman. Hughes's father found he could tie six Beetle Bugs in the same time it took to tie four Royal Coachmen, a significant improvement for a father tying for himself as well as for his three sons.

But as Hughes himself began to investigate patterns from the fly-fishing literature, he discovered the Royal Wulff. Finally, here was a pattern that embraced the visibility and trout-attracting elements of the Royal Coachman, while floating far better than the original because of its moose hair tail and calf tail wing. These same two elements of the fly also made it surpassingly

more durable. The Royal Wulff became Hughes's standard searching dry fly.

That changed, writes Hughes, in the 1970s. Bob Borden of Hareline Dubbin had learned of Hughes's earlier interest in the Beetle Bug; he sent Hughes a few prototypes he had tied "based on the Audrey Joy original." Immediately, Hughes could see that Borden's Beetle Bug would be easier to tie. When he tried fishing it, he also found it caught fish so well that he soon moved it into the leadoff slot of his searching dry-fly lineup, displacing his Royal Wulffs.

There's one last chapter to Hughes's Beetle Bug story, a final twist that shows again how, oftentimes, good flies evolve. Because Hughes wanted his Beetle Bugs to float better in rumpled water, and because he sometimes likes to dangle a little bead-head nymph as a dropper tied to his searching dry fly, he concocted a palmered version of Borden's Beetle Bug. That's his standard tie now, which he doubts catches any more trout than Bob Borden's pattern, and maybe not any more fish than a Royal Wulff will fool if you were to use it in all situations that call for a searching dry fly. Another claim this book makes, again and again, is that you catch fish on the flies you fish with. Hughes seems to agree with that notion as well.

Finishing Hughes's story, I was inspired to try my hand at some Beetle Bugs of my own. The arc of the narrative, as I've said, follows my own belief in where our best—and most interesting—flies come from. I'm also a fan of Dave Hughes; I recognize, in his writing, the kind of water I often fish—and the ways he goes about fishing it.

Of course, unlike Hughes, I can't say I have *any* fly that has "gone all over the world with me" or that "I've yet to find a place where it won't work." I get around—but not like that. Still, when I tied up my dozen Beetle Bugs, I felt I had added an important pattern to my lineup of searching dries, dominated, over the years, by my much-favored Humpys. With its white wing, the Beetle Bug would be much easier to see, and with its hair wing and tail and full-bodied hackling, it would float just as well as the cork-like Humpy. And *buggy*—the last of the three qualities we should look for, argues Hughes, in a searching dry? Well, I've never thought there was anything particularly buggy about the Christmas colors of either a Royal Wulff or a Royal Coachman. But I guess what *I* think doesn't really matter. It's trout, after all, that we're after.

And while you're out there, keep an eye out for that fly box of mine, too.

DAVE HUGHES'S BEETLE BUG

- **Hook:** #10-16 1X fine standard dry fly
- **Thread:** Black 8/0 UNI-Thread, 70-denier UTC Ultra Thread, or similar
- **Wings:** White calf body hair, upright and divided
- **Tail:** Moose body hair
- **Palmer hackle:** Coachman brown (undersized)
- **Body:** Fluorescent red fur
- **Hackle:** Coachman brown

Tying Dave Hughes's Beetle Bug

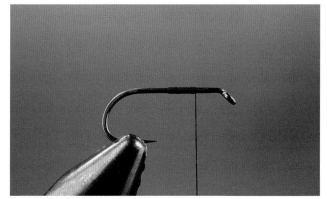

1. Secure your hook; start your thread. Lay down a base of thread over the forward half of the hook shank. Finish the thread base at a point about one-quarter the shank length back from the hook eye.

2. Prepare the calf body hair for the wing. Start with a fairly substantial clump, which will shrink rapidly as you clean out the shorter underfur. I use a cheap makeup brush for removing the unwanted parts in a tuft of hair. Use a hair stacker to align the tips. Measure the hair so that the wing will be just about the length of the hook shank. Secure the hair where your thread is hanging. Start with a couple of soft loops, pulled either directly up or down. Then work your way toward the butt ends of the hair, tightening your wraps as much as you dare. Clip the hair butts well ahead of the bend of the hook. Now wind your thread forward. In front of the wing, build a dam of thread wraps so that the wing hairs stand up perpendicular to the hook

shank. This is not a delicate fly. Don't be afraid to use as many thread wraps as you need.

3. Divide the wing into two even parts with either a needle or point of a bodkin. Lay a wrap of thread between the two halves to keep them separated. Beyond that, I wish I had a magic method to share to help you create perfectly divided and spaced and angled hair wings. I don't. Practice improves your results. I combine two techniques, sometimes making a series of wraps around the base of each individual wing half, and sometimes crisscrossing between halves with figure-eight wraps. You'll get another chance to adjust the vertical cant of the wings when you wind your forward hackle. When you're happy with your wing, place a drop of lacquer or head cement between the splayed halves to help hold them in place.

4. Wind your thread to the bend of the hook. Clip a small tuft of moose hair from the hide. Clean away the underfur and align the hair tips in a stacker. Tie in the moose hair so that you have a tail about equal the length of the hook shank. Wind your thread forward, continuing to cover the moose hair until you reach the butts of the wing hair. Clip the moose hair here. Use thread wraps to create an even taper from the root of the tail to the wing.

5. For the palmer hackle, choose a feather with barbs slightly shorter than the hook gap. Clean off the base of the hackle stem and secure the feather at the root of the tail. Hughes ties in the hackle feather with the concave side facing him, so that the hackle will tilt forward when wound. I face the feather the opposite way, so that the wound hackle barbs point back.

6. For the body, Hughes calls out a specific fluorescent red Hareline Dubbin #04 (last time I looked, fluorescent red is now #06). A fan of seal fur, I tied the bodies of the flies in the photos with red seal fur from FeathersMc.com. Whatever material you choose, you won't need much in your dubbing noodle. The shape and size of the body should already be formed by the thread wraps covering the butts of the wing and tail material. All your dubbing needs to do is cover the wraps to give the body color.

7. Now wind the palmer hackle forward, spacing your wraps evenly until you reach the wing. Tie off the feather at the wing and clip excess.

8. For the forward or main hackle, choose a hackle feather with barbs slightly longer than the hook gap. Secure the feather by the butt of the stem, just aft of the wing. Wind your thread to the hook eye. Wind your hackle feather to the thread, taking this opportunity to adjust your wings if necessary. Tie off the hackle feather and clip excess. Form a tidy head with thread wraps, whip-finish, and saturate the head with lacquer or head cement.

DARK HARE

Dark Hare, variation of nineteenth-century English pattern, the origin of which is still disputed

Off on a weekend trout binge recently, I noticed something odd. Odd for me, at least. Despite a vest stuffed with no less than a half-dozen different fly boxes, each box jammed with row after row after row of carefully constructed flies, many of the patterns tweaked just so for the nuanced demands of the heady trout in this very river—despite these boxes chock-full of good flies, I was gazing into, and selecting from, only a single small box, one of those cheap little six-compartment jobs, maybe two dozen flies in all, not more.

The obvious question: What was I doing carrying those other hundred-dozen flies? This is not the time nor place to get into that, other than to remark I'm not alone: Fly fishers of a certain bent, usually tyers, can be notorious hoarders, unwilling to step into the river without their box of twelve different types of caddis pupae even though they've been fishing over emerging mayflies the past five days. Or is it really just me? On a positive note, fishing out of a single small box, with just a small selection of favorite patterns, suggests an angler who knows the water—someone who has refined his or her game to a few sure strokes that will cover the demands of the day.

I'm a long way from that. Yet now and then I do see evidence of change: I've learned *something* after all. What fly fishing shows us most often, of course, is how

much we *don't* know; there are mysteries unfolding that keep us guessing one moment to the next. Still, when you can step into the water with just a few choice patterns that you know, at *this* moment, are all you really need, you might want to pause and reflect on and even celebrate the fact that you've come a fair distance since you first started waving a rod through the morning air.

You reach this level of confidence on a river when (1) you know where the fish are, (2) you know how to present the fly to them, and (3) you fish with flies you know the fish will eat. It seems pretty simple—until you realize, first, that most places in a river *don't* hold fish; holding water is the exception, not the norm. Second, it's not always particularly easy to deliver a fly to a trout, especially in such a way that the fly ends up behaving like things on which trout typically feed. Finally, the whole notion of fishing a fly that trout will "eat" can be misleading.

My buddy Joe Kelly, the fish biologist, recalls watching a video of trout hanging in a current, each fish constantly taking bits and pieces of this and that into its mouth and then immediately rejecting those things which aren't actually food. Trout don't eat your fly so much as they take it up in their mouths to *investigate* it as possible fare—just as they've learned to forage for food since they arrived in the river without fingers or hands. I know I'm oversimplifying all of this—or stating the obvious. But the point is, your fly goes into a trout's mouth for but a moment, just long enough for the fish to *check it out.* Our job, at that moment, is to stick the fish—which is actually an important aspect of presentation, one that's often overlooked.

Nothing reveals the competence of a skilled trout angler more quickly than the ability to stay in contact with the fly. Good presentation—*on* the surface, *in* the surface, *below* the surface—is always a delicate balancing act; you try to make the fly behave naturally, while at the same time you want to be able to nudge or turn or influence the fly with just the gentlest *adjustment* to the movement of the rod tip.

Nothing comes out of the vise that remotely resembles the feel or, presumably, taste of the live critters on which trout feed—especially when you consider the hook projecting so dramatically from one end of the offering. Reasonably, the most you should ever really expect from a trout is that it tries out your fly because it *could be* food. If I can just get the fish to *pluck* the fly, taking it up for consideration as food, by all counts I should be able to hook the fish—as long as I've remained in contact with the fly.

Now that I think of it, there really is a lot going on. On the other hand, what makes a good trout fly is not so much all that goes into it, but instead what you leave out. It was Gary LaFontaine, I think, who introduced us to the notion that we don't need flies that trout say *yes* to; what's most important, goes the argument, is that there's nothing about a fly the trout rejects. What you need from the fish is only a *could be* response—not necessarily an emphatic *yes.*

The perfect match to a specific hatch—or perfect *moment* in a hatch—is always satisfying; it's also how you can end up carrying a hundred-dozen flies each time you step into the river. A very different approach—and one that can prove equally satisfying—is relying on just a few patterns that, day in and day out, trout will examine with this *could be* grab. Patterns of this nature allow you to stop thinking or worrying so much about your fly and concentrating, instead, on your presentation—and all that presenting the fly implies.

•———————•

It's hard to say, exactly, how an *extra* box of flies develops; just as interesting to me is what I find there, what goes into this separate, immediately accessible stash. Of course, it usually begins with newly minted flies, ones fresh out of the vise. You know you're going fishing—what flies do you know you need *now*?

Fly shops can also contribute to a separate, special stash. That's one of their roles: *Here's what's working today.* Sadly, most shops I visit these days buy from fly manufacturers, so you often don't get those quirky regional patterns—some of them specific to single rivers or even hatches—that you used to find. Guides are a much better source—if you know some well enough that they'll share their secrets.

But the best place to find new patterns to drop into a separate small box is on a river or stream. All you have to do is ask, and most anglers will gladly tell you about a couple of patterns they find indispensable on trout waters they visit. There's a good chance they have one of these flies on the end of their line. You might even end up with an example handed over to you while you chat.

Because it's not just old favorites that go into a separate little stash. There are also experiments, something you got from somewhere or somebody else, something that initiated your own *could be* response—or that you created yourself. Good fly anglers are rarely complacent; few of us are ever completely satisfied with the lineup at hand. While restocking our supply of old favorites, we inevitably try our hand at something new.

Or at least different. For years now, my Wild Hare has often been one of two flies I tie either to the end of my tippet or to a tag end left long from my tippet blood knot, whenever I'm unsure if the trout are actively feeding on any specific insect or stage of an insect's life. A Wild Hare is simply a Gold-Ribbed Hare's Ear that's been tweaked to my tastes, modified and reduced to the components that I feel are essential for the fly to pass as either a preemergent caddis or mayfly or, my favorite criterion, *something else appealing to trout.* In other words, a classic *could be* fly, as generic as an Adams and, in my game, just as effective.

If not more so. Still, you wonder. So lately I've been tying a dark version of the fly, the Dark Hare; the idea is that this dark version is a closer approximation of typical mayfly nymphs and emergers, often a much darker shade than typical caddis larvae or pupae. Or that's the rationale. This is a pattern I actually now use interchangeably with the Wild Hare and Peter Syka's version of a Pheasant Tail—and, lo and behold, the one that spends the most time in the water catches the most fish.

Oh, and one more thing: I just went to my vest and pulled out the single box that I was fishing out of during my recent spell on the river. The box actually contains forty-seven flies—not exactly a bare-bones arsenal. Wild Hares, Dark Hares, flymphs, Pheasant Tails, soft hackles. Plus, an elegant caddis pattern I watched a guy at a shop in British Columbia tie, just for me, when I asked about what he used when the bazillion bugs clouded the horizon each evening above giant macking rainbows.

Could be . . .

DARK HARE

- **Hook:** #12-20 TMC 3671 or similar
- **Thread:** Black 8/0 UNI-Thread, 70-denier UTC Ultra Thread, or similar
- **Tail:** Dark brown elk mane
- **Rib:** Narrow gold tinsel
- **Abdomen:** Soft fur from hare's mask, dyed dun
- **Thorax/head/etc.:** Dun hare's mask guard hairs, spun into dubbing loop

Tying the Dark Hare

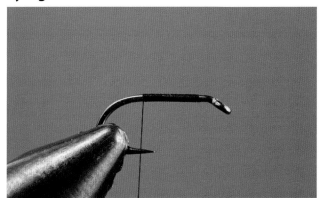

1. Secure the hook in your vise and start your thread. Yesterday, when I tied some Dark Hares with Joe Kelly, I pulled out a half-dozen different nymph and wet-fly hooks, an assortment that reflects both my indecisive nature *and* the wealth of subtle variations available to tyers who like to explore different presentations made possible simply by changing the style of hook you marry to a pattern. If your fly is designed so that it swims at an effective *attitude* in the water, attention paid to the hook on which the fly is tied will prove more effective than just fiddling, say, with split shot on your leader.

2. For the tail of the fly, clip a small tuft of dark hair from the skin. Clean the underfur from the base of the hair. Align the tips of the hair with a hair stacker. At the start of the hook bend, tie in a short, stubby tail; the idea for this type of tail (rather than one made from a few longer feather fibers or the like) is that it suggests a tail while also extending the tapered abdomen of the fly—*plus*, it serves as a substantial rudder so that, again, the fly swims with the proper attitude in the water. Clip the butts of the tail hair and cover with thread wraps, beginning to create shape for the body or abdomen.

3. After covering the tail butts, secure a length of small flat gold tinsel and wind the thread back to the root of the tail. To create the abdomen of the fly, use the soft fur found near the temples and cheeks and forehead of your hare's mask. I use a mask dyed "dun" for this pattern. Wax your tying thread and then form a dubbing noodle by twisting the soft fur onto the thread. Since you've already built up the abdomen with thread wraps over the butts of the tail material, make your noodle so that is starts as sparse as possible, tapering to a slightly thicker diameter as you continue down your thread. Most flies of this style are tied with too much bulk; insects have slender, delicate bodies. Wind the noodle forward, tapering the abdomen as you advance the wraps. Stop the abdomen with *at least* one-third of the hook shank still showing; even *half* the hook shank is rarely too much. Crowding the forward portion of this type of fly is another common error. Once the abdomen is formed, rib the fly with three or four evenly spaced turns of tinsel.

4. Now, what I consider the crux of the fly: You create the thorax, shellback, legs, and head all in one step. The two crucial components to this step include (1) the material you use and (2) creating a "hair hackle" using a dubbing loop and dubbing tool. The material used is the stiff, dark, spiky hair from up and down the edges of the hare's mask; I always cut a bunch of this hair from a mask and keep it in a separate container. Form a dubbing loop with your thread; your tool— even a pair of hackle pliers—hangs from the bottom of the loop. Now wax the loop thread liberally; you're really trying to make the legs of the loop sticky. Then take up a pinch of the spiky ear hair and *dab* it onto the waxed side (facing you) of the loop legs. You're trying to get the hairs to stick perpendicularly to the legs—but don't fuss with it too much or you'll just end up bumping the thread and knocking loose a bunch of hair. After the hair is stuck to the loop legs, spin your dubbing tool. The thread not only catches the hairs, but as you continue to twist the tool, the turns of thread double up on themselves and the loop grows shorter, the hackle more compressed. You don't need to end up with much—unless you're tying a big fly.

5. Now that you've got your hair hackle formed, simply wind it forward. As you do, brush back the tips of the hackle with your fingers and keep one wrap ahead of the other. Wind right up to the eye of the hook, leaving just enough room to tie off the hair hackle loop with the working thread, clip the excess hackle, and then whip-finish. Saturate the final thread wraps with lacquer or your favorite head cement, trying not to soil any of the hair hackle.

HEN & HARELUG

Hen & Harelug, adapted from traditional Scottish wet fly

Fires in my neck of the woods knocked out a little stream that has always been a good place to kick off the traditional trout season. In this day and age, of course, many of us fish for trout nearly year-round, either by travel to distant waters or, more likely, because of the profusion of blue-ribbon, catch-and-release waters throughout the West. For the genuine trout addict, there's nearly always some way to find a fix, while those of us fortunate enough to enjoy a more balanced diet to satisfy our fly-fishing desires will often give trout—or at least our hunger for them—a rest during some portion of what was, in the past, closed season.

Most of us, anyway, carry with us, year to year, the notion that trout season begins sometime as winter loosens its grip on the world around us. And linked to that idea, for some, is a small stream like the one ravaged by fires not far from my home—a place to return to at the start of each season to see again, with our own eyes, that, yes, the trout are still here and, better yet, they're here for no other reason than that this happens to be a trout stream where wild fish live and, on a human scale, have always lived, for no purpose or higher meaning that has anything to do with you or me or one generation or the next.

It's a profound notion. Unlike so many other trout fisheries in the West, the trout in this nearby stream,

pinched between sheer slopes now covered with deadfall and blackened trees, were never manipulated, never managed beyond the simple premise to leave them alone, let them be, *and* protect them. No dams. No stocking programs. Nobody, apparently, paying attention to water quality, cfs flows, macroinvertebrate populations, the number of trout from one mile to the next. Once the season opened, anybody with a fishing license could hike up from the mouth of the stream and catch as many trout as he or she could possibly imagine.

And every time I did this, year after year, without ever seeing anyone else fishing but my own companions, I'd think, *That's cool.*

⚫———————⚫

Another reason I enjoyed fishing this stream at the start of each season, before the fires, was that you could go at it pretty light: Spools of tippet and a handful of Humpys or whatnot were all you really needed. Not that it was easy fishing; I was often surprised, when I brought others to the stream, how much trouble they had wading the slippery rocks, keeping their flies out of the limbs of trees. Or they'd approach a perfect little pool and by the time they managed to get a fly floating merrily down the stream, it was apparent that every trout therein had been alerted to the presence of some terrible danger, and they were no more willing to rise to a fly than to stick their heads, if only figuratively, into a guillotine.

The stream was also a good place, before the fires, to fool around with new patterns, new flies. Or, better yet, to see what I could learn about *old* flies—traditional patterns that, for whatever reason, have gone out of fashion. Of course, I was hedging my bets; any experienced fly fisher could see that the name of the game here was *presentation*, that how you went after these trout was a lot more important than what you tied to the end of your tippet.

Still, you learn a lot when you see fish eat the fly. Just as you learn—or you should learn—how and why it is a nymph is fished differently from, say, a soft-hackled wet fly. Soft hackles, of course, can be great good fun on a small trout stream, in part because rarely are you whacked so hard than when a fly swings downstream, swimming on a taut line riding through the current.

But this year I planned on something different—tying and fishing a fresh assortment of traditional *winged* wet flies. In a rush to embrace the renewed interest in soft-hackled flies, many anglers, I've noticed, fail to acknowledge the historical significance of these old patterns. The upshot is the near complete absence of winged wet flies in the boxes of most modern fly fishers.

There's the sense, of course, that patterns like these belong to a different era, an age, perhaps, of innocence, when trout were plentiful and dumb—to a degree that practically any darn thing dangling from your line would inspire a strike. The earth was still flat, for God's sake. Why in blazes would anyone need to know more than the difference between a nymph and a ne'er-do-well?

Somebody somewhere concluded, however, that flies we fish with are supposed to have wings. Even after the discovery that lots of what trout eat don't have wings, and flies that swim can be just as effective as flies that imitate winged insects, the winged fly persisted into modern times, an irrational tradition seen commonly in decades of winged steelhead flies, innumerable patterns that nobody thinks have anything to do with insects, birds, pterodactyls, or any other creatures with wings.

Or is it irrational? As I've mentioned elsewhere in this book, perhaps the wing on a traditional wet fly has little if anything to do with imitating the appearance of wings or other aspects of a streamborn insect. Instead, the wing creates a mechanical device, much like a sail, that guides the fly through the swing, while at the same time producing subtle, lifelike movements that attract the attention of predator fish.

That's a bold assertion. Nevertheless, I think we're foolish should we disregard, outright, any technique that proved successful for an earlier generation of fly fishers. I've said it too many times already but I'll say it again: The subtle efficacies of downstream presentations are lost to anglers who rely solely on

the dead-drifted dry fly or a nymph or two, usually weighted, fished below an indicator. The reason, I contend, that we see so few traditional wet flies tied to tippets is that, lo and behold, they don't work if you dangle them beneath a bobber. A winged wet fly is designed—by chance or the sublime, who's to say?—to be fished under tension, however slight, on a downstream presentation or swing.

In other words, the flies fail *not* because they're inadequate, *not* because they're from a less sophisticated or enlightened era of the sport—they fail, instead, because many modern fly anglers don't know how to fish the damn things.

Harrumph.

Or maybe they just forgot.

⬤———⬤

Dave Hughes, who makes a living looking at insects and the flies we tie to imitate them, has done as much as anybody to try to remind anglers not to forget or reject traditional wet flies—even the old winged wets. Our nymphs may do a better job imitating early stages of an aquatic insect's life, claims Hughes in his classic work, *Wet Flies*. "But traditional winged wet flies," he adds, "are more effective as imitations of certain emerging insects, *and they still do the best at imitating drowned adult insects, aquatic and terrestrial*" (italics mine for emphasis).

That's another bold assertion, and not one you heard, I suspect, the last time you suited up for a day with a guide or one of your expert trout-fishing friends. Of course, a glance at any of Dave Hughes's books shows him to be something of a generalist; that is, he aims to carry an assortment of fly types that can be used on trout waters anywhere in the world. He favors patterns that rely on broad, clear strokes rather than ones that descend into the minutiae deemed critical by so many of us who fish, year after year, over trout keyed into the same regional hatches. Hughes, anyway, still ties and carries traditional winged wet flies. He recommends we all do. Moreover, he says, traditional winged wet flies allow us to catch trout in circumstances in which we would fail without them.

Yet Hughes holds the idea that the sail- or keel-like properties of the traditional winged wet fly are nothing but a liability. He contends that the traditional wing, usually tied from the stiff quills of mallard primary feathers, is pretty to look at but contribute nothing to a fly's capacity to fool trout. They never "look alive," he says. Worse, he argues, the stiff quill wing usually twists in one way or another, so that its rudder effect causes the fly to swim like nothing a trout has ever seen before—"half the reason," Hughes suspects, that "traditional wet flies fail."

Perhaps. No doubt the hen or other soft-hackle wings that Hughes now employs on his winged wet flies, like the wing used here for the Hen & Harelug, create a fly that looks more like the insects we're trying to imitate, whether in an emerging stage or as adults awash in the water. Hen-hackle wings, like soft-hackle fibers, states Hughes, "quiver and kick . . . with every ripple of current." Yet I still contend that the winged wet fly, fished on the swing, shares with certain swimming insects both an attitude and action that goes beyond the wiggly movements produced by soft fibers bending and flexing in the current. Watch any tiny aquatic animal that feels threatened, be it a caddis pupa or emerging mayfly or even itty-bitty fry or baitfish, and tell me those little guys don't tense up and know how to dart and dive. And in my experience, nothing sparks a strike from predatory fish quite like a lure or fly, or even bait, that acts like it's in danger of being devoured by a monster ten or a hundred or a thousand times its size.

It's a theory, at least, worth further study. Fires nearby have made a mess of things—but I have a hunch this spring I'll be able to get back to that hard-hit stream to continue my research. That's assuming, of course, the trout are still there.

I'm willing to bet they are.

HEN & HARELUG

- **Hook:** #12-16 Mustad 3906 or similar
- **Thread:** Primrose Pearsall's Gossamer Silk Morus Silk, or similar
- **Tag:** Flat gold tinsel
- **Body:** Hare's ear, lightly dubbed, allowing tying silk to show through
- **Wing:** Partridge tail fibers
- **Hackle:** Medium dun hen

Tying the Hen & Harelug

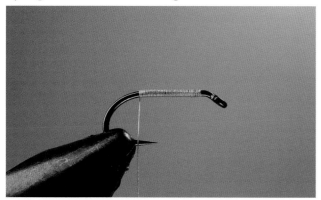

1. Secure your hook. Start the thread directly behind the hook eye. Wind an even layer of thread back to the start of the bend of the hook. Modern hooks notwithstanding, the 3906 (or Mustad's newer S80NP) remains the quintessential wet-fly hook, offering plenty of weight on a relatively short hook. Flies tied on the old 3906 immediately penetrate the surface film and stay down on the swing.

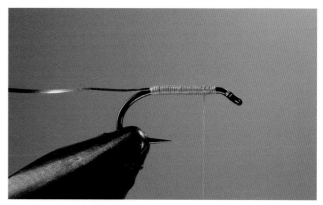

2. Tie in a short length of narrow flat tinsel. Leave the waste end long enough that it lies along the length of the thread underbody. Advance the thread in an even layer back to a point just shy of the hook eye.

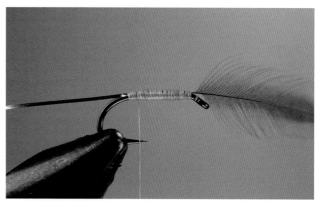

3. Select a hen neck feather with fibers slightly longer than the hook gap. Strip the fluff and webby fibers from the lower portion of the stem. With the underside or concave side of the feather away from you, secure the stem directly behind the eye of the hook. Wind the thread in an even layer to the aft end of the fly, just short of where you tied in the tinsel. Don't clip the excess stem until you've almost reached the tinsel; in that way you have a better chance of maintaining a fair, lump-free body.

4. Create the tag of the fly with two or three turns of tinsel. Tie off and clip excess. If I'm being finicky, I might run another two layers of thread, forward and back, to keep the body as fair as possible. This is especially true when tying with Pearsall's silk thread, which is much bulkier than modern threads.

5. A defining aspect of most "harelug" flies is a touch-dubbed body that allows the color of the thread or tying silk to show through the dubbing material. Apply wax liberally to the top 2 or 3 inches of your tying silk. Use a small amount of dubbing hair, free of any clumps, and simply touch it to the thread. Whatever sticks is enough; don't try to twist the thread or create a typical dubbing noodle. Wind the fuzzy thread forward in loosely spaced wraps, stopping several wraps short of where you tied in the stem of the hackle feather.

6. For the wing, select a tail feather from a partridge skin. Remove the fluff and webby fibers. Stroke the fibers along one side of the feather so that the fiber tips are aligned, perpendicular to the stem. Strip or cut the fibers, keeping the tips aligned. Then gently roll the fibers between your thumb and forefinger, again doing your best to keep the tips aligned. Measure the wing so that it ends up about the length of the hook shank. Secure the wing, leaving enough space between the root of the wing and the hook eye for the hackle. Clip the butts of the wing fibers, being careful not to cut or damage the hackle stem.

7. Attach hackle pliers to the tip of the hackle feather. Wind the hackle back toward the root of the tail, making two to four turns, depending on the size of the fly. Now wind your thread forward, making three or four turns through the hackle wraps, locking the stem in place. In front of the hackle, create a tidy head of thread wraps. If I'm tying with silk, I always wax my thread before I whip-finish, which helps the thread slide through the whip-finish wraps without grabbing. Saturate the final thread wraps with lacquer or head cement.

AMIOCENTRUS

Amiocentrus designed by author

I remember the humiliation as sharply as yesterday. The river was becoming my favorite; I fished it often enough that I had managed to build a game that included the repertoire of flies and presentation techniques you need to catch trout every month of the year. It didn't hurt that success meant contact with the hottest of rainbows, fish possessed of some added dash of horsepower that made 5X tippet a fool's play. There were weekends I saw more backing on sixteen-inch fish than I'd see in a month of successful steelheading.

The moment in question, I had every reason to picture more of the same. Early June, right after the Salmonflies fizzled, the trout seemed heavier, more spirited than at any other time of the year. Just the beginning of the long summer caddis season, I carried a wealth of patterns I had tweaked and kneaded into flies I fished confidently before, during, and, the following mornings, *after* the evening caddis hatch. It was never a sure thing. Is it ever? But I got my share.

Sometimes even more.

So I was shocked that evening, the one in question, when the fish began rising, right below me, in a shallow riffle below an island where I was used to whacking trout that made my heart soar—and for the next hour, maybe two, I failed to touch a single trout.

It's such an old story—perhaps the oldest in the literature. And every experienced trout angler knows it can happen again, even the very next time on the water. Probably not—we do learn a few things, after all. But one of the grand aspects of fly fishing, perhaps the one that keeps bringing us back for more, even after all these many years, is the things we still don't know—especially those we may never learn.

Still, nothing leaves quite the same impression as a run full of feeding trout we fail to move to the fly.

Let's be frank about it. It can drive you nuts.

Or how about this: Failing to fool feeding fish doesn't so much drive me batty as it does *reveal* what's already unsound in my mental game.

The one genuinely great trout angler I've fished with in my career does all those things you know you're supposed to do but few of us rarely practice, even less so in the heat of the moment. I'm not talking about application of a quiet casting stroke or subtle, sparsely dressed flies. Instead, recollections of my own failure remind me how Bruce Milhiser is able to stop fishing, with feeding trout right in front of him, and take the time to consider what is actually going on.

Patience and observation. Here at my writing desk, I'm able to see myself stepping back from those feeding fish during that humiliating scene, studying the riseforms, reaching down in the water and turning over a few rocks, checking my boots and waders to see what may be clinging to them. But I know what really happens: I just keep hacking away.

Sad. I might as well be a dog with someone holding a bone just out of reach. Complete focus—and the inability to pause and observe and reflect on any other evidence at hand.

And here's the irony of it all: Even if you *can't* figure out what's going on, even if you don't know a caddisfly from a mayfly, a pupa from a nymph, a cripple from an emerger from a spinner from a terrestrial, if you simply stop for a moment, quit waving your rod in the air, quit laying your line on the water, rising fish will soon forget all about you and return to the kind of one-dimensional focused feeding that makes them so vulnerable to our crude casts and clumsy flies in the first place.

Eventually almost every savvy trout angler learns this secret: When nothing else you try seems to work, back off and rest the water a while.

Be smarter than the trout, I try to tell myself.

Stop, for God's sake.

* * *

Had I been able to practice this level of self-discipline, of course, I probably wouldn't have suffered the kind of humiliating shutout I'm describing now. At least not that evening. Because as soon as it was over, as soon as I strapped on my headlamp so I could see my way through the shallow riffle and minefield of greasy rocks, I noticed on the legs of my waders the little green caddis pupae that had to have been what was making all of those trout porpoise and boil just beyond the end of my rod tip.

I know, I know: I've claimed throughout this book that your fly doesn't matter—which I still contend, in the grand scheme of things, holds true.

But in trout fishing, I concede, there are times you need something close.

Still, all I would have had to do, sometime before darkness fell, was stop long enough to notice the little green caddis pupae—rather than continue to flail away. Instead, I went home, tail between my legs, and did my research. I had already guessed it was some kind of case-making *Brachycentrus*, the local iteration of which turned out to be what's called the Little Western Weedy-Water Sedge—*Amiocentrus aspilus*. If I had confused it for a Green Rock Worm, the free-living caddis larva of the Green Sedge (*Rhyacophila*), I still should have been able to swing something sparse and green—and probably had action of some sort to keep from feeling I'd learn nothing in decades of trout fishing.

What bothered me most, of course, was that had I stopped for a moment and checked out those pupae gathered on the legs of my waders, I would have taken the time to dig through my caddis box and found *something* that looked right.

Instead, I sat down at home at the vise and cranked out a bunch of green-bodied, soft-hackled little guys, size 16 through 20, Starling & Green, if you need a name for it. A few evenings later, I found the trout more than willing to agree with my rough impersonation of this small green sedge.

* * *

I'm still using the last of that batch of flies. As I've argued elsewhere, the beauty of returning home from a trip and immediately tying up two or three dozen flies is that you know just what you want and now you've got that hatch covered when you run into it the next time—five days or five years later.

On the other hand, you might learn some new tricks along the way.

The Amiocentrus, my latest iteration for fishing during this common early-season hatch, has a few different things going on. Clearly it's old-school, a designation that seems to land on most flies that rely mainly on natural feather and hair rather than newer synthetic materials. It's much like a Gary LaFontaine Diving Caddis as well, a fly I use persistently during the caddis season, whether swinging on the surface or anywhere down through the water column when fished in tandem with a heavier fly or with lead pinched to my leader. The thread body is a classic soft-hackle trait. The touch-dubbed ribbing comes from the Scottish harelug flies. There's also something about this pattern that points back to the old Clyde-style wet flies, tied originally in Scotland for the famous River Clyde, a style of sparse soft-hackled dressing which, if you're not aware of it, might do more to stimulate your creativity at the vise than the tungsten and epoxy fare being served up of late by Czech and Euro-style nymphers.

Then again, the more I look at it, the more the Amiocentrus reminds me of the very first caddis I tied in preparation for a trip, forty-some years ago, to Yellowstone, when I thought a caddis was a type of pattern, not an actual insect—because I'd never noticed caddisflies, nor read about them, in real life before.

AMIOCENTRUS

- **Hook:** #14-18 TMC 3761 or 900BL
- **Thread:** Highland green Pearsall's Gossamer Silk, Morus Silk, or similar
- **Hackle:** Furnace hen
- **Tag:** Flat gold tinsel (small)
- **Body:** Tying silk
- **Rib:** Tying silk waxed and touch-dubbed with dark hairs from natural hare's mask
- **Underwing:** Dark brown partridge
- **Overwing:** Clear Antron yarn

Tying the Amiocentrus

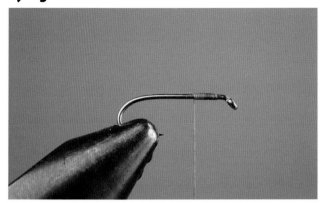

1. Secure the hook and start the thread. I tie most of my wet caddis on the 3761 or similar wet-fly hook. But I also tie a few on light-wire dry-fly hooks, which can help keep the fly, especially when dressed, directly in the surface film, whether dead-drifted or fished on the swing. For size 18 caddis patterns, I usually switch to 8/0 or similar thread, which reduces the bulk created by the thicker Pearsall's silk.

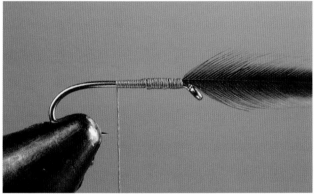

2. Select a hackle feather with fibers slightly longer than the hook gap. Strip the webby fibers from the base of the stem and right up to the first fibers that begin to show the distinctive two-tone colors of furnace hackle. With the convex or shiny outside of the feather toward you, secure the feather with the start of the fibers just behind the eye of the hook and the tip of the feather pointing forward.

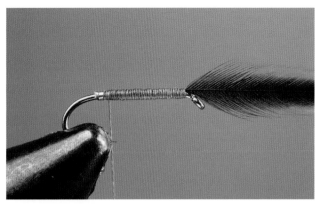

3. Secure a short length of flat tinsel as you wind the thread back toward the bend of the hook. Just forward the bend, create the tag with two turns of tinsel. Before cutting off the excess, lay the tinsel along the hook shank and cut it just short of the lump created by the end of the hackle stem. Cover the remaining tinsel excess and fair the body with an even layer of thread wraps.

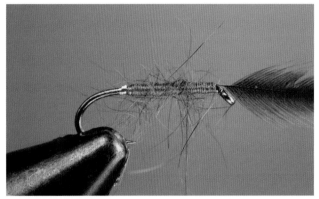

4. I talked about touch-dubbing and harelug flies in the previous pattern. I can't say enough about this body style. It can't be done unless you first thoroughly wax your thread, right up to the fly; if you don't yet employ wax as you tie, watch a Davie McPhail video and maybe he'll set you straight. One trick for touch-dubbing is remembering to touch wax and thread with fingers and thumb on one hand only, so that when you handle the dubbing in your other hand, you don't end up with hairs stuck to your fingers instead of your thread. Once you have a dusting of hairs stuck to the top inch or so of thread, wind the dubbed thread forward as if palmering the body, four or five evenly spaced wraps that end well back from the hackle feather.

5. For the underwing, use a well-marked feather from the middle of the upper back of a partridge skin. English grouse might work as well. Remove the webby fibers from the base of the feather, then align the tips on one side and snip them free of the stem. Measure the fibers against the hook shank; you want the fibers to extend about even with the gold tag. Tie in the fibers, making sure, again, you've left plenty of room behind the base of the hackle feather.

6. For the overwing, use a fairly sparse dressing of fibers separated from a short length of Antron yarn. Gary LaFontaine introduced many of us to Antron (he called it Sparkle Yarn) back in 1981 with his book *Caddisflies*, and I still believe in it, if only because it's been an ingredient in so many flies of mine that have hooked good fish. (I won't bore anybody with Gary's arguments for why he felt Antron was indispensable for imitating caddisflies.) Make the overwing about the same length as the underwing. Clip the excess in front of the tie-in point, making sure you don't also cut the hackle stem.

7. Hold the tip of the hackle feather in your hackle pliers and make two or three turns back toward the root of the wing. Then wind your thread forward, locking down the stem of the hackle feather. Make a couple of turns in front of the hackle, forcing back any untidy fibers. If you are using Pearsall's silk, make sure you wax the thread before whip-finishing. Saturate the finished head with lacquer or your favorite head cement.

GREY DUSTER

Grey Duster, original designer unknown

If you're restless like I am, and you feel life's too short to quit looking around, trying to discover new things, or at least see old ones in fresh ways, maybe it's time you finally move beyond an Adams.

I know it's all but heresy. Famed writers from McGuane to Gierach have sung their praises for the lowly Adams, almost everybody's all-time favorite generic buggy dry fly. And let's be frank about it: If you are a hard-core presentationist, angling under the belief that your fly is the last thing that matters, you could fish the entire season out of an Adams box, with flies sizes 10 to 22, and do just as well as anyone else during all the mayfly hatches you encounter—and probably some other hatches as well.

For one, if you tied nothing but, I have to believe you'd know how to tie an awfully mean and clean Adams, hackle-tip wings and all. And if you owned only a couple of hackle capes, which is part of the appeal of the pattern, you might as well splurge for the deluxe primo platinum grade—or whatever they call the ones that sell for eye-popping prices. In case you haven't yet learned the lesson, good materials really can help produce good flies. Yes, it's easy to go overboard. But it's safe to say that in fly tying, as in all serious crafts, good tools and good materials make the job go more

smoothly, the results far better than trying to get by with dime-store junk.

Still, the last thing required of a timeless all-around pattern would be any suggestion of the need for new or improved materials. The Grey Duster should make that perfectly clear. In its purist form, which goes back at least a hundred years to anglers on the upper reaches of the Welsh Dee, the Grey Duster requires but two components—fur from a hare's mask and a feather from a mediocre badger hackle. Oddly enough, I notice lots of tyers who haven't yet acquired some sort of badger hackle, either a hen's neck or cape of inexpensive saddle hackle. So I take back what I just said about new materials: If you take nothing else from this chapter because you would rather imitate the precise, anatomically correct features of the genus and species of specific mayflies, at least find yourself some badger hackle if you don't already own some.

Precision, here, is not the key. The Duster, in fact, can bring into question how accurate any pattern need be. Author Courtney Williams considered the Grey Duster as good if not better than any other mayfly imitation described in *A Dictionary of Trout Flies*, his classic work first published in 1949. In *Trout & Salmon Flies of Scotland*, Stan Headley claims that some anglers fish nothing but Dusters over any sort of mayflies—and if Dusters fail, they leave the water.

Tiny Dusters have long been used to fish the British *Caenis* hatch, also known as the Angler's Curse, a tiny mayfly that looks a lot like our own Tricos, though experts are quick to inform you the two are not the same. The whole point of the Grey Duster, of course, is that you couldn't care less about the name of the mayfly you find trout feeding on. You just want a fly that's about the right size and about the right color.

You'll take it from there.

That's your Grey Duster. Like most old all-around patterns, it gets tweaked more ways than spaghetti sauce, which I think is the smartest thing you can do for your own bugs and the waters you fish. One common change is to add a wing; Scotsman Davie McPhail ties parachute Dusters with wing posts fashioned out of either deer hair or CDC. Many tyers also add a tail to their Dusters, a move that follows a conventional line of thinking in dry-fly design—but one you may want to think twice about before following it yourself.

Writer and artist Bob Wyatt, a Canadian who lived for years in Scotland before moving to New Zealand, argues that the traditional tailless Duster is actually not a dun or adult mayfly at all, but instead an emerger. He believes that the efficacy of the pattern has to do with how the tailless fly rides low in the water, that the visible hook, hanging beneath the surface, may in fact enhance an imitation of a vulnerable emerging mayfly suspended in the film. In my own experience, I've no doubt that I fool far more snooty trout with flies that sit *in* the water rather than on top of it—even a fly that vanishes into the film, so that all I can do is guess where it is in relation to my leader, until a fish reveals itself in such a way that suggests I should lift—carefully—and see what's going on out there.

With the tailless Duster, then, we return to the trope of *attitude*—that is, the position or posture of your fly in the water. Attitude is a presentationist's concept; the idea is that even the best imitation will fail if the fly isn't presented in the way the bait you're trying to imitate behaves when fish are feeding on it. There's a reason you swing certain wet flies—and you fish certain nymphs with a drag-free drift, even if they are three feet below the surface.

If you think about attitude, you are well on your way to finding a balance between notions of imitation and presentation. Sure, you want a fly that looks right—but does the design include elements that will help the fly do what it's supposed to do once it reaches the water? Which way does the head point, upstream or down? Or, for that matter, should the head point toward the surface or toward the bottom of the stream? Does the bait swim tailfirst? Does it roll over and swim upside down? Does a mayfly emerge with its abdomen sticking up out of the water? How does an egg-laying caddis swim?

These may seem trite or even facetious speculations. But the more I've come to understand what makes some anglers exceptional—and the rest of us fairly mediocre—the more I recognize how often they animate their casts so that their flies present and maintain the correct attitude. This is subtle. Still, we all know the difference between "getting a couple" and actually hammering fish, especially while trout are up and feeding.

But a tailless, wingless fly? You can see why the Duster might be a hard sell to anglers looking for the latest and greatest patterns tied with space-age materials engineered to prick the subliminal longings of unsuspecting fish. Or at least the desires of those of us who cast for them. Trout, however, seem yet to have read the ad copy. Like your soft-hackled wet fly, the Duster, as with similar sparsely dressed old-school or Clyde-style dry flies, has been fooling fish since the dark ages of the sport. And I suspect Dusters, just like those rediscovered soft hackles, will be fooling trout long after anyone reading this is still around and kicking.

One aspect, however, of the *modern* Duster does seem worth noting. Now that anglers view this fly as an emerger pattern rather than an on-top-of-the-surface dun, many of them have taken to tying it on curved, emerger-style hooks. Because I believe so strongly in the importance of a fly's attitude in the water, I'm a fan of many of the technical innovations available in today's fly hooks. By all means, if you have access to them, tie up some Dusters on the TMC 2487 or 206 or 226, the Daiichi 1130 or 1150, the Dai-Riki 125, the Kamasan B-100—or maybe even the Fulling Mill Czech Nymph Hook. I like the looks of all of these hooks. But as you can see in the accompanying photos, I tied my recent Dusters on regular old standard dry-fly hooks—and I don't think that will handicap me in the least.

Tailless, the butt or aft end of the fly is going to penetrate the surface; the canted fly will ride on the length of the hackle fibers, not just the tips. Of course, I don't expect to be able to even see the fly after a drift or two. It will hang, instead, in the film—that vulnerable attitude that trout just seem to love. Many variations of Dusters are now tied not only with different hooks but also with wings, tails, or clipped or doubled hackles. Yet even Davie McPhail, who thinks his parachute-style Grey Duster is an improved variant, is said to, at times, bite off the tails of his new and improved Duster so that the fly sits "well-down in the water."

Like an Adams on top, a Duster well-down is a fly the trout I cast to will generally buy.

GREY DUSTER

- **Hook:** #12-24 standard dry fly or curved emerger style
- **Thread:** Black or brown 8/0 UNI-Thread or similar
- **Body:** Grayish fur from natural hare's mask or similar
- **Hackle:** Badger with well-pronounced dark center

Tying the Grey Duster

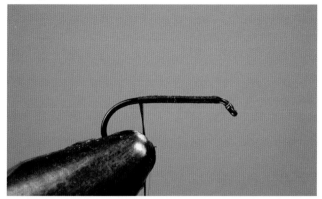

1. Secure the hook; by all means, experiment with curved emerger-style hooks. Start your thread directly behind the eye of the hook and cover the entire hook shank with an even layer of thread wraps.

2. With your thread at the aft end of the hook shank, wax the top couple of inches and twist dubbing onto the thread, creating a slender noodle. McPhail likes mole mixed with rabbit; I like any blend off of a hare's mask because of the mix of colors and textures, which to my eyes always looks more natural than dubbing dyed a single color. Wind the dubbing noodle forward, creating the classic carrot-shaped body. Carry the body forward slightly more than if you were going to include a wing *and* hackle. At the same time, leave yourself enough space for both the hackle and the eventual head and whip-finish.

3. For your hackle, select a feather from your badger cape with plenty of dark fibers toward the lower portion of the center of the feather. If you get sold on Dusters, as I think you will, especially in small sizes (18-24) for late-season Blue-Winged Olives or the like, you'll never pass up a badger cape without inspecting it as a possible source for future Dusters. The right feather does what the pair of two feathers, grizzly and brown, try to do on an Adams; the single two-tone badger feather, dark in the middle and pale as wings at the tips, will startle you, if you've never seen one used, the first time you wind it around the hook. Strip the webbiest material from the bottom of the stem; secure the stem, just ahead of the dubbing, with the underside of the feather facing you. Grab the tip of the hackle with your hackle pliers. As you wind the hackle, don't be worried about winding directly on top of other wraps; you'll see that the fibers splayed around the dark center create just the effect you're after. After four to six turns of hackle, catch the stem with your thread, trim away the excess hackle, form a tidy head, and whip-finish. Saturate the final thread wraps with lacquer or your favorite head cement.

PETER'S PHEASANT TAIL

Peter's Pheasant Tail, adapted by Peter Syka from design by Frank Sawyer

The mayflies are small and few. If you look closely, you see them spotting the water, one here, one over there—but not nearly as many as you would think by the number in the air, which *suggests* a hatch but until you see some feeding fish, you're reluctant to call it that. Still, they *are* mayflies, small and pale, not tiny like a Trico but at least an 18, maybe a tad smaller. Probably a Blue-Winged Olive. *Baetis*. First fish shows itself, you've got just the thing.

Three things, actually, if it comes to that.

But nothing does show. Not a ring, not a dimple, not a rise. The river, you happen to know, is loaded with trout. And this particular run, a textbook bend of perfectly paced water below not one but two riffles, each half as big as a football field, with structure and sunlight and gurgling oxygenated water that pumps out insects like the streamside cottonwoods and alders produce pollen and seeds—this particular run holds trout in numbers that, after two decades fishing it, still boggles your mind.

And trout do have to feed.

As is often the case, my buddy Peter Syka, fishing friend for forty-plus years now and counting, is the first to take a stab in the direction indicated by the evidence at hand. Where I'm one to flog the water with patterns and presentations that have worked in the past, Peter

is much quicker to respond to what's really going on, what's different right now from the norm. *Better casts! Better drifts!* I tell myself—while Peter is one to take a look at things and follow a fresh idea.

He has an advantage, in this case, of also being a visitor; my two decades here may have left me a wee bit complacent. Along with his brother John, Peter has joined me so that as old friends we can, as they say, catch up—and as some old friends are wont to do, catch some hot trout besides. The previous evening, I waded into the whirl of the steaming caddis and did what I know how to do best, whacking more than my share of these scalding trout. "Home field advantage!" I exclaimed, not letting up for a moment because, well, what are friends for?

But this morning there doesn't seem to be the usual number of spent and bedraggled caddis, left behind by twilight emergence and the perilous egg-laying extended into the night. These mayflies, meanwhile, are making me fidget—even if the trout seem slow to respond. Then Peter makes his decision to try something new, and sure enough he's soon tight to a fish, one that's immediately stripping line from his reel—and as I reach for my camera, eager to capture an image of my old friend, I notice he's taken hold of the cork with *both* hands as he starts across the slippery rocks, making for higher ground.

●————————————●

A Pheasant Tail Nymph when mayflies are around? That's nothing new. The move is as routine as a sacrifice bunt to get a base runner into scoring position. Dave Hughes claims that stomach samples taken during a hatch of *Baetis* can show that "nymphs outnumber duns sometimes as much as ten to one"; a Pheasant Tail nearly always gets you into the mayfly game. Some anglers are such strong believers in the pattern that they even *start* with a Pheasant Tail Nymph before they have any idea what's really shaping up, the same way many of us tie on an Adams or a Hare's Ear—or both—just so we have something on the line when we walk down to the water.

Yet many anglers, myself included, don't put a lot of faith in a Pheasant Tail Nymph. We *get it*—we look at the fly and acknowledge its gracious design, simplicity, and overall charm. But we don't immediately reach for our stash of Pheasant Tails—and when we do, usually when nothing else is working, they don't work either, which leaves our doubts about them unchanged.

That's another thing I love about fly fishing—these preferences and prejudices that develop during a career. There's nearly always a story, if not many stories, behind our likes and dislikes, the flies we choose to tie and use and those we reject or refuse to give even a fair chance. Rarely are we offered such an opportunity to see, if we pay attention, how our beliefs can create the reality we experience. We catch fish on the flies we fish with. Beyond that, who's to say where truth lies?

But there's something else going on here: Peter tied on a Pheasant Tail—and I didn't—because he had some with him that he liked. He had fussed with the pattern, turning it into something that looked, in his eyes, how a fly representing a mayfly nymph ought to look.

Or at least how it ought to look if you're trying to fool a trout.

"I was never happy with the legs," Peter explains as we cook, later in the day, a big meal before the evening session. Smoke from the skillet, overflowing with bratwurst and brussels sprouts, onions and peppers and yams, billows through the junipers, rising toward the haze from distant fires. "No matter what you do, it's hard to get those pheasant tail butts to lie like you want 'em."

While he was at it, he made some other changes, too.

●————————————●

In case anybody's still uncertain, let me restate two themes that run through this essay—and show up, to some degree, throughout this entire book and in most everything I've ever written about flies, fly tying, and fly fishing. First, good fly tyers—and by that I mean fly fishers who tie flies that work—are inveterate tinkerers; they fuss and fiddle with patterns, making

them, eventually, their own. These private or personal designs, those that eventually win spots in our go-to lineup, evolve out of the challenges we face in the fish we fish for and the places where we fish. Yet they also reflect an individual style or temperament we bring to the water—how we *like* to fish and the kind of water in which we feel we have the most success. Our flies, like our fishing, should say a lot about who we are—and the best fly fishers I know are those who enjoy a sound yet ever-evolving marriage between the flies they tie and how they fish them. They believe in their flies, they have faith in them, in large part because they've made them their own.

The second thing I'm trying to get at here may in fact just be an ancillary point—how important I feel it is to look at and appreciate flies from the past to develop an understanding of materials and design elements to better inform the choices we make with our own flies. A fly is "beautiful" not when judged against some sort of abstract aesthetic, but when viewed as a working tool that will get the job done in a specific fishing situation. Peter's Pheasant Tail is a pretty little fly that you can tie to your tippet with confidence when mayflies begin to stir—and probably whenever you're trying to present something trout are likely to eat.

That evening, after the midday meal, Peter is still using his Pheasant Tail to good effect. As I said, I don't particularly like my version of the traditional Sawyer pattern—so I've already switched to a size 18 Wild Hare, an old favorite, which proves a fair representation of the little mayfly nymphs or whatever else the trout are feeding on as well. After the sun drops behind the lip of the river canyon, we see a few rises, nothing to get excited about, but fish nosing up to the surface just the same. A few little mayflies flutter past, riding the downstream breeze. The trout are definitely not eating the duns—but something new is going on.

I look through a couple of different boxes. Then I find what I'm looking for, a size 20 Green and Something: floss body, itty-bitty hare's mask thorax, a couple of turns of undersized medium dun hen hackle. I lengthen my tippet, get rid of the small pinch of lead I was using with the nymph. I fish the new fly sort of like a dry, sort of like a soft hackle—sometimes deaddrifting it, sometimes tightening up and allowing it to swing.

The trout, anyway, like this one real well, too.

PETER'S PHEASANT TAIL

- **Hook:** #14-18 TMC 3761
- **Thread:** Black 8/0 UNI-Thread, or similar
- **Tail:** Moose mane fibers
- **Abdomen:** Pheasant tail
- **Rib:** Black copper wire
- **Shellback/wing pad:** Pheasant tail
- **Thorax:** Peacock herl
- **Hackle/legs:** Starling

Tying Peter's Pheasant Tail

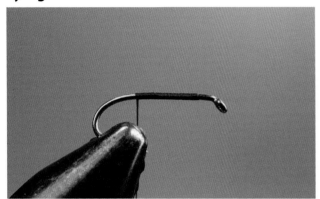

1. Secure the hook in the vise and start your thread. Rather than carry a bunch of different mayfly nymphs, the savvy angler will, with experience, settle on a pattern he or she has confidence in and then be more apt to fuss with hook sizes and *types* of hooks than with pattern changes to cover various moments in a hatch, different water profiles, and the variety of presentations one often needs to employ. Tied on at least three different hook types and in three different sizes, Peter's Pheasant Tail could cover nearly all of your mayfly nymph needs.

2. For the tail, line up the tips of four or five fibers or hairs from a patch of moose mane. Secure the tail just forward the bend of the hook shank, directly above the point of the hook. The tail should be about two-thirds the length of the hook shank.

3. At the root of the tail, tie in a length of black copper wire. At the same spot, secure the tips of three or four pheasant tail fibers. Advance the thread to the midpoint of the hook shank. With a pair of hackle pliers, grab hold of the butts of the pheasant tail fibers and then gently twist them into something resembling a dubbing noodle. Wind the pheasant tail fibers forward, aiming for a tapered abdomen. Secure the fibers and cut off excess. Then wind forward the black wire, segmenting the abdomen with four to six turns of wire. Secure the wire and clip excess.

4. For the shellback or wing pad, tie in four or five more pheasant tail fibers directly ahead of the abdomen. Tie them in far enough from the tips of the fibers that they don't break off when you eventually pull them forward over the thorax. Now tie in one or two lengths of peacock herl. Advance the thread, leaving yourself plenty of room behind thc hook eye. Wind the peacock herl forward, tie off, and clip excess.

5. Ahead of the herl thorax, secure by its tip a small starling hackle feather. If you don't have a starling skin, invest five bucks and get one. It's hard to find smaller, softer feathers for nymph legs or traditional soft hackles. Here you need only one or two turns. Tie off and clip excess.

6. To finish the fly, pull forward the pheasant tail fibers to form the shellback or wing pad. As the fibers lie down over the thorax, they should splay the starling hackle, creating the appearance of legs. Secure the pheasant tail fibers directly behind the eye of the hook and clip excess. Fashion a tidy head with wraps of thread, whip-finish, and saturate the head with lacquer or your favorite head cement.

CZECHISH NYMPH

Czechish Nymph, adapted by author from various popular designs

An old acquaintance of mine, Gary Davis, was kind enough to give me a place to crash for a night at his juniper and ponderosa pine ranchette outside of Bend; that way, there'd at least be beer money left over in the job budget after driving that far to read the opening of a few stories at the downtown Patagonia store. Retired now from managing California projects for a big-deal power or communication corporation, Gary, I should add, is a serious, no-nonsense angler; he's always up on the latest technique or so-called innovation described in magazines or online. Gary's active, as well, in the Central Oregon Flyfishers, the biggest fly-fishing club I know of. He attends workshops and classes whenever they're available, and his fly boxes are filled with intriguing new patterns, often tied with materials I barely recognize or I have never even seen before.

So I was a wee bit flattered when, over a couple of ales in Gary's well-appointed living room, he mentioned thinking of me while he sat through a recent club presentation on Euro nymphing.

"It kept going through my mind," he said, "that this is exactly how you were fishing when you took me to South Junction and we caught all those good redsides on the Deschutes ten years ago."

Well, not exactly. From what I've seen, rigging variations in Euro nymphing don't necessarily mirror the way I go about it. And, by way of context, I can recall, however vaguely, an essay written by James Babb in *Gray's Sporting Journal* maybe two decades ago, in which Babb challenged the idea of new nymphing techniques, describing tight-line methods he and family and friends used long ago on the Tennessee River. Or, if I've got the details wrong, that was the general idea.

And, anyway, what was Charles Brooks talking about when he taught us how to nymph for larger trout forty-plus years ago and counting?

I know, I know: Readers out there will contend that this is different, that Euro nymphing is something entirely new. On the other hand, Gary Davis actually attended the workshop—and he's the one who claims I was doing it way back when.

We can at least agree on this: Nothing successful I've ever done on a trout stream is more than an interpretation of techniques I've seen or read about elsewhere, methods practiced by anglers with much more experience than I'll ever have, despite the many decades I've already squandered in this far-fetched game.

What I like about the attention given to so-called Euro nymphing is that it's prompting anglers to put away their bobbing strike indicators and get back in touch with their flies. It's about time.

Learning to stay in touch with a sunk fly dead-drifting naturally downstream, and then even leading it through the drift without dragging it downstream or across the current, is the telltale stuff of successful nymphing. I'm less enamored, however, by the notion of a brightly colored "sighter" inserted somewhere in the leader; with your butt-section nail knot and the two or three blood knots that make up your leader, don't you already have plenty of things to "sight"—or watch—to indicate even the subtlest change in the drift of your cast? And, anyway, by the time you register this type of visual clue, you should probably already be lifting or swinging or in some other way tightening your line with the rod tip—while at the very same instant softening your grip in case that's a pig down there that has every chance to make mush out of you and your 4X tippet.

Fun stuff. And how else get to know your prey and how it feeds better than when you actually feel the way it eats the fly? This is priceless information—a source of insight and even enlightenment, as different from indicator fishing as fly fishing is from fishing with bait.

That's saying a lot—and it's sort of why old-schoolers like me have been harping about nymphing *without* bobbing strike indicators all these years. Guides, on the other hand, often prefer clients to fish with nymphs suspended beneath strike indicators; unless an angler has experience without an indicator, he or she is likely to hook more fish using one. Also, presenting nymphs from a boat, with the rower, not the angler, controlling the drift, might well be more effective with flies dangling under a bobber.

I don't know much about *that*. And as far as I can tell, it has little to do, either, with the Czechs or the Spaniards, or even the French, carrying home the gold from the latest world championships, the venue that brought so much attention to high-stick, short-line nymphing and what now seems like the Euro nymph craze. To win, team anglers must follow the strict rules laid down by the Fédération Internationale de Pêche Sportive Mouche, which make it illegal to add anything—neither sinking nor floating device—to your leader. That means no strike-indicating bobber *or* split shot—the rule that's done so much to inspire a style of fly that must do double duty as both a sinking device and a fish-fooling lure.

When I got serious about nymphing, a quarter century ago and counting, that double-duty fly was often a heavily weighted Stone Nymph, tied to the point of the leader, with a much smaller immature caddisfly or mayfly imitation tied to a tag end of my blood knot connecting the tippet to the leader. That big weighted nymph gives you the all but taut line that's so critical in short-line nymphing—and because I often fished where Salmonflies and stoneflies lived in abundance, that big dark fly, working its way downstream amongst the rocks, was often gobbled by good trout.

But so was the much smaller Hare's Ear or Wet Caddis or some sort of soft hackle. In fact, as time went on, I grew more confident fooling bigger fish with smaller flies, especially when nymphing—so it wasn't long before I was fishing with a brace of small flies, adding split shot in various ways and positions to my leader to do the job of the weighted and now discarded Stone Nymph.

At this point, we're one step away from what's now being hailed as Euro nymphing. And it's a very, very small step indeed. Because the competition rules say that you can't add split shot to your leader, you add it, instead, in the form of a metal bead, preferably tungsten, to the fly. A little epoxy and lead wire will help that puppy sink as well. In fact, the more streamlined you make the fly, reducing drag and surface area associated with rough dubbing or hair and feather fibers, the more quickly it sinks, too—which means it doesn't need to be as heavy as a traditionally dressed fly of the same size.

Picture, as an example, a Copper John: The mechanical properties, described above, of this jig-like pattern allow anglers to fish smaller flies in faster water, or in deeper lies, maintaining contact with the fly without resorting to split shot—which, sadly, often ends up in the stream. Of course, it also works under a bobber or suspended beneath a high-floating dry fly as well. In my eyes, the Copper John is the progenitor of most flies associated with Euro nymphing. Now, tie it on a small jig hook, one that best fits a bead with a slot in it as well as a hole, and you have a fly that swims or drifts upside down, able to probe the depths of a stream with less chance of hanging up or snagging on the bottom—and a near replica, sans epoxy, of countless Euro nymphs fished today.

Granted, I'm oversimplifying each and every aspect of Euro nymphing. My thesis, as is often the case, is that the latest and greatest method or technique or movement in fly fishing is rarely anything new at all, but instead a return or slight refinement to something out of the sport's long and storied past. Or, as my father used to say about my mother's tangents along her convoluted spiritual path, "Same candy bar, different wrapper."

Nonetheless, it's true that at one time, long ago, nobody weighted a fly, much less squeezed lead to the leader. Nymphing, of any sort, was considered contrary not only to the rules but even the spirit of the sport. Yet at the same time we know as well that there were always "up" or north country anglers who didn't give a lick about rules written by upper-class sports, and from the very start they found that sparsely dressed wet flies, tied on stout hooks and fished on a taut line, could be *murder* when the trout weren't rising. Carry that thinking forward far enough and—with a few adjustments to casting angles, mends, and then lifting all of that useless slack line off the water—you're more or less there, Euro nymphing with the best of them.

No doubt, new commodities deemed necessary to execute so-called new techniques will always be part of the sport. After all, I bought jig hooks and replaced my old brass beads with tungsten—slotted, no less—to experiment with nymphs for this chapter. And I don't suppose it will be long before we find ourselves styling our latest and greatest creations on hooks made out of some sort of new, fourth-dimensional metal that's denser and heavier per unit size than anything used before, just so we can gain that fraction or half percent of sink rate with our sleek and slender Hot Spot Hare's Ear that will finally—*finally*—show those damn Czechs or Spaniards, or even the French, who's boss on a trout stream.

CZECHISH NYMPH

- **Hook:** #12-16 TMC 2457
- **Bead:** Copper tungsten (⅛" for #12, ⁷⁄₆₄" for #14, ³⁄₃₂" for #16)
- **Thread:** Camel 8/0 UNI-Thread or similar
- **Legs:** Fine (comparadun) dark deer hair
- **Tail:** English grouse or similar
- **Rib:** Copper wire (small)
- **Body:** Golden olive Crystal Splash
- **Thorax:** Dark brown squirrel with guard hairs, or similar

Tying the Czechish Nymph

1. Slip the bead over the hook. Secure the hook in the vise and start the thread. Even though I experiment with jig hooks, I prefer the profile of the curved, 2X heavy TMC 2457 for this and other bead-head patterns.

2. Clip a small tuft of extra fine or "comparadun" deer hair. If you don't have any of this type of deer hair, get some; it's much easier to work with for many applications, especially on small flies. Clean and stack the hair. Measure the hair length so that it's about equal to the length of the hook, then tie it in directly behind the bead with the tips of the hair pointing forward past the eye of the hook. As you tighten your thread wraps, squeeze the hair forward against the bead, causing it to flare like the wing of a comparadun. Then make a couple of thread wraps between the standing hair and the bead, creating a small space for dubbing later on.

3. Secure the butts of deer hair. As your wind toward the aft end of the fly, clip the butts a bit at a time to help with the taper of the fly. Wind the thread deep into the bend of the hook and then tie in a short tail. Clip the butts of the tail material so that it fairs in with the forward half of the body. Now wind the thread forward and back a few times to create a smooth carrot-like taper for the body of the fly.

4. As you wind the thread to the back of the hook the last time, secure a short length of copper wire. When you reach the root of the tail, also secure a couple of strands of the Crystal Splash. Wind the thread forward, then touch a tiny amount of superglue to the thread wraps before winding the Crystal Splash forward, covering the entire abdomen. Stop the Crystal Splash just short of the deer hair. Now rib the abdomen with three or four evenly spaced turns of copper wire.

5. For the thorax, wax your thread and create a slender, tapered dubbing noodle. Make a couple of turns of dubbing behind the standing deer hair. Now pull the tips of the deer hair back and away from the bead and wrap dubbing over the base of the deer hair, creating legs that extend back toward the abdomen. Use enough dubbing to hold back the hair and fill the gap between the deer hair and the bead. Touch the top of the thread with a drop of superglue, make two or three more wraps between the dubbing and the bead, then whip-finish.

BIG JELLY

Big Jelly, designed by Joe Kelly

My buddy Joe Kelly is a hunter, noted within a small circle of friends as the guy who finds animals when everyone else spends most of his or her time wandering about the woods, engaged in vigorous hiking, and little else, throughout the season. Joe doesn't always put meat on the ground; year after year, nobody in our busy neck of the woods can claim much in the way of success. But Joe nearly always returns from a hunt with stories of *encounters* with animals, how he found them, what they were doing, what he saw and heard, how the animals eventually reacted to his presence—even if he didn't get a chance to pull a trigger.

I bring up the matter of Joe Kelly's hunting skills because he also happens to be an angler who hunts, hooks, and lands big fish. Most of the fishing we do together involves trout of one kind or another; Joe has teenage daughters, and on weeks or weekends they're with their mother, Joe and I often head off together, occasionally with his raft in tow, a tool that also comes in handy for a guy who likes to track down big fish. Joe, in other words, is just about the ideal fishing partner, a guy who gets after it whenever he can and who's always on the lookout, with one ear to the ground, for inside dope on the whereabouts of exceptional or at least promising sport.

One difference, however, looms large between Joe and me. While I like to catch big fish, especially trout, as much as anyone, I also like nothing better than chasing hatches, casting to rising fish or bringing fish to the surface with patterns that mimic something the trout are looking for. My fly boxes reflect this itch; not only do I stuff my vest with a half-dozen boxes of patterns aimed at different families or genera or even species of insects, I also include other separate stashes of *types* of flies—soft hackles, attractor dries, or, simply, Humpys.

Joe, on the other hand, carries just one box of flies—or maybe two sometimes, I'm not really sure. Let's just say he's nothing like the fly junkie I am. And even though I'm confident he's got all of the bases covered, there's one fly that's nearly always on the end of his tippet. A hunter with a penchant for big fish, Joe maintains that something big and black and wiggly will keep you in the game—especially when trout are on their lies, with nothing specific in the way of insects showing. I have my own ideas about how to go about finding trout at such times—but Joe considers most of these approaches beside the point. Big trout, claims Joe, are always on the lookout for a mouthful.

It's hard to argue with success.

I call Joe's favorite trout fly Big Jelly. It's quick and easy to tie, and I've seen it in the mouths of more good trout than perhaps any other single pattern I fish or I've seen fished throughout my lifetime. It probably gets eaten as a stonefly nymph, although there's nothing obvious about it that distinguishes it from a half-dozen other common stonefly patterns you can either tie or buy.

Except maybe the legs. Or not just legs per se, but all eight appendage-like gewgaws that dangle from the fly like so many feathers down a heron's breast. Years ago Joe stumbled upon a supply of this freaky rubber material; each strand is so thin you need a small sharp needle, and a pair of reading glasses, to separate a single strand from the remaining material. The stuff reminds me of the strip of rubber that goes inside the narrow rim of a high-end racing bike—except it's made out of those separate pieces that can be pulled apart one fibery strip at a time.

Does it matter? Can you substitute, instead, the usual thicker rubber leg material sold at your local fly shop or online dealer? I'm the last guy to worry about changes made to any pattern—I'll readily swap out one material for another so that I don't have to search out something rare or hard to come by just so I can replicate the original. But in this case I tend to think Joe may be onto something. His Big Jelly makes the legs on, say, a Girdle Bug or a Pat's Stone look like they're made out of toothpicks. If the movement you get from a rubber-legged fly is important in the first place, the legs on Big Jelly are akin to giving your fly the moves on the dance floor of Michael Jackson rather than those of Shaq O'Neal.

Still, I hesitate to make claims about any specific material—especially one you may not be able to readily find. (Joe got his legging material at our local fly shop; I don't know what he's going to do if he eventually runs out.) Because the truth is, the biggest reason Big Jelly ends up pinned to the mouths of so many good trout is that Joe Kelly knows how to hunt up fish with his favorite fly.

The first thing worth noting is that Joe often uses Big Jelly to catch fish on the swing, not as a dead-drifted nymph. He'll pitch it upstream, allow it to sink a bit, and then lift all of his line off the water so that he's tight to the fly as it sweeps downstream. It helps that Joe happens to be six foot five; by the time he raises his rod hand overhead, with the rod tip nearly vertical, he's got more than fifteen feet of line in the air rather than lying on the surface, where currents can mess with his presentation. All of that line in the air also means that Joe is able to keep his fly from swinging hard across the current, an unnatural presentation that often prevents us from pulling fish off a far bank or other holding lie on the other side of swifter water directly in front of us.

These are all subtle manipulations. And Joe has a host of others, often employing several of them on a single cast. One of them, the Stony Creek mend, named after a piece of water he used to fish as a kid in Michigan, involves repeated mends, at the end of his swing, into which he feeds line so that his fly reaches farther and farther downstream, often toward a logjam or overhanging branch or some other obstruction that prevents any sort of conventional cast. Eventually, the fly is off in the distance swimming in some dark, hard-to-reach hole, those wiggly legs doing what all to entice a strike.

I've seen that one work a time or two, I can tell you that.

My point here, however, is not to instruct the reader how to fish Joe Kelly's favorite fly. Instead, these examples serve as evidence that the last thing Joe worries about is what he's tied to the end of his line. He has absolute faith in Big Jelly—which leaves him free to go about hunting big fish in the many ways available to an experienced fly angler.

For Joe, like a lot of good anglers, it's not about the fly. It probably has little to do with the fly's legs either.

What matters most, instead, is the hunter at the other end of the line.

BIG JELLY

- **Hook:** #4-8 TMC 200R or similar
- **Weight:** .025-.030 lead wire
- **Thread:** Black 8/0 or 6/0 UNI-Thread, or similar
- **Tail/legs/antennae:** Thinnest, limpest black rubber you can find
- **Underbody:** Black chenille or black yarn (small or medium)
- **Body:** Black rabbit fur mixed with peacock black Ice Dub

Tying Big Jelly

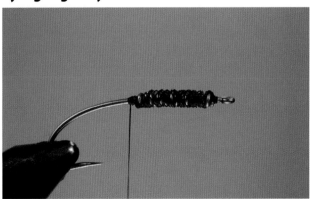

1. Secure the hook. Start the thread directly behind the eye. Wind a layer of thread back to the middle of the hook shank. Cover the thread wraps with ten to fifteen wraps of lead, depending on the size of the fly and thickness of the lead. Cover the lead wraps with wraps of thread, then build a small tapered dam at the aft end of the lead to help keep it from sliding.

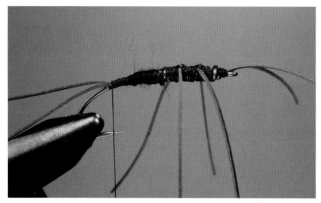

2. Strip off a long length of legging material; if you are tying more than one Big Jelly, strip off several pieces. Cut the lengths into 2½-inch pieces; you'll need four of these for each fly. For the tail and forward antennae, fold the pieces in half and secure with thread wraps, one piece at the aft end of the fly, the other just behind the hook eye. For the legs, tie in the other two pieces on top of the lead in the thorax region, leaving space between each piece. Don't fuss too much at this point with the length of these parts or their precise position. They can be moved when you wrap the dubbing and trimmed to length after the fly is constructed. To help reduce the amount of dubbing needed with this fly, Joe covers the entire abdomen with a layer of black chenille. Because I like to get a pronounced taper through the abdomen, I tie in chenille or yarn at the midpoint of the abdomen, wind it forward so that it fairs in with the lead, then wind my thread back to the tail.

3. For dubbing material, Joe mixes small doses of something brown or gray with the black rabbit fur to give texture and contrast to what would otherwise be a solid uniform color. My favorite additive is currently some chopped-up peacock black Ice Dub by Hareline. A pinch will do. You'll probably have to form three or four dubbing noodles by the time you make it all the way forward through this big fly. I try to taper the abdomen, then create a beefy thorax while positioning the legs just so. Create a tidy head and then whip-finish under the root of the antennae. If you think it matters, you can even up the length of the appendages with judicious use of scissors. Also, if you think a more realistic fly is important, create a more pronounced thorax by pricking out dubbing fibers with your bodkin needle or teasing them out with a dubbing brush. Saturate your whip-finish with either lacquer or head cement.

NEO-FRESCHI BULLDOG

Neo-Freschi Bulldog, adapted from design by Don Freschi

I don't write much about stillwater patterns. My attention rests on flies I use, and the truth is I've never been much of a lake angler, even if lakes promise some of the biggest trout we might encounter in any given year. I know anglers as well who clean up on anadromous fish that gather during summer and early fall in pools of cool water formed by tributaries backed up by dams on main-stem rivers, a crowding together of anglers and their prey that encourages a circus-like atmosphere and, at times, fisticuffs.

Because I don't fish much in lakes or reservoirs, I'm not very good at it. I look at all of that quiet water and nothing tells me, immediately, that the fish are here or there or somewhere else. I'm quickly befuddled, often confused, more likely than not at a loss what to do next. Beyond the obvious signs of fish feeding on the surface, I struggle to conjure up images from below the two-dimensional plane, unable to grasp narratives into which I might insert my fly.

It can be humiliating. Two years straight, for example, my buddy Jeff Cottrell and I had access to a string of high-desert, spring-fed impoundments that a rancher had stocked with trout and largemouth bass in hopes of creating the sort of pay-to-play fishery that was proving, regionally, as lucrative as renting rangeland for wind

generators. Jeff, a fly shop owner, was there to suss out the ponds so that he knew what he was selling when he booked clients, through his shop, at two or three hundred dollars a day. I got to tag along because, well, that's just what writers do.

We did catch fish—even a few trophy rainbows. But mostly I remember wandering around the ponds, often dangling inside a float tube, wondering why we couldn't figure out some way to stimulate steady action. Fish have to feed. Yet even the bass, which hung out near small patches of shoreline weeds, sometimes sending up showers of tiny baitfish as you headed that way, eluded us more often than not. Time and again we left the ponds frustrated—yet all the more determined to tie up a batch of winning flies.

It never happened; we finally just sort of quit on the place. It still bugs me we didn't do better. The ranch owner, too, eventually lost interest, giving up on the idea he could start raking in the big bucks, like some of his neighbors, without so much as lifting a finger.

The problem, as I see it now, was that neither Jeff nor I, nor the rancher, was all that interested in the process: We just wanted to stick some big fish, and the guy just wanted the money. I never could get excited about the fishing—dragging a fly behind a float tube; casting and retrieving; anything, especially, to do with chironomids. The rancher, meanwhile, had no real interest in the fish *or* the fishing, his attention directed, instead, toward cattle weight, heavy equipment, and the pickup scene at the local tavern.

⏺————————⏺

Things felt like they were leaning differently last year when I found myself getting towed in circles by another heavy rainbow out east where roads fade and finally fizzle into sky. My friends the doctor and his wife, the two best trout fishers I know, had finally convinced me to rattle my way out to a small impoundment where, for reasons I can't explain, the trout are plump, plentiful, and sassy.

And not particularly hard to fool.

The doctor had told me it's a scud game. Nice chunky ones, too, so that anything tan or green on about a size 10 hook gets you in the game and keeps you there. To be frank, there was nothing about this fishing that challenged the intellect; once you slipped into your floating device and figured out where the trout were, it was a touchy-feely thing, waiting for the fly to sink and then inching it back your way, ready for the line to straighten.

Still, when it worked, which it did more often than not, you had a heavy fish somewhere down there on the end of your line, a few of which felt as good as small tuna sounding toward oblivion, without the anguish such fish can eventually spark as the fight drags on into the later rounds. No, this was pretty much just straightforward fun—at least until I began to sense that nothing else was bound to happen unless I tried to change up tactics as well.

Don't get me wrong: I'm not greedy. Well, okay, when it comes to fish, maybe a little. But at this stage of my life I do have a tendency to grow inattentive, or at least a wee bit complacent, in the face of expected results. Let's find out, instead, what happens when we try *this*.

From my limited bag of stillwater tricks, however, I don't have a lot to reach for. My longtime favorite is a little olive bugger, a pattern that, tied sparsely, does a fair job representing the often-present damselfly nymphs flitting about any weed beds. More important, the little olive bugger offers an excellent imitation of SEAT—*something else appealing to trout*—a "hatch" I find as significant as any other when I go looking for our favorite coldwater species.

Still, the slender profile I give my little lake buggers fails to cover another option—that is, the BM, or Big Mac. This is a fly you turn to when you give up trying to finesse the opposition; sometimes it works to just throw 'em, instead, a Big Mac.

I was reminded of this option on that remote rainbow reservoir when, coming ashore for a midmorning break, I spotted, near a stand of cattails, the husk of a dragonfly nymph. *Hmm.* If you've ever poked around

in ponds or kept a small aquarium filled with stillwater critters, you've no doubt seen the impressive dimensions reached by many dragonfly nymphs, a size commensurate with the damage they'll do on any other swimming or bottom-crawling neighbors, especially in the confines of a private observation tank.

That's your Big Mac. You can go to town trying to create an exact imitation of a dragonfly nymph. Or you can take another tack and just make sure you have something big and gnarly that might suggest not only these bodacious nymphs, but perhaps also crayfish, leeches, tadpoles, or salamanders or a host of different forage fish. That is, *something else appealing to trout*—only in this case, something even *bigger*.

I know, I know: It's a lot more fun to home in on a hatch or bait and fool fish with an irresistible imitation. Meanwhile, back in a real world, where most of us reside, it's good to carry a stash of those all-around patterns that seem to work wherever you go fishing. Clearly, there's no such thing, not even a Clouser Minnow, that fools fish everywhere. But on a stillwater impoundment where rainbow trout grow fat and happy feeding on everything under the sun, you really should carry something you think qualifies as a genuine Big Mac, a fly that represents a mouthful of nutrition that just might stimulate a strike from an otherwise inattentive or even complacent old trout.

Don Freschi's Bulldog could be that pattern. I've tweaked it here, because that's what I do to most every pattern I fish, and also because I encourage readers, or anyone else who ties flies, to do the same. The Bulldog, after all, is simply a Woolly Bugger—with a little of this and a little of that thrown in. Freschi's two-tone hackling offers provocative shading; I'm also a fan of burnt orange (or rust or the like) in many of my generic patterns, from the smallest nymph to the biggest dry. Color, of course, probably means a lot more to the angler than it does to the trout. Then again, the first thing a fly has to do is win over the angler—or else it will never end up tied to the end of your line.

NEO-FRESCHI BULLDOG

- **Hook:** #6 Daiichi 2220 streamer or similar 4X-long
- **Weight:** .015-.025 lead wire
- **Thread:** Black 8/0 UNI-Thread, or similar
- **Tail:** Marabou, dyed burnt orange
- **Rib:** Copper wire (medium)
- **Hackle:** Pair of Bugger Hackle, grizzly dyed burnt orange and grizzly dyed olive
- **Body:** Holographic gold Diamond Braid
- **Collar:** Guinea fowl, dyed olive

Tying the Neo-Freschi Bulldog

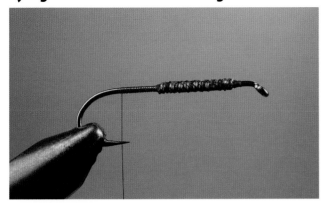

1. Mount the hook. Starting just aft of the midway point on the hook shank, make twenty or so wraps of lead wire. Stop well short of the hook eye. Start your thread directly behind the eye and build up a small dam of thread wraps to keep the lead wraps from crawling forward. Now secure all of the lead wraps with widely spaced turns of thread, plus another small dam of wraps at the lead's aft end. Finish covering the hook shank until your thread is slightly aft of the point of the hook.

2. For the tail, secure a substantial tuft of marabou fibers about in line with the point of the hook. I like those tidy pin fibers toward the tip of a marabou feather; others like the bushier fibers farther down the sides of the feather. The tail should be about the length of the hook shank. Once the tail is in place, clip the excess so that you're left with a wad of stems that will cover the hook shank behind the lead wraps, helping to create an even foundation for the body. Return the thread to the tail's tie-in point and make a couple of turns behind and under the root of the tail; this helps prevent the floppy tail from fouling on the hook.

3. Secure a length of copper wire just ahead of the root of the tail. Leave enough excess wire to reach the aft end of the lead; cover the excess with thread wraps, again keeping the underbody fair. Now select two bugger hackle feathers with fibers about equal length. Splay the individual feather fibers, leaving only the tips lying in line with the stem. Don Freschi, from Trail, British Columbia, the inventor of the Bulldog, sets the olive hackle feather on top of the burnt orange feather before tying in both feathers by their tips. The goal is to have the two feathers positioned so that they can be wound simultaneously, one against the other, after the body is formed.

4. With both the copper wire and pair of hackle feathers out of the way, secure a length of Diamond Braid at the root of the tail. Advance the thread to the forward end of the lead wraps. Wind the Diamond Braid forward, creating an even body that covers the lead.

5. Now hold the hackle feathers, olive on top and in front of the burnt orange, and wind them forward simultaneously. Leave a small gap between each turn, while at the same time stroking the feather fibers toward the aft end of the fly and also maintaining the same feather orientation, olive in front, burnt orange behind. End the hackle wraps well back from the hook eye; you want plenty of room for the collar and head.

6. Secure the palmered hackle feathers with counter-wraps of copper wire. I always dislike doing this after working so hard to get the hackle feathers to lie just right; no matter how hard I try, I always end up scrunching some of the fibers with the copper wire wrap. But these counter-wraps are the best way of preventing your fly from unraveling if it actually ends up fooling a fish, which is what we want, rather than trying to win a beauty contest. Now, select a well-marked dyed guinea feather; tie it in by the tip directly in front of the last turn of hackle feathers. I like the guinea feather fibers long enough to eventually extend just beyond the midpoint of the fly. Fold the feather along the stem, fibers pointed aft, as you make two or three turns going forward, each turn directly in front of the other. Catch the stem of the feather with your thread and secure it. Clip excess. Tidy up any errant fibers with thread wraps, then form a clean head, whip-finish, and saturate the head with lacquer or your favorite head cement.

PERDIGÓNERO

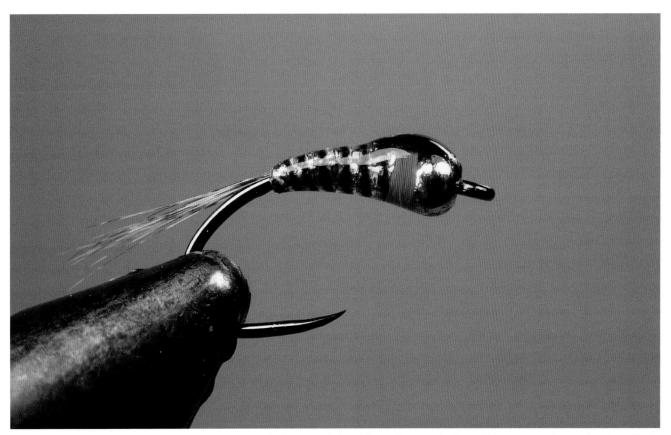

Perdigónero, variation of popular nymph allegedly by competition anglers from Spain

In a scene almost identical to one I wrote about before, I was tying flies this past fall in Bob Hoyt's Whale's Tale Inn in Magdalena Bay, replenishing supplies after two weeks getting knocked about by big roosterfish, when guide Jeff deBrown showed up at the bar and immediately assailed me from across the room.

"What the *hell* are you doing?" he hollered, beer bottle in hand.

What I was doing was securing the eyes on the sides of the heads of several baitfish patterns, fiddling with five-minute epoxy dribbled onto the flies with a wooden match. This tiresome task was followed by the laborious and clumsy job of forming the heads of the fly, which required a second and sometimes third batch of epoxy, then lifting and turning flies this way and that while at the same time adding more of the runny goop to another fly, juggling everything in hopes of creating two or three fair heads, free of unsightly drips, bulges, or eyes knocked askew.

"*Five-minute epoxy?*"

DeBrown, incredulous, approached my table, stationed alongside the front window for adequate light.

"I'm not trying to tell you what to do. But don't you have better things to do with your time than working with that shit?"

I twirled another fly, its sides held flat by a pair of needle-nose pliers with a rubber band wrapped around its handles.

"Come on, man. Join the modern age."

This isn't the first time it's been suggested to me that I drag my sorry ass into the twenty-first century. Immediately on arriving home I ordered up the appropriate UV light and quick-cure resins. *Voilá.* I began to think about coming to terms with a smartphone.

Before I went *that* far, however, I decided I finally had one of the most important tools for getting serious about fabricating any number of the quintessential Euro nymphs so popular in the sport today. In another development from last year, the esteemed publisher of a magazine I write for had asked if I would share my thoughts about Euro nymphing. The piece I wrote, "Czechish Nymph," argued that the technique actually points back to short-line nymphing techniques practiced long ago *before* the reliance on indicators impeded the development of so many anglers' presentation skills.

Anglers now, of course, associate a particular style of fly with Euro nymphing techniques—flies that grew out of rules governing fly-fishing competitions especially popular in Europe. The most important rule states that you can't add anything that floats or sinks to your leader—that is, no floating indicator or bobber-like device, as well as no split shot or similar aid. The job of getting the fly down to where fish are holding falls to the fly itself—and the skill of the angler. If you're fishing small flies, often the most effective way to move pressured fish on pressured waters, you look for flies that offer every possible advantage to penetrate the water column as quickly as possible, while also helping you maintain that all but taut line so important in this kind of nymphing.

———————•————————•————————

Rules, like scorecards and standings, are anathema to many fly fishers. What's competition got to do with how the sport enlivens or enriches my soul? Yet fly fishing itself is a set of specific if loosely defined rules, the likes of which provide parameters for innovation and, in some cases, grounds for arguments about cheating.

It's hard to claim any moral high ground. Robert Frost, who loved the rules of formal poetry, claimed that writing free verse was like playing tennis without a net. Sailboat design, on another tack, has often been marred by attempts to find loopholes in handicap rules. Closer to home, we now have rules on the North Umpqua, for example, that were initiated in part because of Californians who showed up and, with big black weighted flies, nymphed the bejesus out of those famous and previously hard-to-fool summer steelhead.

And just this past year, I might add, while swinging flies for big river trout, I had the best one-fish day in memory, losing more than a half-dozen other fish after my friendly guide reminded me of the rules and pinched down the barb on my fly.

The point, of course, is that some rules can make you a better or more skilled angler—and in that way increase the enjoyment you get out of the sport. Three decades ago, when Bill McMillan published the essays he had been writing the previous dozen years in reaction to a school of thought that claimed that sinking shooting heads were the most effective way to catch steelhead, many steelheading careers—mine included—were invigorated by the notion that the best all-around tool for catching these elusive fish was, instead, a floating line.

In his collection *Dry Line Steelhead and Other Subjects*, McMillan rejected the idea of the so-called mechanical advantage of sinking or lead-core lines, especially in the face of evidence that, at times, surface presentations were the most effective way to move steelhead to the fly. There was also the question, never stated but implied, of how often steelhead were *snagged* by anglers using quick-sinking shooting heads, even fish hooked in the mouth after they were "flossed" by a swinging, deep-running line.

Innovation or cheating? One of the things I like about the latest and greatest Euro nymphs is the way they marry technique and technology. There's no other way, to my knowledge, that you could get tiny flies that

sink so quickly without the UV-activated resin that creates a smooth, hard-bodied nugget ready to penetrate the water column with little in the way of extremities to resist its descent—the difference between, say, a drop of frozen rain and a snowflake drifting down from the sky. That's clever. Whether it's actually a jig, not a fly, is an argument I refuse to entertain. What does the Fool say in *Twelfth Night*? "For, what is 'that' but 'that,' and 'is' but 'is'?"

I'm reminded, finally, of a conversation I had recently with a young fellow, an ex-student of mine, now a teacher himself, who was convinced his recent and newfound success on the home river we share is a direct result of his discovery and practice of Euro nymphing techniques. Before, as a novice fly angler, he'd struggled to catch anything on a river I know, from experience, does not offer up secrets freely, especially to beginners. Now, however, my ex-student was whacking plenty of good trout. He was flush with success. He had the latest Euro nymphing rod; he'd learned to tie the right flies on the appropriate hooks; he had tossed aside his indicators and learned to stay connected to the fly, line lifted off the water, eyes trained on his leader throughout each drift.

"I've got three good spots along the road. I get fish at one until it slows down, then I drive to the next spot and get some more. One day, in less than two hours, I hooked—"

I turned away, inspecting the rush of clouds riding the wind above the river below. When my ex-student was finished recounting his exploits, I found my best teacher voice, free of the patronizing tone that eventually spirited me out of the profession, and I suggested that maybe he was simply learning to fly-fish—that his success wasn't a result of discovering Euro nymphing techniques at all but, instead, about learning to read the water, where the fish are, and how to handle and manipulate subsurface presentations.

He wasn't buying it.

"You make it sound too simple," he said. "There's a lot more to it than that."

I nodded in agreement. There *is* a lot to it—more than you can learn in a lifetime.

"So tell me," I added. "With that nymphing rod in hand, what do you do when the fish start rising?"

My ex-student gave me a look; he'd heard me enough times in the classroom to know something was up.

"You know what?" he said. "I don't even worry about dry flies anymore. Those fish won't eat dries. The evening caddis hatch? I put on a dry fly and it never works. I get all my fish on nymphs."

I nodded again.

"Do you ever try a little soft hackle? Fish it just like a dry fly? Fish don't like to stick their noses out of the water if they don't have to. It's like crossing the threshold into an alien world."

My ex-student gave me another look.

"What's this?" he asked, all but sniffing. "Sounds like some kind of old man wisdom."

We soon shook hands, parted ways.

Who can argue with reasoning like that?

PERDIGÓNERO

- **Hook:** #12-16 Gamakatsu J20 Jig Nymph, Firehole 317, or similar
- **Bead:** Copper or gold tungsten ($7/64$-$1/8$" or 2.5-3.5 mm)
- **Thread:** Fluorescent orange 14/0 Veevus or similar
- **Tail:** Coq de leon
- **Body:** Gold holographic tinsel (medium)
- **Rib:** Stripped peacock herl, small dark edge Magic Quills, or similar
- **Collar:** Tying thread or hot red UV Fly Finish
- **Finish:** UV-activated clear resin
- **Wing case (optional):** Black Sharpie dot covered with drop of clear UV resin

Tying the Perdigónero

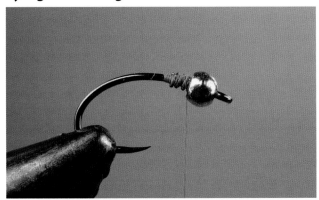

1. Slip your bead onto the hook. Secure the hook in the vise. Brush a dab of quick-drying glue right behind the eye of the hook and then slide the bead into position and let things sit for a couple of minutes. You can also take a few turns of .010 lead wire to help secure the hook and add weight to the fly. Start your thread directly behind the bead. (I'll note right here that for all their alleged mechanical advantages, I'm still not a fan of jig hooks. Whatever they might do in the way of helping the point of the hook ride upward, with less chance to hang up on the bottom, I find the finished fly sort of homely, not nearly as graceful as a standard bead on one of any number of curved hooks available today. When I reach into my fly box, I invariably grab the prettiest fly of any pattern—and I fish that fly with greater confidence or at least commitment. Aesthetic appeal remains a big part of the pleasure I get from the sport.)

2. Wind a layer of thread back to the bend of the hook. Those wraps of lead directly behind the bead, if you used them, help to begin to build up the taper you eventually want to run from the bend up to the bead. At the bend of the hook, tie in ten to twelve fibers from a coq de leon feather.

3. Build up the appropriate taper, working with even layers of thread wraps up and down the hook shank, each layer ending, at the aft end, farther and farther forward. Once you're happy with the overall shape of the body, tie in tinsel for the underbody. There are a million different materials you can use for this step, including just your tying thread if you're aiming to suggest a specific species of insect. Holographic tinsels, used in this example, are especially popular. Leave the tag end long enough that it covers the length of the body; cover it all the way up to the bead, maintaining the even taper. Now wind your thread back to the root of the tail, and secure the tip of your stripped peacock herl. You can make your own or buy them, real or synthetic; there is also a variety of other materials available to give that two-tone effect we associate with abdominal segmentation. And since you're eventually going to encase the entire body in resin, you don't need to worry about your segmenting material coming unraveled after your first fish.

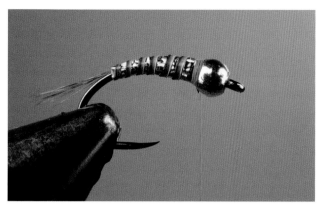

4. Wind your thread up to the bead, then first wrap the tinsel underbody, followed by the stripped herl, leaving a small gap between turns so that the underbody shows.

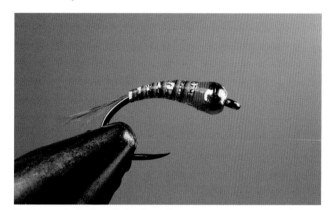

5. Directly behind the bead create a narrow band, or hot spot, with your tying thread. You can also get the same effect with the various colored UV-curing resins now offered by Loon Outdoors. After finishing the bright band, whip-finish and clip the excess thread. Finally, cover the entire body of the fly with a thin coat of UV-curing resin, being careful not to overdo it and end up with bulges or drips. As soon as things look good, zap the fly with your UV light.

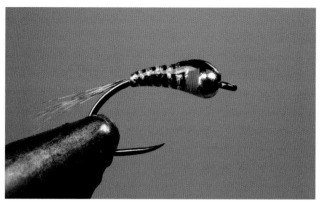

6. The classic Perdigón features a wing case—a spot of black, made with a Sharpie or other marking pen, that's then covered with a single drop of resin, immediately cured, so that you end up with a small black bulge where, on a mayfly nymph, the wings develop. Does it matter? If you think it does, you should also consider how the fly will ride in the water: Should the wing case be on the point side of the body? Or on the side we generally think of as the back of the fly?

LIGHT CAHILL WET

Light Cahill Wet, wet fly variation of design by Dan Cahill

Has there ever been a lovelier material for tying flies than wood duck lemon flank feathers? In our search for the latest and greatest iridescent scream, a space-age ingredient that will attract wary or jaded fish as if flames spotted across an empty sea, we often lose track of or forget about these elegant old-timey natural fibers that played such a large part in the original seduction. The romance of fly fishing has always included the alchemy of actual fur and feathers fabricated into a formal impression of life, a transference capable of animating primal responses from creatures we sense, even from afar, suggest a heaven sublimer than any we might possibly imagine.

Some of us have never recovered. Was it ever really just about catching fish? Like countless moments from my distant past, I can't recall the first time I used or bought any wood duck lemon flank feathers, yet they seem to have been somewhere in my supplies ever since I started tying so many decades ago. One look at these pretty feathers, with their wispy fibers and delicate dark bars, and you know immediately that they're going to find their way into one pattern or another, even if you can't imagine mastering the wings of a classy Catskill dry.

All tyers have materials that speak to them at some profound and perhaps even organic level; you recognize colors or shadings that mimic life in the natural world, or there's a feel that promises properties of motion you don't sense in other visually similar materials. Or perhaps, as Tom McGuane has suggested, just as certain flies can inspire one's conviction, when we inspect various materials we are subject to emotions that reflect the fact that like fish, we too are a species of prey.

Peacock herl. Partridge and grouse feathers. The versatile hare's mask. Ring-necked pheasant tails. From the moment we begin tying flies and paying fresh attention to what bugs look like on the water, many of us recognize that it's an impression we want on the end of our leaders, not an exact representation, and that certain materials suggest what we're looking for without asserting claims of infallible imitation. There are very few tan or cream or yellow mayfly or caddisfly patterns that couldn't be enhanced by a few judiciously placed wood duck lemon flank feather fibers; the few innovative tyers I know are the ones who make these subtle adjustments with tried-and-true materials, avoiding attempts at wholesale changes to proven patterns.

After all, the smartest tyers I know are pretty darn good anglers as well. They don't place excessive faith in precise imitations; they want something close enough, while leaning toward patterns that also suggest an all-around bugginess that inspires confidence even when fish aren't up and visually feeding. Mostly, they understand that the fly tied to their tippet is only one aspect of the game.

Dave Hughes, who likes the old Light Cahill wet fly as an imitation for the Yellow Sally stonefly hatch, will fish this pattern just as he would a dry fly, a drifting nymph, a swinging emerger—or even a likely looking lure dangling downstream on the end of a taut line. The point is, the pattern, tied with that lovely wood duck lemon flank feather wing to originally imitate either Pale Morning or Pale Evening Duns, crosses over nicely to the Yellow Sally hatch, especially when fished in the variety of ways that trout might encounter these seasonally important bugs.

A host of other traditional wet flies, tied with traditional materials, assume this same logic: good enough for one hatch, but quite possibly effective in other situations as well—as long as the angler is ready to employ a range of techniques that present the fly in the different ways fish may recognize such food in the stream. Clearly, it's never *wrong* to attempt to imitate the precise stage, say, of a specific hatch. The suggestion here, however, is that a traditional fly like the Light Cahill wet can cover not only different hatches but also different stages of a hatch, allowing the angler to explore the different casts and presentations that are often the real key to triggering a strike, while at the same time keeping the fly in the water, the only place I've ever found they actually catch fish.

———•———•———

If you're inspired to tie up a few Light Cahill wets, I should make you aware of a curious aspect of those pretty wood duck lemon flank feathers: Unlike so many things we purchase today, including much of our food, wood duck lemon flank feathers are available seasonally. If you go to buy them in spring or summer, there's a chance, depending on the year, that your local fly shop or even online site will be out of stock. I searched this past March and was told by every single supplier I contacted that, sorry, I would have to back order.

Despite the inconvenience, I was somehow heartened by this shortage. One of the reasons I enjoy fishing so much is that it anchors me within the cycle of seasons. Bugs and fish and birds move with the changing cant of the sun, and though I might believe, thanks to the internet, that I can do anything or be anywhere any time of year, I can, in reality, only fish for trout feeding on Yellow Sallies for a very brief period in any given year. Such limits tend to make me appreciate these moments—more than if I could obtain them, like so many other things in life, simply by sharing the details of my Mastercard.

If I were to posit a guess, I might also suggest that part of the enduring appeal of tying and fishing traditional patterns like the Light Cahill wet is the use of genuine fur and feathers, often procured seasonally from hunters afield. The idea of those pretty flank feathers

plucked from a downed wood duck, carried shoreward in the mouth of a happy retriever, may not appeal to everyone—but for some of us it opens a wider window onto the history and lore of the sport of fly fishing.

For a number of reasons that I don't need to go into here, it's easy to forget at times that some of the materials we secure to our hooks to imitate insects or other baits were once part of the bodies of living and breathing creatures, some of them as wild as the fish we hope to fool. For those of us with an appreciation for and fascination with the natural world, there's a certain symmetry to all of this, one that seems a little less balanced when employing, say, carpet fibers produced in million-ton lots by the likes of Dupont, or colors derived by use of chemicals created by their friends at Dow.

Which is only to say that trying your hand at a half-dozen or so Light Cahill wets just might help you recall some larger purpose to this frivolous game.

LIGHT CAHILL WET

- **Hook:** #12-16 2X stout or 1X fine
- **Thread:** Primrose Pearsall's Gossamer Silk, Lt. Cahill 8/0 UNI-Thread, or similar
- **Hackle:** Light ginger hen
- **Tail:** Light ginger hackle fibers
- **Body:** Cream fox fur or similar
- **Wing:** Wood duck lemon flank fibers

Tying the Light Cahill Wet

1. Secure your hook and start your thread just behind the hook eye. As for most traditional soft hackles, I tie this one on a variety of hooks, from the short, stout, old Mustad 3906 to any sort of fine-wire dry-fly hook. The idea, of course, is to enhance the versatility of the pattern so that it can be offered up in a range of different presentations. A fine-wire size 12 is just about perfect for little Yellow Sallies. Also, I continue to use the last of my Pearsall's Gossamer Silk for size 12 and 14 soft-hackled wet flies, switching to finer modern threads for smaller sizes. Now, choose a hen hackle feather with fibers about the length of the hook shank or twice the width of the hook gap. Strip the downy waste from the base of the feather. With the concave or good side of the feather facing you and the tip pointing forward from the hook eye, tie in the stem along the top of the hook shank. The goal is to have the feather positioned so that when you wind it, later, back from the hook eye, the hackle fibers slant back without having to be tortured into place with your thread.

2. Wind your thread or silk to the aft end of the hook shank, stopping just above or slightly behind the point of the hook. Clip a long feather from the top or sides of your hen neck. Remove six to eight fibers from the feather, keeping the tips aligned. Measure the fibers against the hook shank; the tail should end up about that length. Tie in the fibers as a tail, adding a turn or two under its root to cock the tail slightly upward. When tying with silk, I cut the excess butts of the tail fibers so they extend forward the length of the body, then run my silk in even wraps all the way forward and then back to the root of the tail, in this way creating an even foundation for the body dubbing with a strong layer of thread color underneath.

3. Wax your thread and twist on a wee bit of dubbing. I saved some underfur from a patch of fox used for winging steelhead flies and ended up with a pile of beautiful material. I find you can never dub lightly enough, especially when tying with silk. A touch is all it takes. Wind your dubbed thread forward, creating an evenly tapered body. Stop the body well short of the forward end of the fly, leaving plenty of space for the hackle, the wing, and the head.

4. With your thread well back from the eye of the hook, secure the tip of the protruding hackle feather and make three turns back toward the thread. Then catch the stem of the hackle feather under a turn of thread and continue winding the thread forward, directly through the hackle fibers. Take a few turns of thread in front of the hackle fibers, directing any errant fibers rearward while maintaining space for the wing.

5. Finally, those lovely wood duck flank feathers. Align the tips of eight to ten fibers from one side of a feather and clip or pull from the stem. Measure the wing against the hook shank; I like my wing about the length of the body, perhaps longer, to the midpoint of the tail, if I'm really trying to imitate those little Yellow Sallies. That's getting pretty fussy, but it might be just the thing to get you to tie on the fly, even if the trout don't seem to care. Tie in the wing directly behind the hook eye, clip the butts, then create a tidy head, whip-finish, and saturate your thread wraps with lacquer or your favorite head cement.

ZUG BUG

Zug Bug, designed by Cliff Zug

I'm standing at the open tailgate of my brand-new seventeen-year-old fishing pickup, pawing through the contents of more fly boxes than any sane angler needs, gathering a fresh assortment of just the right flies before I plunge into a canyon where, for the past two days, heavy trout have done a number on my first-team supply of heavy-water nymphs.

More to the point, I'm looking for flies to match the Zug Bug hatch.

I know I've said this often enough before, but few things delight me more in this sport than fishing with flies that make no pretense of imitating anything you can identify, with certainty, that fish might be feeding on. Or, just as good, a pattern that seems to work because it comes out of left field, startling fish into sudden reckless behavior that nothing in your match-the-hatch lineup has been able to provoke. Of course, I'm making that part up: Who knows why a fish eats a Zug Bug, other than the claim, however oblique, that when presented just so, the fly looks, to a trout at least, good enough to eat.

No doubt, we can always speculate why. My success the past two days at the bottom of the canyon has traced a proportionate decline in a lineup of Zug Bugs, tied years before, in a box loaded with the big black nymphs I associate with trouting in this sort of steep, deep canyon in the early part of the season. Oddly,

there's also been a prolific number of medium-size gray mayflies, a smattering of chunky tan caddisflies, and, hovering around the reeds and grasses knocked flat by high water, thick swarms of delicate damselflies—none of which has stimulated any of the thick-bodied rainbows to show themselves feeding on the surface.

Not one. Does it have something to do with the off-colored water, dark enough to hide my boots once I'm knee-deep in the vigorous current? The Zug Bugs I've been using to clobber good fish—and, in many cases, get clobbered myself—are slender unweighted versions, sizes 10 and 12, that have been waiting patiently in the same box from which I usually pull the gnarly beasts crowding the opposite leaf.

What's made me turn to those neglected Zugs? First off, the big black stone nymphs haven't exactly lit up the scoreboard; more often than not, they end up clinging to a river bottom filthy with sharp boulders hidden by the opaque currents. Plus, there are very few stonefly shucks displayed on rocks or weed stocks above the water line when, at this time of year, I expected to find the edges of the river littered with the nymphs' crunchy remains. And the few shucks I have found are much smaller than I usually encounter on my home river.

As I often do when I'm on a new river and uncertain what's going on, I'm also fishing with two flies—in this case, because of the time of year, the big stone nymph on the end of my tippet, with something smaller on a tail of the tippet knot above. That's where I eventually attach the first Zug Bug. Beforehand, I've gone through my usual assortment of soft hackles, a couple of different Pheasant Tails that seem appropriate nymphs for the mayflies sailing on the water, and my wet or swimming caddis patterns that generally produce some sort of action whenever those lively, size 14 tan caddisflies are fluttering about.

That first Zug Bug, anyway, soon disappeared, after a big trout performed three spectacular belly flops before that tag end parted, leaving me free to retrieve but one of two flies.

What is it the Zug Bug represents? Could the slender profile of this particular batch possibly imitate the nymph of the swarming damselflies? I like to think that after all these many decades searching for trout I'm capable of making this kind of subtle connection—when in my heart of hearts I know it's often pretty much a crapshoot. That didn't work? Try something else.

On the other hand, I'm absolutely certain that changing flies doesn't mean squat if you don't present your cast in the appropriate, effective manner. In the case of deep, fast-water nymphing, in marginal conditions with not a single fish revealing its whereabouts with any manner of telltale rise, that means getting your fly or flies down to fish and aiming for a drag-free drift, while at the same time remaining in close, strict contact with those flies, capable of detecting, immediately, any sort of touch, whether from rock, fish, or anything else that stops downstream progress of the cast.

Easier said than done. When fly anglers talk about challenging *technical* fishing, they're often referring to the kind of "fine and far off" sport we associate with gin-clear chalk streams or eerily quiet spring creeks, fooling snooty trout with application of, among other things, long gossamer leaders and sneaky flies perhaps best tied under a microscope. I agree: That can be awfully tough fishing, demanding an assortment of subtle skills and techniques acquired through keen observation, practice, and often years of frustrating experience. But over the course of a lifetime spent trout fishing, I've come to appreciate as well how "technical" big-water nymphing can be, requiring a set of skills just as challenging, in their own right, as those needed to get tough trout to rise—and the reward, as Charles Brooks told us long, long ago, is often the "larger trout" that so many of us love to encounter in our fishing.

●━━━━━━━●

We all know some anglers, of course, who say they just don't like this kind of fishing—which always sounds to me a little like that kid in class who complains about a lesson he's having trouble with because it's *boring.* You don't like to hook big trout? I understand a preference for good fish tipping up to take a seductively drifting size 20 Go-Go Dun. But I don't see this as in any way superior to sticking a beast down deep in heavy current amongst the rocks, one of those thick, overweight trout somehow still capable of throwing its entire self three feet out of the water not just once but four straight times right in front of you, the end of your fly line barely beyond your rod tip, the sound of the fish, each time it lands, splatting as if a plastic gallon jug, filled with lead, hitting the water.

Maybe a Zug Bug, in all its unrefined glory, is no more sophisticated—nor technical—than that. As I continue to dig through my many fly boxes, trying alongside my new truck's tailgate to supplement a much diminished Zug Bug supply, reduced in part by encounters with just this sort of bounding rainbow, I'm suddenly tickled by the thought that I'm searching for flies that imitate another fly, one that doesn't look much like anything I've seen in or on or along the water. What I'm looking for, instead, are flies I hope might work as well as the Zug Bug has been working.

That's a pretty funny way to match the hatch. But there you have it. To sophisticates out there who need to draw a clean line between what they do and what happens at the business end of their cast, a clear cause-and-effect relationship that explains how and why fish do or don't end up connected to the fly, the Zug Bug may not be the pattern for you. It implies, for one, that you forgo certainty, accepting outcomes that you can't legitimately explain. From a personal standpoint, I've long believed that's one of the appeals of the sport: Things happen for mysterious reasons.

In fact, I've always thought that's kind of the whole point.

ZUG BUG

- **Hook:** #10-16 1X- or 2X-long standard nymph
- **Weight (optional):** .015 lead wire
- **Thread:** Black 8/0 UNI-Thread, or similar
- **Tail:** Peacock sword fibers
- **Rib:** Oval silver tinsel (small)
- **Body:** Peacock herl
- **Hackle:** Furnace or brown hen, sparse
- **Wing case:** Mallard flank fibers, clipped short

Tying the Zug Bug

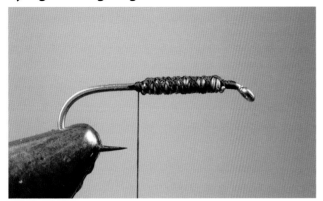

1. Secure the hook and, if weighting the fly, cover at least two-thirds of the hook shank with ten to fifteen wraps of lead. Leave plenty of room between the forward end of the lead and the eye of the hook. Start your thread, build small dams at each end of the lead to hold it in place, then cover the lead with a base layer of thread wraps.

2. For the tail of the fly, use three or four fibers from a peacock sword feather. Make the tail about half the length of the hook shank. Tie in the tail so that the curve of the fibers sweep upward. Cover the butts of the fibers up to the aft end of the lead and clip the excess.

3. Secure the oval tinsel for the ribbing as you wind your thread back to the root of the tail. For the body of the fly, create a dubbing loop, slide four or five lengths of peacock herl between the legs of the loop, then spin the loop until it forms a tight herl rope. With

your thread hanging in front of the lead, wind the herl rope forward. Secure the herl just ahead of the lead and clip excess. Then rib the body with four or five evenly spaced wraps of tinsel.

4. From a furnace hen neck, select a feather with fibers about half the length of the hook shank. Brown hackle will also work. Secure the hackle feather by the tip. While folding back the fibers, make a single turn of the hackle feather and then tie it off and clip the excess. Use wraps of thread to force any errant fibers so that they lie back along the body of the fly.

5. Patterns for the original Zug Bug call for a wing case tied from a wood duck lemon flank feather. As I mentioned writing about the Light Cahill wet, these feathers can prove hard to find; tyers have now taken to substituting mallard flank feathers dyed lemon for the wing case. Or, better still, simply pull a bunch of fibers from one side of any mallard flank feather, tie them in, and clip the fibers to create a pronounced wing case that extends about one-third the length of the body behind the hook eye. I doubt very much that this slight change of color will be the reason a trout either accepts or rejects the fly. Now clip the butts of the wing case feathers, create a tidy head with thread wraps, and whip-finish and saturate the head with lacquer or your favorite head cement.

ALDER FLY

Alder Fly, adapted from design by Charles Kingsley

When my fishing buddy Joe Kelly shot a turkey last spring, I felt complicit enough to lay claim to a few of the big tom's tail feathers. We'd spotted birds while out with some gals hunting for early season morels, the tasty mushrooms that offer a good reason to wander about in the woods when the trout in our home rivers are just coming off their spawning redds, in no need of pestering from anyone. A week later we were driving backroads to a jump-off point into a canyon reach of a local steelhead river when a pair of hens scurried away from our approaching truck. We were all set to fish again the next afternoon, only to discover that overnight rains had blown out the river, turning it from a milky, snowmelt green to the color of cardboard or khaki trousers.

"Guess I'll go look for a bird," said Joe, as I finished unloading my gear from the back of his truck.

He phoned that evening and said he got one.

I hurried over to Joe's house to inspect the kill. I'd been looking for feathers, not the usual quills from the wing, commonly used for muddlers, but instead the dark, copper-and-chocolate striped tail feathers. But *not* the longest primary tail feathers either, the ones that create the striking halo-like display if you find a tom posing for a bunch of hens. Just forward of the longest tail feathers you can find another sweep of quills

that are about half as long, these ones almost symmetrical, heavily barred, with just a splash of ginger along the uppermost margins—the perfect feathers for tying the wing of an Alder wet fly.

The pattern, claims Dave Hughes in his book *Wet Flies*, was first tied in 1858 by one Charles Kingsley, who fished the fly on the River Itchen, hallowed waters in Hampshire, England. I don't know that I've ever seen a real alderfly—in England or anywhere else. In photos they look a lot like big caddisflies, which I do see a lot of where I look for trout. Hughes tells us that alderflies, unlike caddisflies, are lousy swimmers; they don't float and they tend to sink without really swimming. Hence the wet-fly pattern, one that Hughes believes fishes most effectively without giving it any action, allowing it to sink through the water column, where it often gets eaten, until you finally retrieve enough to start your next cast.

This is usually on lakes or other stillwater fisheries, ones where trees line the shore. Hughes says he's had little experience fishing the Alder Fly in moving water; where it's proven most successful, he says, is where "a current tongue peters out into a deep pool." Then, in the very next sentence in this discussion of the Alder, Hughes offers what I feel is his most important thought on the matter: "But I'm never sure when I do this whether I'm imitating a natural alderfly or just showing the trout a fly that looks like something good to eat, as likely to be mistaken for a dark caddisfly as for an alderfly."

Exactly.

We return, once more, to a trope that describes many of my favorite trout flies: *looks like something good to eat.* Very often that's close enough. Just this past weekend, on a reach of unmolested water where I was pretty certain the caddis would stir once the sun went down, I inspected my lineup of Alder wet flies and thought, *Yes, that should do nicely.* Like many anglers, I often fish light-colored caddisfly patterns, for the simple reason that most caddisflies, although certainly not all of them, tend to be pale. But most everyone I know who fishes on or near the surface in low light agrees that trout and other fish, looking up, see dark flies best because of the silhouette they create while backlit by the sky above—even when we reach the point when we can no longer sight flies ourselves.

Whether the spectacular trouting that followed, after I tied on a little Alder Fly and began swinging it through some likely chattering caddis water, had anything to do with my choice of fly will probably remain a mystery. Downstream Joe Kelly said he caught thirty fish that evening without moving from a certain rock, all with a big ugly nymph that could have eaten a dozen of my Alder flies if it were an actual bug alive in the water. You never know. But I liked the looks of my offering as an approximation of a small dark caddis—and I certainly liked how the trout, many of which ended up taking me into my backing, came to the surface and smacked the swinging cast with the ferocity trout often take caddisflies swimming through their feeding lanes.

You know what those evening head-and-shoulder rises look like—the ones that actually reveal trout pivoting back toward deeper water *after* they rush to the surface to nab swimming caddis pupae or ascending or egg-laying adults. In my eyes there's nothing prettier—if only because I feel an unusual amount of confidence swinging sparse little wet flies downstream to this sort of rising trout. That evening, they climbed all over my Alder Fly.

Of course, who's to say? They might have taken a size 14 Hare's Ear just as well.

• ———————— •

When I returned home and sat down to refresh my stock of Alder flies, I was struck by the simplicity of the original pattern: three common, natural materials—although all of them might not be on every tyer's bench. I believe in substituting materials whenever I don't have, immediately at hand, what a specific pattern calls for. Yet now and then I also recommend acquiring certain materials, if only because I think tyers will find them useful for more flies than the one I'm describing.

A cape of furnace wet-fly hackle, for example. Like badger hackle, furnace feathers sport a dark stripe along the stem, which gives you that saucy two-tone effect when you wind the feather around the hook shank. Contrast between parts of a fly has always seemed to me a critical element—more important, perhaps, than actual color. Of course, all such notions may have more to say about what *I* like rather than what interests a trout. I can go on and on about how that dark patch at the center of a wound furnace hackle feather creates the impression of both the head and the thorax of an emerging or adult aquatic insect—but I'm really only telling you why I reach for a certain pattern, one I believe will do the job when I know I have fish feeding in front of me. When the fly works, I want to say "See? I told you!"—when, in fact, all I really know is that I didn't scare the fish away.

And what about those turkey tail feathers? Do you really need them to tie a successful Alder fly—especially if you are actually going to use the fly to fool fish feeding on caddis? In the end, these may well be rhetorical or theoretical or even philosophical questions, answers to which might not prove forthcoming if we haven't yet resolved them over the 160-plus years since Mr. Kingsley first flung his latest concoction from the banks of the lovely Itchen. I'm okay with that.

When I stumbled into camp at dark after clobbering fish with the Alder fly, I found Joe sipping a beer; he waited politely for me to describe my success before he related the slaughter in which he had just participated. Nevertheless, I was moved to suggest that I may have hit upon a new—for me—red-hot pattern, one that was sure to terrorize trout up and down the river.

"Just like your flymphs," said Joe, handing me a bottle. "Or was it the Dark Hare last time? The Wet Caddis? The Zug Bug?"

He had a point. Fishing had been pretty good the past couple of seasons. Maybe I had it right from the start—your fly is the last thing that matters.

But unless you try them all, how will you ever know?

ALDER FLY

- **Hook:** #12-16 standard wet fly
- **Thread:** Black 8/0 UNI-Thread, or similar
- **Hackle:** Furnace hen hackle
- **Body:** Peacock herl, twisted into dubbing loop
- **Wing:** Secondary turkey tail feather

Tying the Alder Fly

1. Secure the hook and start the thread directly behind the eye. Now's as good a time as any to review the traditional method for tying soft-hackled wet flies, with the hackle lashed to the hook *before* creating the rest of the fly. The technique calls for orienting the hackle feather so that when you wind it back to the body of the fly, the feather fibers curve toward the aft end of the fly, while also allowing you to lock the hackle stem under wraps of tying thread. Strip any waste from the stem of the feather up to a point where the fibers are about one and a half or twice the length of the distance of the hook gap. Point the tip of the feather ahead of the hook eye with the good side or convex curve of the feather facing you. Directly below the lowest fibers, lash the stem of the feather on top of the hook shank, just behind the hook eye. Some soft-hackle feathers—especially traditional Hungarian partridge—are easier to deal with if you first flatten them with the tips of your thumbnail and the nail of your middle finger.

2. Now wind your thread in even wraps back to the start of the hook bend. One of the reasons I like traditional wet-fly hooks like the old Mustad 3906 is that the hook shank is surprisingly short; you don't have room to oversize the body, a common mistake with many patterns, especially imitations of caddisflies, the bodies of which should be disproportionately smaller than the wing. You should end up with a small fly on a size 14 hook, a hook still large enough, however, to sink plenty of steel into the business end of a large trout. For an Alder Fly I create a dubbing loop; that is, hook a dubbing loop tool (or hackle pliers) around the tying thread about 3 inches below the fly; then, while maintaining tension with whatever tool you use, catch the thread at the top of the loop with a wrap at the bend of the hook. Lay down an even layer of thread wraps forward to a point about one-third the hook shank back from the eye of the hook. Wax the legs of the loop and insert a couple of strands of peacock herl. Spin the loop so that the herl gets trapped by the twisting legs of the loop and, as the twists tighten, you end up with a rope of herl woven into the twisted thread, which will prevent the herl from breaking as soon as a trout begins to gnaw on the fly.

3. Wind the herl rope forward to where you've positioned the tying thread, catch the rope under thread wraps, and clip excess.

4. Now attach your hackle pliers to the tip of the feather extending ahead of the fly. Make several turns of hackle, starting behind the hook eye and progressing back to the body of the fly. Catch the hackle stem under a wrap of thread and then advance the thread through the hackle two or three times until the thread is directly behind the hook eye. Trim the excess hackle feather and, if needed, stroke back the hackle fibers and tidy up the hackle with a few more wraps of thread.

5. For the wing I use ⅛- to 3/16-inch-wide sections of fibers from both sides of a secondary turkey tail feather. Much as I try to fashion a pair of those classic wet-fly wings, however, the thin tips of the turkey feathers generally lose their shape and I end up with a ragged bundle of fibers, much like you get when tying a caddisfly with stacked elk or deer hair. The fish don't seem to mind. These bundled feather tips are generally quite supple, which means you get a lot more movement than you do with hair, and, of course, they allow the fly to sink a bit more than hair does, although a couple of nights ago I kept noticing that my Alder Fly was waking, in swift current, just below the surface before trout pounced on it. Tie in a wing that extends at least to the bend of the hook, clip the butts of the wing fibers, and create a tidy head.

6. Whip-finish and saturate the thread wraps with lacquer or your favorite head cement.

MUDDLER MINNOW

Muddler Minnow, adapted from design by Don Gapen

If you haven't done this lately, let me remind you what you're missing. You come out of the high country, transported by some sense of purpose, one no deeper perhaps than a wish for beer or maybe, just maybe, a longing for home—when suddenly you find yourself, in quick succession, along the shores of a broad impoundment, then skirting a dam, then tracing at length the banks of a tumbling stream or river all but hidden below road or highway by a tangle of brush and riparian willows. Immediately you stop—or at least duck into the first pullout you can find. Below you the water runs cold and clear, spilling out from the depths of the reservoir above—and the question before you now looms as large, in context, as any other question in your life.

Are there trout down there?

The answer is obvious if you can see them. But, really, how often is that? Trout, we know, enjoy the capacity to vanish, or remain invisible, while in plain sight. Don't ask me how. What's important when looking for them, especially where we're uncertain if they actually exist, is a way to entice them to reveal themselves—a straightforward ruse that puts the question to rest and may well prove, for the moment at least, all the answer you really need.

The Muddler Minnow is such an iconic fly pattern, the perfect tool for exploring rough-and-tumble new

water, that I'm surprised how rarely I see the fly in other anglers' boxes. I know flies go in and out of fashion; this book is often dedicated to patterns I sense have all but vanished from the lexicon, patterns that anglers of a certain age or breadth of experience might reject as old-school. Or, worse, they may have never discovered the fly in the first place, or—worst of all—they have no clear notion when and how to actually fish it.

Streamers, as a whole, seem to have fallen out of favor. I get it. In many waters, especially those that receive heavy pressure from the bobber-and-nymph crowds, swinging a downstream streamer, or launching the same fly tight to shore from a drifting boat or raft, can wear out your arm while producing nothing in the way of meaningful results. For reasons I still can't explain, streamers rarely work on my home river; over nearly three decades, I've caught fewer fish there on streamers than I can count on one hand, although this probably has something to do with the fact that I never tie on a streamer unless everything else has failed, a moment of resignation that all but ensures the next option won't work either.

Of course, I do know local anglers who have taken to swinging streamers for trout with two-handed rods. I'm all for that. Nothing is more pleasant than a session launching long casts with a lightish double-hander, although the problem, as I see it, is that you've restricted yourself to a range of presentations not nearly as broad as those you enjoy with a traditional single-handed trout rod.

The Muddler Minnow, anyway, should not be viewed as some sort of specialty fly. It belongs, instead, in a lineup of other proven traditional patterns that work in hand with presentation techniques they're designed for, in order to fool trout in one or many of the wide variety of situations in which we find them.

Which is no more to say than that a Muddler Minnow catches trout. And it catches them for reasons about which we can speculate but I'm not sure we can all actually agree on. Does it matter? The common logic has always argued that the pattern imitates a sculpin, those small, big-headed baitfish that inhabit cold shallow streams, the same environment favored by trout. No matter that on many streams and rivers neither you nor I have ever seen a sculpin; we take it on faith they're in there someplace—which is why our Muddler Minnow keeps getting rocked.

Or maybe it's just a generic baitfish pattern, no more specific to a small sculpin than a Gold-Ribbed Hare's Ear is to either a mayfly nymph or caddis pupa or some other immature aquatic insect. There does seem to be a moment in the lives of many trout when they become something more than mere insectivores; we recognize this change when we witness certain predatory behaviors that leave us convinced the larger trout in a stream are hungrily chasing baitfish—or even the young of their own kind.

Return, for a moment, to our opening scene: You climb down the bank of the tailwater or tailrace stream, claw your way through the willows, and pitch your Muddler Minnow into the frothy current. What we know about so many of these below-dam, below-reservoir waterways is that they're lousy with bait, downstream remnants of all sorts of nonsense that gets dumped into impoundments by fish and wildlife managers trying to *improve* recreational fishing. Who can blame them? Once the dam goes in, any system has been degraded to such a degree that we have, essentially, a man-made fishery. Let the managers have at it. Should the downstream fish populations include trout, we'll often find either rainbows or browns, or both, that have keyed into the young of other species or, especially, forage fish that proliferate in seasonally warm surface waters above the dam, only to get flushed, on occasion, into the stream or river below.

Hence, the efficacy of your Muddler Minnow. If there are trout below the dam, a Muddler Minnow will find them, sculpin or no sculpin in the stream. Of course, there are a host of other streamers that can work in these situations. I'm just suggesting the Muddler Minnow is one pattern you can tie and carry if you wish to be prepared for this common western scenario.

But there's more. Summertime, when grasshoppers abound along many western rivers and streams,

a Muddler Minnow does a fair job of mimicking a drowned or drowning hopper. Few things are more exciting in trout fishing than seeing a good fish smack a high-floating hopper pattern. But trout anglers everywhere know of occasions when their carefully constructed grasshopper fails to stimulate a response, only to grow waterlogged and sink, or get dragged below the surface, and immediately a heavy trout is throbbing at the end of the line.

That's a reason not to weight your Muddler Minnows—at least not all of them. Sculpins, yes, like to hug the bottom of the stream; other forage fish perhaps less so. If it's hopper season, however, I want my Muddler Minnow high in the water column; sometimes I'll even aim my cast directly across stream and fish the fly on the surface on a slack-line drift along the far bank before it begins to drag—at which point I'll throw one last mend into the line as the Muddler settles into a downstream swing.

Which sets the stage, at times, for the Muddler Minnow's greatest glory of all. If you're a steelheader, you're probably already familiar with the wonders of waking flies. Trout anglers, I find, are less inclined to employ the technique. I'm not sure why. A sparsely dressed wet caddis pattern swung downstream so that it bumps up against the underside of the surface, creating a wake behind it, can be a devastating ploy as daylight fades on a summer eve; some grabs practically yank the rod from your hand, as though the trout attack the fly out of a reckless passion rarely exhibited by such skittish creatures. A Muddler Minnow, waking downstream on a taut line, can elicit a similar reaction. Sometimes these wild strikes come up short—at which point a strip or two of line, or even a slight lift of the rod, will often provoke an even more committed rise.

At the very least, a rise to a waking Muddler Minnow will offer evidence of trout in a stream. That's a start. A big fly swimming across the current, the Muddler Minnow also has a long history of moving big fish, often the biggest fish in a given river or stream. Exceptional fish may not always be your goal when trout fishing. If so, I have but one question: *Really?*

MUDDLER MINNOW

- **Hook:** #2-12 3X- to 6X-long standard streamer
- **Weight (optional):** Lead wire approximately same gauge or slightly smaller than hook shank
- **Thread:** Brown 8/0 UNI-Thread, or similar
- **Tail:** Mottled turkey feather
- **Body:** Flat or oval gold tinsel
- **Underwing:** Gray squirrel tail
- **Overwing:** Mottled turkey quill sections
- **Collar:** Deer hair, spun
- **Head:** Deer hair, spun and clipped

Tying the Muddler Minnow

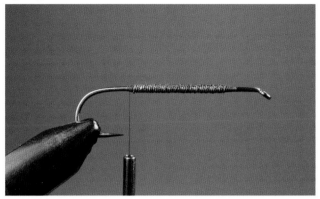

1. Secure the hook in the vise. If weighting the fly, stop your lead wraps about one-quarter the length of the hook shank back from the hook eye; that way you'll have room later on to spin the deer hair for the collar and head. Frankly, if I weight a Muddler Minnow at all, it's with thin (.010-.015) lead wire. An unweighted or lightly weighted fly is much more pleasant to cast than a fly that feels like a sparkplug on the end of your line. Also, by employing the appropriate presentation techniques, you have the option of fishing an unweighted fly at a variety of depths, from the surface down through the water column.

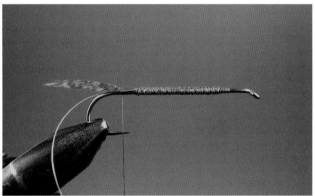

2. For the tail, cut a single section from a mottled turkey feather. Measure the tip of the section one-third to one-half the length of the hook shank. Tie in at the start of the bend of the hook. By using a single section of feather, you don't have to try to match up a pair of feathers; nevertheless, the goal is to secure the feather section so that it remains positioned on edge vertically, in line with the spine of the hook shank. Clip off the butts of the tail to create an even underbody for the tinsel. At the root of the tail, tie in a length of tinsel.

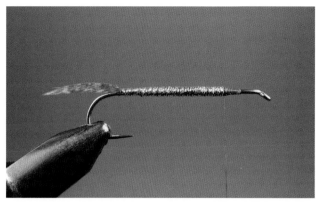

3. Advance the thread to the forward end of your lead wrap—or to a point about a quarter of the hook shank back from the hook eye. Wind your tinsel forward in tight, even wraps. Medium instead of small tinsel allows you to pull tighter on your wraps and will stand up better to toothy trout. Tie off the tinsel and clip excess.

4. For the underwing, clip a small tuft of hair from a gray squirrel tail. Before you clip the hair, align the tips by lifting the hair at an angle to the tail. The aim is to create an underwing that tapers slightly at the tip rather than having the hair tips precisely aligned as if the hair were stacked. Measure the hair so that it reaches about the midpoint of the tail. Tie in securely at the forward end of the body. Squirrel tail hair is slippery; pay attention to lashing it tightly. Clip the butts at an angle to create a smooth taper forward of the body.

5. For the overwing, clip quill sections from either a pair of turkey wing feathers or the two sides of a symmetrical tail feather. I find the tail feather quills easier to work with than quills from wings. Align the tips of the paired quill sections; measure to a point beyond the underwing but short of the tip of the tail. Secure the wing directly in front of the root of the underwing; like the tail, the wing should end up standing vertical along the spine of the hook shank. Some tyers tie in one quill at a time, favoring a slightly different-looking wing. Either way, clip the wing butts, leaving a bit of bare hook shank forward the root of the wing.

6. The collar of the fly is fashioned out of a substantial tuft of deer hair, cleaned and stacked and spun. Easier said than done—I hope you've already mastered this important technique. If not, here are a few tips: Hair should be absolutely free of underfur; it won't stack or spin properly if those tiny kinky fibers are clinging to it. I use an eyebrow brush to comb out the fur. After aligning the tips of the hair in your stacker, measure the tuft about the length of the hook shank. Now switch the hair to your off hand and clip the butts into an even edge with the butts extending something shy of ½ inch beyond the hook eye. Trimming the butts before you spin the hair makes it easier, later, to shape the head without cutting away the collar. In order to spin the hair, hold the tuft on top of the hook shank and make one or two loops of thread over the tuft while pinching the loops between the thumb and forefinger of the hand holding the tuft. Now, as

you pull the thread, allow the loops to slip free from your thumb and forefinger; as the thread tightens, it will cause the hair to spin around the hook shank. If the hair tries to bunch up unevenly in spots, ease the tension on the thread and then pull tight again; you might even find you need to help the hair spin with the tip of your scissors or bodkin. When you are happy with the coverage of the spun hair around the entire hook shank, make several more turns of thread directly through the hair butts, which will cause them to flare at right angles to the shank. Finally, push the flared hair back from the eye of the hook and hold it upright with a tightly wound dam of thread wraps.

7. On larger Muddler Minnows, I often add a second tuft of spun deer hair for the pronounced, bulky head we associate with the pattern. If I decide to go that route, I find it easier to use finer, comparadun-style deer hair for spinning the head. I also like the effect you can get with contrasting shades of hair. Clip a tuft of hair and clean and stack it as before. Again, clip the butts even, but also clip the tips, so that you end up with ½- to ¾-inch hair in the clump. In front of the previously spun deer hair, spin this new clump just as you did the first clump. After winding the thread through the flared hair, draw back the ends of the hair and whip-finish between the eye of the hook and the hair butts. You can treat these finishing wraps at this time with lacquer or your favorite head cement. Finally, shape the head of your Muddler with either scissors or a razor blade. Because I don't aim for a tight, compact head like you might find on a deer hair bass popper, I use scissors. I think most commercially tied Muddler Minnows are overdressed, in fact. That tightly packed head and full skirt of collar hair detracts from the effect I'm looking for, an opinion which is based on nothing more than my preference, in general, for sparsely dressed flies.

SILVER SEDGE

Silver Sedge, adapted by author from traditional Irish wet fly

I'm not an expert on anything—except maybe postures of self-deprecation. So when an editor at a magazine I write for invited me to chime in with my two cents on the topic of fishing for trout with two-handed rods, the subject fashionably referred to as *trout Spey*, plus perhaps a couple of thoughts on the flies this fishing entails, I hesitated to offer a response.

What I know about fishing for trout with two-handed rods is that it's a great way to swing wet or waking flies, especially on big rivers where casting distance can sometimes matter. Also, a long rod offers greater line control as you set up for and manipulate a downstream swing. These same attributes explain why Spey rods so quickly became the tool of choice once Pacific coast steelheaders began to get their hands on them. Few of us can make hundred-foot casts with a single-handed rod, a shot made even more difficult with backcasts blocked by trees or brush or whatever other obstacles line the bank behind us. Standing in water up to the top of your waders and then, hands overhead, hoping to double-haul and shoot an entire fly line are, for most of us, equivalent to a slam dunk in basketball—doable for some no doubt, or maybe that was a few years back, but a stunt not found in the repertoire of the rest of us.

Fortunately, most trout fishing occurs at more pedestrian distances. And even if we spot trout feeding near the horizon, we eventually discover that on most moving water, the dry fly is better fished close, where intervening currents aren't so apt to disrupt the natural, drag-free drift of the cast.

Which brings me to my first objection against embracing, wholeheartedly, the trout Spey movement: I've never liked fishing dry flies with a two-hander, and I absolutely hate carrying two rods along river or stream.

And I do enjoy dry-fly fishing—which I want to be prepared for at any moment I'm on the water.

I've often been quick to point out, of course, that the soft-hackled wet fly can prove the best way to fool trout poking their noses through the surface and feeding on floating caddisflies or mayfly duns. Yet even when fishing "wet," I often present the fly on a drag-free drift, just as though it were a dry fly, an effective presentation that's difficult, especially at short range, with a long two-handed rod.

Short, accurate casts to rising fish with either a true dry fly or a soft-hackled wet fished like a dry can even be difficult with many modern, fast-action single-handers, which fail to load properly unless you have a fair length of fly line outside the rod tip. If you've ever fished beside a skilled bamboo rod aficionado while snooty fish are sipping right in front of you, you know how effectively he or she can aim and fire tight, deadly loops that unfold directly over a nose that's nudged the surface only a rod's length or two out in the current.

Of course, I'm oversimplifying all of this. And there are exceptions to every scenario I might devise. The vagaries of fly fishing are all but infinite, the reason, for many of us, it remains so appealing no matter how long we've been at it. In the face of so much uncertainty—those countless variables we can't even identify, much less control—we eventually learn that the key to success is rarely a matter of choosing the right fly or even the right answer, but instead good trout anglers, especially, make choices they believe in and then direct their full attention, unencumbered by indecision, to making that choice work.

Which is actually one good argument *for* the two-handed trout rod: It doesn't do everything. Carry a two-hander to the river for a day of trout fishing and you've pretty much made your decision how you're going to fish. Granted, there's still plenty of room on that stage for experiments, creativity, even far-fetched improvisation. But in my fairly basic skill set, as it's called, I generally prefer to rely on my trusty one-hander for the range of techniques I might need in a day's trout fishing, whether nymphing, swinging wet flies or streamers, casting dry flies to rising trout, or any and all techniques in between.

There are enough choices already. Two rods in hand, I'm suddenly pushed to the point of indecision, the surest state of mind for me, like most anglers, to fail.

Do I reject *trout Spey*—or whatever you want to call fishing for trout with two-handed rods? No, I don't. In fact, let me make myself perfectly clear. In certain situations, on certain rivers, when fishing for certain fish, I *love* fishing the two-hander. It's a great angling tool. It offers a host of delightful ways to cast, ones that will come in handy even when you pick up your single-hander again. Yet those long elegant loops you learn to throw across the wide blue river are, truth be known, rarely the answer to catching more or better trout.

Again, the best trout anglers I know put little stock in a particular fly, a must-have rod, or any other specific piece of equipment. It's the carpenter, not the hammer—that sort of thing. If there is any infallible reason I can get behind for embracing trout fishing with two-handers, it's that it's a fun way to fish, simple as that.

What more need be said than that?

———•———•———

The flies I like to cast when fishing for trout with a two-hander are generally traditional wet flies, most of them inspired by years of moving steelhead to the surface with swinging and often waking flies. Hence, the *fun* I just mentioned. With steelhead numbers throughout the West continuing their disconcerting decline, fishing for big-river trout with two-handers may be the closest some of us get anymore to the pleasures of employing traditional dry-line techniques for summer steelhead. Right before COVID hit I finished tying up a bunch of simple surface patterns generally used for Atlantic salmon, a lineup I planned to try out the first week of spring fishing with John Gierach for big-river British Columbia rainbows. Then John phoned and said his doctor told him he wasn't going anywhere, the first clue I got that the virus was serious.

My notions about swinging surface patterns for both trout and steelhead have often been inspired by caddisflies, especially the big October Caddis, which I always associate with fall fishing for summer steelhead. Yet nearly all caddisfly hatches I know of invite the use of a swinging soft-hackled surface pattern, especially in the swift, bouncy currents we find so often throughout the West, the same kind of water that favors vibrant caddisfly hatches. In their pupa stage, most caddisflies are vigorous swimmers; as adults, many caddisflies also do a lot of swimming, at this stage rather clumsily, especially when depositing eggs back into the water.

What all these swimming caddisflies mean, of course, is that they are available to hungry trout; the swinging caddis pattern, we hope, mimics some of the real caddisfly's vigor, eliciting emphatic reactions from fish. God, how I look forward to those grabs. With your line downstream, all but taut in the current, the strike passes immediately through rod and into hand and often starts the reel singing. With leader and fly line now dragging through the water, you feel every movement if not emotion of the fish, an intimacy with wildness I needn't belabor.

The Silver Sedge is a simple Irish pattern, one that translates nicely into summer sessions fishing over an evening caddis hatch, swinging wet flies downstream to rising fish. No room to speak here about the subtle manipulations employed by soft-hackle aficionados; it's enough to say that a long two-hander helps in lifting your line off the water and allows you to easily mend the cast, whether to slow down or speed up the swing. And on a big river, need I add, the two-hander can produce a most magnificent swinging arc, one that swims the fly through vast reaches of water, hunting or being hunted all the while, as you await a jolt that vibrates all the way down to your knees.

SILVER SEDGE

- **Hook:** #12-14 Fulling Mill 5025 or similar
- **Thread:** Gray 8/0 UNI-Thread or similar
- **Rib:** Oval silver tinsel (small)
- **Body:** Silver fox underfur
- **Hackle:** Light ginger hen hackle
- **Wing:** Bronze mallard
- **Head hackle:** Medium dun hen hackle

Tying the Silver Sedge

1. Secure the hook and start your thread directly behind the hook eye. Choose a hen hackle feather with quills slightly longer than you would use for a dry fly. Strip the webby fibers from the stem. With the good side of the feather facing you and pointed beyond the hook eye, secure the stem directly behind the eye; the feather should end up on edge, quills vertical, the stem in line with the hook shank.

2. Continue winding your thread aft. About one-third of the way back from the hook eye, secure the tip of a short length of oval silver tinsel. Continue winding aft, covering the tinsel. At about the two-thirds point of the hook shank, secure the stem of a light ginger hen hackle feather with quills shorter than those on the forward hackle. Again, position the feather so that it ends up on edge, quills vertical.

3. Carry your thread wraps back to the start of the hook bend. Form a dubbing loop and wax the legs of the loop. Lightly dab the silver fox underfur onto the loop thread; you don't need much. Spin the loop to form a shaggy dubbing noodle. Now advance the thread to the original one-third point on the hook shank and then wind the dubbing noodle forward, forming the body. End the body at the one-third point, leaving room for the wing and the forward hackle.

4. Using hackle pliers, grab the tip of the aft hackle feather and palmer the body with evenly spaced wraps of hackle. Tie off the hackle and then lock it in place with three or four wraps of oval tinsel. Don't worry if your body and palmered hackle and tinsel end up looking a little disheveled. That's sort of the point of the traditional soft-hackle wet fly: Rather than trying to mirror our image of the insects in question, these patterns offer fish a complexity of impressions as they swim at the end of the swinging line.

5. Before creating the wing, trim the palmered hackle tips along the back of the fly; this helps the wing lie flatter and offer a denser profile. For the wing itself, align the quill tips of a fairly broad section of a bronze mallard feather. Cut or strip the feather quills from the stem. Keeping the tips aligned, tie in the wing of the fly just ahead of the forward end of the body, with the tip of the wing extending beyond the body of the fly and about even with the hook bend.

6. For the forward hackle, use your hackle pliers to secure the tip of the feather you tied in for step 1. Wind the hackle back to the wing, making a turn over the butts of the wing fibers. Catch the stem of hackle feather with a turn of thread and then advance the thread through the hackle and up to the eye of the hook. Form a tidy head, whip-finish, and protect the thread wraps with lacquer or your favorite head cement.

LITTLE BLACK CADDIS

Little Black Caddis, adapted from Fluttering Caddis designed by Leonard M. Wright Jr.

The river's famous and I'm holding my own, slipping downstream after the morning drift boat hatch while raising fish, here and there, with a big green Humpy. Summer grasses reach headfirst for the water, and beyond the banks squalls of young grasshoppers erupt along the trail. The sun leaves the tops of the tall cottonwoods and at some point ceases to rise, soaring west across the blue, opaque sky.

I get two heavy rainbows by wading deep into a wide eddy beneath an island, drifting the fly at the end of long casts along the edge of the main current. While I'm landing the second fish, a guy shows up at the bottom of the island and makes a big stink, to his buddy, about me standing *in the exact spot where the fish are.*

"Guy gets his first pair of waders and he thinks he owns the river!" he hollers, keeping his head turned as though I'm not supposed to hear.

I release my fish and blow on the Humpy to dry it. I can see the guy has a strike indicator on his leader—a different approach to this fair and blossoming day. Naturally, I'm insulted by his show of scorn—*Didn't he just see that fish!*—while at the same time I know better than to invest one bit of time or emotional energy defending my old-fashioned game.

A couple of little weighted nymphs drifting through the eddy where I'm standing certainly *would* work.

Instead, I swing the head of my line out of the rod tip and, gently as I can, set the fly, in the guy's direction, back into the current, where it rides, prettily, my way.

Famous rivers, I remind myself, can be a bitch.

You learn to take what you can get.

●————————————●

After lunch and another mile of river, I slide into a long channel running behind another island, water you'd never fish or even find from a boat unless you already know it's there. Which is probably *only* fifty guys today, I immediately calculate, considering the number of boats that keep drifting by. Oh, well. Yet sure enough, up along the inside edge of the current, right at the top of the channel where a boat swinging in would be turned around, guys casting at the *other* bank, the big Humpy gets eaten by a very big trout—one of those takes that's so slow, and so confident, that besides being the loveliest sight the sport has to offer, it immediately inspires your deepest fears because you know, by this time, how genuinely big the fish in this river could get, and the weight through the rod feels absolutely insane as the shocked and astonished trout gets directly into the heavy current that created the channel and now just acts *pissed* as it blows downstream in a head-shaking, cold-blooded huff.

I try to regain some control.

Oddly, in the midst of first chasing and then fighting the fish, I twice hear guys in passing boats holler, "You need a net?"

Turns out they're not talking to me.

Everybody, it seems, catches fish here.

This one, when I finally land it, seems about as good as they get, a great slab of trout with all the brilliant features the family shares, as precious in every way as the details of a musical instrument you've learned to play. The river, too, has begun to take on that subtle appearance of great water you're falling in love with even though you don't yet know much about it. It's just big and wide and full of the color of the sky—and apparently a hell of a lot of big trout besides.

At the bottom of the channel, where I free the fish, I notice there's this weird triangulation of currents created by a break in the tail of the island.

If things have been fishy up to now, this could be the Buddha's navel.

But it's deep—more like a swimming hole than a spot to get fish that aren't rising to move to the dry fly.

I'm easy—and interested, too. So I reconstruct my leader into a nymphing rig, sans indicator, and run a little Wild Hare and green Sparkle Pupa down the slot, allowing a bit of weight between the flies to keep things tight, which I sort of lead downstream with the rod tip in that way so many of us have mastered, in one form or another, over the years.

Only one problem: I forgot to remove the 5X.

And I swear I hardly even leaned on him! I whine, a little while later, to no one in particular while reconstructing my nymphing rig again.

The next time I break off, I fabricate an excuse that has to do with the depth of the grab and *all that line* underwater, so that you can hardly ease off enough and a big trout, in the current, is virtually unstoppable.

It's kind of embarrassing.

Anyway, I'm 0 for 2 in the hole, not exactly fishing how I like to fish, but it seems like I should at least land *one* here before I head my merry way.

And, besides, the sun is out, the swallows swirling, the hot dry breath of the West fragrant with cottonwoods and sage—and one of these days, maybe sooner than later, I'll be too old to wander along a new river and cast a fly, even two, and see what happens or what I might find.

I'm halfway through rerigging again when I glance downstream—and there, in a patch of dead water where the current below the deep hole suddenly bends and reconfigures and heads back toward the main course of the river, I notice, in the long slick lying right beside a steep bank of tall willows, what appears to be, from this angle, a gang of sea otters poking their heads up and down through the surface . . . or maybe it's the ticking of a big kelp bed moving up and down in the . . . *waves?*

No, those are trout, I tell myself.

Holy shakes, I think.

I hold still long enough to get the scale and perspective right. What I'm looking at, I finally realize, are the snouts of two or three dozen trout rising up and down through the surface as though crates of jettisoned cargo bobbing again and again into view.

They look like black triangles, slightly rounded at the top, moving up and down like kids on a carousel.

They look like big trout feeding like crazy.

●————————●

I gather in my nymphs and head downstream.

Coming around the willows, I enter the periphery of a fog of little black caddis. This is no time to get technical. They're small. They're black. They're caddis.

I happen to have some of those.

I rebuild the end of my leader, lengthening it with both 4X and 5X. I tell myself to stay cool. The fly I tie on looks good, not perfect, but the size is right, the profile close. The real bugs, I can see, are resting on the slick water, just sitting there, and the trout have moved out of the current and are feeding. It's sort of obscene—either a great bacchanalian feast or a slaughter of biblical dimensions. The bugs look like whiskers on the water. The trout are big, and they are eating.

Fortunately, I pay attention to what I just told myself and I don't let my excitement get the best of me. There are so many fish feeding that it's difficult to pick out just one, to figure out what it's doing. I'm pretty sure there's absolutely no way to make this work unless I aim directly at a fish's nose. They're not going to move one way or another for the fly. They're going to get a perfect look at it.

I make a half-dozen short casts, trying to get the distance just right, the leader to fall perfectly straight. Every time a fish rises anywhere near the fly, I lift the rod, and when there's nothing there, I backcast once and put the fly down again, aiming for another snout.

When I finally lift and connect, it feels like I came tight to a brick that's now sinking and, now, ripping line off the reel.

Sweet Jesus, I think.

They're all big. They're all good. Rainbows and browns both, feeding right together so that, after a couple of each, I begin to wonder if I can tell them apart by the way they rise or take or fight. I haven't a clue. The light is low, funky, everything taking on the same shade of gray. I can't even really see the fly, only the spot it should land as the leader falls at that certain distance from the end of the line. I see a fish rise and my rod goes up as if to ask, as Dave Hughes says, "*Is anybody there?*"

When there is, you sure as hell know it.

What's most startling to me is that the fish just keep right on feeding—even after I've clomped around fighting and landing a few. I move up higher in the pool, and then I move down low. I wonder if my buddy from earlier in the day would suggest I've positioned myself all wrong. I wonder if I've *owned* more pairs of waders than the number of years he's been fishing in his life.

But who needs thoughts like that?

The water is crotch-deep, dark as shade, and still—except for the feeding trout. Near the bank, after failing to stop a fish that headed directly upstream, never once pausing until the hook pulled free, I notice that both legs of my waders are discolored, thigh to calf, by a dark green film—two slimy bands of green caddis pupae, pressed together tight as seeds in a tomatillo.

I've got plenty of those, too.

Yeah, right, I think. As if this—casting little dry flies to big feeding trout—isn't precisely what forty years of fly fishing has taught you to do?

● ●

In the morning in camp I set up to tie a dozen Little Black Caddis. My lineup has taken a beating. I'm also devoted to the notion that after you've actually seen a hatch on a new river, you can do better than the flies you brought, no matter how well the pattern you used has worked.

Of course, if I had genuine responsibilities I was supposed to take care of this morning, I'd be perfectly okay with returning to the river, later on, with the flies already in my caddis box. But isn't tying flies in camp while drinking coffee in the cool of the morning and the oats cook and the quail hurry by and the scent of the soil rises with the sun and your anticipation of a hatch like yesterday yet another reason you've been at this all this time?

Here's what I do for a Little Black Caddis. On a size 16 or 18 dry-fly hook, I tie in what amounts to about a third of a strand of black Antron yarn, which isn't really black at all but more like root beer or chocolate. I twist the fibers and wind a slender body. For the wing I use moose hair; it lies flat, never flaring like deer or elk hair, so it gives you the right profile as well as a dark color. For the hackle, in front of the wing, I use two or three winds of something undersized and brown.

That's it. It's a simple tie, and I crank out all dozen, six 16s, six 18s—and then six 14s for good measure—in the time it takes the oats to cook. By then I'm also on my second pot of coffee, which is okay, I figure, since I expect to spend about eight hours on the water if things go like yesterday.

If they don't, I suspect something else good will happen—another chance to do this my own way.

Which is the best reason of all, I think, for enjoying this silly game.

LITTLE BLACK CADDIS

- ▢ **Hook:** #16-18 TMC 900 BL or similar
- ▢ **Thread:** Black or camel 8/0 UNI-Thread, or similar
- ▢ **Body:** Black Antron yarn
- ▢ **Wing:** Moose hair
- ▢ **Hackle:** Brown

Tying the Little Black Caddis

1. Secure the hook in the vise and start the thread. Cover the hook shank with an even layer of thread wraps. At the bend of the hook, secure a length of Antron yard; on a sparse little fly like this you want to use only six to ten fibers separated from the heavier strand of yarn. Advance the thread to a point about one-third back from the hook eye. Twist the Antron fibers into a tight noodle; wrap the Antron forward, secure with the thread, and clip excess.

2. Clip a dozen or so strands of moose hair from the skin. Clean out any short hairs or underfur, then drop the hair, tips down, into your stacker and align the tips with a few raps of the stacker on your bench. Carefully remove the moose hair, keeping the tips aligned, and secure at the forward end of the body as a wing that's about the length of the hook shank. Moose hair lies flatter than deer or elk; the tips of moose hair are also finer. This is a wee fly that we don't want to overdress.

3. Prepare a hackle feather by stripping the fibers from the base of the stem. Secure the stem just forward of the root of the wing. Make only two or three turns of hackle. Tie off and clip excess. Whip-finish and saturate the thread wraps with lacquer or head cement. And do yourself a favor: Take a needle and clear the eye.

MY FAVORITE TERRESTRIAL

My Favorite Terrestrial, adapted from design by Randall Kaufmann

The river, like so many in this part of the country, seems really a stream. Or, better perhaps, a creek, up here in its broad headwater valley, all empty rangelands and expanding vistas save for the vast puddle of blue-green willows, each glimpse through which offers but a suggestion of the wide river pulling at the arid landscape somewhere beyond the horizon below.

Small water, anyway, it brings us up short, prompting a brand of offhanded disdain. *That's it?* A dozen miles downstream we've found good fish, big fish—but that was below the reservoir, stalking the margins of a spring-creek-like tailwater meandering through private land. This, too, is private land, yet with public access, the sort of mindful arrangement that allows us to feel particularly clever all the way through a half-mile of pasture, from the barbed-wire gate to the gap in the guarding willows—until we fan out along the lip of the bank, practically pooh-poohing prospects of the meager run gliding by beneath our boots.

Still, there's the grudging consensus that small water—and, presumably, smaller, easier fish—is exactly why we're here this fair summer morn. The scale of our interest favors a day of relaxing sport—in sharp contrast to the drama of our recent outings downstream, the sort of spellbinding angling that can leave one's nerves rubbed raw as wind-chapped flesh. Today why not let's

just go . . . *fishing*, we've all agreed—yet another example of the kind of remarkable accord that seems available on trout streams and practically no place else in any of our lives.

We—my old friends Peter and John Syka, plus Patrick, my younger son—split into pairs and head our separate ways. I'm delighted, of course, to fish with Patrick—more so because in water this size, protocol dictates that we leapfrog upstream, sharing first licks on successive runs rather than plunging off on tangents of our own. At the same time, Patrick's readiness of late to fish by himself, and his success while doing so, has bolstered my fragile sense of parental worth—if for no other reason than I feel vindicated by tangible proof that, come what may, I've raised a child who knows how to, well, fly-fish.

Please, let's not anyone bring up questions about the value of *that*.

•———————•

I'm drifting a cast in the vicinity of a shaded eddy, a patch of still water rooted to a tuft of willows draped over an undercut bank, when Patrick, a dozen yards upstream from me, releases a sound that anglers everywhere have been making, in one form or another, for as long as they've hooked good fish.

I'm startled. For a quarter-mile now we've been dinking around with little trout—most of them too small to get their mouths around our flies. So far, in fact, the best decision we've made is to wade wet, allowing us to march right up the creek channel, free of the heat and dense willows while wading cool as toddlers in our boots and soggy leggings. Braided and curled, the stream here seems ideally suited for one of those fashionable micro-line rods—while our standard-issue 5-weights require us to stand well back from water's edge, trying to tighten our loops in the direction of obvious lies that have offered nothing to dispute our curt first impressions.

Until now. The fish, by the look of Patrick's rod, is the genuine article, a trout not unlike the big rainbows we found, sparingly, below the reservoir. That a fish this large should be in water this small shocks both of us—although I'm the one who ends up hollering as if a lizard's loose in the kitchen, while Patrick patiently wears down the trout and, eventually, slides it to hand.

When he returns the trout to the water, I ask Patrick what it ate.

"The Green Humpy," he answers. "A big one."

The fly he holds up, broad as a thimble, looks like nothing in nature I've ever seen. Patrick himself, I also notice, now stands eye to eye to me, his long limbs and angular features unlike those of the boy I've been raising for the past sixteen years.

"Wait a minute," I say. "I thought I told you those things don't work."

Or not, at least, as well as *my* favorite terrestrial.

My research, informal at best, had been conducted during those past two days of nervy fishing over big trout downstream. The water, slick and clear as a nightcap, gave up nothing in the way of hatches, except for a brief flurry of twilight midges that left everyone grumbling like gamblers. Two locals had a trick up their sleeves, a big ant or a little beetle, depending on how you looked at it, with a bright orange rubber indicator on its back so they could see it at the end of their long casts—but that only proved what we all suspected, that the trout were hungry and looking for terrestrials, something big to float by and give them cause to rise.

Hence my first choice, the Green Humpy, size 10—the same fly Patrick has just used, to some effect, against my sound parental advice. In my case, I'd had good reason to try it. I was inspired the first morning after gazing upstream and spotting, off in the distance, something the size of a small hummingbird skittering on the surface, only to witness it disappear in a rise that brought to mind those fuzzy, slow-motion, newsreel first moments of an atomic bomb test off a South Pacific atoll. Hmm. Later, I was able to conclude that the insect that sparked said explosion was a crane fly—a creature for which I was carrying no reliable pattern, although in this case it didn't seem to matter, thanks to responses

I soon generated with that oversized, Gravenstein-green Humpy.

Responses—but repeated failures to connect.

What's with that? you ask.

The reflex reaction finds you kicking yourself for having *missed* the strike. Others claim *the fish* just missed. Both reactions, I contend, fall entirely off the mark.

Trout don't miss. Especially big trout. Especially when they rise with intent to eat a big dry fly. Unless you jerk the fly away from a trout, or a trout rises to an insect that suddenly flies away, the times trout miss beg an infinitesimal improbability that defies the existence of trout at all.

Trout don't miss. Instead, they refuse—or reject—the fly.

But, you argue . . .

But, nothing. If they want it, they eat it.

Still, those were stirring rises inspired by the Humpy—great boils of disturbed water rupturing the slippery current, the trout themselves revealed as violent predators flashing brilliant and sleek through the shattered surface of the stream—rises grand enough, almost, to claim your money's worth. For it's hardly a novel idea that nothing in the sport of fly fishing surpasses the thrill of a good trout rising to the drift of a big dry fly—just as nothing, I'd like to add, invites more spirited and elegant rises than a big terrestrial riding down a quiet summer stream.

Yet nobody—absolutely nobody—can go long raising big trout and not hooking them, without an itch on the trigger finger that begins to feel like a hole in the heart itself. What was going on here? I was moving fish—fish *not* actively feeding, so clearly they were fooled, rising to the surface only to refuse the fly within inches, it looked, from their nose. Two different trout appeared to actually *jerk* their head away from the fly at the last instant, a maneuver that produced even greater shock waves reverberating downstream—while at the same time leaving me all but limp, as if grabbed by my wading belt and worried like an old sock.

Or maybe, I ventured, these were the gestures of trout that were simply pissed off, angered by the sudden disappointment of desire denied following the momentary stimulation that had pulled them from the safety of their lies.

Sometime, I suspected, I might want to run that one by Patrick, too.

My answer, anyway, to all of this rejection proved simple enough. Throughout the course of our second morning on the private tailwater, I experimented with Humpys of different colors, getting rises to the green one alone. The very best green, of course, in the history of flies is peacock herl—and I happened to have along with me a couple of experimental Stimulator-like

Skwala Stones with just such bodies. (You should also know that I recall reading once a claim by Randall Kaufmann, the creator of the Stimulator, that the green Stimulator is his favorite—but I've never been able to find the reference again.)

By lunch, two trout had risen to and eaten one of these peacock herl Skwalas. Convinced I was onto something, I spent the short-shadow hour of the day at a vise affixed to my van's steering wheel. Mostly, I tried to replicate what had just worked. Besides color, the wing seemed to me the telling feature. But who knows? Where the big Humpy had ridden high atop the water, asking the trout to breach that terrible margin between stream and sky, the fly just eaten had rested low in the film, suspended from a flat, greased wing. To me this reflected perfectly my notion that the trout—some of them over twenty inches, all of them immaculately configured for launching themselves high into the air— were feeding on whatever random bugs came drifting by—as long as they were bugs big enough to make it worth the trout's while to rise to the surface and intersect the path of its prey.

That afternoon, five trophy rainbows rose to and ate My Favorite Terrestrial. Of the three I landed, two came under such exquisite conditions—long casts; long drifts; profound, ponderous, confident takes—that I began to think of the session as the best bit of big dry-fly fishing I've experienced in all my life. Of course, I often grant good outings this kind of hyperbole. It's probably the same inclination that inspired me, after releasing the second fish, to remain on my knees in the low-angled light, eyeing the long blue run and precise fold in the wrinkled current where the drifting fly had disappeared—all the while wondering what I'd ever done to deserve this kind of elegant sport.

On the small water with Patrick the next day, we each land three trout as good as any we could possibly imagine from a stream in which, most places, a twelve-inch fish would earn you bragging rights. I get mine on the newly anointed MFT; Patrick, sticking to his hunch against my generous counsel, gets all of his on the big Green Humpy. His fish are bigger than mine—a breach of authority neither of us feels any need to address. The last fish—hooked in a narrow channel cut between sharp head-high banks—comes so far out of the water it *clears* a streamside bush into which we both think, for a moment, the trout is about to land.

As we thread our way through the willows, heading downstream to look for Peter and John, I dub the morning the best day of small-stream dry-fly fishing we've ever shared. Somewhere behind me, Patrick doesn't protest.

- **Hook:** #10 Mustad 94831 or similar 3X-long dry fly
- **Thread:** Highland green Pearsall's Gossamer Silk or Morus Silk
- **Tail:** Moose body hair
- **Body hackle:** Brown
- **Body:** Peacock herl
- **Wing:** Moose mane
- **Thorax:** Green Pearsall's Gossamer Silk
- **Thorax hackle:** Brown

Tying My Favorite Terrestrial

1. Secure the hook in the vise and start the thread behind the eye. Cover the shank of the hook in an even layer of thread wraps. For the tail, clip and clean and stack a tuft of moose body hair. Forward the bend of the hook, tie in a short bushy tail. Clip the butts of the hair at an angle and cover with thread wraps so that there are no unsightly lumps under the body.

2. Strip the fibers from the stem of a hackle feather long enough to palmer the body of the fly. Secure the stem at the root of the tail. Now create a dubbing loop, wax the legs, and spin two or three lengths of peacock herl into the loop, creating a tight, dense peacock herl rope. Wind the rope forward to a point about one-third back from the hook eye, leaving yourself plenty of room for both the wing and the thorax hackle.

3. Hold the tip of the hackle feather with your fingers or a pair of hackle pliers. Palmer the body with four or five evenly spaced hackle wraps. Tie off the hackle at the forward edge of the body. If the hackle feather is long enough, you can position the tip out of the way so that you can continue wrapping it later over the thorax. It's easier, however, to clip the excess from the body palmer before tying in the wing and building up the thorax.

4. For the wing, clip a generous tuft of moose mane hair. Clean away any underfur or short hairs and align the tips in your hair stacker. Measure the wing length so that the wing extends to a point about even with the tips of the tail. Wax your thread and tie in the wing at the forward edge of the body, using tight wraps so that the wing won't spin on the hook shank. Clip the hair butts and cover with thread wraps. Build up an even thorax with more thread wraps.

5. For the thorax hackle use either the feather from the body hackle or tie in the stem of another feather forward the root of the wing. Make two or three hackle wraps; the green of the thorax thread should show between and beneath the hackle wraps. Now create a tidy head with thread wraps, whip-finish, and saturate the thread with lacquer or your favorite head cement.

COCK ROBIN CADDIS

Cock Robin Caddis, adapted by author from traditional Irish lough pattern and Scottish variant

We were up north, just across the border, swinging flies on a wide river for rising trout, when I was struck again by the peculiarities of the waking fly. Nothing hews more sharply against the grain of conventional fly-fishing wisdom than the idea of a fly, swung downstream on a tight line, that creases the surface of the current as a means of stimulating a strike. That evening I was fishing two flies, a soft-hackled caddis pupa and, above it, a wet caddis that kept riding up against the lid, or ceiling, of the river; even in the low light, the abnormal V trailing the top fly stood out as if a contrail behind a jet in blue sky, clearly visible despite the sad range of focus of my aging eyes.

All of my best fish that evening, a handful of them, came to the waking fly. A session later in the week, on the same water, offered much the same. We can only speculate why. One trout in particular erupted through the surface, at the apex of the V, and instantly broke off—without a discernible trace of weight passing through line or rod. (I know it ate the waking fly; that's what was missing on inspection of the apparently undersized leader.) But after two decades since initiation into the juju of waking patterns and presentations, back when I first witnessed their remarkable efficacy in provoking grabs from summer steelhead, I wonder if the question *why* serves any real purpose—beyond the need to fabricate a narrative for the stranger-than-fiction or otherwise hard-to-believe.

How, it seems to me, might be the better question. Most fly anglers approach river and stream well versed in dry-fly doctrine and, to a lesser degree, a rudimentary understanding of basic nymphing techniques, although for many anglers their subsurface studies have been short-circuited by a reliance on various iterations of strike indicators. If an angler has woven the wet-fly swing into his or her game, it probably means he or she has explored the literature—or been lucky enough to fish with an experienced hand, a parent or other relative or perhaps older friend who doesn't necessarily know about the latest and greatest flies and gimmickry, but who somehow manages to catch at least as many fish as anyone else on the water.

But who includes waking flies in their repertoire of tactics? I'm referring here to trouting—although the question pertains as well, of course, to steelheading, to saltwater surface presentations, and to bass and other warmwater species. Not that fishing a waking fly is difficult. It's just that many anglers don't include the tactic in their playbooks, especially in the running waters—the rivers and streams—that make up so many of our traditional trout-fishing opportunities.

This may change as more and more trout anglers take up two-handed rods and begin to explore with greater frequency the subtleties of downstream presentations. But don't get me wrong: I'm the last person to argue the need for new equipment to expand your angling skills or artistry. The favorite rod and cared-for floating line remain the core components of nearly every solution you'll ever need while trouting on river or stream—and as soon as you recognize and accept these basic tools for the job at hand, you can turn all of your attention to the aspects of presentation that matter most and that make you a better fly fisher as well.

Like which direction to cast your line. I'm not trying to be funny. Inexperienced anglers are often confused by or unaware of the sharp difference between upstream and downstream presentations—or how seasoned anglers might change the way they manipulate casts that begin with a natural drift in the upstream quadrant and then come under tension as fly and leader and line pass downstream. Schooled only in traditional dry-fly tactics, anglers see the fly begin to drag and they know they should pick up and cast again. Practiced in a full range of presentation techniques, however, an angler becomes adept at utilizing drag or *tension* to offer up the fly in ways that might actually prove more lifelike, or at least enticing, than the fly during a drag-free drift.

Which brings us to the matter of the waking fly. What, in real life, we may be trying to represent is anyone's guess. These days, as mentioned, I prefer to limit myself to the thought that I'm hoping to catch fish—and the waking fly is one way that sometimes works. And by *works* I mean it's a technique that often yields the best fish of a session, a day, a trip. Again, I don't know why, other than to note that nothing else we do with the fly behaves quite like a waker—and its mysterious appeal to fish feeds my own desire for surprise, wonder, and delight, ingredients that have always seemed essential to the point of fly fishing.

Here's what I do know. First off, waking should not be confused with skating. If you can see your fly riding on top of the water, your fly is either overdressed or the water you're fishing has too much current. You want your waking pattern to fish *beneath* the surface; it rises to the extreme top limit of the water column and leaves its wake by scraping or scoring or otherwise distorting the *underside* of the surface film. Obviously, it's the tension created by current that makes the dragging fly press against the ceiling of a river or stream and leave its telltale, V-shaped wake. Still, one of the best things you can do when fishing a waker is slow down its movement or swing *across* the current, beginning with a straight-leader cast that's followed by judicious mends, preventing the sort of crack-the-whip swing that plagues so many downstream presentations.

Long straight casts aimed farther down than across the current work best. Even if you want to begin with a drag-free drift and then have the fly wake through the

swing, a cast that begins with a straight leader nearly always spends more time fishing effectively than one that uses up much of its swing before settling into a smooth, even pace. On the other hand, let your waking fly fish. Too much mending, like too much picking up and recasting, disturbs the water and, presumably, the fish. Nothing improves your chances more in trout fishing than stopping and doing nothing at all for a while. Wait until you see a fish rise—then swing your waker right over the trout's nose.

Is there more to it? I'm not sure. Clearly it's reasonable to assume that if our waker looks something like the bugs the fish are feeding on, we have more chance to provoke a strike or stimulate a grab, than if we attempt to imitate, say, a lawn chair or plastic bath toy. But I've seen too many fish respond to waking flies that are simply attractive lures to take that logic too far. Fish, like most animals, can be curious; there's probably some deep biological imperative that demands trout, like steelhead, set caution aside now and then and *get up there and check it out.* Of course, the crucial fact about fish is that they don't have hands or paws or other appendages to do their investigative work. Fish explore their world with their mouths.

Lucky us.

⎯⎯⎯●⎯⎯⎯●⎯⎯⎯

The Cock Robin Caddis is the latest iteration of a long line of waking muddlers I've fashioned over the years. Earlier versions of this style of fly were for targeting steelhead; this is the first one I've created with trout in mind. All of these muddlers belong to a lineage that originates with Bill McMillan's Steelhead Caddis, the fly that sparked interest in surface flies for summer steelhead at a time, forty years ago, when most anglers were convinced that the best way to hook these elusive fish was to deliver the fly, by whatever means, *down* to the level of the fish rather than expect the fish to rise to the surface and grab.

McMillan's Steelhead Caddis was originally developed with some idea of imitating the big October Caddis so common in fall on West Coast rivers. He soon concluded, however, that in steelheading, at least, "method outranks precise pattern in importance." My own waking muddlers have nearly all evolved to the point that they make no pretense of imitating anything found in nature; they're simply mechanical devices designed to wake, with the sparsest of dressings and just enough color and flash so that *I* believe in them.

The Cock Robin Caddis, on the other hand, would seem to imitate, or at least suggest, the genuine October or Fall Caddis (Limnephilidae). In truth, however, it owes its design and name to the original Cock Robin, a traditional Irish lough pattern and a Scottish variant of the same name. Like so many other patterns I fish, some of them with a great deal of success, the Cock Robin simply looks right to me; it took little in the way of imagination to conform it into the style of my other waking muddlers and picture it, in fall, moving some of those same big trout that grabbed so greedily the smaller wet caddis waking on a summer eve.

Whether I end up swinging the Cock Robin Caddis through a steelhead lie as well remains to be seen. If the trout are big enough, and they rise to a fly on a waking swing, you might find yourself capable of ignoring, for a while, fish that swim from the sea.

COCK ROBIN CADDIS

- **Hook:** #6-10 Partridge Single Wilson or similar
- **Thread:** Antique gold Pearsall's Gossamer Silk or similar
- **Tag:** Oval gold tinsel (small)
- **Rib:** Oval gold tinsel (small)
- **Body:** Rear half, golden olive seal fur; forward half, burnt orange seal fur
- **Underwing:** Bronze mallard
- **Overwing:** Squirrel tail
- **Head/collar:** Sparse deer hair, spun and trimmed with a few strands left to extend back over body

Tying the Cock Robin Caddis

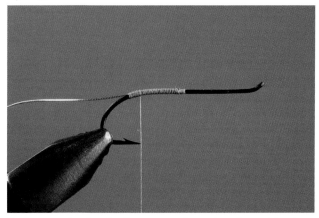

1. Secure the hook. Start your thread at the midpoint of the hook shank. Tie in the end of a length of oval tinsel. Align the tinsel with the top of the hook shank and cover it with thread wraps back to a point directly above the barb of the hook. Now advance the thread to a spot directly over the point of the hook.

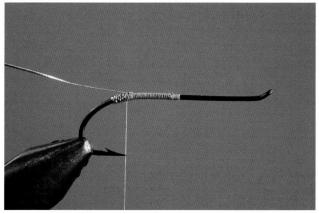

2. Starting above the barb of the hook, create the tag of the fly by advancing the tinsel five or six turns. Tie off the tinsel, then fold it aft and cover the folded portion with several more thread wraps. Don't cut off the remaining tinsel, as you will use it later for ribbing the fly.

3. To begin the body of the fly, wax your thread and create a small dubbing noodle with golden olive seal fur. Wind the noodle forward, from the tinsel tag to the midpoint of the hook shank. For the forward half of the body, create another dubbing noodle with burnt orange seal fur and wind it forward, stopping well short of the hook eye. Now wind the tinsel forward, ribbing the fly with four to six evenly spaced turns. Secure tinsel and clip excess.

4. For the fly's underwing, align the tips of a small tuft of bronze mallard wing fibers and then roll them between thumb and forefinger. This disorganizes the inherent bend in the fibers so that they end up looking *more* coherent once tied into place. Tie in the fibers by the butts with the tips extending about even with the tag end of the fly.

5. The squirrel tail overwing should extend just beyond the underwing. Because the entire wing, underwing and overwing, is fashioned in two parts, it's easy to end up with an overdressed wing. Remember: Waking flies work best when *sparse.* Clip a small tuft of squirrel tail, comb out any underfur, and align the tips in a hair stacker. Tie in the squirrel tail hairs directly on top of the bronze mallard fibers. Clip excess butt material of both wing parts.

6. The essential component of all waking muddlers is the last step, creating a sparse, spun, deer hair head, with a collar of stray hairs extending just beyond the butt of the fly. Practice, practice. Your aim, again, is a lightly dressed fly. Some deer hair works better than other deer hair; there's also personal preference. Clip a fairly substantial tuft from your patch, comb out the underfur, then align the tips in a hair stacker. Lay the tuft along the top of the fly, check the length against the bend of the hook, then take one or two very soft turns of thread just forward the tie-off point of the underwing. The trick now is to slowly continue the next thread wraps while at the same time creating thread tension so that the hairs spin around the hook shank and begin to splay. Continue to wind the thread through the splayed butts of deer hair until you finally have all of the butts standing erect behind the final forward wraps of thread. At this point you can whip-finish and saturate the exposed thread wraps with lacquer or head cement. Then grab your scissors, trim up the head of the fly, and reduce the aft-pointing hairs to a number far fewer than you may think you need. A good buddy of mine calls my wakers "Six-Haired Muddlers." That's an exaggeration—but not by much.

Once two-handed rods found a new home in Pacific coast steelhead fishing, suddenly the sky was the limit. *Nobody* has looked back since.

PART TWO

Steelhead Flies

When I moved to the Northwest as a starry-eyed fly fisher, I naturally took immediate steps to join the ranks of serious steelhead anglers. The idea of swinging flies for sea-run fish is hard to beat, and even before I crossed the Oregon border for good, I was under the spell cast by old photos of Bill Schaadt with exquisite Russian River fish, the elegant prose and frontier adventures of Roderick Haig-Brown, plus a handful of North Umpqua steelhead I had encountered firsthand during visits to my then-wife's hometown of Roseburg.

I remember walking into the old Kaufmann's Streamborn store in Tigard, near Portland, thinking I might pick up some inside dope. The clerk looked me over, no doubt recognizing my dubious immigrant status. He shared the names of a few obvious coastal winter-run rivers, pointed out several different flies I had already read about and even begun to tie. We were both just sort of going through the motions—he, I assumed, because of my scruffy surfer mien and dinged-up framing carpenter's hands; I, because those same two working hands earned just enough to support the then-wife, now teetering on the brink, and our two young sons.

Then suddenly, as if in a fit of pity, resignation, I'm not sure what, the clerk turned and pointed to a display of books and said, "Of course, *this* is what we all really want to do."

Thirty-five years since publication, Bill McMillan's *Dry Line Steelhead* remains my guidebook to this fickle sport. Two-handed rods, articulated Intruder flies, Skagit heads you can cast into trees on the far side of the river, even crashing fish runs—none of it has diminished my enthusiasm for moving steelhead to or near the surface with traditional swinging flies, especially sparsely dressed muddlers that leave that telltale wake as they scurry or creep at the end of a well-mended line.

The clerk at Kaufmann's was right: Everybody *wants* to catch steelhead swinging flies on floating lines. But who believes it's even possible anymore? Just as the number of steelhead seems to decline each year, so does the number of anglers willing to stay committed to surface presentations and the thrill of the surface take.

Who can blame them? Fishing pressure and drastically reduced numbers of fish do seem to make steelhead increasingly reluctant to rise to the surface or chase the fly. Or is that just the opinion shared by so many anglers who have given up, or never even attempted, the voodoo of swinging patterns designed to tremble along the enigmatic margin between river and sky?

I confess I often find myself joining the ranks of the nonbelievers. In winter, we assume, cold water slows the metabolism of sea-run fish. The other confounding truth that steelheaders eventually learn about their prey is that much of a steelhead's behavior and riverine whereabouts is associated with spawning salmon. Steelhead, claim what you will, are egg eaters, and a fly that offers any semblance to the lowly salmon egg

The author releases a steelhead hen hooked and landed with a single-handed rod on a small creek on the Oregon coast, just hours after she had crossed the sandbar and escaped a gauntlet of sea lions, one of which left teeth marks on her head.

There's a reason steelhead have captured the imagination of Pacific coast fly anglers since long before any of us was alive. Their uncertain future in the region threatens to diminish the possibilities of the sport by an all but unimaginable degree.

is a form of hatch matching at least as sophisticated as presenting a generic Gold-Ribbed Hare's Ear or Adams dry fly to resident trout.

A lot of ink and digital screen-space will be wasted again this year in discussions or arguments about the probity of resorting to egg patterns when fly fishing for steelhead—as though anyone has been appointed to dictate what does or doesn't constitute a fly, much less earned rights to claim authoritative insight into the motives for steelhead grabbing or striking or eating a fly in the first place. Can I get a witness? This past winter I hooked and landed two of the biggest winter steelhead of my life, both on big yarn balls fished exactly like trout nymphs guided through drifts beneath a floating line. Today, this presentation technique is commonly championed as Czech or Euro-style nymphing—and it's awfully close to how traditional gear fishermen have always caught steelhead, with their longish light-tipped rods, level-wind reels, and treated salmon-egg "berries" drifting alongside a bit of parachute cord packed with lead.

That's a far cry from Bill McMillan's waking muddlers. And the then-wife is long gone, my two sons grown up with lives of their own. I still fish waking patterns, some as sparsely dressed as fruit trees before they flower in spring, and I like nothing more than swinging an impressionistic shrimp pattern an inch or two beneath the surface, best tied on a double, although that's still illegal in most waters outside the range of

Just one of them can change your life. All they need are healthy rivers running free.

what we were told, as schoolkids, had once been called the British Empire. Change happens. But for now, at least, the steelhead keep returning, climbing rivers along the northern reaches of the eastern Pacific, and a fly in the water, no matter how you fish it, can still bring these remarkable fish to hand.

CLARET & HOPE

Claret & Hope, adapted from the old Irish salmon fly, Claret & Jay, designer unknown

It's hard to know at this moment what to even think about steelhead flies. With runs falling this year to record lows throughout the fish's historic range, who can say with certainty we should even cast where wild steelhead still swim and spawn? We're not quite there yet, but if trends continue, I can imagine hiking into remote watersheds armed with nothing more than binoculars and a camera, hoping to catch sight of a steelhead, perhaps paired up on or near a redd, a story to tell one's grandchildren as though having encountered, firsthand, a condor, a trout in Baja, or the bark of the spotted owl.

Given the state of the fishery, tying steelhead flies can come to seem like an abstraction, the creation of an object, elegant or otherwise, that may never do what it was intended to do. Of course, the vast majority of flies tied for steelhead, even those tied by serious steelheaders, never catch a fish; many of them will never even find their way into the water. The very best steelhead anglers, those who fish all day with confidence, never worrying about fly selection once a choice has been made, go through very few flies. Yet like most dedicated anglers, these same steelheaders will happily tie flies night after night, a form of creative exploration that leads, now and again, to a fly that seems just right.

Yet there's little reason to believe that any of us needs a new steelhead pattern. The flies don't represent much in the first place; most of us simply mimic patterns we've had success with in the past. Over time, we settle on a handful of patterns that we feel will cover any conditions we might encounter on steelhead rivers near to or far from home. We fall back on these patterns because they've worked in the past, accepting the grim truth that they worked—and they will no doubt continue to work—because these are the flies we keep swinging on the end of our line.

This is the kind of logic that can drive half-hearted steelheaders nuts. What eventually becomes apparent is that this is fishing for someone other than the faint of heart. Bearing down takes on a whole new meaning when you fish for days on end without sign of a fish, without any discernible reaction to the fly. Wondering if your fly is the problem is the surest way to start down a road that leads nowhere other than yet another fishless day.

Successful steelhead anglers do, of course, change flies. They recognize different river conditions, different lies, and they adjust accordingly. Most steelhead anglers have a collection of winter flies and another stash of patterns for summer-run fish; flies for high dark water, flies for water low and clear; flies to use with their floating line and flies for getting deep when attached to a short leader and ten or fifteen or twenty feet or more of thin, dense, "sink-tip" material powered by a plump heavy Skagit head or the like that flies from the rod tip as though a two-ounce pyramid sinker.

All of these different fly types indicate a process of selection more sophisticated than some of my initial comments might suggest. I'll stand by my argument, however, that in any given season, under such-and-such conditions, successful steelheaders don't spend a lot of time worrying about fly selection. They've seen what works—and they assume the same will work again. Few of us approach the level of disregard for different patterns as an angler once described by Tom McGuane, a fellow steelheader who, allegedly, if I remember correctly, fished only with flies given to him by other steelheaders. I love that attitude, knowing full well I suffer far too many anxieties to embrace such a radical tack.

Anxiety may not be the right word. What we all tend to hold somewhere in our minds, however, is the belief that there just might be a fly out there, one we still haven't stumbled upon, that will work like magic, a silver bullet that provokes a response from any steelhead anywhere in a given river. We know that belief is absurd. Yet nearly all of us continue to hold on to it somewhere in our psyches, more so, perhaps, the longer we go without any sign of fish.

The real issue today, no doubt, is whether those fish we long for are in the river at all. A *big* issue, to say the least. It's hard to know how we reached this point. But for anyone who has invested the time and energy to find these iconic West Coast fish in the past, the one fish that has driven so much in the way of innovation both in gear and technique throughout the entire sport of fly fishing, the current spate of crashing runs and river closures, from California to British Columbia, feels like nothing short of a tragedy.

So who needs another steelhead fly?

My guess is we all do. A new steelhead pattern places a claim on hope, that precious attitude at the heart of every successful steelheader's game. The sport is littered with anglers who gave up hope and quit, their attention diverted to more plausible pursuits, anything besides the grim prospect of never finding another steelhead again. It could happen. But a new steelhead pattern demands we don't surrender to this fatalistic view, that we still believe it possible a fly can move a fish from the realm of mystery, or abstraction, to a concrete visceral experience with the clearest expression of unfettered wildlife many of us will ever know.

Is it too late? I don't think so. River closures and unprecedented angling restrictions mean that somebody is paying attention, that wild steelhead won't vanish overnight, eclipsed from the face of the earth as though the last of the passenger pigeons. But the threat is real. Something happened to this year's age group of West Coast steelhead: they left their natal waters in apparently normal numbers—but on return

from the ocean, there are far fewer fish than anyone has ever counted.

Will your new fly help? I won't answer that, other than to state that if you go ahead and tie it, and it gives you pause to consider the fate of these remarkable fish and what it might take to keep them an important part of any comprehensive West Coast fly-fishing career, then it's served its purpose—improving your odds, however small the increment, of catching a steelhead in the uncertain future ahead.

CLARET & HOPE

- **Hook:** Partridge low water Wilson or similar, size 6-10
- **Thread:** Claret Pearsall's Gossamer Silk, Morus Silk, Ephemera, or Wine 8/0 UNI-Thread
- **Tag:** Silver tinsel and orange floss
- **Tail:** Golden pheasant tippets and topping
- **Rib:** Oval silver tinsel
- **Body:** Seal fur, claret, spun into a dubbing loop
- **Hackle:** Grizzly saddle hackle dyed red
- **Throat:** Guinea fowl dyed blue
- **Underwing:** Golden pheasant tippets
- **Wing:** Bronze mallard

Tying the Claret & Hope

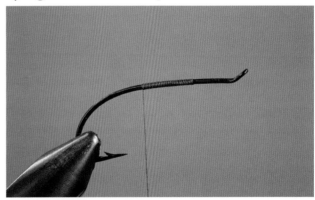

1. Secure the hook and start your thread. If you didn't stock up on Pearsall's Gossamer when they quit the business of producing silk thread a decade ago, you can find the exact same product now from Morus Silk. Their reproduction of the original Pearsall's colors may not yet have reached an outlier such as claret, dark or light—but another silk thread, by the French company Ephemera, is a good substitute. The "wine" UNI-Thread is another perfectly good option.

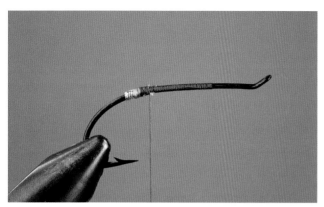

2. Above the barb of the hook (which you may need or want to flatten before fishing), secure a length of oval or round silver tinsel for the tag. Make two or three wraps of tinsel, secure with a wrap or two of thread, then secure the floss and add a couple of wraps of orange at the forward end of the tag.

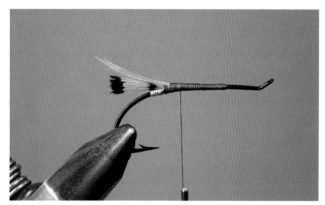

3. The tail is made in two parts. First, just forward the tag, secure a single small orange and black "tippet" feather from that golden pheasant skin I'd really like you to buy if you haven't done so already, so that you have a wealth of the beautiful and varied feathers found on such a bird. (These birds, I should note, are now raised in captivity, which makes the skins remarkably inexpensive and no more harmful than the killing of chickens or turkeys raised for food.) Secure the tippet feather so the tail extends just past the bend of the hook. Now, for the second part of the tail, use a single yellow feather from the crest of the bird, located on the skin above the two-tone tippet feathers. Position the feather so that the tips curl upward, then tie it in so that these tips extend just past the reach of the tippets below.

4. The body of the fly is also composed of two parts, the dubbing and the rib. Start by securing a length of small oval tinsel just ahead of the tail. Now create a dubbing loop, wax the legs, and spin in the dubbing material. Wrap the dubbing noodle forward, stopping just short of the tip of the return wire from the hook eye. Then rib the dubbing body with four or five evenly spaced wraps of tinsel. Secure the tinsel and clip excess.

5. Forward the body tie in a single hackle feather with barbs about 1½ times the hook gap. Tie in the feather by the tip and advance your thread several wraps. Wind the hackle forward, trying to fold the feather lengthwise and hold the barbs rearward as you wind. Make 3–4 hackle wraps, secure and clip excess. Now a few judicious thread wraps can help aim those hackle tips rearward rather than sticking out as if constructing a bottle brush.

6. The throat of the fly is a single guinea feather dyed blue—in this case Silver Doctor Blue. Secure the guinea feather along the bottom of the hook just forward the hackle, with the tips of the feather pointing aft. After taking a turn or two of thread to secure the feather, you can tug on the stem and slide the feather forward until the length of throat tips seem appropriately proportionate to the length of the hackle barbs.

7. The wing of the fly is also two parts. For the underwing, just forward the hackle, tie in a small tuft of fibers from one of those two-tone golden pheasant tippet feathers. The tip of the underwing should just reach the root of the tail. For the wing itself, select sections about three-sixteenths of an inch wide from two different bronze mallard feathers, the feathers from opposite sides of the bird. Hold the feather sections as a pair, dull sides facing each other, and secure along the top of the fly with the tips of the wing extending to the end of the tail. Easier said than done. You are better than I am if you can tie a symmetrical pair of wings that embrace the rest of the fly as if arrow fletching. But I try to tell myself I've learned other important things in my life while I wasn't at my bench trying to master this skill. Once the wings are finished, create a tidy head, whip finish, and saturate the final thread wraps with lacquer or your favorite head cement.

GREEN BUTT MUDDLER

Green Butt Muddler, adapted by author from Bill McMillan's Steelhead Caddis

I spent some time on the phone the other day with one of those film guys who has done so much of late to redefine the fly-fishing experience. We resolved the business end of our conversation pretty quickly—and before long he asked about the steelhead season. Last year he made it out to the coast, and for the first time in his life he had hooked and landed sea-run fish. This year he's feeling the pinch of the hobbled economy—and like a lot of us, he's had to resign himself to finding sport closer to home.

I didn't suggest he try to imagine keeping a fishing career afloat writing stories.

Instead, I confessed that this was one of those years I catch a few more steelhead than other years. I didn't go into it much; I didn't want him to feel bad for not making it out this season. And the truth is, the increased success I've enjoyed has had little to do with the fishing itself.

In a way, it's sort of sad. Or discouraging. For from all I can tell, the only reason I've caught more steelhead this year is because I've spent more time fishing for them.

Odd though it may seem, this direct proportion between the time spent fishing for steelhead and the number of steelhead caught is perhaps the single biggest reason anglers back away from the sport—even if they've enjoyed steelheading success in the past. For tell me: Who wants to come out a "winner" just because you take more turns rolling the dice? Is it really nothing

more than an endurance contest? The longer you stay out there, the more fish you catch?

Because if that's all there is to it—

Well, it is.

And it isn't.

Somewhere in the twists and turns of another recent phone conversation, I mentioned to my old pal Peter Syka that steelheading reminds me of casting flies in the surf: You spend all this time without anything happening—and then, out of nowhere, something shows up.

"Well, that might be true," said Peter. "But there's a big difference."

"What's that?" I asked.

"When you do catch something, it's a steelhead."

He had me there.

All of which suggests the sort of cryptic steelhead "wisdom" that can seem artless and obvious on the one hand or, on the other, profound as a Zen koan.

I talked to a guy recently who begged me to give him advice. He's fished three winters for steelhead and failed to hook a fish. He explained how he was nymphing, drifting weighted Egg-Sucking Leeches and egg patterns under an indicator—pretty much de rigueur on the local beat, even if a few of us continue to swing flies all winter, just to keep our loops in shape. The guy had run into me at a downtown bookstore; he wanted to set up a meeting, a chance to talk when I might have a little more time. I assured him that wouldn't be necessary. It sounded like he was doing everything right. I wouldn't be able to add anything more.

"The only problem is," I said, "you're not catching any fish. Other than that—"

"I *know* I'm not catching any," he said, a wee bit exasperated. "Three winters. So what do I do *this* winter?"

"You still want to catch a steelhead?" I asked.

"Of course I do."

"Then keep fishing. That's the only way you will."

———•———•———

Fortunately, I long ago reached the age when stating the obvious could lead to fisticuffs. Now, I'm generally acknowledged as (1) old-school or (2) old fart.

It's hard to know which label fits best.

Clearly, the more time spent steelheading, the less certain one becomes about any and all notions beyond a few obvious truths. Among the serious steelheaders I know on rivers I frequent throughout the steelhead season, it's perfectly apparent that there are *no* silver bullets, *no* secret recipes, and *no* magic formulas for success. The default wisdom is that nobody knows shit. Of course, the fact that these same anglers catch a fair number of steelhead each year undermines this modest assessment of insight and knowledge—leaving novices and newcomers with the sneaking suspicion that somebody's holding out on them.

They're not. Instead, successful steelheaders embrace—sometimes with fatalistic glee—the simple truths available to all of us, while at the same time rejecting any and all superfluous notions about how to execute the business at hand. This attention to the obvious is why steelheading so often gets folded into impressions of a spiritual practice—or at least the ideas of such rigors held by angling laypeople, often those with a bent for tawdry weeds, spirits, and other forms of hedonism.

Don't worry. I won't go there. Mention of spiritual practice is simply a way of illustrating that steelheading, like life, demands nothing of us we don't already know. Which isn't to suggest there's a single thing *easy* about either of these pursuits. When's the last time you really tried to treat *everyone* as you would like to be treated?

And when have any of us been able to maintain our focus, cast after cast, on the only two truths we need when steelheading?

You don't catch fish without your fly in the water.
You catch steelhead where steelhead are.

———•———•———

So few truths, I'm trying to suggest here, are precisely what makes steelheading all but impossible to master. Instead, steelheading is a *practice*. You show up; you do the things you know you're supposed to do. You keep at it. Now and then you catch fish. Sometimes things go well, sometimes exceptionally well, and you catch plenty of fish.

But the best steelheaders I know fish within a very tight range of options. Essentially it's the same casts, the same flies, the same lines, the same lies—over and over and over again—regardless of whether they're catching fish or not. As I mentioned earlier, this is the reason many anglers *quit* steelheading; they come to view it as nothing more than a chore—or an act of humility, even submission, to all that they can't control.

Most of us waver as well when faced with doing what we know we should do when things seem to go contrary to our desires.

Our practice suffers.

Or we shitcan the whole deal.

Because the truth is, it's hard to stick to it—especially in the face of inconclusive or even nonexistent results. Remember, now, I'm talking about steelheading. The most difficult thing about it is that often—very often—you shouldn't do anything other than what you're doing, because you're already doing everything right.

Naturally, we can all grow frustrated when we fail to catch fish. But if the trials of steelheading were as tidy as catching or not catching fish, it would have never left behind the trail of troubled and confused and occasionally defeated anglers that color the course of its relatively brief and recent history. For steelheading has proven to be, again and again, a merciless taskmaster, enervating at times the strongest of anglers among us, while driving no small number of them to drink.

A couple of examples. My buddy Jeff Cottrell was in the throes of a midseason slump this year, the kind we all seem to suffer at one point or another. He was tempted to run a nymph down the throat of a favorite run. Instead, he tied on a big, dark articulated thing, on the theory that—well, the truth is, there's never a theory worth the time it takes to repeat it, because that's all you have, another theory in the face of the insufferable mysteries of steelheading. Anyway, preparing cast number 9,999 without a fish, Jeff put the fly upstream with a Snap-T, and then he circled around with his rod tip to form his D loop. While the fly was lying dead in the water, nothing more than a big black clump of fuzz, a pretty little hen came up and ate it—and just like that, Jeff was out of his slump.

Example two. It wasn't exactly a slump I was in, but I'd had three or four good pulls in a row on which I'd failed to connect. You begin to wonder if you're leading the fly too hard, or following it too much, or holding too long or too short of a loop, or dropping your loop too soon or too late. I came down through a treasured piece of water, one perfectly designed for a swinging fly, with boulders and slots and ribbons of current—and as the fly swung into the shallows, something grabbed, straightened the line, turned the reel once, and vanished.

Yuck.

I went through all the usual steps, backing up, fishing through again, changing to a smaller fly, a bigger fly, etc., etc. Forty-five minutes later I was all set to leave, hike up to the next run. I even had my daypack on. But once I climbed up onto the bank, I suddenly decided to turn around and try again. I started back in with the same fly I had used earlier, the one that was grabbed and dropped—and before I made a real cast, while I was swinging the fly about a dozen feet below me to clear the short sink-tip I had on, a big fish grabbed. Not *really* big, but well past the thirty-inch mark, the first of six fish, it turns out, I've landed there in the past three weeks, the last one this morning, on the same twelve-foot cast that worked the first time.

This time I did it on purpose.

My point, of course, is that this kind of thing can drive you absolutely bonkers. You do everything right, you get a grab, you miss the fish. You do everything wrong, the fish eats, game's on.

The more you steelhead, the more this kind of thing happens.

There's a lesson there—but I have little or no idea what it is.

●———————●

Still, I believe there *is* hope for steelheaders. We're not entirely at the mercy of the gods. In my own convoluted thinking about the sport, of which this essay is yet one more example, I've fashioned a corollary to offset some of the grimmer ramifications of the notion that the surest way to catch more steelhead is to spend more time fishing for them.

To wit: *You catch more steelhead when you fish for them in the manner you enjoy catching them.*

No doubt, this is not a profound piece of wisdom. What it suggests, however, is that you'll keep at it, and keep at it longer, if you enjoy the hunt as much as the kill—metaphorically speaking, of course. In my own career, like so many others today, "enjoying the hunt" has meant learning to cast a two-handed rod—and continuing to learn about the elegance of the tool as rods and lines evolve. I'm not a casting junkie—one look at my loop will tell you that—but I'm a firm believer that better casts make for better presentations, and better presentations catch more fish—despite the squirrelly illogical nonsense that invariably creeps into different moments of our steelheading days.

A good Spey caster, of course, can cast anything. But I don't know anyone who enjoys throwing a leader jacked up with weight or a bobber affixed to it. I do it—sometimes. But it's never fun.

Or pretty.

Occasionally, I even catch fish this way. But not as often as I might because, truth be known, I usually tire pretty quickly of such efforts, as nothing about them seems elegant in the way that fly fishing generally invites me to feel. *Catching* a steelhead is always fun. But in the meantime . . .

So it goes. If you enjoy *how* you're fishing, you will fish more and, in the long run, catch more fish.

I think that's pretty much the point of fly fishing in the first place, isn't it?

●———————●

My favorite way to fish for *and* catch steelhead is, as I've often mentioned, with a waking fly, patterns I've shared elsewhere as both the Remuddled and my Waking Muddler. The window for fishing surface steelhead flies, however, is painfully small—and this year I found myself spending more and more time with traditional Spey flies on the end of my leader, as I failed to raise fish with the unconventionally sparse muddlers I've relied on over the years.

Now, another truth shared by veteran steelheaders is that your fly doesn't matter—a notion that can only contribute to the nuttiness of the sport. Yet the more steelheading you do, the more you understand about the meaninglessness of fly patterns. Eventually, everybody knows this—but almost nobody believes it.

What a new pattern is mostly about is rekindling your stoke. Do you think for a minute I would have tinkered with the Waking Muddler had fish been rising to it as they had in the past? There are countless reasons my tried-and-true patterns might not have moved fish. Or no reasons at all. All I can do is report is that as soon as I created the Green Butt Muddler, I caught my first steelhead of the season on a surface fly. For the next month, it was the only waking fly that rose fish.

Of course, it's the only pattern I tried.

GREEN BUTT MUDDLER

- **Hook:** #8 Wilson dry fly
- **Thread:** Highland green Pearsall's Gossamer Silk or Morus Silk
- **Butt:** Light green silk floss
- **Rib:** Lagartun flat silver tinsel (small)
- **Body:** Peacock herl
- **Head/wing:** Sparse spun deer or elk hair, trimmed, with strands straying back toward bend of hook

Tying the Green Butt Muddler

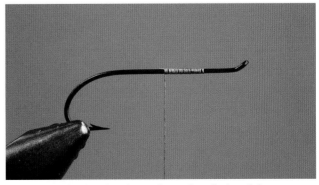

1. Secure the hook. The Wilson dry-fly hook by Partridge of Redditch remains the lightest wire hook I know. Fighting a steelhead, I remember that I can bend this same hook with a stout tying thread. Start your Pearsall's silk directly behind the eye wire and lay down a solid layer of thread wraps that ends at the midpoint of the shank. Pearsall's has become difficult to find, but I may die before I run out of my stash. I like this thread because it's strong enough to spin deer hair, plus it shows through the peacock herl when I spin my dubbing loop. Also, it's totally old-school.

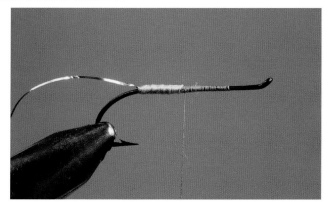

2. Secure the tip of the tinsel at the midpoint and cover the tinsel evenly back to where the thread is directly over the point of the hook. Good French tinsel can withstand time in a toothy steelhead's mouth. Same with silk floss—which is *much* tougher than nylon/rayon material such as UNI-Floss. Secure a length of silk floss and wind your thread back to the midpoint. Now cover the aft half of the hook shank with tight wraps of floss, tie off, and clip excess.

3. Create a dubbing loop. Advance the thread to the head. Insert three or four strands of peacock herl into the loop. Spin your loop, creating a peacock herl noodle with silk thread inside. Create the forward half of the body by winding the herl noodle forward to the return wire of the eye; that will leave you room to spin the head and collar. Tie off and clip excess.

4. Rib the fly with the tinsel, making an equal number of evenly spaced turns around both the butt and the body. Tie off short of the head and clip excess.

5. Spin and clip the deer hair head, leaving a dozen or two strands extending back to the bend of the hook. This step is the crux of the fly. I use the softest deer hair (or thinnest elk hair) I can find. Do not overdress. What many anglers seem not to understand is that a waking pattern this sparse creates the wake from *beneath* the surface. This fly has none of the bulk or flotation elements of a skating pattern. You don't see the fly when it's swinging. In fact, now that we're nearly all making 80-foot or 100-foot or longer casts with our two-handed rods, you probably won't be able to see this fly wake—unless, late in the day, in a slick tailout or run, you catch glimpses of that telltale V opening across the water. Often, seeing the wake will only get you into trouble: Focusing on the exact placement of the fly, you see something disturb the surface of the water, and instinctively you lift the rod tip to see what's going on. Unfortunately, this is the precise moment you should, instead, be *giving* the rod tip, the line, and the fly to the fish. If you don't, chances are you've already pulled the fly from the fish's mouth—or you've stuck the fly on the very front of the fish's mouth or the tip of its nose, which nearly insures an eventual unbuttoning if the steelhead behaves in the manner you hope to see. After you spin and trim the collar, create a tidy head with thread wraps, whip-finish, and saturate with lacquer or your favorite head cement.

THE MIRACLE FLY

Miracle Fly, variation of design by Jeff Cottrell

The rock sits in the middle of the current, a big rock, the size of a household appliance, a dishwasher or clothes dryer, or maybe a piece of furniture, a recliner or small bed. The current sweeps around both sides of the rock, frothy whitewater bouncing toward the end of a long riffle, with a small wave folding back from the implacable basalt face. But below the rock stretches a slender arc of smooth dark water, a graceful narrowing sliver or half crescent or comma outlined on both sides by the white and writhing current—the precise spot from which, many years ago, I took an exquisite steelhead, a wild hen well past the thirty-inch mark on my first Spey rod, the first of many fish taken over the years from the lowest pool—this one with the rock—at the mouth of the wooded canyon.

Remember the rock.

The cast is delivered from far upstream of the rock, a long cast that, like all casts made with a two-handed rod, has a name. But the name doesn't matter. The cast stretches far downstream and across the river, but because it was made from well above the rock, and because the cast is straight, when it lands the line lies almost parallel to the current, allowing the line and the leader—and the fly—to hang beyond and below the rock, between the current and the smooth water in the rock's wake. The cast is the same as the cast used

to catch that wild steelhead years ago—and though over the years I have fished near the rock on countless other occasions, and I have caught many steelhead from this, the last pool of the canyon, I have never, until now, made the exact same cast again.

Remember the cast.

The fly is big and dark, big like a crow is big when compared to a robin or a warbler, which in this comparison are the steelhead and trout flies you might normally tie to your tippet. The big dark fly hangs without swinging at the edge of the frothy current and smooth water below the rock—hangs without swinging but still moving, its long webby hackles and bold marabou wing fluttering or writhing or pulsing in the fluid and dynamic push and pull and press of the river. The fly is a Green Butt Spey, a fly very similar to the Spey Car that the wild hen ate in the same spot near the rock so many years ago—and when a fish grabs the fly and it threatens, soon afterward, to disappear with the fly out of the far end of the pool, I remember fearing the same thing could very possibly happen with that similar fly years ago.

But forget the fly.

No form of fly fishing seems richer in paradox than steelheading. Ask most serious steelheaders if flies really matter, and they'll tell you, emphatically, they don't. Yet ask these same ardent practitioners to give up their own favorite flies for someone else's patterns, and the very idea may well make them laugh.

Or worse.

One of the quietly held secrets shared by most serious steelheaders, anyway, is that fly fishing for steelhead is simple. Simple, of course, does not mean easy—as most of us know as we struggle to succeed in this maddeningly difficult sport.

Still, come November each year, after enjoying the relative ease of autumn steelheading and looking forward, with confidence, to the winter runs ahead, I'm often tempted to suggest I've learned a few things, the kind of heady wisdom we're all looking for to help us unravel the mysteries of this puzzling game. The inclination, however, grows increasingly suspect. For a career in steelheading can often come to seem but little more than a collection of remembrances carried forward from the past, an accumulation of empirical data, none of which means anything at any particular moment, yet in aggregate is the stuff of experience that brings, now and then, another fish.

In other words, unlike so much other fishing, where success offers insights which we transfer to later fishing and, hopefully, more success, I feel, at times, that everything I know about steelheading adds up to virtually nothing that really matters.

It's easy to become a fatalist. Usually, this feeling is accompanied by what can only be labeled a *slump*. Every year, in fact, there's a spell during steelhead season when I feel quite certain I will never catch another steelhead again. This feeling is softened, of course, by the rational understanding that if I keep fishing, I will eventually catch another fish, an understanding borne out by a decade of remissions while in the terminal grip of this maddening game.

Some anglers appear never to suffer such ills—the very same anglers, it often seems, who report catching steelhead in numbers I find absolutely staggering. No doubt such exploits deserve applause. Somehow the mere possibility of racking up mind-numbing totals should give us all hope in the midst of our own private despair.

All slumps *do* end. One day, once again, there's a steelhead on the end of your line. So perhaps the more interesting question is this: When do slumps *begin*?

In steelheading more than any other kind of fly fishing, you can be sure you're very close to a slump—if you haven't entered one already—when you begin to experiment with flies.

The logic can work the other way, of course: You've been catching so many fish, why not play around, see *what else* they'll eat? But for most of us, a situation like this remains a theoretical problem, like having too much money or all the time in the world to fish. Okay, it's possible. But how many of us are genuinely puzzled by what to do with an overflow of fortune, fame—or too many steelhead grabbing our flies?

Instead, we just want one—the *next* one. Given that goal, nearly all steelheaders look to a fly that has worked for them before—unless they're mired in a slump, having lost faith in what's worked for them in the past.

We turn, then, in desperation, to something new: the Miracle Fly. Older hands recognize this as pure folly— yet every one of them has done it before.

And every one of them will do it, no doubt, again.

When you tie on the Miracle Fly, you admit confusion, loss of direction, a dark sense of defeat. Over the years, I've copied and created—and knotted to my tippet—dozens of these flies. I've got two or three new miracle flies lined up in my fly box each year. Yet here's the telling detail: So far this fall I've caught all my fish on three patterns, and the newest one, my Green Butt Spey, is now four years old—tied in four different sizes.

Is that any way to increase market share?

Still, there must be something more than the dour uncertainties of the sport that I can offer in the midst of this year's steelheading.

To wit:

Remember the rock.

Remember the cast.

Do not take lightly the old adage that you catch steelhead where you find them. More than anything else, I believe, we don't catch steelhead because we don't know where they are. We end up fishing, in other words, where there aren't any fish.

On a grand scale, of course, there need to be fish in the river for you to find them at all. Given the *presence* of steelhead, however, we still spend far too much of our time fishing the wrong water. We shoot into the forest, hoping to hit something, rather than recognizing the most likely targets, taking aim, and trying to nail them.

Or remembering, precisely, where we've found steelhead in the past. The very big difference between the novice steelheader and the experienced hand is that those who catch steelhead with any regularity acquire a larger and larger map of spots where steelhead have grabbed the fly in the past. This map does much more than delineate specific holes or pools or runs. Instead, it pinpoints specific *lies*: that is, the exact spot in the run where fish hold—the ledge along the bank, the depression in front of a logjam, the slot in the tailout, *the big rock in the throat of the current.*

On the small rivers I often fish, most runs have, at most, two specific pieces of holding water—one low in the run, one up high. There's no guarantee, of course, that either of these lies will hold a fish. But when fish are in the run, more likely than not you'll find them, again and again, in these same specific lies.

Even on large rivers, if you fish with a guide, you will notice, if you pay attention, that very often your guide is near you when you hook a fish. How is that so? He wandered off to smoke a cigarette, prepare lunch, fiddle with the boat—and then right when you touch a fish, there he is, standing at your side.

The answer, of course, is that your guide knows where fish generally hold. It's worth it, no doubt, to continue investigating an entire run, for steelhead can be highly individualistic fish, some of which behave in unpredictable fashion. But guides see the same runs repeatedly—and if clients catch fish, it soon becomes clear where fish hold, or at least which lies fish well when addressed with the fly.

Then there's the matter of the cast. In this era of refined nymphing techniques—when the manipulation of slack line and an indicator dead-drifted above an egg pattern, bead, or God knows what has proven incomparably effective over the wide range of possible steelhead lies and the conditions in which fishing for steelhead occur—it's little wonder that the cast fails to get the same attention it did in the past.

Even two-handed rods, surprisingly enough, have contributed to the lack of close attention many anglers pay to the delivery and presentation of the fly. Because two-handed rods can throw such a long cast, sending the fly to the far reaches of sight, anglers often fail to consider how their line and leader land, whether the fly turns over directly in line with the leader, whether or not the fly begins fishing effectively the moment it hits the water and the line begins to swing. Instead, they just try to chuck that sucker as far as they can. Of course, they know enough to mend the line as it starts to swing—but if the line and leader didn't land straight in the first place, the fly inevitably goes through all sorts of weird gyrations at the start, and by the time it settles down and begins to swing smoothly and effectively, you've already missed a large percentage of the water you meant to cover with the cast.

Here's the deal: Anglers who catch more steelhead than other anglers do so by keeping their flies in the water more than other anglers, by keeping their flies in the *right* water, and by having their flies spend more time doing what they're supposed to be doing cast after cast after cast.

Successful steelheading, in other words, is not about the fly. Instead, it's about being a better fly fisher.

Reach for the Miracle Fly and you place your hopes in a charm or totem or fetish that has little or nothing to do with whether or not you catch a steelhead. No doubt, you have to believe in your fly—to the point that you forget that the fly is even there on the end of your leader. What you *should* be thinking about, instead of your fly, is fishing—where the fish are, what your cast is doing, how well you're presenting the fly.

Remember the rock.

Remember the cast.
Forget the fly.

When it all works—as it always eventually will—remember the fish, too. Especially the wild ones. If you need to believe in miracles, put your faith where it belongs.

THE MIRACLE FLY

- **Hook:** #2 TMC 7999 or similar
- **Thread:** Black 8/0 UNI-Thread or similar
- **Tag:** Lagartun flat silver tinsel (medium)
- **Tail:** Pink/pearl Sili Legs
- **Abdomen:** Dark green Krystal Flash
- **Rib:** Lagartun oval silver tinsel (small)
- **Wing:** Pink/pearl Sili Legs
- **First hackle collar:** Purple schlappen (small)
- **Thorax:** Purple Ice Dub
- **Second hackle collar:** Black schlappen (small)
- **Throat:** Purple Ice Dub, tied in and left to trail

(Note: Proceed at your own risk. Just because this pattern allegedly caught seven steelhead in one day this fall, do you really believe it's somehow special?)

Tying the Miracle Fly

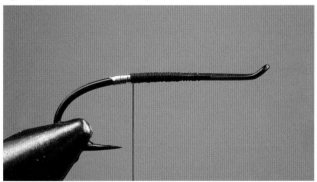

1. Secure the hook and start the thread. Establish the midpoint of the fly by tying in the tip of the tinsel for the tag halfway back from the hook eye, then cover the tinsel tip all of the way back to a point above the barb of the hook. Make a tag with two or three turns of the flat tinsel. Tie off and clip excess.

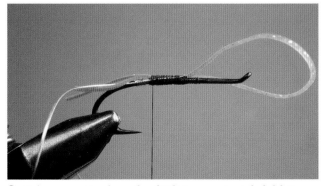

2. Take an entire length of Sili Leg material, fold it in half, and tie it in directly in front of the tag with the two tips extending beyond the bend of the hook.

Wrap the thread forward over the two legs of the Sili Leg loop until you reach the midpoint of the fly. Start your thread back toward the tail, covering the end of a piece of oval tinsel that will become the rib of the abdomen.

3. Advance the thread to the midpoint, ahead of the abdomen. Rib the abdomen with three evenly spaced wraps of tinsel. Secure the tinsel ahead of the abdomen and clip excess.

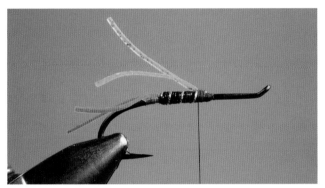

4. Fold back the loop of Sili Leg material and lash it down with thread wraps. Clip the loop so that the legs of the loop, now separate, extend just short of the tips of the tail. Don't worry if you can't get the wing to lie down flat; you can fuss with it in the next step.

5. Forward the wing, then tie in a small schlappen feather by its tip. If you find you have trouble tying in a folded feather so that the fibers flare back rather than stick out, bottle brush fashion, strip the fibers from the top side of the feather. When you wind the feather forward, the fibers on the opposite side of the stem will lie pointed neatly in the direction you want them.

6. Spin a small amount of purple Ice Dubbing onto your thread and create a pronounced but not overly heavy thorax. You can use the first turn or two of your dubbing noodle to help position any errant hackle fibers from the previous step. End the thorax leaving plenty of room for the forward hackle and throat.

7. Ahead of the thorax tie in the forward hackle. Choose a schlappen feather with fibers longer than those used for the first hackle collar. Prepare the feather as you did the last one, tie it in by the tip and, winding it forward, make three or four wraps before securing it with thread wraps and clipping the excess.

8. The throat of the fly is just a bit of dubbing material lashed in place and teased out to leave a sparse accent, proving once again that tyers will try anything in hopes of a miracle. To finish the fly, create a tidy head, whip finish, and saturate the thread wraps with lacquer or your preferred head cement.

BLACK AND BLUE

Black and Blue, adapted from design by Marty Sheppard

This past fall I spent a weekend at a literary event in eastern Oregon, a gathering of writers and poets that wouldn't have anything to do with fishing had it not been held at the casino on the Umatilla Indian reservation.

Weird: Is *everything* analogous to fishing anymore? Let me explain.

Between readings and panel discussions, I wandered out onto the casino floor. Lights flashed. Colors blinked. Bells and whistles fought like mating birds. The clientele, many of them smoking, sat all but still, quietly staring at video slot machines. Play consisted of a touch of the screen, a moment of waiting, winning and losing against odds over which the hopeful had absolutely no control.

A friend of mine followed me onto the floor. She selected a machine, sat down to try her luck.

"It's a lot like steelheading," I warned.

This friend, whose eyes I've come to know quite well, looked at me with patience I've tested before.

"*Just* like it," I said.

—————— •—————•——————

Two decades ago, when I was still relatively new to the game, nothing seemed more important to me than the sight of a fly of mine pinned to the hinge of

a steelhead's firm-lipped mouth. I'd travel far and frequently for that moment, fish long and hard for each brief encounter with these fabulous creatures that offered intimacy with forces both mysterious and wild. And sublime. When I wasn't actually chasing steelhead, I did everything I could to learn about them, the rivers they returned to, the fish's habits, its haunts, the anglers who fished for them, the tools and techniques of the game.

Now, every year, it gets harder and harder for me to take steelhead fishing seriously.

In my best seasons, I caught dozens and dozens of steelhead—enough, anyway, that when I look back on those years and I compare the number of steelhead I caught then with how many I catch now, I wonder if I was just lucky—in the right places at the right times—and maybe not a particularly skilled steelheader at all.

Because at some point steelheading began to feel like a spiritual paradox: The more I knew, the less this knowledge seemed to matter.

Today, when I go steelheading, I feel I'm at the mercy of the gods, a victim of chance or fate. I feel like those gamblers on the casino floor, compulsive pilgrims with no control over the outcome of their efforts, regardless of longing or hope. How can you take fishing like this seriously? Cast your line, swing the fly—and occasionally something grabs it.

This is no way to improve your game.

The temptation, you see, is to embrace these feelings, to languish in a state of mind in which we argue to ourselves—often quite sensibly—that the only thing between us and our next steelhead is the time we spend on the river and an untold number of casts. The default claim is that pretty much everything else is out of your control. You don't know if there's a fish in the run. You can't tell, in most cases, if there's a response to your fly. You certainly can't keep those other ninety-nine guys off the river—nor prevent a host of new guides from instructing clients in the subtleties of dead-drifting egg patterns beneath bobbers cast all of ten feet to one side of a boat's bow. And God only knows who've got their nets in downriver—and what the hell's happening, anyway, to the temperature of the Pacific these days?

All of this assumes that you already know how to catch steelhead—where to find them, how to present the fly. Now it's just a matter of time on the river, covering water, covering lies. Cast, swing; cast, swing. Keep moving. Given a degree of proficiency, sooner or later you'll feel another steelhead on the end of your line.

Still, is that *all* there is to it? Shouldn't it matter as well how *good* you are—not just who can put in the most time?

Here's the reasoning, of course, behind Tom McGuane's famous quip that what's required of a successful steelheader is a strong right arm and a room temperature IQ. McGuane also noted, I should add, the utility of a large stipend—an asset shown to work for many successful fly fishers I've met over the years.

———•——————•———

The question, then, that serious steelheaders must finally ask themselves is what, if anything, they can do to improve their odds. How can they continue to work on their game rather than submit to the vagaries of chance? What is it, finally, steelheaders have control over—and what remains outside our influence, belonging instead to the hapless realm of card playing, dice rolling, or supplications for mercy against the tyranny of the angling gods?

The Gear

Let's start with something simple: Have you got a good stick?

I think it's terrific that there are longtime steelheaders who still use single-handed rods—anglers who claim these same rods caught plenty of fish in the past, so why do they need to change now? If that's you, great. If not, get over the idea—right now—that there's any viable substitute for two-handed rods and the elegant manner in which they cover most steelhead lies.

I won't bore you with a long list of attributes you've already heard about that make Spey rods superior tools for steelhead fishing. Instead, let me remind you that any double-hander is only as good as the balance attained by matching its size and action and your own casting style with the appropriate line system. I know it can all seem bewildering—especially as new lines and new nomenclature flood the sport almost yearly. But you simply have to take the time to sort out a system that you understand and that works for you and the kind of steelheading you do. A poorly balanced system will do more to frustrate an angler than any number of fishless days. You are, after all, going to spend most of your time casting—and not much else.

The good news today about Spey rods, especially for winter fishing, is how well they work with the right compact Skagit line. In much the same way that thirty-foot shooting heads suddenly made it possible for surf fishers and other distance seekers with single-handed rods to launch casts toward the horizon, a short heavy Skagit head makes effective Spey casting relatively easy, regardless of what school or style of casting you favor. The right Skagit head loads the rod effortlessly; it's easy to manage throughout the various gestures of the cast; and once headed in the right direction with a reasonably shaped loop, it will pull ungodly amounts of running line toward the river's far bank.

There's more. Take 500, 600, or even 700 grains and squeeze them into less than thirty feet of line, and you create such a concentrated *mass* that, once accelerated, it has the *force* to pull either long dense sink-tips or big heavy flies—or both—off the water and out across the river. In winter I carry a wallet full of tips chopped out of spools of both T-14 and T-17 sinking line—and even with twenty feet of such ugly stuff hooked to the front end of my Skagit head, I rarely have trouble making things perform the way they're supposed to perform.

A good two-handed rod balanced with the right line is a joy to cast—even if you're throwing heavy artillery. The pleasures of casting help keep your fly in the water—the only place it can hook a fish. Working on your stroke—striving to improve each one of the medley of casts the accomplished steelheader regularly employs—offers reason to *keep* casting, even when the fishing itself suggests reeling in and exploring other options, none more obvious than the local tavern or bar.

The Ride

Age does a lot of weird things to many of us and our minds—but nothing seems stranger in my own angling career than a recent conversion to the charms of boats. For most of my fishing life I considered boats, at best, a necessary evil; in most cases they seemed actual obstacles to angling success, requiring time and attention that was better spent on bank or beach making casts. I won't dwell on my continued distaste for certain boating practices, especially those that ask so much of the person on the oars while so little of the person holding the rod. And I should come clean and confess that

I still have nothing but disdain for anyone anywhere who resorts to fishing for steelhead with egg patterns beneath bobbers, a no-doubt effective way of angling but one that has absolutely nothing to do with the spirit of the sport of fly fishing.

Still, nothing makes more sense on a steelhead river than a boat or raft or other watercraft to carry fly fishers run to run. Learning to handle a boat, to navigate a river's currents, can open up an array of possibilities that give one a sense of ever-improving odds. Whether these efforts claim more hookups or more fish remains a question—but few things give one a greater sense of *doing everything possible* than backing a boat into a river, climbing in, and pulling on a pair of oars.

The Flies

Perhaps the hardest thing for experienced steelheaders to believe in is any sort of "new and improved" fly. Over the years they see patterns come and go, many of which they give a try, usually when nothing else has worked, which means the new pattern, finally tied to the tippet, has little chance of success. By the time most steelheaders start tallying their second dozen fish, they've already settled on a couple of patterns that they will return to for the rest of their careers. Changes to this trusted core do occur; certainly fresh auditions are always waiting in the wings. But the longer they're at it, the more serious steelheaders grow convinced that their fly is the last thing that matters, that a new fly is *not* going to alter the odds.

Still, few of us are immune to the intoxicating promise of a new pattern taking shape in the vise—either one that we've heard or read about other steelheaders having success with or a fresh idea we've stumbled upon ourselves. Of course, our steelhead boxes are crowded with these new patterns and fresh ideas; I need hardly mention that these are the flies we rarely use for long or need to replace. I'm often embarrassed by the number of flies and even fly boxes I carry to a steelhead river. I dream of a late-life epiphany or future incarnation where I slip but a handful of flies into the breast pouch of my waders and head to the river knowing I'm carrying plenty to fool the fish I'll find—with more than enough as well to share.

Meanwhile, new patterns continue to insinuate themselves into my inner circle of go-to flies. I'm not sure how this happens; efficacy *and* simplicity seem significant features in my well-used patterns. I'm also unclear how or why a fly falls *out* of favor—especially a pattern with plenty of fish to its credit—becoming part of the background scenery in the composition of a particular box. What I do know is that the lineup eventually changes, a slow evolution that may well have less to do with the challenges of steelheading than it does with the wandering journey toward nothingness that I grow increasingly aware of, gambling my life away one cast at a time.

BLACK AND BLUE

- **Hook:** #1/0-2/0 TMC 7999 or similar heavy steelhead iron
- **Thread:** Black 8/0 UNI-Thread or similar
- **Tail:** Black bucktail tied long, topped with a few strands of black Angel Hair or similar sparkle material
- **Body:** Black Polar Chenille
- **Wing:** Black marabou plume feathers
- **Collar:** Guinea fowl, dyed Silver Doctor Blue

Tying the Black and Blue

1. Secure the hook and start the thread. Clip a tuft of hair from a dyed black bucktail and clean any underfur from the hair. Place the hair in a stacker and give it a few sharp raps; remove the hair from the stacker and pull out any short hair. Measure the hair so the tail will end up at least twice the length of the hook. Pinch the tuft of hair and clip the butts before tying the tail in place, leaving plenty of hair to lash to the hook shank. Tie in the hair by first covering the clipped butts, then work your thread back toward the bend of the hook, pulling on the tail so that the hair remains on top of the shank.

2. Secure a few strands of Angel Hair or similar spicy flash material on top of the tail, allowing it to extend just beyond the tips of the tail. I don't like a lot of flash aft of the sparkly body; small amounts of Angel Hair seem sufficient.

3. Create the body of the fly with wraps of black Polar Chenille. Tie in the tip of the chenille at the root of the tail and then advance your thread to the point of the return wire of the hook eye. Now wind the chenille forward, stroking the crinkly fibers back along the hook shank as you wind. Secure the chenille at the point of the return wire. Clip excess.

4. For the wing, select an entire marabou feather and strip the fibers from the lower half of the stem, leaving the straighter, more aligned plume fibers at the top. Tie in this entire portion of the feather so that the wing extends to a point somewhere between the root of the tail and the bend of the hook. Clip the butt of the stem and any excess marabou fibers.

5. For the collar, select a single guinea fowl feather. Strip the webby fibers from the base of the stem. Stroke the fibers down along the stem, leaving a few pointed toward the tip. Tie in the feather by the tip. Now fold the side fibers away from the hook eye and wrap the feather forward; two or three turns will be all you get, which give you a more than adequate collar. Secure the butt of the feather, tidy up the head with thread wraps, and whip-finish.

6. Saturate the head with lacquer or cover with head cement.

PARK'S SPECIAL

Park's Special, designed by Parker Stenersen

Steelhead season arrives slowly at the Roost. Nobody really needs any more steelhead flies—our boxes show that most of us tie a half-dozen flies for every one we lose—and usually everybody's been out a few times, occasionally with fish to report, before anyone gets serious about a pattern he needs to tie.

But there might be more to it than that.

Favorite steelhead flies are based on—what? It's widely observed that the fly an angler uses to catch his first steelhead will return to his tippet, again and again, throughout his steelheading career. Just as troubling is the "brilliant steelheader" mentioned in a McGuane essay—an angler who only fishes "with flies he finds or is given."

Try as we might, nobody gets far with claims for a must-have or can't-miss steelhead fly. Experience has proven that there is no such thing. At best, we settle for the belief that a fly that has worked in the past will eventually work again. Far less magnanimous is one of steelheading's sourest truisms: You catch fish on the flies you fish with.

●━━━━━━━●

Bruce Milhiser, the trout fisherman, seems only to dabble in steelheading. In season, he adopts an off-the-cuff manner that shares none of the drama and high-minded cant favored by so many of us who set off in pursuit of anadromous fish. Bruce, I should add, catches more steelhead in less time on the water than any other angler I know.

I'm pretty sure Bruce's success has little to do with his favorite fly, a small nymph he ties in a variety of colors from a lifetime stash of seal dubbing he bought off a guy who recycled the lining from a bunch of surplus overcoats discarded by the Russian army. Bruce, a quiet left-hander with the fishing instincts of an osprey, catches steelhead because he's learned their lies and the casts that present his flies just so, an aggregate of experience and skills that have more to do with his catch rate than any favorite fly.

And "favorite" may even be misleading; most *effective* fly is probably a better way to describe this simple size 6 nymph that I see Bruce use most often in red, although he claims he does just as well with versions in purple, brown, and a rusty orange. Still, as a cane rod collector and enthusiast, Bruce tends more and more to fish traditional steelhead flies on the swing, if only because the method seems so well suited to the rods he loves to cast.

"I use the nymph as a last resort," says Bruce. "And—well, you can guess what usually happens then."

Without the talents or streamcraft of a Bruce Mil-hiser, many of us still fall prey to the belief that we just need the Right Fly. How else deal with the heavy toll on our spirits? The sport measures our faith. Not a small number of steelheaders become cynics or fatal-ists, resigned to the hopeless dread, between strikes, of yet another ten thousand empty casts. Just as many, I suspect, simply quit, convinced by loved ones—or the shadow of mortality—that there are better ways to spend one's time.

Still, a great many steelheaders embrace the sport because of the very aspects that make it so difficult. Like romantics who seem to crave the trials of love, serious steelheaders reveal a willingness to experience the profound doubts and uncertainty of most moments spent on the water. Who really knows where the fish are—or if they are—or what makes them grab the fly? At the same time, survivors in the sport—those who return to it each year no matter how many steelhead they've caught, no matter how many times they've been reduced to despair—approach the tying vise with their own hard-bitten strategies, most of which say more about the angler than they do about the next fish he or she hopes to find.

My old pal Fred Trujillo returns again and again to the Roost to tie an oversized but by no means exotic Egg-Sucking Leech. A professional, Fred ties all of the usual steelhead standards to sell to guides and online customers and audiences attending a circuit of fly-fishing shows he takes part in each year. But Fred never, ever fishes those patterns. His ESL is noteworthy for little more than a pair of dumbbell eyes so large they give the head of the fly the appearance of the front end of your grandfather's Studebaker. He uses mara-bou blood plumes for the tail and red copper wire to rib the fly and keep the palmered black hackle in place, and those big eyes give him room to create a head to rival anybody's single egg pattern, a series of figure-eights employing enough chenille to repair both cuffs of a raglan sweater.

Fred catches a lot of steelhead, too. An ex-wrestler, he doesn't feel there's the least bit of mystery to getting the job done. "Get it down there and hit 'em right in the nose," he says. "That's the way to make steelhead pay attention to your fly."

Which leaves me—the only other tyer at the Roost this week with the kind of long-term steelheading career that warrants genuine street cred. The young-sters, I'm sorry, just don't count. At their age, anything seems possible. But without a certain number of steel-head seasons under your belt, both good years and bad, it's impossible to know for sure if you're indulging a fantasy—or if you're in the sport for the long haul.

Sadly, I'm convinced I've learned little more about steelheading than that I need to keep my fly in the water. I never do that, not for long, when I fish with nymphs, egg patterns, and sucking leeches. Not that I don't fish such patterns now and then. But when-ever I do, I think I should immediately catch a fish—and when that doesn't happen, which is usually the case, I generally say the hell with it and retreat to higher ground.

Like the fish I hope to catch, the steelhead flies I'll keep in the water hour after hour, day after day, are flies I find beautiful, however loose my criteria for beauty may be. No doubt a fly's success in the past contrib-utes to its appeal. And enough seasons spent chasing steelhead, occasionally even catching a few, gives us all some idea what works and what doesn't. Some—because we're still on squishy turf. A fly I consider beautiful looks like it *ought* to catch fish.

Because I don't tie to sell, nor for clients or an audi-ence other than fish, I tie fairly simple patterns, focus-ing on fundamentals and the best hooks and materials I can find. Different patterns tend to share a common look. Most of my flies are derivatives of proven patterns, tweaked just so to match the kind of water I like to fish, the equipment I like to use, the casts I like to make—and a private aesthetic that boils down to flies I hold up and think, *That's a good-looking fly.*

Which brings us, finally, to the Park's Special. A fan-cier pattern than I'm used to tying, it's still relatively simple once you assemble the long list of quasi-exotic materials. Peacock breast feathers. Silver pheasant. *Golden* pheasant tippets dyed red. Is any one of these essential? You know my answer. Still, the fly melds so many elements from different classic steelhead patterns that it seems worthwhile to follow the recipe—if only to find out if Parker Stenersen, the creator of the fly, has hit on a magic combination.

Chances are, I've said, no magic combination exists. That's sort of the whole point. Still, we are all quite sure that some steelhead flies work better than others—and if you carry that notion far enough, there remains the possibility that a true killer fly lurks somewhere just beyond the horizon.

And the Park's Special *does* work.

At least for me.

This morning, for example, on a favorite run tucked up a twisted canyon where I have more than my share of steelhead memories, encounters with native fish that seem lit with the spark of some impractical genius that makes them willing to jump a fly. Not all steelhead are created equal. First light today, however, revealed the river dark, discolored, soiled by recent rains; I might have fallen into a funk were it not for a Park's Special, the perfect contrasting hue. Knotted in place, it worked so well that I had no trouble keeping the fly right where it belongs, swinging through the heart of the run, rekin-dling my faith as I raised the rod tip and pivoted and cast again.

PARK'S SPECIAL

- **Hook:** #4 purple MFC (Montana Fly Company) 7099
- **Thread:** Black 8/0 UNI-Thread or similar
- **Tag:** Mirage Tinsel (large)
- **Butt:** Fluorescent yellow Lagartun Mini Braid
- **Tail:** Golden pheasant tippets, dyed red
- **Rib:** Oval silver tinsel (small)
- **Body:** UV purple Ice Dub
- **Hackle:** Silver pheasant body feathers, dyed purple
- **Wing:** Blue peacock breast feather (body plumage)

Tying the Park's Special

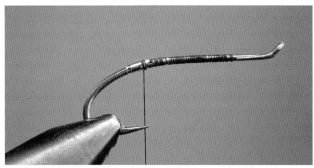

1. Secure the hook and start your thread. Create a tag the width of one or two wraps of the large Mirage Tinsel.

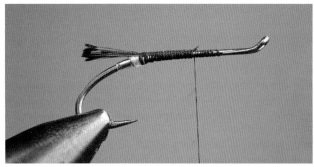

2. Secure a short length of Mini Braid. Create a butt no wider than a couple of wraps. Clip a dozen or so red golden pheasant tippets and tie in a tail.

3. Secure a length of oval silver tinsel for the rib. With the purple Ice Dub form a dubbing loop or dubbing noodle and create a body that ends just about where

the hook is doubled to form the eye of the hook. For the ribbing, wind the oval tinsel forward with four to six evenly spaced wraps.

4. Prepare the hackle feather. With the convex, shiny side of the feather facing you and the tip pointing up, strip the fibers from the left side of the stem; leave enough of the fibers at the tip so that you can tie this portion of the stem to the hook shank. Secure the feather perpendicular to the hook so that the remaining fibers point toward the butt of the fly. Holding the feather by the butt of the stem, wind it forward, twisting it slightly so that the feather fibers form a graceful curve around the body of the fly. When there are no fibers left, tie off the butt of the stem and clip the excess.

5. For the wing, clip a bunch of fibers from a peacock breast feather. Tie the feathers in a tight bunch over the top portion of the collar. Clip the butts, whip-finish, and saturate the wraps with lacquer or your preferred head cement.

PINK WOOD

Pink Wood, designed by Jeff Cottrell

There's a spell during every steelhead season when I readily consider any means imaginable a viable option for hooking a fish. These are the schemes of a covetous angler. Up and down rivers spilling toward the sea, each one rising and falling to the rhythm of winter storm and blue-sky chill, anglers of all stripes fashion their private temptations, stopping short of nothing when it comes to the chance of hooking a steelhead on a fly rod and some-thing—anything—that resembles a fly. If you go long enough without a fish, nothing seems too far-fetched. Now and then, you might even discover—old dog or not—something genuinely new . . .

It was early yet to get a fish on the local steelhead river, so when I did, I phoned Jeff, who doesn't come this way often because he has plenty of good water out his way.

We met at the turnout and hiked into the canyon and up to the run where, the morning before, the pretty hatchery hen had grabbed a Green Butt Spey and per-formed admirably beneath the mist and the shadowy pines. Today, we were later than I like to start—but since Jeff feels the same about dawn patrols as he does about giving up cigarettes, I at least got the honors while he smoked and rigged up. Also, despite my recent success, Jeff had no intention of swinging flies. Instead, he had brought his one-hander—along with the usual assortment of nymphs and egg patterns and other nefarious gewgaws that the short rod now implies.

But age has made me a tolerant man, and I don't mind if my fellow angler resorts to chopsticks or chew-ing gum—as long, that is, as no rules are broken—*and* I get first licks at a hundred yards of boulder-strewn holding water where, in recent memory, I went dancing with a handsome silvery maiden who stood on her tail and shook for me.

Still, we must all know by now that steelhead—like children, bird dogs, and lovers—will always find ways to break our hearts. Which was why, on this gray but mild early-run day, forming my D loop beneath the reach of the leafless riparian hardwoods, I remained fairly detached from the outcome of my efforts, trying my best to throw a tight loop and straight line, enjoying recollections of the previous day's grab without worry-ing yet when the next one might come.

Then Jeff hooked a fish. A big man, high in the slot-ted throat of the run, he held his rod up like a trout fisherman, his glowing strike indicator surging back and forth above the surface of the river as if attached to a length of bungee cord. His guide, more or less, this morning, I felt pleased I had done my job, glad to have put a friend on a fish in a river he rarely visits. I hur-ried along the bank, skipping over exposed roots, and reached Jeff in time to admire his fish, another hatch-ery hen, not as pretty as mine from the day before, although for some reason—I can't explain it—that's nearly always the case.

Then Jeff hooked and landed two more steelhead.

He hooked and lost one, too.

All of these fish came out of the same deep slot beyond an underwater ledge that Jeff, high-sticking, could run a nymph along by guiding his indicator precisely down a slender ribbon of current. This is exactly the sort of pocketwater that makes traditional fly-swinging techniques as ineffective as casting chrome Kastmasters to trout sipping emerging mayflies. Still, anybody who knows anything about steelhead will tell you that more than one fish taken from a particular lie is exceptional, and four fish—or three landed and one lost—is not only out of the ordinary, but practically absurd.

Or obscene.

I figured he must be cheating.

Or not actually *cheating*, but—well, what *do* we feel when the guy nearby absolutely clobbers fish where we feel we're lucky to pick up one, maybe two if all the stars align? That he's in the right spot and you're not? That he's a better angler, a Real Guy? Or that he or she's in possession of some secret technique, the new and improved line, a covert item of revolutionary equipment? Or—worst of all possible fears—that this somebody else has *the Right Fly*?

And you don't.

Of course, I shouldn't have to point out to anyone by now that I rarely believe the Right Fly offers the real solution to the problems of catching fish. And when it comes to steelhead, anglers who claim the superior performance and enhanced satisfaction of their World's Grooviest Juju Bug are simply tooting their own horns—or blowing smoke up yours.

Believe me: I've tried them all.

Still, I finally decided it was time to at least—well—take a *look* at Jeff's fly. I mean, for the record. For the data. For *the science*.

Or maybe—you never know—for a story.

———•————•———

Jeff Cottrell's Wood Series began as part of a Christmas present he received years back from a sister in Whittier. The gift—some unremembered trifling that middle-aged sisters love to send their wayfaring brothers—was wrapped in holiday paper, bound by a strange, sparkly, elastic material that caught Jeff's attention. A tyer as well as a painter, carpenter, and free-thinking *artesano*, Jeff has a nose for new and unusual materials, and this rubbery, tendon-like twineage spoke to that part of Jeff's mind that may well reflect more closely what goes on in the brains of fish than most fly anglers care to admit.

Jeff clipped a length of this rubbery stuff and threw away the rest—an act of neglect he soon came to regret. For experiments proved his initial reaction correct: Integrated into a few new patterns, the material, whatever it was, caught fish—or at least seemed to increase a fly's efficacy.

"Of course, I wasn't surprised," explains Jeff, while we talk along the river, smoke climbing through the bare limbs of alders bankside beneath the pines. "I'm an old Rocky Mountain trout fisherman. You fish there so much with flies with rubber on them, you learn to recognize the Bra Snap—when a trout grabs the fly, holds on for a second, and then lets go."

Still, it was what Jeff found he could *do* with this new material, the *look* he could create, that really inspired him—especially when he started using it to fashion a pattern specific to steelheading. Unfortunately, he soon ran into a problem: All of the material from that first cutting was finally gone.

He and his wife, Jan Sage, also an artist, looked everywhere for something to replenish Jeff's original stash. They tried gift shops, fabric stores, arts and crafts suppliers. They tried stationers. They tried scrapbookers. They tried Home Depot. They tried Walmart.

"We even went to L.A.," says Jeff, knitting his blond brows as he recalls a visit to his sister and a futile, freeway-to-freeway search.

In time, Jeff grew weary of hunting for something that seemed not to exist—at least not anywhere this side of the Pacific. There are always other ways to catch steelhead. He honed his Spey fly-tying skills, practiced casting Skagit heads, and resisted, as much as he could, the temptation to start nymphing whenever he felt his steelhead mojo grow cold.

Then one day Jan returned home with a new toy.

It was actually something she bought with the dog in mind. Or Humpy—a little white Lhasa Apso that got dropped on its head at a young age and had suffered fits of dementia ever since—decided right off that the toy was his, appropriating it for his own private use.

"It was some kind of kiddie toy," says Jeff. "From the Dollar Store. It came with a light in it."

Humpy, who was named for his tactless behavior, not after the fly, grew so found of the toy that he hated to share it. More than anything, he seemed infatuated with the simple fact that every time he squeezed the toy, the light inside came on, illuminating the pink tendrils dangling from its surface membrane.

"Humpy really liked that," says Jeff, giving in to that easy smile that dog owners all seem to share. "He'd carry it around and his whole mouth would light up."

What *Jeff* liked about the toy, however, and the reason, it turns out, that Jan had bought it, was all of those pink, wiggly appendages that seemed to move with a life of their own. Humpy was no fool. He knew the right stuff when he saw it.

For finally, it seems, Jeff again had a material that replicated the one he had been playing around with since he received that forgotten gift from his sister years ago. Not only did he have *some*, he had as much as he wanted—as long as he kept Humpy from devouring the whole toy.

———•————•———

After Jeff's four hookups and tale of the origins of the Pink Wood, I led him downstream to another bit of holding water, a short, deep run that gets hammered by gear guys yet produces fish, now and then, practically any month of the season. Three separate chutes cascade into a single pool, and after years of experimenting with casting angles, depths, and weights of flies, I've managed to find fish on the swing in a hole that begs for dead-drifted nymphs and egg patterns. Still playing host, however, I allowed Jeff first whack—and while I stood alongside him, pointing out the complicated currents and subtle lies from which I'd moved fish in the past, Jeff flipped his leader and a rod's length of line into the pool, and I watched a steelhead rise up out of the depths and swim over and eat his fly, the diminutive yet unmistakable Pink Wood.

Later, up on the highway, Jeff showed me his second pattern in the Wood Series, this one tied out of the same rubbery material, but a shade of blue reminiscent of Walmart branding.

"*Blue* Wood?" I asked, holding up the fly and moving it to activate the wiggle of its signature feature.

"Balls," said Jeff, a little sheepishly.

"As in—" I hesitated, fearing the worst. "What I think?"

"'Fraid so," Jeff said, lighting a smoke. "Name recognition—it's everything."

PINK WOOD

- **Hook:** #2-4 Gamakatsu C14S Glo Bug or similar
- **Thread:** Pink Danville 140 Denier or similar
- **Tail:** Pink tendril from Dollar Store Squishy Ball, Walmart Aqua Culture Anemone, or similar
- **Eyes:** Pearl painted lead dumbbell eyes (medium)
- **Membranes:** White small round rubber leg material, Life Flex, or similar
- **Body/egg:** Hot or fluorescent pink Angora goat, pseudo seal dubbing, or similar

Tying the Pink Wood

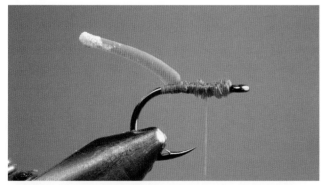

1. Start your thread. Affix the tip of a Squishy Ball tendril, about ⅝ to ¾ inch long, directly above the barb of the hook. Use your thread to give the tail the appropriate attitude.

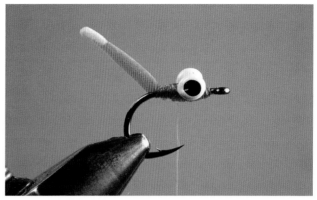

2. Attach the dumbbell eyes between the tail and the eye of the hook. Use lots of thread wraps and cover these with a bit of UV-activated epoxy or Zap-A-Gap or similar cyanoacrylate glue.

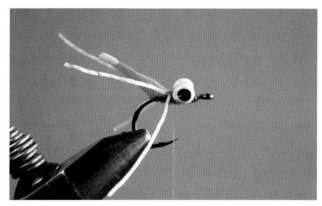

3. The so-called membranes are nothing more than a pair of short rubber legs extending from both sides of the hook. Cut two pieces of leg material about 3 inches long and tie them in at the midpoint of the material directly behind the eyes. I leave the two rubber legs long until the fly is tied, at which point I trim them to length.

4. Create a dubbing loop with the dyed Angora goat hair or your favorite sparkly pink dubbing. Spin your dubbing tool and create a fuzzy noodle. Crisscross around the eyes, forcing the rubber membrane material into the appropriate position. Tie off the dubbing and clip excess. Whip-finish and add head cement. Trim the membrane material to length.

ANADROMOUS STONE

Anadromous Stone, adapted by author from 20 Incher, original designer unknown

It had been a while since I thought much about salmon. They were around, of course, especially during fall, but never in the kinds of numbers that drew my attention off of steelhead, that most bedeviling autumn sport. Now and then I encountered a big chinook or feisty coho, usually after I gave up on surface patterns and laced on the meaty Skagit head and started swinging my 1/0 and 3/0 marabou-winged Spey flies—but these were dark, late-season fish, not salmon I would target, much less kill.

All anadromous fish are interesting to catch. Their life histories give them the appropriate degree of mystery and, for many of us, sea-run fish offer the chance to hook our biggest fish of the year, if not also our careers. Still, it's difficult to remain too excited after landing a fish, however big, that looks a lot like a worn-out pair of Levi's—and when you see the lead weights and psychedelic bling the gear guys use for salmon, you can be excused for sidling out of the scene and retreating, say, in search of a pod of spirited trout worrying a late-season hatch of Blue-Winged Olives.

Plus, there's the sense these days, true or not, that salmon runs everywhere have declined to the point that one more perfect storm may send local populations plummeting into the abyss of extinction. Do they really need my flies contributing yet another tug on the thin thread of their existence?

But last year all of that changed. What started as the usual trickle turned into an unprecedented flood. By September, tens of thousands of salmon were swimming in the river right below my house. For a while I remained keen on steelhead, out of habit if nothing else—until one morning, after getting blanked through a favorite run, I decided to see if maybe I could find one of these salmon everybody up and down the river was, by now, talking about.

But how? Fly fishing, we all know, is never as simple as the decision to target an unlikely fish that suddenly appears within reach of a cast. And salmon, of course, pose their own host of challenges: What do you use for a fly for a fish that no longer eats?

Or do they?

And if so, what?

And if not—we're back where we started.

Which is how, perhaps, I came to tie on a pair of big stone nymphs. I say "perhaps" because, at that moment, I was more concerned with *how* I was going to go about catching a salmon than any pattern that might do the trick. By now, readers should recognize the tack. Despite the promise or reputation of any fly, I invariably return to my original thesis: It's presentation, not patterns, that catches fish.

What I tied to the end of my tippet, and also to one of the tag ends of the blood knot between tippet and leader, weren't big stone nymphs so much as they were, simply, *big* nymphs—versions, in fact, of the 20 Incher, a trout fly I had written about earlier. But the patterns themselves seemed entirely beside the point. A pellet of split shot pinched to the tippet halfway between my flies, my hunch was to nymph up a salmon.

Half a century lost to this silly sport has convinced me, among other things, that the shortest route to a hooked fish remains what I consider the oldest trick in the book—a couple of sunk flies led on a tight line through an obvious lie. Floating line, long leader, no indicator. Variations to the method are many, and the technique gets named and renamed again and again. But it's the same candy bar, regardless of changing wrappers. Get down to where the fish are. Establish contact with your flies. Your rod tip, moving, travels one iota *ahead* of your flies. Read your line. Do what it tells you to do.

It's as basic as fishing a worm. And usually just as deadly. The longer the rod, the better, as you want to lift as much line as possible off the water, reducing the play of currents on both leader and fly. At the same time, the last thing you want to do is *drag* the fly through the lie—or do anything that restricts or changes the fly's natural course.

The profound insight about this most basic of fishing techniques is that it's essentially the same way you swing a *surface* fly through a steelhead run or a soft hackle through trout water—and if you can make that connection between these seemingly disparate methods, you're well on your way to understanding the principles that apply to nearly all aspects of presentation.

Easier said than done. I can't count the number of times I've stood next to friends or students and failed to get them into fish while they try nymphing through a proven lie. Time and again I think they've got it: their casts land just right, they pick up the slack off the water, flies appear to travel perfectly through the slot. But nothing happens—no take, no grab, no sudden thudding jolt just at the moment you thought you might be hung up on the bottom.

These days I refuse to touch the rod in these situations. I can make as many mistakes as the next angler, but given a couple of good-looking nymphs and a little split shot on a good piece of trout water, chances are I'll find something. For students, nothing is more discouraging than running a nymph through a slot for fifteen or twenty minutes, then having the teacher take the same rod and reel and fly setup, stand in the exact same spot, and immediately hook a fish. Nobody likes that. If it's your sweetheart you're fishing with, you've really blown it.

Still, short-line or tight-line nymphing—or whatever you want to call it—is part of a long and oftentimes frustrating learning curve. Then again, at some point, you just *get* it. Unless the only reason you go fishing is to catch fish, you probably won't become a full-time nympher, no matter how effective the technique may be—but from the point you master the basics of fishing weighted flies with split shot on your leader, you've got *that* to rely on should all else fail.

⸺•⸺⸺•⸺

I insert this long digression on the basics of nymphing because I want to impress upon the reader the idea that more times than not, catching good fish—even salmon—is not about having the Right Fly. Intent on nymphing for local chinook, I tied on a pair of flies I know how to fish in a particularly effective manner. I waded in up to my knees, lobbed a rod's length of line and leader upstream, and as the cast followed the tip of the rod, I got an idea how deep I could fish in how much current, whether I needed less weight or more, how far I could swing into the soft water before tangling with the bottom. By this time I wasn't even thinking about my flies anymore—a subject that does you absolutely no good to consider once you step into the river and start casting.

I wouldn't share all this, of course, if none of it worked. What surprised me, however, was how much the salmon liked a big stone nymph—or were at least agreeable to eating them. Within two days I had the smoker going full-time, and I was passing out salmon fillets to folks who had been sharing summer produce from their gardens, the kind of thing that happens with increasing frequency to a single man approaching his dotage. At the same time, I began refining my nymph, transforming it into a pattern that I wanted to believe proved more and more effective as I beached more and more salmon.

Maybe. By the end of the salmon season, I was calling the fly the Anadromous Stone—but when I sat down at the vise this summer in anticipation of what was predicted to be an even bigger run of salmon, I was struck by how much my "refined" pattern looked like the trout fly Kaylee's Stone I described earlier in the trout section of this book. There were definite changes, and I was sure I had never had salmon take the fly so aggressively, strikes that *felt* exactly like feeding fish. "They *want* it," I claimed to no one else in the kitchen, spreading smoked salmon mixed with cream cheese on a shingle of Rye Krisp bread.

I was reminded, anyway, of a classic line once spoken at the Tyers' Roost: *All nymphs are Hare's Ears; they're just tied with different materials.* But with the Anadromous Stone, I wondered, did I finally hit on some magic combination, one that salmon can't refuse?

You know the answer. Rather than the Right Fly, I happened upon a pattern that worked, one I came to believe in when fished in a manner I trust in a spot that I knew held plenty of fish.

That's the real combination, right there.

ANADROMOUS STONE

- **Hook:** #2-4 Mustad 79580
- **Bead:** Gold brass
- **Weight:** .025-.030 lead wire
- **Thread:** Black 8/0 UNI-Thread or similar
- **Tail:** Dark brown goose biots
- **Rib:** Oval gold tinsel
- **Underbody:** Fluorescent chartreuse chenille (medium)
- **Abdomen:** Peacock herl, spun into dubbing loop
- **Wing case:** Turkey tail feather
- **Legs:** Brown round rubber
- **Thorax:** Purple or orange chenille (medium)

Tying the Anadromous Stone

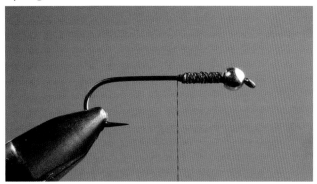

1. Slide the bead over the point of the hook (you may have to pinch down the barb) and up to the hook eye. Secure the hook in the vise. Make about fifteen wraps of lead wire over the front third of the hook. Press the coils of wire tight to the bead. Start your thread and lash the lead wire so that it doesn't spin on the shank.

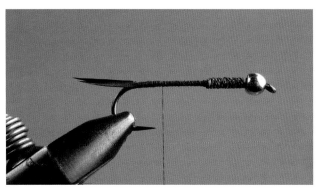

2. Wrap your thread so that it hangs near the point of the hook. Hold a pair of goose biots back to back and align the butts with the hook shank. In order to get the biots to sit correctly, start with the pair held about a quarter turn in your direction, take a couple of loose thread wraps around the butts of the biots, and then allow the biots to spin into place as you continue wrapping your thread. Some anglers claim that fish don't inspect the tail of your fly. However, as an old surfer, I believe that the rigid biots affect how a fly travels through the water, and I aim to create a profile that remains in *trim* while riding the current.

3. Secure the tinsel ribbing at the root of the tail. Then tie in a length of chenille for the underbody. Wind your thread forward up onto the rear portion of the lead wire. Wrap the chenille forward to the same point and tie off and trim excess. The purpose of the chenille is to add bulk to the abdomen; it will also begin to show as the herl that covers it, in the next step, begins to wear. Spiral the thread back around the underbody to the root of the tail.

4. Create a dubbing loop; wax the legs. Insert the tips of four or five strands of peacock herl at the top of the loop and spin your dubbing loop tool at the bottom to form a rope of herl. Advance your thread and follow with the herl rope to form the abdomen of the fly. Because these are such big flies, you may have to repeat the dubbing loop process halfway up the abdomen. The abdomen should end about a third of the way back from the head of the fly. Then spiral four or five open wraps of the tinsel from the root of the tail over the abdomen and secure it just ahead of the abdomen with your thread.

5. Clip out a ⅜-inch-wide section of turkey tail feather. Clip off the tip of the feather so that you're using the tougher, thicker fibers. Tie it in, dull side up, by the forward end of the feather, directly in front of the abdomen.

6. Clip a pair of 3-inch lengths of rubber leg material. Tie in one piece, at its midpoint, directly in front of the abdomen, and the second piece midway through the thorax. Don't worry, at this point, about the exact orientation of the legs. You'll hold them in place with material wraps when you create the chenille thorax.

7. For the thorax, secure a length of chenille directly in front of the tie-in point for the turkey feather wing case. Then wind your thread forward to just behind the bead. Now wind the chenille forward, wrapping between the pairs of legs so that they end up fairly evenly spaced, extending perpendicularly from the thorax. Tie off the chenille directly behind the bead. Clip the legs if necessary.

8. Pull the turkey feather over the top of the thorax. Tie off directly behind the bead, clip excess, and cover the clipped ends with thread wraps. Whip-finish and saturate the exposed thread wraps and the turkey feather wing case with lacquer or head cement.

WAKERS

Steve's Waker, designed by Steve Wrye

Once the middle-school girls finish their cross-country season, Coach Wrye starts packing for a trip to the Snake and the Grand Ronde. For most of us, it's pretty late to be swinging surface patterns, but Steve Wrye's one of those guys who's been doing it for so long, it's as though he doesn't know any other way to fish for steelhead. Can you blame him? Whether fishing for trout, bass, roosterfish, or backwater bluegill, most everyone agrees that moving fish to the surface and seeing them eat the fly offer the defining moment that separates fly fishing from all other forms of angling, while going a long way to remind us why we fell for the game in the first place.

But there's more to it than that. This fall, when steelhead began showing up in river conditions that give surface presentations their best odds, a young hotshot I know got his first-ever fish on a waking pattern—and then, from the same pool, two more steelhead that rose through the river's silky sheen and ripped the fabric to shreds. This is one of those guys who came of age during the onset of the modern Spey rod era and who now throws those tight, immaculate loops that seem constrained by nothing but the size of the river itself. He catches tons of steelhead—and you figure an angler like this has been waking steelhead to the surface like my lawn gives up dandelions. *His first ones?* Naturally, he was blown away: "I can't believe I haven't tried it

before," another buddy reported him saying. "What have I been doing with my life?"

When I tell this story to Coach Wrye, he shakes his head. Kids. Wrye, it should be noted, belongs to that generation of sportsmen in which juvenile behavior has, for many of us, segued seamlessly into senior discounts, Medicare, and, of late, disturbing intimations of senility. Plus, there's not a one of us who hasn't been made more aware of death than we've ever been aware of death before. Life's short and getting shorter, says the reproachful wag of Coach Wrye's white-whiskered bald head.

A steelheader who doesn't fish wakers?
What has *he been doing with his life?*

●———————●

It's a mindset, I suspect, more than anything else. Or maybe a matter of style. Why do we go fishing? Once we throw off the shackles of bait, we're free to imagine all manner of seductions, the best of which demand the most of us as casters, hunters, naturalists, and savvy or even sanguinary sportsmen. When an angler chooses a fly rod and flies, he or she commits to a path that leads elsewhere than the simple goal of catching fish. Of course, we all want to hook and land our share. But there's something much larger at work, I'd argue, for those of us who have given up so much to have so little to show for an angling life.

Old sailor, surfer, and boatman, Steve Wrye contends that it's a matter of form following function. What are you fishing for? What are you trying to get from the sport? From a day on the water?

You use a waker when steelheading because that *is* steelheading.

At least in fall.

At least when there are enough fish around to give you a fair shot.

"And there's always a chance a fish will rise to a waking fly," says Wrye.

Despite his scheduled departure, Wrye has conceded to a visit to the Roost. He usually hates this kind of scene. His strict opinions about virtually everything to do with sports include a general disdain for flies with names or the specifics of any pattern. He fits right in. Ask him about any aspect of any fly in his box that he's tied and he'll say it doesn't matter. Practically any fly will wake, he claims, if you riffle hitch it, fish it on a floating line, and swing it in the kind of current in which steelhead generally lie.

Really?

By way of illustration, Wrye hands me a fly he says is pretty much all he uses these days. With its tinsel ribbing and white wing, the fly looks a lot like something Randall Kaufmann might have tied thirty years ago for the Deschutes—and not at all like the sensuous Spey flies or antagonizing Intruders now so popular in watersheds along the northeastern Pacific. Wrye seems perfectly at ease with my suggestion that even the traditionalists who frequent the Roost might find the pattern a wee bit old-fashioned.

"I guess I'll worry about what the fish think," he says.

Although this is a fly-tying book, I feel once more a mention of presentation tactics is in order. Form follows function. If you know how you intend to fish a fly, you'll do a better job creating the look you need.

In his rightfully famous tome *Steelhead Fly Fishing*, Trey Combs offers a concise description of his own introduction to the "riffling hitch" and his eventual understanding of fishing waking flies. "When a properly dressed wet fly with a turned up eye has been hitched and brought under tension," he writes, "the head pulls up until it breaks through the surface to create a V wake."

This *head breaking through the surface*, however, is somewhat misleading. Many anglers confuse this idea with skating rather than waking. A true waking fly isn't seen; the notion that your fly is poking its head out of the water like a curious otter or seal is a different technique—effective, at times, but never as consistently as a fly underwater that touches the surface just enough to leave a trail-like wake as though scratching the underside of a ceiling of glass.

A hitched fly, anyway, is the surest way to get a fly under tension to create a wake. The hitch is nothing more than one or two half-hitches formed with the tippet around the head of the fly. Cast across the river and to some degree downstream, the fly drags against the current, doing what any wet fly does on the swing but with exaggerated fluctuations of movement caused by its misaligned attitude to the leader.

Despite its unnatural track, a true waker makes a subtle offering, nothing like the raucous gyrations of your heavily dressed skaters. In fact, many traditional steelhead dressings will do. "I prefer a somewhat sparse and drab wet fly to hitch," says Combs, "one that entices rather than startles."

This gets to the heart of the matter—and the stance Steve Wrye takes with his own flies swung waking through classic steelhead lies. Nobody really knows why this is such an effective way to move steelhead—but then nobody really knows why anything besides egg patterns and big stonefly nymphs get steelhead to bite. What most of us who employ surface presentations *imagine*, however, is that a fish looking up at the surface of the river, a vast screen backlit by the sky, can see a waking fly and watch it swing toward it, for a long, long way. In the specific sort of current that steelhead favor, it requires virtually no energy for the fish to pivot or rotate its pectoral fins as though they are ailerons and rise to the surface and intersect the course of this swinging fly.

Why one cast and waking swing produce a strike and hundreds or even thousands of others don't is a question that should, by all counts, bedevil us forever. What are we fishing for if not the ineffable and the sublime?

For many old-school stylists, the answer begins with the mesmerizing V spreading behind a waking fly. Hitched, "almost any conservatively dressed fly will work," states Combs. It's a bold assertion, one difficult for the uninitiated to embrace. For Steve Wrye, it's an obvious truth—and the reason he disregards any serious questions about this kind of dubbing or that kind of tailing material.

Still, it's a real fly tied from honest-to-god materials that Coach Wrye feels obliged to leave behind at the Roost. And when I take Steve's Waker to the bench and cut it apart for closer inspection, I begin to sense all of the usual prejudices and superstitious tendencies that infuse the patterns of so many longtime steelheaders. Steve doesn't own up to this material or the other, I suspect, because these are *his secrets*—not necessarily things that other anglers don't know, but a private recipe born out of a lifetime of unprovable theories developed while watching the fly swing like the hand of a clock through one season and the next. Whatever it is Steve Wrye's fishing for, it's all come to this—some fur and feather and faith in a waking fly.

And it's a faith, I'm happy to report, that still pays off. In the following week in a well-known stretch of river that most readers could reach in a day's drive, Wrye uses his old-fashioned waker to land three fish over twelve pounds—plus a buck that noses past the forty-inch mark, his biggest steelhead ever.

Wakers, of course, aren't for everybody.

It depends on what you're fishing for.

STEVE'S WAKER

▥ **Hook:** #4 TMC 7989 or similar
▥ **Thread:** Black 8/0 UNI-Thread or similar
▥ **Underbody:** Strip of thin (2 mm) fly foam
▥ **Tail:** Bronze Antron yarn
▥ **Tag:** Narrow gold tinsel
▥ **Body:** Black seal fur or other dubbing
▥ **Rib:** Narrow gold tinsel
▥ **Wing:** Polar bear or appropriate substitute
▥ **Hackle collar:** Ringneck pheasant nape

Tying Steve's Waker

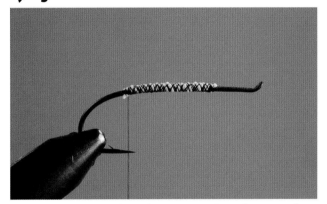

1. Secure your hook and start your thread. Cover the shank of the hook with a layer of thread. On top of the length of the hook shank attach a strip of foam (2 × 2 mm, or ¹⁄₁₆ × ¹⁄₁₆ inch). Lash and compress the foam by working your thread forward and back along its length.

2. With the thread above the point of the hook, tie in a length of tinsel and create a narrow tag. Secure the tinsel, pull it out of the way, and tie in a short length of Antron yarn for the tail. Take one or two turns of thread behind and under the root of the tail to make it stand proud.

3. For the body, create a dubbing loop at the root of the tail. Wax the legs of the loop liberally. The seal fur dubbing I use (from old Russian army coats) is stiff and spiky; you want it to just sort of lie on the waxed thread until you spin the dubbing tool. Eventually you'll end up with a bristly rope. Wind it forward, stroking the wild hairs toward the back of the fly. Tie off and trim at the front end of the compressed foam.

4. Spiral the tinsel in five or six evenly spaced turns to the front of the body. Tie off and clip excess.

5. Calf tail, bucktail, bleached deer hair or elk hair, or even synthetic material all make perfectly good white hair wings on steelhead flies. But many old-timers came upon some polar bear hair long ago in their lives—and it's pretty hard to stop using it while there's any still left in the stash. Whatever you use, tie in a fairly sparse wing, one that extends to about the root of the tail.

6. Ringneck pheasant have a lot of different kinds of feathers, and when I asked Steve Wrye which ones he uses for the hackle collar, he gave his usual noncommittal, disdainful shrug. But when I offered up the skin of a whole bird I had hanging out in the boatshed, Wrye pointed specifically to the eyed, jungle-cock-like feathers in the patch directly at the back of the bird's neck. This was my first clue that Steve pays a little more attention to the details of his pattern than he lets on. Strip one side of the feather and tie it in by its tip. Wind the feather forward, taking no more than two or three turns to create a fairly sparse hackle collar while leaving plenty of room behind the eye of the hook for the possible use of a riffling hitch. Form a tidy head and saturate it with lacquer or your preferred head cement.

AQUA BUDDHA

Aqua Buddha, designed by Jeff Cottrell

Is it too early to begin thinking about steelhead? My buddy Jeff Cottrell doesn't think so—but that's probably because he's reached the point in his career where steelhead have become a year-round game. Or curse. In all things angling, nothing seems surer to deprive claims of mastery, much less a sense of peace, than a calendar dedicated to finding steelhead, month after month, anywhere in their native range. It's an aim sufficiently difficult—or onerous—that I would worry about Jeff were he not possessed of a certain pragmatic optimism, the fatalist's hope that all steelheaders must embrace if they want to stay in the hunt for the long haul.

The roosterfish fancier can grow desperate when, day after day, his casts are rejected by fish lashing the surface in reckless attack on anything but his flies. Yet at least he keeps *seeing* fish—feeding fish, no less, which generally makes the thing seem doable, even when you can't get it right. And if his spirit fails completely, the roosterfisher can always tell his *pangero* to go find some skipjack tuna, mindless sport into which he can plunge his steaming frustrations.

But a steelheader knows few such mercies. The fishless day means—what? Far too much claptrap has been freighted onto the sport, yet nobody has a deeper sense of staring into a meaningless void than a steelheader

in the midst of a protracted skunk. Are there fish here? Has one even *seen* my fly? Does my next cast matter?

Few anglers endure many of these spells without suffering lasting damage. Some steelheaders simply quit: Why go fishing if you're not going to catch any fish? Others find it easier to keep plugging away—albeit in reduced doses—rather than accept a life in which they'll never hook a steelhead again. And then there are steelheaders like Jeff, who, in the face of empty casts and fishless runs, ends up spending more time on steelhead rivers each year because, to his way of thinking, you still never know what epic fish might suddenly come your way.

Good steelheaders are often possessed of this sort of loony buoyancy. Jeff and his wife Jan found a little house a cast away from a favorite steelhead river shortly after his fly shop went belly up for all the usual reasons; not even Jeff's silver goatee and feel-good charm could cover the lease. The river opens in June—but for much of the summer things are spotty as runoff from snowmelt and mountain glaciers stains the river, turning it the color of dusty yucca leaves.

Jeff, like other locals, fishes the river in summer; some even claim there's a daily cycle that sees a period of increased water clarity from colder nighttime temperatures in the high country. But it's not until around, say, the first of September that the river clears and fishing really lights up—at which point Jeff is in the thick of an annual gig as camp host at a steelhead lodge a half-hour upriver from his flower-lined house.

I should also mention that earlier each summer Jeff spends weeks at a time working at another lodge, a spot that anadromous fish no longer reach because of downstream dams—but where the trout are often just as big as steelhead, and on a stretch of river as big as any steelhead water in the world.

Jeff's home river closes the end of November. That's just about the time the coast begins to see its first spate of heavy rains. Winter steelhead soon follow. And for the last two or three winters—I can't quite keep track—Jeff's had another camp host gig, this one on a stretch of reservation water never before opened to non-Native sport anglers, the final miles of a brawling rain forest fishery where twenty-pound fish, covered in sea lice, don't take anyone by surprise.

Which is not to say they're taken for granted. A twenty-pound steelhead is, after all, a hell of a fish—especially when hooked so close to the Pacific you can smell salt clinging to the old-growth forest looming at river's edge. Also, because they're steelhead—even steelhead taken from essentially private water at the tail end of a 200-square-mile drainage protected from headwaters to the sea—they're never easy to find, never found in abundance, and rarely a week passes when the river doesn't blow out, unable to handle what adds up, each winter, to something on the order of twenty *feet* of rain.

It's not, anyway, a cakewalk. Then again, I don't believe steelheading ever is. Even Jeff, in all his tireless optimism, comes up against it now and then. What do you say to a group of high-dollar clients, all of them soured on big trees and rain, who have gone an entire week without so much as a touch, a take, a grab? The real guys, he says, can deal with it; experience has taught them that sea-run fisheries are *always* a roll of the dice. But there's a whole new breed of fly fisher, Jeff claims, convinced that if they spend enough money, and they find the remote word-of-mouth lodge, they should be guaranteed fish wherever and whenever they arrive.

"They think it should be Alaska," says Jeff. A big man, broad-shouldered and fair, one who has spent his entire adult life dealing with guides, lodge owners, sales reps, the sporting parvenu, and clients from the privileged class, Jeff holds his ground by balancing his good nature with a faint but very real hint of ferocity should anyone ever get too far out of hand. "I don't tell them that if they were hoping for Alaska, that's where they should have gone."

Good advice. More to the point, if you really don't like what it takes to catch steelhead, you probably shouldn't set much store in getting one now and then.

Serious steelheading—year-round or otherwise—seems always to lead back to these obvious truths. What's even more telling is that this so-called wisdom was probably passed along to most of us early in our steelhead careers—only we just didn't believe it. You catch fish on the fly you fish with. Your fly doesn't matter. You don't catch fish unless your fly's in the water. Atlantic salmon fishing and, in recent decades, the quest for sea-run browns can also inspire a tenor of this self-evident if slightly paradoxical repartee. From another lifetime, Jeff remembers the advice he got from Tom Brady, the first guide to hang out his shingle in Tierra del Fuego, where Jeff had just arrived to cater to angling luminaries on the Río Grande. "The longer you do it," said Brady, referring to flies cast for the river's anadromous browns, "the less you know."

Still, steelheading gets much of the blame for these grainy observations that smack of a kind of Asian or Zen-like truth. You can see how it happens. Steelheading isn't hard so much as it is a discipline or ritualized practice. You learn to do it correctly—read the water, recognize holding lies, deliver the fly—and then you're required to do it over and over again, often with little or no feedback that suggests in any way you're doing it right.

Sort of like life—which I won't say any more about other than to mention that many of us remain confused, believing that we're somehow meant to be rewarded for our good deeds, responsible citizenry, and a reasonably clear conscience.

What steelheading makes obvious, anyway, is that each of our many admirable skills may, on any given day, add up to squat—at least in terms of recognizable *action* with the fish we so desire. This desiring, some would argue, is part of the problem—although if that's the secret, fishing without desire, I think we're all pretty much hosed.

———

The Aqua Buddha comes out of a collection of flies that Jeff—along with Trey Combs, Jack Mitchell, and Michael Davidchik—designed for Rainy's Flies, a series they call the Steelhead Underground. The name, I suspect, is an appeal to the latest generation of steelheaders who want to see themselves as gnarly, radical, hard-core, dirtbag—or whatever other current adjective captures an attitude it often takes to catch steelhead with any regularity. Oddly enough, few serious steelheaders I know have ever bought their flies, much less settled for patterns tied commercially overseas.

Which isn't to discount this particular lineup. I'm sure all of these patterns will catch fish. The trick is deciding which fly to choose—which one to hang your faith on and when.

Like many of the patterns in the Steelhead Underground collection, the Aqua Buddha offers the impression of a simplified Intruder, that beast of a fly so popular with Spey rodders on steelhead rivers today.

With their undulant tendrils and seductive color combinations, these flies go a long way in approaching the size and action gear anglers get with their wobbly plugs. The Intruder, of course, came in the wake of any number of patterns that employed trailing "stinger" hooks, a way to create a big-profile fly without resorting to a full-length hook better suited to fishing for sturgeon or triple-digit halibut. Whether tied on tubes or on hookless shanks, most stingered flies are also tied "in the round," offering that distinct impression of a curve-handled parasol, a concession to the uncertain orientation such flies will take as they swim on a tight line without the keel-like properties of a traditional hook.

Does it matter? Tyers who like to think their stingered flies have a top and a bottom, or who care about the orientation of the trailing stinger hook in relation to the rest of the fly, will now use dumbbell eyes on the *under*side of the fly's head, hoping to keep the fly from flopping over on its side as it swings in the current. But this is a long, long way from the notion that in steelheading, at least, your fly is but a small piece of the puzzle—and I have to confess that at some point, talk of this sort sounds to me like discussions of where to part your hair, or whether the Scotch is too peaty or has too much smoke and leather on the nose.

Jeff's a little like that, too. Yet when faced with the mysteries of steelheading across the long reach of a year, he can fall prey to the usual prejudices and jingoism that afflict anglers trying to make sense of their seemingly senseless successes and failures. More power to him; it's a tough game. At the same time, Jeff's under no illusions about his black and blue Aqua Buddha—nor any other fly that's ever been created for steelhead. When it all begins to seem a bit too complicated, he's fond of quoting his old mentor, Tom Brady, along the banks long ago of the Río Grande: "If something pulls, pull back."

That's about all any of us really knows.

AQUA BUDDHA

- **Hook:** 25 mm Waddington Shank with #4 Owner bait hook looped onto black standard Senyo's Intruder Trailer Hook Wire
- **Thread:** Black 6/0 Danville Waxed Flymaster
- **Eyes:** Mini lead eyes (1/80 oz.)
- **Tail:** Kingfisher blue Finn Raccoon Zonker
- **Butt:** Kingfisher blue SLF Dubbing or blue steelie Ice Dub
- **Underwing:** Ostrich plume, mix of black and dyed kingfisher blue
- **Lateral line:** Herring back Krystal Flash
- **Overwing:** Black marabou
- **Topping:** Kingfisher blue Lady Amherst tail
- **Collar:** Guinea fowl, dyed blue
- **Head:** Black fur dubbing

Tying the Aqua Buddha

There are countless ways of constructing flies with trailer or stinger hooks, some of them involving sophisticated tools that really do make the job easier. At the same time, it takes but a little foresight and innovation to get by with existing tools. In the photographs it's difficult to see that I swung the head of the fly in the port direction, then pivoted the upright shaft of the vise so that the fly was positioned appropriately. Experiment. Adapt. Both skills remain at the heart of the game.

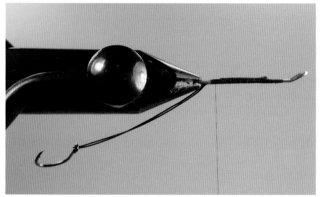

1. Secure the Waddington shank with the straight eye in the vise jaws and the cocked eye at the front of the fly pointing down. Start your thread. Lace your trailer hook onto a 4-inch length of trailer hook wire. Lash the wire to the top of the Waddington shank with the point of the trailer hook positioned downward. Then feed the wire through the forward eye, fold it back below the shank, and continue lashing. Clip off the excess wire and fair the shank and lashing with wraps of thread.

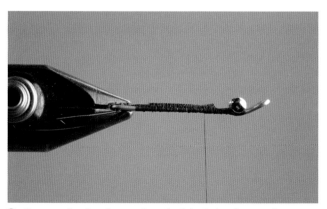

2. Secure the lead eyes just behind the forward eye of the fly.

3. Starting at the middle of the Waddington shank, create the tail out of two tufts of Finn Raccoon Zonker fibers that extend just past the back of the trailer hook.

4. Create a dubbing loop and spin in your blue butt material. Wind the twisted strand of dubbing into a plump round ball just forward of the root of the tail.

5. In front of the dubbing ball, tie in a half-dozen black ostrich plume fibers spaced around the top half of the shank. Do the same along the bottom half. Then repeat with fibers from a blue ostrich plume.

6. For the lateral line, tie in a single strand of Krystal Flash along both sides of the fly.

7. For the overwing, secure the tip of a single marabou feather. Holding the butt of the stem, make two complete turns around the hook shank. Tie off and clip the excess. Stroke the plumes toward the rear of the fly and help them lie properly with judicious wraps of thread.

8. Forward the butts of the marabou, secure a dozen Lady Amherst tail feather fibers spaced evenly around the fly. Because of the unruly marabou, it's often easier to tie in small clumps of the Lady Amherst feather fibers top and bottom, rather than try to spin one big clump around the entire fly.

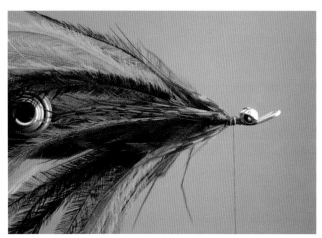

9. For the collar, strip one side of a dyed guinea fowl feather. Tie in the feather by the tip. Make two turns of the feather, positioning it so that the fibers lie tight to the fly rather than splaying like the bristles of a bottle brush.

11. Saturate your finish wraps with lacquer or your preferred head cement.

10. Create a small dubbing loop and spin in a bit of seal or possum or hare dubbing. Wind the dubbing strand forward and make a single figure-eight around the eyes. Secure the dubbing strand in front of the eyes, clip the excess, and whip-finish.

GABE'S FLY

Gabe's Fly, designed by Gabe Cunningham

When it gets you early, there is no escape.
—Paul Gartside, designer and boatbuilder

They're building a hotel where you used to be able to park before climbing down to the river, a backdoor approach below the pedestrian bridge that put you out on a bar on the wrong side of the run except right on top near a pocket of holding water, no bigger than a pair of drift boats, where the first guy through will often find a fish. The hotel, currently plywood sheathing and an armada's worth of Tyvek flapping in the breeze, put an end to this inside move. Now that you have to park on the other side of the river, in the little lot by the county history museum, very few of us are willing to cross the bridge for those few quick casts into that little bucket and, in doing so, risk losing the spot we might have already claimed in the lineup parading through the heart of the run.

Unless you're Gabe Cunningham. Gabe's of an age, either wretched or enviable, when no shot is too long—when any spot in a river a steelhead might lie is worth visiting, no matter the time, energy, or forfeited opportunity it takes to give that wheel a whirl. Gabe goes fishing the way you hope your bird dog smothers a field. Sometimes, when he's on the water the same hours I am, I think there are two of him.

A while back I was into a bunch of good fish in the eastern part of the state with Mr. Kelly, another teacher from the high school. I asked him, rhetorically, if he could imagine Gabe with us getting into this remarkable wilderness sport. Mr. Kelly shook his head—he knows Gabe as well as I do—then he proceeded to re-create the scene that had passed before his eyes, descending into images far more graphic than anyone wants me to depict here.

How many of us can remember what it was really like when we were young? In retrospect, it all makes perfect sense; at the start, fish just drove us crazy. I find it laughable when I hear or read old-timers worry about the future of the sport: Where is the next generation of fly fishers? By simply asking this question, the old-timer reveals he's forgotten the furious passion that once consumed him, a restless desire a certain type of youngster finds impossible to resist. Where you *won't* find kids crazy to fish is hanging out where old farts sit around brooding about the future of the sport—or their distaste for texting, tattoos, body piercings, or the shit kids call music these days.

Last spring I arrived at school one morning and was swept up in the excitement surrounding "Gabe's fish." Before the first bell rang, half a dozen kids came by my classroom to show me pictures on their phones. Two of the students were especially eager to share; their inclusion in the photo was offered up as evidence that they had played a part in landing the fish, a role I didn't doubt when, on closer inspection, I counted five teenagers, side by side, holding up a sturgeon that extended head and tail beyond the boys, all smiles, at either end.

Finally Gabe arrived. He was already grinning, sure I had heard the news, his eyes lit up beneath his black eyebrows and unkempt shock of dark hair. There were actually two fish; his buddy Russell broke one off. They were out on the end of the sand spit; you can get right to the edge of a forty-foot-deep hole in the main stem when the water's low enough or they open the downstream dam. He and Russell and the other guys had brought beach chairs, sand spikes, bait—a goofball teenage fishing expedition were it not that Gabe had been waiting for just such a spring afternoon.

Next thing he knew his salmon rod was getting dragged across the sand.

"I thought you had sand spikes."

Gabe looked at me as if I were a teacher who expects way too much.

"They were just sticks we found on the way."

Asked what happened then, Gabe raised his right hand across his body and, with a pair of backhand thrusts, mimicked coming up tight to a fish, a gesture complemented with clenched teeth, pressed lips, muscles showing at the hinges of his jaw.

And?

Back in the moment, Gabe grew starry-eyed.

"Big fish," he said, shaking his head. "It took a while."

If it troubles readers to learn that Gabe Cunningham doesn't fish exclusively with flies, let me remind them that nearly all good anglers began catching fish by less sophisticated means. The first chapter of Roderick Haig-Brown's *Primer to Flyfishing* is titled "On the Virtues of Worms." Although it's possible, of course, to become an accomplished fly fisher without having ever fished with bait, lures, nets, spears, diving ducks, or domesticated sea otters, I've generally found that those whose fire burns hottest to fool fish with flies—and to do whatever it takes to protect these fish and the habitats in which they live—discovered that passion before they ever picked up a fly rod.

Gabe's appetite seems limitless. Smallmouth bass, carp, tiger muskie—not a weekend approaches when he doesn't have a plan on the burner. An understanding mom with a willingness to visit every corner of two states hasn't shorted Gabe's rations either. This past summer Gabe held a job as an intern at a lodge at the mouth of one of British Columbia's most famous steelhead rivers. Okay, *the* most famous BC steelhead river. In exchange for cleanup and maintenance chores, Gabe got room and board—and lots of opportunities to experience firsthand the steelhead for which the river has gained its widespread fame.

"You should really try to fish there," Gabe tells me—after describing yet another fish, festooned with sea lice, cartwheeling back to the sea. He swipes through his phone and shows me pictures of cradled spacecraft, their exquisite profiles sparkling without hint of color beyond that of a goblet of gin. In a pinch he learned to plunge Spey rod and reel into the river, strip off twenty-five yards of line, and let the current carry the loose line downstream; pressured from a new direction, the fish comes back upstream, your chance again to try to control it. Fish in the high teens aren't so much routine as they are the size that actually get landed.

"Any bigger and they don't stop," says Gabe, smiling like a teenage surfer washed up on the beach after getting swallowed by the first big barrel of his life. He's sure, of course, that fish like these will grab his fly forever.

Will he ever suffer loss so joyfully again?

"You really ought to try to go there," repeats Gabe.

He often has advice for me. Besides his certainty that I should dip into my writing riches and set aside $10,000 for a week of summer steelheading, he visits my classroom each week to suggest a river or fishery I should consider in the more immediate future. What possible reason could anyone have for not driving three hours to the coast for a shot at a pod of coho seen ascending Panther Creek? And a grown-up, no less. Now that he has an imported pickup of his own to drive, Gabe is more convinced than ever that any week that passes during which I don't fish proves some sort of sad truth about me. Like there's anything else but fishing I'd rather be doing?

He's just trying to help. Why? Because Gabe also happens to be one of those bright young anglers who understands that old farts have something to offer, that they actually know a thing or two—that if he wants to solve the mysteries of evening hatches on the Wolf, or how and when and where to fish a riffle-hitched waker, it's worth putting up with the rambling tales of twenty-fish days and forty-steelhead falls. Much as it's easy to believe that old-timers weren't good so much as they were just lucky—lucky to be around when rivers and beaches were uncrowded, the fish abundant and dumb—Gabe recognizes that fifty years on the water can add up to inside dope that no amount of money can buy.

And no doubt the opposite is true: Kids on the water stumble into their own insights and inspirations. Better yet, this latest generation of fly fishers—Gabe and his pals—finds itself with opportunities that others have never had. Right here in our own neighborhood, dams are coming down; across the bridge, an entire watershed has been given back to the full rainbow of anadromous fish. Blocked by unprecedented summer temperatures, sockeye salmon turned up in local tributaries where they've never been recorded before. An hour to the east, conservation groups continue to purchase outdated ranches to increase public access on the longest undammed river in the west. This weekend a local angler landed—and released—a five-pound bull trout, a fish nobody's seen the likes of since the species was listed as threatened nearly twenty years ago.

Opportunities—or portentous anomalies? The obvious answer is that nobody knows what the future holds. Except this: Kids like Gabe Cunningham have a vested interest in the shape of what's to come, and I'm willing to bet that Gabe, for one, will go as far as he needs to go to help keep our waters alive.

In the meantime, he dropped by this week to see if I'd been out since the last big rains. Chinook, he reported, were spawning just above the mouth, spread out on fist-size gravel that has built up in the two and a half years since they took out the upstream dam. I asked how the new fly worked. Gabe's got a pattern he's been tweaking all season, a concoction he's pretty proud of because of the number of fish it's brought to hand. It may not be much to look at—whether it's clownish or sublime, it's hard to say—but when you're a teenager tying flies for sea-run fish, looks are probably beside the point.

It turns out, however, Gabe saw all of those spawning salmon and decided to tie on a little bead that he could swing down below the redds. Steelhead, of course, love to hang out in just such lies, picking up salmon eggs that wash downstream.

"Is that even fly fishing?" I asked.

Gabe looked at me and frowned.

It was as if he hadn't understood a word I said.

GABE'S FLY

- **Shank:** 15 mm Waddington
- **Thread:** Wine 6/0 UNI-Thread
- **Trailer hook wire:** Black Senyo's Intruder
- **Trailer hook:** #4 Owner Straight Eye Bait Hook
- **Body:** Opal Mirage Tinsel (large)
- **Thorax:** Mint Antron dubbing
- **Wing/tail:** Olive variant black-barred rabbit strip
- **Tentacles:** Bronze Flashabou
- **Collar:** Pink schlappen (small)
- **Lateral line:** Natural Lady Amherst

Tying Gabe's Fly

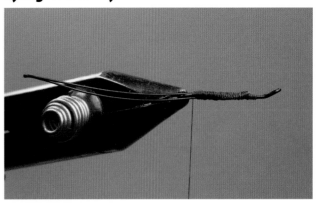

1. Secure the Waddington shank in your vise. Start your thread. Fold a length of trailer wire in half and lash the forward quarters to the shank. The loop for your trailer hook should be about equal to the length of the shank.

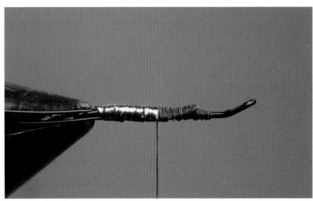

2. Secure a short length of tinsel to the aft end of the shank. Advance your thread about two-thirds the way toward the eye of the hook shank. Wind the tinsel forward and tie off with several wraps of thread.

3. Wax your thread and create a dubbing noodle. Wrap the noodle over the front portion of the tinsel body, creating a chubby dubbing ball.

4. Cut a rabbit strip long enough to reach just past where the bend of your trailer hook will eventually ride. Trim the fur off the forward tip of the rabbit strip and taper the tip to a point. Tie in the forward tip of the rabbit strip just ahead of the Antron dubbing ball.

5. Fold three or four strands of Flashabou around the thread and secure just forward the front tip of the rabbit strip. Jockey the strands of Flashabou so that they lie along each side of the hook shank. Trim the Flashabou to about where the trailer hook will ride.

6. To prepare a schlappen feather, hold the tip in your right hand with the outside of the feather facing you. Strip the quills from what's now the top half of the feather above the stem. Secure the tip of the feather directly in front of the rabbit strip. As you wind the schlappen forward, try to twist the stem so that the remaining quills lie back along the hook shank rather than springing outward like a bottle brush.

7. For lateral lines, tie two or three quills from a Lady Amherst feather along both sides of the fly. Whip-finish and lacquer the head. To attach the stinger or trailer hook, squeeze the loop through the hook eye, then run the loop around the bend of the hook and past the hook point and pull the loop tight. Gabe is still young enough to wonder if it matters whether the hook rides point up or point down.

DESIGN SPIRAL DOUBLE

Design Spiral Double, designed by author

We'll get to flies in a moment. First, some background.

The idea of a design spiral comes from the boat designer and boatbuilder Paul Gartside. Gartside, from Long Island via Canada, and before that England, refers to the idea as the practice of looking back at his older boats and applying their characteristics to the new design on his drafting board. (Yes, drafting board, not a computer screen.) Over time, as Gartside creates designs for similar types of boats, say cutters or pulling boats, he's able to plug in existing numbers as a starting point for a new design rather than calculating those numbers from scratch. Based on the known performance of previous hulls, he can adjust the characteristics of the new design to achieve the aims he's after.

It's a fairly simple idea: Use past work to inform the new. On a broader scale, Gartside's design spiral includes a respect for and understanding of traditional boats from his childhood in Cornwall, plus the Northwest work and pleasure boats designed by the prolific Bill Garden, whom Gartside worked for early in his career. Now, more than thirty years later, Gartside remains loyal to what might best be described as a timeless aesthetic; many of his boats still look as if they should be leaving the quay at Falmouth and making for the English Channel.

I bring up this notion of the design spiral as a way of introducing this chapter's fly, the Design Spiral Double.

Each year I produce a fresh batch of waking muddlers, a type of fly I've written about often and one I turn to frequently during the early reach of every steelhead season. Some waking muddlers I tie new; others I recycle, refurbishing them to whatever new standard I've come up with in response to books and articles I've read, new or rediscovered materials, what's worked for me or hasn't worked in the past.

But this year, determined more than ever to explore every aspect I can about the almost magical efficacy of waking steelhead flies, I've added something new to the arsenal—muddlers tied on double hooks.

Doubles?

I don't want to start any arguments. But if we're going to talk about doubles, flies tied on hooks that look like two hooks aligned side by side, one canted approximately 45 degrees to the other, strong opinions both for and against will inevitably arise. The discussion includes, but is in no way limited to, the question of a fly's fish-hooking abilities, its capacity to stay hooked while fighting a fish, whether one fly is more harmful to a fish than the other, how a fly rides in the water, and the relative dangers of singles and doubles to anglers themselves.

My default answer to any of this is to know the regulations wherever you fish. "Single" means just that. But doubles can be barbless—or have their barbs smashed down—and on some rivers, especially where gear fishing is allowed, your doubles, barbless or otherwise, are just as legal as fishing two flies at once.

Still, a discussion about doubles leaves legal turf quickly and can land you in an argument faster than your opinions about politics, technology—or how to educate the youth of America today. It can be almost as bad as talking about dogs on trout streams. No matter that doubles are a long-held tradition throughout the British Isles, where the ethics of fly fishing are most deeply rooted, and in Atlantic salmon camps on both sides of the pond.

My buddy Jeff Cottrell, who gave me my first doubles, began tying them while guiding for sea-run browns in Tierra del Fuego on the Río Grande. This was back when most of the double-handed rods seen on the river were owned by the Brits, who could never stop joking, it seems, about the Yanks and their silly little one-handers.

Guess they were right about that, too. Because say what you might about doubles, nothing else swings on a tight line quite like them, and their work as waking flies is unique. I won't go so far as to contend that a double is *better* than a single. My point is simply that if you wish to explore the full range of waking presentations for steelhead, and maybe even tight-line downstream presentations of any kind, you would be smart to check out how doubles do the job in lies not necessarily suited for your light-wire or traditionally dressed singles.

•———————•

That's your design spiral. Take a look at the past, both what's come before you and what you've done yourself during your own career. I think most fly tyers do this, to some degree, intuitively; most of us are inveterate tinkerers, searching incessantly for ways to improve patterns, even ones we feel work as well as they possibly can in the specific situations for which we tie them. Those of us who believe it's almost never the fly that catches the fish still feel it's worth doing everything we can to nudge the odds our way.

And maybe more so in steelheading than any other sort of fly fishing. Outside of egg patterns and stonefly nymphs, little about steelhead flies points to any actual life-form—or at least our perception of life in the natural world. Nearly all steelhead flies are part of a design spiral, approximations of patterns that have worked in the past, coupled with our own ideas of features we hope will improve the fly.

Hence the Design Spiral Double, my latest in a long line of muddlers. To review: I came to steelheading in the wake of Bill McMillan's seminal work, *Dry Line Steelhead*, which advocated the use of floating lines and surface patterns at a time when most steelheading was done with sinking lines (and one-handed rods), in the belief that "steelhead are uninclined to move from river depths." Like McMillan, I caught my first steelhead on the surface using a traditional Muddler Minnow, and I soon started tying McMillan's Steelhead Caddis, a pared-down, sparsely dressed muddler that McMillan relied on, in various colors, from May through October—and sometimes even during warm spells in winter.

I learned the basics of a variety of surface presentations with the Steelhead Caddis. But it wasn't until I created my own waking muddler, replacing the dubbed body of the Steelhead Caddis with floss and tinsel and eliminating entirely the mottled turkey wing, that I began to consider that there might be truth to McMillan's claim (one made by Roderick Haig-Brown as well) that given water temperatures common in late summer and fall, surface methods will move more steelhead per hour of casting time than any other single level of presentation.

I've been fiddling with my waking muddlers ever since. Some years I believe in them more than others. This year, when I arrived home after spending another summer in my beach yawl *Madrina* on Magdalena Bay, I took a morning off from end-of-season boat maintenance and pedaled my bike into a favorite run. I tied on a Green Butt Muddler, a later pattern to come out of my own muddler design spiral. In the heart of the run, a big fish came up and ate.

A really big fish.

I'm still astonished when it happens. And for some reason I often believe that surface patterns generally move smaller, feistier steelhead—not a thirty-five-inch wild buck that's clearly closer to fifteen pounds than twelve.

Back at the tying bench, I sorted through a pile of waking muddlers from previous seasons. Some I stripped completely down to the bare hook before retying; others I simply replaced the spun deer hair head and collar. After sifting through the whole lineup, I spiraled back to both my earliest and latest muddlers—and came up with a new pattern, as of yet unnamed, a pretty little thing with a red floss abdomen and a thorax of peacock herl dyed red.

The next morning, on a fresh stretch of river, none of these waking muddlers—neither the revitalized nor the new—touched a fish. How could they refuse?

Then I turned to my doubles.

That evening, while steelhead baked in the oven, I called Jeff Cottrell. When I told him I rose a fish on a waking double, he was as delighted as if I had announced I had a new girlfriend.

"Things move the water, don't they?"

Two states away, I could still see Jeff smiling while shaking his head.

"I couldn't believe it," I said. "Came out of nowhere and ate it."

"It's a miracle every time."

DESIGN SPIRAL DOUBLE

- **Hook:** #6-8 Wilson 02 Double, Daiichi D7131, or similar
- **Thread:** Black 8/0 UNI-Thread
- **Tail:** Natural deer hair
- **Abdomen:** Gold Mylar tinsel (large)
- **Rib:** Oval silver tinsel (extra small)
- **Thorax:** Peacock herl
- **Wing:** Squirrel tail, dyed green
- **Overwing (optional):** Peacock Krystal Flash or other bit of flash
- **Head/collar:** Sparse deer hair, spun and trimmed with a dozen or two strands left straying back

Tying the Design Spiral Double

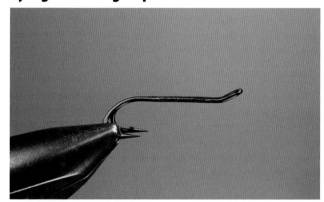

1. Install the hook in the vise. The hook shown in the photos is the Daiichi D7131, heavier than the Wilson 02. Most modern vises can be swung forward and aft as well as rotated so that your double hook is positioned appropriately, just as it will ride in the water.

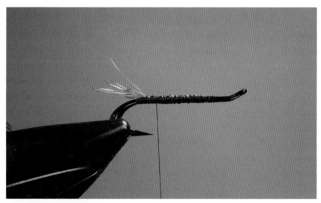

2. Before tying in the tail, wind your thread all the way back to the bend of the hook, then forward so that your thread hangs even with the points of the hook. Tie in a short tail of about a half-dozen deer hair tips. Set the tail on top of the thread wraps that extend back to the bend of the hook so that your tail doesn't slip down between the hook bends.

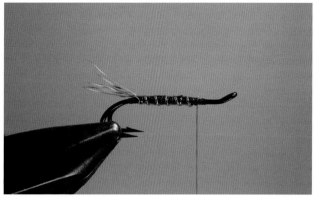

3. Just forward the root of the tail, first tie in a 4-inch length of Mylar tinsel and then tie in a 4-inch length of oval tinsel. Advance your thread so that it's about one-third the shank back from the hook eye. Wind the Mylar forward, secure, and clip excess. Then wind the oval tinsel rib in the opposite direction, making four to six evenly spaced wraps before securing and clipping the excess.

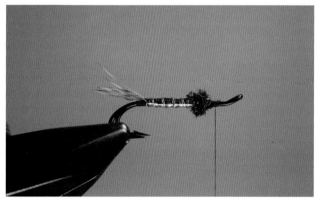

4. Create a dubbing loop, wax the legs of it, and slip in a pair of peacock herl. Spin your loop to create a tight, dense rope of peacock herl. Wind the rope to create a pronounced peacock herl thorax.

5. Clean and stack a small tuft of squirrel tail. Tie the tuft as a wing directly in front of the peacock herl thorax. The thorax will help the wing stand proud.

6. For the optional overwing, tie in two to four strands of Krystal Flash on top of the wing. I've experimented with other materials, none of which—including the Krystal Flash—offer conclusive evidence that it matters.

7. Selecting and spinning deer hair for these and other sparsely dressed muddlers is the skill you want to master. It's the essence of this genre of waking fly; at times I think the rest of the dressing is inconsequential, a thought that does nothing to keep me from trying to improve these patterns. For all of your waking muddlers, clean and stack a tuft of soft deer hair. Not too much—you're not trying to tie a skater. In fact, on a slack line, this is a fly that will sink. Lay the tuft of deer hair on top of the hook; take two *very loose* wraps around the deer hair just back from the eye hook. Slowly tighten the thread, encouraging the deer hair to spin around the hook shank. If you don't get an even distribution of hair around the hook, gently loosen tension on the thread and tighten again. Then make several tight wraps through the flared ends of the deer hair while working the thread forward. Finally, force back all of the butt ends of the hair and hold them back with thread wraps and your whip-finish. Trim the butt ends and most of the hair that extends back along the rest of the fly; trim to form a small, sparse muddler head. Leave just enough stray hairs to enclose the fly; I like the stray hairs to extend anywhere from the point to the bend of the hook. Lacquer the thread wraps at the head.

BRUCE'S LITTLE RED STEELHEAD NYMPH

Bruce's Little Red Steelhead Nymph, designed by Bruce Milhiser

There's a certain kind of day on a certain kind of water when all I try to do is catch a fish.

I know it sounds goofy. What am I trying to do the other days? But most anglers know what I'm talking about, a technique or style of fishing they turn to—oftentimes reluctantly—when all they care about is bringing a fish to hand.

Suddenly the fantasies and far-fetched schemes no longer matter. You're not a character in a story. I'm reminded of how, way back when, I used to claim if I were in Baja with a family to feed, I could get the job done with my nine-foot jigging rod, a Penn Jigmaster filled with 20-pound-test Maxima, and a handful of chrome Krocodiles and rubber Scampis.

But at that point in my angling career, I no longer wanted to fish that way. Instead, I wanted to hurl a heavy shooting head out beyond the surf line, eager to discover what a concoction of colorful fur and feathers, lashed to a big fly hook, could deceive.

I'm still a fool for the fabulous. It's not the two-foot wild rainbows that hold me a second week this summer in a tent and hundred-degree heat—but rather the chance, at dusk, to raise one more of these beasts to a size *8* dry fly.

And I refuse, on all counts, to calculate the hours I've wasted watching the wake of a sparsely dressed muddler wrinkling the glossy stream, hoping once more for a steelhead to enliven this feckless dream.

●————————●

It's hard to say what brings me down from the clouds. Sometimes it's a friend catching fish while, casting about, I feel like a lost cause sitting in right field watching the butterflies. Or there's a woman involved. Or it occurs to me that time is finite: Before the story unfolds, who's to say I don't up and die?

Usually, however, it's a matter of simple curiosity:
Are there fish here?
What kind?
What do they look like?
How big?

Given I've a fly rod in hand, the surest way I know to answer these questions is with a couple of nymphs—sometimes weighted, sometimes not—and a technique that I call, just as others do, tight-line nymphing. This isn't anything new. For most accomplished fly fishers, in fact, this kind of nymphing is second nature: sink the flies, come up tight by lifting line off the water, *lead* the cast through the lie without actually pulling the flies out of their natural, drag-free drift. Of course, sometimes there's split shot involved. The aim is to *stay connected* to your flies. If a fish eats, or if you touch rock or bottom, you know immediately—while at the same instant the tip of the rod has already begun to rise.

It's as subtle as bait fishing. And just as effective. Yet for many fly fishers, this type of presentation remains mysterious. Or, worse, held in disdain or disregard. They believe the dry fly—the most elegant aspect of the sport—is also the most challenging way to catch fish. Actually, dry-fly fishing is much, much easier than effective nymphing.

To recognize a practiced nympher, all you have to do is watch how long it takes the angler to notice a bottom-stalled or hung-up fly. The novice or inexperienced nympher won't be aware the fly has stopped moving until current draws the leader tight—oftentimes long after the fly stopped fishing. The experienced hand, however, lifts immediately—just as he or she would were it a fish that intercepted the drifting fly.

All of which comes to mind recently as I scramble at first light down a steep embankment, crowded with oaks, above the mouth of a tributary still frequented, on occasion, by sea-run fish. Along with these anadromous species, it's also rumored that resident trout have shown up in the final mile-long stretch now that obstacles to in-stream migrations have been removed. I really don't know what I'm fishing for—although any time anyone mentions steelhead, I'm hard-pressed to ignore even the remotest possibility.

Faced with no clear objective, I carry a ten-foot 6-weight, a rod I found years ago on the bottom of the Poudre River, in Colorado, while peddling books through the West. The rod isn't quite right for any of the fishing I do; by that I mean I nearly always have a diffcrent rod I choose when I know what I'm fishing for. But with a little more length and a little more backbone than normal, this is a rod I can fish practically anywhere and feel like I'm in the game, whether it turns out I need to deliver a dry fly at sixty feet or muscle up on a fish I would have rather dealt with on a double-handed rod.

And it's a terrific nymphing tool. One problem with a longer single-handed rod is the extra effort it takes to wave it through the air. If you're just plopping nymphs upstream, the added length hardly matters. And once the cast is made and it's time to lift line off the water and come into contact with your fly or flies, and then you begin to fish the cast as if trying to paint a floor with a brush dangling from a string, that extra foot of rod gives you that much more control while probing the depths of a moving stream.

Even if you fish with a bobber, you want to establish and maintain contact with your float, which usually means keeping as much line off the water as possible.

I reach the river with the help of a rope someone has tied to the trunk of an oak and left dangling down the trail. The river has cut a deep slot tight to the base of the bank; a wading staff and a cinched belt above my belly get me to the start of a broad tailout, formed by freestone tumbling out of the canyon now that the upstream dam has been removed. The river here is a hundred yards wide. It braids its way through channels and shallow riffles as if water from a hose running across sand, the patterns and contours of hydrodynamics as easy to read as a grade-school primer.

Cool air hovers above the chill currents. Against the far bank I find another deep slot, this one as perfectly proportioned as a meadow stream. *Well, let's just see what we have here*, I think, standing ankle deep in a spill of water tumbling over a lip of loose stones. And because of the hints and rumors, and my feel for these things, I add a length of tippet to the bend of the hook of an October Caddis pupa, and to that I tie on a little red nymph that I learned about from the best fly fisher I've ever known.

●━━━━━━●

I've mentioned this before: Bruce Milhiser doesn't think much of steelhead. "They're dumb," he says. "Put a fly in front of them, they'll eat it."

Of course, finding steelhead to put a fly in front of is another matter altogether.

Bruce considers his nymph a last resort. (He also ties it in black, purple—and probably other colors he hasn't shown me.) Like many traditional steelheaders, he prefers his flies served up swung. If there's irony whatsoever in this streamy fly tale, it's that I'll tie on Bruce's little red nymph not as a final option, but as a first choice when I just want to catch *something*.

It's a good fly for that. Obviously, there's something *eggy* about the pattern, a crucial aspect in any attempt to insert deceit into the food chain of a drainage with sea-run fish. What *are* fish doing, anyway, down in the final reach of a freestone wash spilling out of a deep, forested canyon?

Bruce's little red nymph can help answer that question—plus the others you might have when you feel the point really is to catch a fish. A couple of drifts down the far-bank slot and my plucky nymph fools a slender, square-headed steelhead, all of twenty-two inches, a wild fish aimed who knows where. Just below this, I hook and land a chunky fourteen-inch trout. Then another ten steps downstream, where the current slows, a standard-issue whitefish resigns itself to the tug of my line, the red nymph pinned to its lip as though the glowing ember of a cigarette in a 1950s Hollywood movie.

For a start, at least, that tells me all I need to know.

BRUCE'S LITTLE RED STEELHEAD NYMPH

- **Hook:** #6 TMC 2457
- **Bead:** Gold Cyclops Bead Eye (³⁄₁₆")
- **Weight:** .025 lead wire
- **Thread:** Red Danville 140-denier Waxed Flymaster
- **Tail:** Red rabbit fur from Zonker strip
- **Shellback:** Lagartun flat gold tinsel (small)
- **Rib:** Copper wire (small)
- **Abdomen:** Red UNI-Mohair
- **Thorax:** Seal fur, dyed red, or red Angora goat

Tying Bruce's Little Red Steelhead Nymph

1. Slide the bead over the point of the hook and up tight to the eye. Secure the hook in the vise with the eye tipped down. Wrap ten turns of lead directly behind the bead. Slide the lead wraps tight against the bead. Start your thread directly behind the lead. Build a dam of thread wraps to hold the wraps of lead in place. Advance the thread over the lead and up to the hook eye; return the thread to the built-up dam. Continue to wrap thread behind the lead, creating an even taper between the lead and the shank of the hook.

2. Wind your thread deep into the bend of the hook. Adjust the hook as necessary so that you can secure the tail almost perpendicular to the eye of the hook. Clip a tuft of hair from a Zonker strip. Tie in a tail, no more than the length of the hook shank behind the bead. Cut the excess tail material at an angle and continue to use thread wraps to create a fair taper throughout the length of the hook.

3. For the rib and the shellback, first secure a length of copper wire forward the root of the tail, then a length of small gold tinsel. With your thread still near the root of the tail, secure a length of UNI-Mohair. Advance the thread to the lead wraps. Create the abdomen with wraps of mohair, again trying to create an even taper throughout. Leaving yourself plenty of room for the thorax, secure the forward turns of mohair and clip excess.

4. Pull the gold tinsel over the back of the tapered abdomen. Secure and clip excess. Now make five or six evenly spaced wraps of copper wire around the abdomen, keeping the tinsel shellback straight along the back of the fly. Secure the copper wire forward the abdomen and clip excess.

5. Create a dubbing loop. Wax the legs of the loop. If you like seal dubbing as much as I do, you can get it through John McLain at FeathersMc.com. (The story is that somebody got a hold of old Russian army coats, lined in seal fur, and harvested and dyed the stuff.) Angora goat is a fair substitute. Spread the fibers along the legs of the dubbing loop, then spin your dubbing tool to create a spiky rope. Wind the rope forward to create a plump, hairy thorax that pushes up tight against the bead. Secure with your thread.

6. To tie off behind a bead, I always wax my thread and whip-finish, which helps the thread slide through the hitches. A drop or two of lacquer behind the bead is useful if you can avoid the thorax dubbing.

ALLY'S SHRIMP

Ally's Shrimp, designed by Alastair Gowans

Deep into steelhead season, it's easy to grow fidgety. Among those of us who practice faithfully, who hasn't buckled beneath the temptation to abandon whole hog what's worked in the past, to discard the very flies and even techniques we've relied on in the past? It's a grim moment when we unfold our treasured leather wallets and every fly inside looks as tantalizing as a beach ball. Yech. You might as well have flung open your closet, anticipating a hot date, and found yourself staring into a tangle of paisley shirts rimmed with scimitar collars, jumpsuits jeweled with studded lapels, and bell-bottom slacks sporting hems inside which you could hide a pair of spirited Yorkies.

I would like to advise you to resist: In steelheading, more than any other type of fly fishing, your fly is the last thing that matters. I know the thesis is heretical; that doesn't make it any less true. Still, avid steelhead anglers will often find themselves in need of some sort of elixir, a new pattern that promises fresh results in the face of futility and frustration, protracted failures that threaten to sap one's will to simply suit up and cast a line. *We are fueled by hope, nourished by new rhymes.* By all counts, successful steelheaders keep their flies in the water, the only place they've ever worked, believing in what can seem, at times, nothing short of a

miracle—a religiosity that returns, again and again, to the idolatry paid the new fly.

•————•

I came to this one by way of doubles. As mentioned in an earlier section, after years admiring some sparsely dressed double-hooked flies tied and given to me by Jeff Cottrell, who had seen such patterns used to great effect by British anglers fishing for sea-run brown trout in Tierra del Fuego, I finally knotted one to a leader and immediately hooked and landed a small steelhead.

I went home and tinkered with Cottrell's patterns, eventually settling on a design of my own, the Design Spiral Double, a fly that incorporates materials and design elements from other patterns that have proven successful for me on the handful of steelhead rivers I frequent throughout the year. Did I catch more steelhead with this pattern? More than I've caught in other years? Don't be silly. But I fished the fly often enough, and so when fish were caught, it was often the catcher, if not necessarily the cause.

What intrigued me most about the fly, however, was that pair of canted hooks on which it swam so seductively at the end of my line. *What's up with that?* I wondered. Why is it, in fact, the Brits and Scots and Irish remain so enamored with doubles, while stateside you can hardly find hooks on which to tie such flies, much less anglers who fish doubles—or who have any sense at all of their place and purpose in the long history of the sport.

I bought some books, tied some more flies, caught some more steelhead. As an old surfer and practicing boatbuilder, I began to recognize how significant it was to have a fly swimming in current with two hooks—aligned symmetrically, along a fore-and-aft center line—instead of just one. For decades now we've heard the claim that the most important concern in fly design is size and profile—with color a distant yet still important consideration. What you don't hear much about, however, is *action and attitude*—the two attributes that go so far in distinguishing those flies we know as doubles.

Action is a pretty simple concept to get your mind around. A dry fly needs to float. Wet flies, fished downstream, come alive in current. Tension on the line causes either the materials out of which the fly is tied to flex and bend and sway, as if laundry in the wind, or the entire fly itself to respond, which is the real point of those big keel-like quill wings on so many traditional patterns.

Action, in other words, generally refers to a fly fished under tension. In the case of steelheading, that means a fly fished on the swing. Much attention, of course, has been paid to getting more and more action out of our steelhead patterns, a trajectory that reaches its sublimest orbits in the realm of modern Spey flies, and an all but ungodly outer limit with the octopus-like Intruders. What these patterns share, of course, is their focus on soft or pliant or willowy materials. That creates one kind of action.

But if you want a very different kind of change of action in an object moving through the current, whether water or wind, drop two fins or keels off the hull—and watch what happens then. We're not just talking about wiggles and squirms, twists and shivers and shakes. Now you have an aerodynamically designed creature that *swims*, not one merely dangling from the end of your line. If I'm overstating my case, it's not by much. Watch a Brit with a two-hander hang a fly tied on a double down into the current of an Atlantic salmon run. If the fly's swimming, it's fishing. If it's fishing—well, you know what can happen next.

Along with action, we have attitude, a second often-overlooked aspect of fly design. Attitude has nothing to do with any anthropomorphic or metaphorical behavior of your fly. Instead, attitude is the position of the fly in the water; it's the reason that a properly designed nymph, like a Hare's Ear, rides in the water column the same way as the naturals rising from the bottom on their way to emergence.

In the case of a steelhead fly, attitude pertains to whether the fly stays upright—or at least how it was designed to ride in the current—throughout the course of its swing. Many modern flies are designed to eliminate this problem by offering up a profile with no top or bottom nor even sides. That's pretty much your Woolly Bugger, your Egg-Sucking Leech, or again, an Intruder. Flies meant to imitate salmon eggs are tied "in the round" as well. I don't think there's one thing wrong with that. But if your fly is supposed to mimic something that's alive and that live critter has a front and back, a top and bottom, a head and tail or the like, you probably want it to behave like the real thing behaves, which means it doesn't swim with its belly pointed toward shore—nor practices spontaneous capsize drills wherever the current quickens.

Along with the swimming action imparted on swinging flies, patterns tied on double hooks stand the best chance of maintaining the upright attitude they hold while secured in your vise. Does it really matter?

Sheesh . . . Do I have to answer that *again*?

How I happened to end up with Scotsman Alastair Gowans's famous shrimp pattern, the Ally's Shrimp, as my go-to double this season remains anyone's guess. Like all successful steelhead patterns, this one offers the visual and even visceral appeal so necessary in order for the angler to commit to and maintain faith in a fly. It's also fairly easy to tie, with just enough in the way of old-school materials to make you feel like you've tapped into something timeless and true, not the latest craze pushed on us by marketers.

Shrimp patterns also make a lot of sense for fish that have spent much of their adult lives in tidewater and at sea; the great A. J. McClane said it took him years to find a good shrimp imitation before discovering the old Horner Shrimp, the Eel River classic from nearly eighty years ago. My friend the fish biologist Joe Kelly did point out to me, however, that there's a good reason shrimp patterns in general are so much more popular in the British Isles than here in the States: In Ireland and the UK, he noted, you're rarely fishing for anadromous fish beyond sight or scent of the sea.

Still, any pattern that brings steelhead to hand with any regularity soon finds itself getting nudged toward the top of the private and generally short lineup that most serious steelheaders employ throughout the year. I recommend you choose at least one double, Ally's Shrimp or not, to insert into that select group. Always check the regs to make sure such flies are legal—and if they are, give one a try. Just as learning to cast a two-handed rod can keep you amused enough that your fly stays in the water, the only place it will eventually hook a fish, exploring the unique capabilities of a swinging double-hooked fly can stir your interest, curiosity, speculation—necessary ingredients for staying keen during the hunt.

Keep a double fishing, it will eventually catch a fish. I guarantee it.

ALLY'S SHRIMP (VARIANT)

- **Hook:** #6-10 Daiichi 7131 double salmon
- **Thread:** Red Pearsall's Gossamer Silk or fire orange 8/0 UNI-Thread
- **Tag/rib:** Oval silver or gold tinsel (small)
- **Tail:** Bright orange bucktail
- **Body:** Rear half, orange or red floss; front half, black floss
- **Underwing:** Natural gray squirrel tail
- **Overwing:** Golden pheasant tippet, tied horizontal
- **Hackle/collar:** Orange hen hackle

Tying the Ally's Shrimp

Note that I'm labeling this a "variant" because I'm including options, and I don't want to be accused by any classicists out there of tweaking the original pattern. The Alastair Gowans Ally's Shrimp was mostly red; I've had as much luck with an orange variation tied by another Scotsman, Davie McPhail. A quick online search will lead you to videos of both men tying versions of the fly.

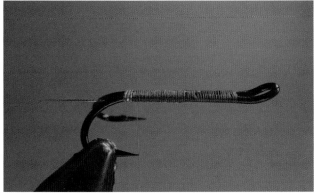

1. Secure the hook in the vise. I can find the Daiichi 7131 at most places I buy tying supplies, though it has nothing in the way of the elegant curves seen in many doubles sold overseas. Start your thread directly behind the eye of the hook. After a half-dozen turns back along the hook shank, lay your tinsel along the top of the shank and continue to wind over it until the thread hangs directly over the hook points. Catch the tinsel at the Y where the hook splits and make three or four turns for the tinsel tag. Then pull the tinsel forward under the hook shank and wrap thread over it, then pull the tinsel back toward the bend of the hooks and wind your thread back along the hook shank to the front edge of the tag. The extra tinsel will later be used for the rib of the fly.

2. Use a small bunch of orange bucktail for the tail. The tail should be about twice the length of the hook. Stack the hairs, then secure the root of the tail directly in front of the tag, beginning with light wraps of thread so that the bucktail doesn't flare. Trim the butt ends of the bucktail at an angle, then work your thread forward and back with tighter wraps, trying to maintain an even substrate for the floss body.

3. Secure a length of orange floss for the rear half of the body. Advance the thread halfway up the length of the body. Wrap the aft half of the body with the orange floss, secure it with thread wraps, and clip excess. With black floss, do the same for the forward half of the body. Proportions are always easier to get wrong on larger flies; this half-and-half body should end well back from the hook eye, leaving yourself plenty of room for the wing, the hackle, and the head.

4. Rib the floss body by winding the tinsel forward in evenly spaced wraps, about two turns for each half of the body.

5. There are two ways to go after the squirrel tail underwing. You can either tie in a small bunch of hairs on top of the fly and then on the underside or "spin" a larger tuft of hair around the fly, much like spinning deer or elk hair around a muddler, teasing and combing the squirrel hair as you tighten and loosen and tighten and loosen your first few wraps of thread. Either way, you want the tips of the underwing to extend no farther than the middle of the length of the tail.

6. Select a single small golden pheasant tippet feather, either the natural orange or one dyed red, for the overwing. Both Gowans and McPhail have a method to get the tippet feather to lie flat or horizontally atop the fly. I find it easiest to spin the feather back and forth between thumb and forefinger, rolling the barbules into a bunch, and then tying in the feather so that the tips extend to the tinsel tag. Now tap the tippet feather with your finger—it should open up flat on top of the fly.

7. Select a hackle feather with barbules that, when the feather is tied in, will extend to about the hook points. Prepare the feather by stripping off the barbules opposite the side of those that you want to extend back toward the aft end of the fly when you tie in the feather by its tip. Secure the tip of the feather. Make three or four turns of the hackle feather, one in front of the other, using your fingers to help the barbules lie toward the aft end of the fly. Catch the hackle stem under a few thread wraps and cut off the excess. Then create a tidy head, whip-finish, and saturate the thread with lacquer or head cement.

BADGER SHRIMP

Badger Shrimp, adapted by author from various Irish patterns derived from Pat Curry's original Red Shrimp

One of the grave misconceptions shared by many inexperienced or misled fly fishers is that the best flies are those that look most like the insect or other animal we hope to imitate or represent. Experienced hands have just as much appreciation as anyone for a fly that looks exactly like a real mayfly or caddisfly or whatever, yet on the water they're generally more inclined to reach for patterns that appear, in hand, to replicate nothing at all encountered along the stream. The list is long, but one need only glance at a lineup of well-loved patterns—from soft hackles to Humpys, Hare's Ears to Beetle Bugs and Chernobyl Ants—to resist the dubious claim that the flies we want on the ends of our lines are the ones that look the most, through our eyes, like what we see floating on or swimming in the water.

Take a Wulff, for example. Ignore the royal version, those absurd Christmas colors that make it and, say, the Royal Coachman such ridiculously effective searching dry flies despite nothing in any stream I've visited that resembles tree ornaments fluttering about the surface. Instead, perch a Gray Wulff in your palm, and now try to tell me that chunky body and those frizzy calf tail or deer or moose hair wings look anything like any part of any real mayfly you've seen. Even an Adams puts a Gray Wulff to shame. Yet how well I still remember, forty years ago and counting, the look of a Peter Syka Gray

Wulff wobbling down amongst the big drakes sprinkled about a ribbony pool on Yellowstone's Pelican Creek and thinking, *My God, it's a perfect match*—when suddenly Peter's fly disappeared in a swirl of fish and current that simultaneously pulled me under, a dunking from which, apparently, I've never quite emerged.

The notion, of course, is that rather than replicating exactly what we see when we look at an insect or other potential fish fare, many successful patterns are made up of elements that give fish the *suggestion* or *impression* of something on which they feed. And even that's a fairly bold presumption. We often know what fish are feeding on, yet just as often the pattern that does the trick isn't one in our box that has anything to do with a particular hatch or whatnot going on. Or maybe it does, but we just don't see the connection.

And it's also no small matter that we catch fish on the flies we fish with—*not* ones that remain in our box.

All of which brings me to a new pattern—or, better, pattern *type*—that's trying to insinuate itself into my steelhead lineup. And maybe even into my select corps of saltwater flies as well. The Badger Shrimp comes out of a long tradition of Irish salmon flies, the first of which appears to have been created over a hundred years ago by a fellow named Pat Curry, from Cleraine, on the River Bann. Curry's Red Shrimp has spawned dozens of other similar Irish shrimp patterns, none of which look particularly shrimp-like, at least not to the degree of imitations favored by American tyers, patterns with eyes, antennae, and realistic carapaces, shiny and segmented, just like the shells that pile up while we enjoy our fresh boiled shrimp and a pitcher of mojitos.

Maybe it's a cultural thing. Across the board, flies tied and fished throughout Ireland and the UK are rarely the sort of precise imitations that we often favor stateside. One glance at, say, a Grey Duster, Greenwell's Glory, Iron Blue Dun, or any of the Yorkshire or North Country Spiders, and it's easy to shrug your shoulders and think—*whatever*. Whether patterns fashioned for lough trout, resident river or sea-run trout, or even Atlantic salmon, Irish and UK tyers seem less inclined to attempt a photocopy-like image of bug or beast than they are an impressionistic suggestion of the critter—or even just the essential elements of the bait.

It might also have to do with a historical perspective. Given the long reach of the sport of fly fishing in Irish and UK waters, anglers may be less apt to chase after the latest and greatest pattern or fly-tying product. (Of course, they *would* if somebody could prove the latest and greatest actually fooled more fish.) I think it's also safe to say that, for whatever reason, you don't see in Irish and UK fly-fishing circles nearly as much hype about synthetics and other technologically advanced tying materials as we commonly embrace this side of the Atlantic.

What I'm really trying to get at, however, is this notion that the Badger Shrimp and other shrimp patterns popular for decades in Ireland and Scotland and England trace a lineage inspired by a very different approach to fly tying than many American fly fishers favor. Like the Ally's Shrimp, the Badger Shrimp caught my attention simply because it appealed to some sense I've developed, over two decades of serious steelheading, of what makes a good steelhead fly. Or what *I* like in a steelhead fly. Truth be known, I'm not sure whether the efficacy of these patterns has anything to do with their shrimpish attitude or appearance. All I know is that the first time I dangled an Ally's Shrimp, tied on a double hook, in a steady but no way strong current, precisely the speed that holding steelhead favor, I thought, *Wow, look at that thing swim.*

Same with the Badger Shrimp. Only in this case, it wasn't just the *action* of the fly. Rather, something unique happens when the two individual badger hackles get wet and work against the current. These two dark-centered hackles, along with the tail wound from a single golden pheasant red breast feather, common to most Irish and Scottish shrimp patterns, certainly wave and waggle and pulse in the current. But what I had never seen before was how those wet two-tone hackles create the illusion of a much bigger, semitransparent, segmented body—exactly what you expect a real, live swimming shrimp to look like in the water.

That's my point. Since 3-D printers, say, can now produce perfect models of eyes, elbows, and other human organs, I'm sure they could create a precise facsimile of a lowly shrimp. But would it fool fish? Aren't there, in fact, other elements besides photocopy realism that make some flies more successful than others?

Certainly, we'll never know much more than that some flies work better than others. And, often, one day's different from the next. That's the good news; few of us go fishing because we like to step in the river to do exactly what other anglers do.

In *Flies of Ireland*, author Peter O'Reilly offers a list created by "renowned gillie" Robert Gillespie of his top ten shrimp patterns. To my eyes, all ten of these flies look pretty much the same—variations, that is, on the same basic theme. And none of them looks particularly shrimpy—not as something you would set, say, on a shelf and expect people to look at and recognize as the animal in question. But obviously Irish and UK fly fishers have come to an agreement on the general *look* of their shrimp patterns—and we can rest assured they wouldn't have arrived there if these flies didn't work.

The Badger Shrimp might well open eyes—and minds—to new ideas about the compelling aspects of a successful fly. Maybe it's time some of us moved beyond the one-dimensional idea that the pattern that looks the most "realistic" in the vise is one that will catch the most fish. The inherent alchemy of successful patterns in different regions and different waters should be embraced, not ignored. If nothing else, the Badger Shrimp and many other shrimp patterns from Ireland and the UK should inspire you to go out and purchase a complete golden pheasant skin, one of the great deals left for creative fly tyers anywhere. (I paid just over $10 US a couple of years ago.)

And, for the record, a Badger Shrimp does catch steelhead.

BADGER SHRIMP

- **Hook:** #6-12 single or double salmon
- **Thread:** Fire orange 8/0 UNI-Thread
- **Tag:** Oval or flat silver tinsel
- **Tail:** Red golden pheasant breast feather, wound
- **Rear body:** Golden olive seal fur
- **Rib:** Oval or flat silver tinsel
- **Middle hackle:** Creamy badger
- **Front body:** Black seal fur
- **Rib:** Oval or flat silver tinsel
- **Front hackle:** Creamy badger
- **Head:** Fire orange thread

Tying the Badger Shrimp

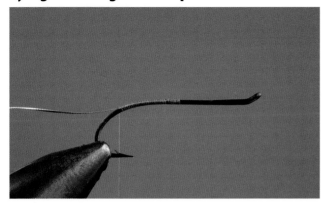

1. In *Flies of Ireland*, Peter O'Reilly claims that many anglers "make the mistake of fishing too big a Shrimp Fly." Size 10 are the most popular. Secure the hook in the vise and start your thread in the middle of the hook shank. Starting your thread in the middle of the hook helps clarify where the rear body ends and the middle hackle is placed. Secure a length of silver tinsel, covering it as you wind the thread back to the bend of the hook or, in traditionally curved hooks for sea-run fish, back to the point where the thread hangs about even with the barb (not the point) of the hook.

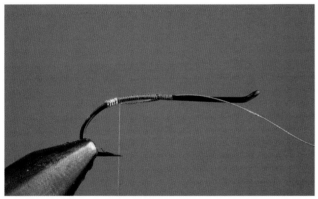

2. Advance the thread a half-dozen turns, then create your tag with three or four turns of tinsel. After securing the tinsel with thread wraps, leave the tinsel lying forward for now, so that it doesn't get in the way while tying in the tail of the fly.

3. The common feature in almost all Irish shrimp flies is the tail created by winding a single reddish feather from the breast of a golden pheasant. There are many ways to go about this; all of them share the problem of the delicate stem, especially toward the tip, which is the part of the feather with the best color. What you're trying to do is much the same as winding any soft hackle, with the barbs of the feather lying, in this case, aft of the bend of the hook. I tie my feather in by the tip and wind forward two or three turns, trying my best to stroke the barbs of the feather so they don't get caught under the stem wraps. At the same time, the tail should end up splayed; that's part of the reason for the tag, which keeps the tail from lying in a tight bundle. A look at other Irish shrimp patterns will show you just how bold and untidy this tail is generally tied.

4. Before dubbing the rear body of the fly, make sure you catch the tinsel under the thread and get it back where you can use it for ribbing. With the thread at the root of the tail, add your dubbing material to your thread. Here I'm tying what's really called a Badger & Golden Olive Shrimp; there are, however, endless variations of body color combinations, although most are a lighter color in back than in front. Wind your body to the midpoint of the hook shank, then rib this portion of the body with two or three turns of tinsel.

5. Clip a large hackle feather from a creamy badger neck; you're looking for those feathers with pronounced dark centers running down the length of them. You want the hackle fibers to be one and a half times the hook gap; if your feather is long enough, hold the convex side toward you, tip pointing to your right, and strip the barbs off the top side. Tie in the feather by the tip; hold the base of the stem and wind forward, each turn tight against the last, trying to keep the stem twisted so that the hackle fibers point aft, not perpendicular to the hook shank as in a bottle brush. Make four to six turns of hackle, secure, and clip excess.

7. For the forward hackle, repeat steps for the middle hackle. Clip the excess, then form a tidy head with thread wraps. Again, at this stage, you can also use thread wraps to help shape the lie of the forward hackles. Then whip-finish and saturate the head with lacquer or head cement.

6. Again, make sure your tinsel is now aft of the front body. Add dubbing material to your thread. When you start winding the body, you can force any errant hackle fibers you just tied in to align in a rearward direction. Wrap the front body, leaving plenty of room for the hackle and head. Then rib the body with two or three turns of tinsel.

RUSTY RAT

Rusty Rat, designed by Clovis Arseneault as a variation on the original Rat flies tied by Roy Angus Thompson

Few things capture the spirit of fly fishing quite like the school of thought that directs us to flies that look like nothing seen in nature. Once you forsake bait, of course, all angling becomes an abstraction—an artificial game that provokes the imagination because of a set of rules that limit the means by which we're allowed to attack the goal.

Just as fly anglers have all agreed you don't affix living creatures to the hook or fly to help catch fish, we're all pretty much in agreement that certain mechanical devices—small explosives, say, or even a cleverly arranged gill net—are, if not illegal, at least beyond the pale. As for the snagging capabilities afforded by small hooks dangling behind beads or the body of a fly, I've settled on the notion that fish attack the head of their prey, not the tail, bringing into question whether I actually fooled any fish that ends up pinned to a trailing hook.

Fooling fish, need I argue, is at the heart of the game. This is in large part why the dry fly—or any surface presentation, for that matter—is the quintessential and no doubt most satisfying aspect of our otherwise trivial pastime. When a fish moves to the surface and eats your fly, there's no question that you fooled it—although the reasons it fell for your ruse may remain very much in question. By way of contrast, watch, say, on video or in an actual stream, a trout holding near the bottom and plucking from the current this and that, bits and pieces that are immediately eaten or rejected as food—plenty of time for a tiny hook inside the interesting morsel to end up embedded in the fish's flesh.

But I'm not here to split hairs; readers should know by now that I'm a big fan of doing whatever it takes. Instead, my interest here lies in flies that make little or no pretense of replicating anything that inhabits the real world as we know it, but that are somehow intended to fool fish by power of an alchemy we can, at best, only intuit. Of course, followers might also note that I often argue the fly is the least important aspect of the game. True. Still, you do have to knot something to the end of your line.

Atlantic salmon flies, we know, have long epitomized patterns that seem concocted out of the imagination of tyers without regard for anything that exists in river or stream. Steelhead patterns can be much the same. Most experienced steelheaders eventually come to recognize that egg patterns, representing the spawn of various Pacific salmon, match the hatch, so to speak, better than any other type of steelhead fly. Yet few dedicated or ardent steelheaders stop there. Odd as it may sound, simply catching these elusive fish is rarely enough to keep us engaged over the long haul.

It's hard to say, however, what we're really after. That may be part of the appeal of a genuine steelheading career: If you are unclear what you're looking for, chances are you'll never claim to have found anything that leaves you with the sense of having arrived, of completing some finite goal, the sort of popular bucket list mentality that prompts so many of us to wipe our hands of one thing and move on to the next, as though what we were doing, in the past, was somehow not good enough, too shallow or, worse, not really what we wanted to be doing in the first place.

That's a long ways from fishing with flies that don't represent anything fish eat—or flies that might work when fish have little or no interest in eating at all. But I'll contend, vigorously, that it's the angler interested in fashioning baits or lures that have no apparent equal in the natural world who comes to fishing with the kind of creative energy that lasts a lifetime. There's *always* a new idea—or a long look back at what's worked in the past for reasons we might only now begin to glimpse or understand.

●————————●

The Rusty Rat is an old proven Atlantic salmon fly, especially popular in Canadian provinces along the Eastern Seaboard. It has several elements, however, that have found their way into steelhead patterns I've had my share of success with over the years. I actually first tied the fly to fish for landlocked migratory trout in water best covered with two-handed rods—more or less steelheading, without the cachet of fish returning from the sea.

The history of the pattern offers the sort of origin story, often apocryphal, common to so many old-timey flies. The first Rat-style flies, claim Dick Stewart and Farrow Allen in *Flies for Atlantic Salmon* (Lyons Press, 1991), were tied by Roy Angus Thompson—R.A.T.—in the early part of the twentieth century. The development of the *Rusty* Rat, goes the story, fell to the New Brunswick tyer Clovis Arseneault after Joseph Pulitzer (whose dad the prize was named after) had a Black Rat, tied by Clovis, begin to disintegrate following several hooked fish. This same fly, claimed Pulitzer, became even more effective when the rusty orange thread used beneath the black body started to show. A forty-plus-pound salmon, taken that same day from the famous Restigouche River, no doubt helped support Pulitzer's claim.

By the way, if you're interested in this kind of historical context, you might want to get your hands on one of the original 105 copies of *The Ristigouche and Its Salmon Fishing with a Chapter on Angling Literature*, first published in Edinburgh in 1888, with etchings and engravings and page decorations that combine to make some experts call this "the rarest and most beautiful book on salmon fishing." A copy sold in 2007 by Bonhams, of London, went for $18,000. Another copy is currently available at James Cummins Booksellers for $50,000—which, you'll be glad to hear, includes free shipping.

Even if you aren't inclined to delve so deeply into the history of flies and fly-fishing techniques that, surprisingly enough, still prove relevant today, you may find the Rusty Rat a step along the path toward a more expansive view of steelhead flies. Why one pattern works, and another one doesn't, will no doubt remain a mystery; it's also likely that when a steelhead does end up on the end of your line, it has little to do with the actual fly you chose to tie to your tippet.

In the face of what can often seem like variables beyond our control—a sense, even, that you've descended into a game of chance—the best advice I know is to fish flies that please you and leave it at that. The Rusty Rat is a fly I always feel good about; it looks like nothing but a fly that will catch fish. It's hard to go wrong with a feeling like that.

RUSTY RAT

- **Hook:** #2-4 Bartleet Salmon, TMC 7999, Alec Jackson Steelhead Iron, or similar
- **Thread:** Fire orange 8/0 UNI-Thread or similar
- **Rib:** Oval gold tinsel (small)
- **Tail:** Peacock sword fibers
- **Rear body:** Rust orange rayon floss, pumpkin UNI-Floss, or similar
- **Underwing:** Same as rear body floss
- **Forward body:** Peacock herl
- **Main wing:** Silver fox guard hairs, gray squirrel, or similar
- **Hackle:** Soft grizzly

Tying the Rusty Rat

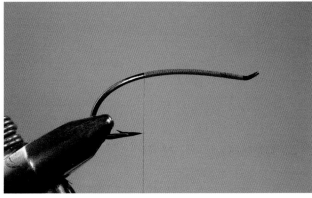

1. Secure the hook. Start the thread directly behind the eye of the hook. Cover the entire hook shank with an even layer of thread wraps. Stop wrapping the shank where the thread hangs even with the point of the hook.

RUSTY RAT | **181**

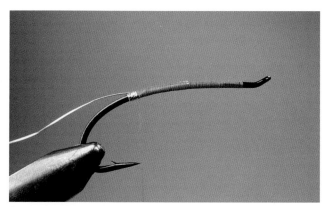

2. Measure the tag end of a generous length of tinsel so that it extends midway up the hook shank. This helps delineate the two halves of the body. Secure the tinsel directly above the hook point. Make eight to ten thread wraps toward the bend of the hook, then advance the thread back to the tinsel tie-in point. Now form the tinsel tag with five or six wraps of tinsel. Catch the tinsel with a turn or two of thread, then pull forward the long leg of the tinsel alongside the hook shank. Advance the thread forward to the midpoint of the hook shank, covering both the short tag length and the long leg. At the midway point of the shank, fold the long leg of tinsel back along the hook shank and start back with the thread until you reach the forward edge of the tag. The remaining tinsel, dangling aft, will be used later to rib the body of the fly.

3. For the tail, use five or six peacock sword feather fibers. Take advantage of the curl in the fibers, securing the bunch just forward of the tinsel tag so that the tail sweeps upward. The tail should end just shy of the bend of the hook.

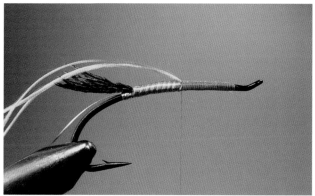

4. Tie in a length of floss just ahead of the tinsel tag. Advance the thread to the midpoint of the hook shank. Wrap the rear half of the body with floss; try to get the floss to lie flat. At the midpoint of the hook shank, catch the floss with a turn or two of thread. Clip the floss, leaving about 3 inches. Pull the floss forward and cover with even thread wraps up to the forward end of the body. Then pull the floss rearward and cover with thread wraps back to the aft half of the body.

5. For the front half of the body, secure two or three lengths of peacock herl. Clip the tips so that they reach the forward edge of the body, helping to keep the entire body fair and balanced. Advance the thread. Then wrap the peacock herl forward, in the opposite direction of your thread wraps, to the front of the body and secure with thread wraps.

6. Rib the body. Pull the floss underwing material out of the way (you can pull it forward and catch with a temporary turn of thread) and make three or four evenly spaced wraps of tinsel around the back half of the body. Then pull the underwing rearward and make three turns of ribbing through the peacock herl forward body. Now clip the underwing to length; it should end at about the midpoint of the tail. Certain flosses look better if you comb out and separate the individual strands.

7. For the main wing, clip a tuft of fur with plenty of guard hairs from the skin of a gray or silver fox. Hold the guard hair by their tips and pull away the underfur. (Save the underfur for dubbing other flies.) Align the guard hair tips in your hair stacker. Clip the butts of the guard hairs so that the wing, measured from the tie-in point, will end up just shy of the floss underwing. If you clip the guard hairs to length beforehand, you can catch the butts with your thread and, working your way aft, secure the wing with a smooth transition between the hook and the threads holding the wing.

8. For the hackle, choose a soft webby feather from the top or outside edge of a hackle neck. You want the hackle barbs to be about half the length of the main wing. Directly in front of the root of the wing, tie in the feather by its tip—tip pointing forward, good side of the feather facing you. Pull the hackle fibers rearward as you wrap the feather forward. Make three or four wraps, secure with your thread, and clip excess. Finally, tidy up any errant hackle fibers with thread wraps. Create a fair head, whip-finish, and saturate the head with lacquer or your favorite head cement.

PART THREE

Saltwater Flies

Jeffrey Feczko enjoys a moment admiring a handsome jack crevalle, aka *toro*, that he hauled through the surf outside of Bahía Magdalena, far from the madding crowd.

It seems remarkable that less than three decades ago, when Frank Amato published my first book, *Angling Baja*, fly fishing along the shores of the eastern Pacific remained an anomaly, sport favored by a small but growing number of anglers who finally realized they didn't have to drive to the High Sierra or Montana to cast a fly. I'd been at it a dozen years, at least, before the book reached print, but by then I had moved to Oregon, my sights on trout and steelhead, and the truth is I had begun to lose touch with the saltwater scene.

Then Gary Bulla called. The way he tells the story, his friend Yvon Chouinard, with whom Gary worked and fished, read *Angling Baja* and said something to the effect of "Who is *this* guy? Why don't we know him?" I flew south a couple of times and spoke at Gary's local fly-fishing club, and then finally we worked out a deal so that I could join him on one of his hosted kayak trips in the Sea of Cortez in exchange for a story I would write for *Fly Rod & Reel*.

That trip I realized what I had been missing. After getting dragged around atop kayaks by skipjack tuna and the like, the paying clients left and Gary and I found ourselves with an extra day to fish together. We hired Israel Lucero, one of the panga captains Gary uses for his bluewater trips, and a day of fighting dorado and small yellowfin tuna convinced me that this sort of sport was too much fun to ignore any longer.

Like a lot of Gary's friends and clients, I especially liked those big roosterfish his captains could find.

The wild coast of Isla Magdalena, on the Pacific side of the Baja California peninsula. It's hard to believe, but true, that there are still beaches in the region where nobody has ever cast a fly.

Roosterfish, *Nematistius pectoralis*, the stuff of every fly fisher's dreams. This average-size surf-caught specimen is the sort that has kept the author, and his home-built boats, haunting the Pacific beaches of Baja California Sur.

When my second son graduated from high school, I decided I needed to give both him and his older brother a taste of Baja before they slid further into the exigencies of their own lives. We joined Gary on a kayak trip he hosted each summer in Magdalena Bay. Much as I enjoyed the raucous panga fishing in the Sea of Cortez, there was something very different about Mag Bay that captured my imagination and sense of adventure. The untold miles of mangrove esteros, the dramatic tides pouring in and out of the wide surf-lined bocas, the sheer magnitude of a place that showed little evidence of gringo intrusions of the sort transforming the shores of the gulf—all of it begged for exploration with fly rods and flies.

Of course, there were plenty of other fly anglers before me with the same idea. Gary Graham had already written his *No Nonsense Guide to Fly Fishing Magdalena Bay*. But after I built my Iain Oughtred Sooty Tern, an open row-and-sail beach yawl I named *Madrina*, I began to explore Mag Bay and its islands and Pacific beaches in ways that led to fishing I'd never read about nor even dared to imagine.

It's been the best sport money can't buy.

Now there's a new boat cradled on the shop floor; I'm old enough I get tired of stretching out on *Madrina*'s floorboards, squeezed in between her starboard bench and centerboard trunk, my legs tucked under the rowing thwart. And cooking on a little stove positioned just so between my knees. Damn this age thing, anyway. Plus, here I am with another new job, with deadlines and duties and all the rest, and it feels like it's just going to get harder and harder each year to pull the plug and disappear into the mangrove for a month or two at a time, sliding this way and that on the swing of the tides.

Harder, perhaps, but not impossible.

I just need a day or two beforehand to tie up a few flies.

SOMEBODY'S MINNOW

Somebody's Minnow, author's adaptation of various saltwater baitfish patterns

The captain's knot is worth learning. Tied a little like a Palomar knot, a little like a Jansik special, it ends up resembling a perfection loop from which you've dangled the fly. A lot of anglers today like their fly hanging from a loose loop, the idea, of course, being that you get more movement or action or simply a more realistic presentation out of your cast. The captain's knot does all that, plus it has the advantage of using, when tied right, very little tippet material.

But I use it because I believe in it.

Panga fishing in Baja, you better believe in your knots. A big part of bluewater fishing anywhere, in fact, is finding out, over and over again, the weak link in your system—very often a knot that fails. If a knot gives, you need to learn how to tie it correctly—or try something new.

Still, like a kid who only gets to go fishing a time or two a year, I never seem to remember how Valente and the rest of the Lucero captains hang the fly off the tippet—at least not until I return to Baja and get back into the panga groove. At the start of a trip, I always feel like I'm trying to catch up, figuring out my rods and lines and reels, some of which I still borrow each year because, in case you haven't noticed, the shit's expensive—despite the economic drawdown.

One question, however, is why don't I use the captain's knot when I'm fishing for anything else—trout or steelhead or smallmouths or . . . whatever. And that's a really good question, an answer to which might go a long ways in revealing aspects of my character that I think we should just stop fishing for right now.

I have my reasons.

Well, okay . . . since *I* brought it up: The reason I haven't changed knots in my freshwater fishing is because I *never* change knots—or anything else in a system—that already works.

Or, to put it another way, I believe in knots, like most things, as long as they don't fail.

I told you an answer was going to reveal way too much about me.

But this isn't an essay about knots, anyway. Instead, I'm trying to ease my way into the subject of flies, flies that work and flies that don't work—or at least that don't work as well as others—and especially flies tied for panga fishing in Baja, or probably anywhere in the ocean as far as that goes, where the fish you're fishing for feed on other fish.

In other words, this is about minnows.

Now, traditionally, nearly all baitfish patterns were referred to—either in name or style of fly—as minnows.

Even when the fly was created to imitate a sardine or herring or other type of baitfish, the fly pattern was still, essentially, a *minnow*. Mostly this meant that the fly in question wasn't a crab or shrimp or some other crustacean pattern. Nor, significantly, a popper. Because there really aren't a heck of a lot of different things that fish feed on in the ocean (I mean that at the class/order level of taxonomy), a minnow became a basic *style* of fly, almost like classifying a trout pattern as either a dry fly, a wet fly, a nymph, or a streamer.

A minnow or other named baitfish pattern shares certain fundamental properties, so that regardless of color or materials or size or combination thereof, you still have a minnow or minnow-like pattern—a fly that represents small schooling fish that are preyed upon by the larger fish we're trying to catch.

This is all pretty obvious—just as obvious, for most anybody who thinks about such things, as how to fish such flies. If it's a minnow, you throw it out in the water, try to make it look like it's swimming (or maybe struggling to swim; or maybe dead, drifting, floating, or in some other fashion that makes it easy pickings) and hope the fish you're after, or anything else, mistakes it for a baitfish and eats it.

This isn't higher order thinking.

Which should not suggest, either, that it's necessarily easy.

There are a lot of things besides fooling fish with a minnow pattern that go into successful panga or bluewater fly fishing. I mentioned knots. I mentioned equipment. Of course, you have to know how to use this stuff to cast to fish, to hook, fight, and land them. These skills still probably don't employ the most sophisticated aspects of our thinking. Neither, perhaps, does hunting fish in the wide reaches of the oceans, along beaches and channels and reefs, through the movement of the sea as current and waves and tides under the influence of weather, wind, seasons, the sun, and the moon. Very little in this equation, in fact, seems to demand much in the way of reason, articulation, the subtleties of language, or the precision of music or math.

But it's still not easy.

Much of this fishing, I'd like to suggest, is more physical than mental, more intuitive, maybe even more emotional, than the logical problem-solving asked of us in trout fishing, say, as well as in our daily or living-earning lives.

A lot of times, out on the ocean blue, we just sort of seem to be winging it. And though that's probably truer, as well, about our day-to-day lives than most of us care to admit, it should go a long way in explaining why many fly fishers can't get enough of the sport I'm describing—that is, casting minnows to wild fish on the feed.

Many of us find it a relief sometimes to get out of our heads.

A minnow is just a minnow. Find fish. Throw it at them. If it's right, it'll work.

If not?

The fish will let you know.

●————————●

Minnows, in whatever color, size, or configuration, are the quintessential style of saltwater fly because they work. Lefty's Deceiver is a minnow pattern—which is probably sufficient evidence that a minnow will nearly always get you in the game. A Clouser, too, don't forget, is actually a Clouser *Minnow*. Here on the West Coast we also have, among many others, popular patterns such as Jeff Priest's Sardina, Gary Bulla's Tuna Tux, Larry Kurosaki's Larry's Minnow—all good flies, all available in a variety of sizes and colors, all essentially minnow patterns, all variations on the same theme.

And before Lefty's Deceiver, there was Joe Brooks's Blonde Series, simple minnows you might want to look at—and maybe even tie a few and fish—the next time you're wondering where to turn when faced with an overwhelming choice of different must-have minnows available, at five dollars a pop, from the catalogue or fly shop nearest you.

Or even that *really* old saltwater classic, the Hy-Tie.

Trying one of these early minnow patterns is kind of like knotting on a simple nineteenth-century soft hackle that, surprise surprise, ends up fooling its fair share of trout while looking like nothing, exactly, on which you've ever seen trout dine.

Still, we all know that *not just any minnow works*. Not all the time. Not everywhere. Which is how this drifting essay returns to the thesis, introduced in the subject of knots, that the right thing is whatever works.

Failure to catch fish—or, better, to *hook* fish—is the primary evidence most of us use in determining whether or not things are working. (I'm talking here about angling—not the larger ramifications of what it means when we aren't catching any fish at all in our lives.) Given the presence of fish, especially fish getting caught by others, when *we* don't catch fish, the first thing we generally question is the fly.

Fling your minnow in the path of a charging roosterfish, watch rooster rush the fly with its comb of spines erect and twitching, and now see said fish pivot like a barrel-racing pony and vanish in one instantaneous move, and you can be sure you'll wonder if you have the right fly affixed to the end of your line.

This fly doesn't work! goes the logic.

Or: *This fly sucks.*

Hence, the change of fly.

Hence, *Somebody's* Minnow.

Now, most experienced fly fishers know that the fly is rarely the issue. Or they *should* know that. Casting and presenting the fly have a lot more to do with your success than your choice of fly.

But it's easier to change flies than suddenly improve your game.

Still, when that roosterfish turns away, you *know* the right fly could have fooled him.

Or at least you think so.
Somebody's Minnow works.
And if it doesn't?
You'll probably want to try somebody else's.

Somebody's Minnow is no different than anybody else's minnow—besides the fact that it's tied to look like the baitfish you happen to be fishing around at any given place and time.

I'm reminded of the strange evolution of the Gold-Ribbed Hare's Ear in my trout fishing. Generally tied to represent a mayfly nymph, a Hare's Ear didn't become part of my regular lineup until I tied it in such a way that it looked more like certain caddis pupae common on the Deschutes—at which point I started fooling so many fish with it that my pal Fred Trujillo dubbed it my Wild Hare. Later, after I had worked up a pattern to use as a mayfly nymph for some snooty brown trout east of home, I showed Fred the fly, claiming it was exactly the same as a Hare's Ear, only tied out of *completely different materials.*

He knew exactly what I meant.

Somebody's Minnow is just like that. It's tied pretty much the same as every other minnow or baitfish pattern, except that you use certain materials unique to the pattern. Of course, color and size can change dramatically and you're still tying a *Somebody's* Minnow. In fact, *whose* minnow or baitfish pattern you choose to tie or use is hardly the point. What you want is a fly that swims through the water without any attributes that make fish refuse it.

That's a little bit of a different way to look at the problem. And it's not an original idea. Instead, Gary LaFontaine used to talk and write about it, the idea that fish are hardwired to say *yes* and only refuse our casts when we cause them (poor presentation, something about our fly) to say *no*. Fish need to eat. That's pretty much what they're built to do—that *and* reproduce, which requires most of the energy from the food they consume. So it's not like fish, by nature, are picky eaters—nor do they adhere, like vegans or those of us on the latest health-enhancing diet, to a prescribed list of foodstuffs they will and won't eat. Fish try to eat shiny metal lures, for crying out loud. You think that's on the menu?

Yet every fly fisher is acutely aware that fish do say *no*—that, in fact, they often refuse the fly. Thank God for that, I say. Wouldn't be much to think about (nor talk *or* write about) if fish always obliged our devious ways.

When I fish with one of the Lucero captains, I let him look through my flies and select those he likes best. More and more, they're nearly always *Somebody's* Minnow. If I'm fishing with Valente, one of the senior captains, he lets me finish my captain's knot and then he swings the leader over the side of the panga and pulls the fly through the water, inspecting how it looks—the size, the shape, the color—whether it *looks like the bait.*

What a concept. Most significant, however, is what Valente *doesn't* like to see—usually some kind of typical flashy saltwater material that shows up in the water like bits of neon light. Look at baitfish in the water and they practically never look like that. *Somebody's* Minnow is a simple, almost drab pattern tied with plain natural materials—sort of like an outfit of a good pair of khaki chinos and a no-nonsense cotton dress shirt. I'm all for the new, the bright, the space-age high-tech next-generation kumquat-fusion DNA fiber for tying flies. But I like it more when Valente pulls my *Somebody's* Minnow through the water alongside the panga, and then he turns to me and smiles and says, "*Ay, Papi.*"

SOMEBODY'S MINNOW

- **Hook:** #2/0 Owner Aki, Trey Combs Big Game, or similar
- **Thread:** White Danville 140-denier Flymaster
- **Tail:** White bucktail
- **Belly:** White calf tail
- **Upper body:** First layer, white bucktail; second layer, tan or light olive or dirty yellow bucktail or yak hair; third layer, natural brown or dark olive bucktail
- **Eyes:** Yellow or silver hologram (5/16")
- **Head:** UV-curing or five-minute epoxy

Tying *Somebody's* Minnow

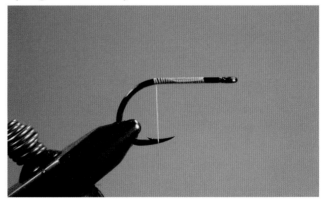

1. Secure the hook in the vise and start your thread. Of countless saltwater hooks on the market, I still have the most confidence in the classic, forged Owner Aki bait hook, adopted by saltwater fly fishers for both its strength and penetrating sharpness.

2. Clip a small tuft of hairs from a natural white bucktail. Even the tips of the hairs in an oversized hair stacker. Secure the hair just ahead of the hook bend; use light thread tension on the first few wraps to prevent the hairs from flaring, then increase the tension as you move the thread forward. Trim the hair butts and cover with an even layer of thread wraps.

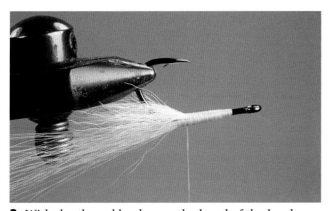

3. With the thread back near the bend of the hook, invert the fly in the vise jaws or by spinning the jaws of your rotating vise. Clip a small tuft of hair from a calf or kip tail. Remove any underfur from the longer hair fibers. Secure the hair to the underside of the hook; the tips of the belly hair should extend to about the middle of the tail.

4. Return the fly to an upright position. Select another tuft of white bucktail, align the tips in your hair stacker, then tie in the hair ahead of the root of the tail. This new layer of hair should extend approximately one-half or two-thirds the length of the tail.

5. Invert the fly again and tie in another bit of calf tail. Go easy here. Calf tail is dense; too much and the fly gets bulky and doesn't look—or swim—right. Now spin the fly upright again and select a tuft of tan (or light olive) bucktail, usually hair from the center of the same tail from which you find your white. Stack and tie this hair so that the tips lie just short of the previous layer.

6. The last layer of bucktail or similar material should be the darkest—brown or dark olive, depending on the bait you are trying to imitate. Again, the tips of this layer should extend just short of the previous layer. With the hair butts clipped, form a tidy head with thread wraps and then securely whip-finish.

7. Much can and maybe should be said about adding eyes and creating the epoxy head of a conventional saltwater fly. My caveat, right here at the start, is that I know one exceptional guide who doesn't bother with any of it, and he fishes circles around me, in large part because he sees fish and casts far better than I ever did or ever will. And he's swift afoot, has exceptional stamina, and has lots of other attributes that support a thesis that argues your fly is just a small part of the success equation, especially in salt and surf. Anyway, before the advent of UV-activated epoxy, I used needle-nose pliers with a rubber band around the handles to hold the front of the fly flat, making it easy to affix the eyes before creating a fair and solid head with five-minute epoxy. Fussing with five-minute epoxy, of course, is a pain in the neck, no longer necessary with the modern, UV-activated epoxies. I must add, however, that I find the new material a lot less durable than the earlier, messier product.

TRILOBITE

Trilobite, designed by Peter Syka

I've been fishing with Peter Syka, my latest guest at the Roost, for over forty years. Nobody needs to listen to a couple of old farts reminisce—yet it's worth noting, by way of context, that a friendship this long dates back to an era when, say, you could still grill a pair of Yellowstone cutthroat while meandering about the park. In the San Diego and Baja California surf, where Peter and I were lured into uncharted waters, the sport of saltwater fly fishing was not so much an anomaly as it was a kind of secret witchcraft concocted by bands of rogue anglers who, in their own isolated haunts, had fallen under the spell of midnight jinn or other potent spirits.

Time and experience, of course, are the sport's two great teachers. Which is why I feel especially lucky to have an old hand like Peter agree to drop by the Roost and share what he's been tying lately for the surf—specifically what he uses these days for targeting barred surfperch, day in and day out the species the southland surf angler can expect to catch between far-flung encounters with yellowfin and spotfin croaker, sand bass, corbina, halibut, or other more illustrious prey.

Savvy readers may question the intent. Does anyone really need a perch fly? Can't you catch them on *anything*?

Peter dismisses the question with a patient smile. This late in life, he's adopted a far-reaching generosity toward a kind of unfathomable ignorance and outright stupidity that once threatened to drive him mad. An important aspect of our friendship has always been his reluctance to buy into my own high-pitched shenanigans and half-baked schemes. He was the first person to point out to me that my second book, the screwiest of jury-rigged novels, was "unreadable." A lifelong scientist versed in the pop culture and political absurdities of the past half century, he asks little of others beyond a willingness to pay attention to what's going on.

Adjusting a Padres cap above the shadow-like reach of his still-dark and all but conjoined eyebrows, Peter reminds me that when he and I first tried perch fishing near home, flush with the big streamers and burgeoning baitfish tactics we had done so well with in the Baja surf, we made little if anything happen.

"Then I tied up a bunch of Skykomish Sunrises with bead-chain eyes," says Peter. "Tied them on, like, a number 4 regular 3407 Mustad hook—and one day, in one of those rips at Black's, I started catching perch until I realized, *Okay,* this *is how it happens.*"

He's been making discoveries like this for as long as he's fished. Still, many anglers refuse outright to fish for perch, as though the species were somehow beneath them, unworthy of their efforts and time. I've heard Peter wonder as well if he's ever going to catch something *besides* "another damn perch." But the key to all of this, especially surf fishing, is keeping your fly in the water. If you don't catch perch, it means you're going to end up not catching anything at all.

The latest stage in the evolution of Peter Syka's perch fly, the Trilobite, has fooled all of the glamour species available in the southland surf. Like most experienced surf anglers, however, Peter knows that it's not your pattern that's going to get you your next spotfin or halibut or maddeningly spooky corbina. But it *will* be a fly that quickly penetrates the strike zone and offers, in Peter's words, "something that fish will see and eat in a turbulent, foamy, and sometimes murky environment." Before claiming a name for the fly, Peter once described the Trilobite to me as his "Hare's Ear for the surf"—a generic template that covers, regardless of size or color, three out of four flies he ties for the surf, flies that fish don't refuse if you find them.

The Trilobite, explains Peter, is named for "the extinct arthropods, a class of animal that lived for about 270 million years, managed a wide array of sizes and functions—grazers, predators, filter-feeders—while retaining an easily recognizable form." *Trilobite*, adds Peter, means three-lobed. "The flies I've been tying and using are really a simple assembly of three components: eyes, hair, and legs."

At the vise, Peter handles himself, the tools, and his materials with that quiet attention to detail of someone who's been practicing his craft a long, long while. But there's more to it than that. Decades ago, when we both first got out of college, Peter made a living operating on rats, part of the research done at the lab where he worked; for the past two or three decades, he's operated on a scale that goes right down to the tiniest components of life. His skill as a tyer reminds me of the time I fished with a retired dentist in Baja; after admiring an elegant collection of saltwater patterns he had tied, I realized I shouldn't be surprised.

"I guess if you're a decent dentist," I noted, "you ought to be able to tie flies."

I've tied next to Peter up and down the length of Baja and throughout the West. I've tied on picnic tables, at vises hooked to beach chairs, in the front seat of nearly a dozen different trucks and vans, one vise hooked to the steering wheel, the other to the open door of the glove compartment. Tying in camp or on the road, in anticipation of the next session on the water, has been such an integral part of our fishing trips that I'm surprised when I come across guys who don't indulge in the practice—the luxurious delight of carefully constructing three or four specimens fashioned precisely for the showdown ahead.

I suppose you could drink, instead.

The Trilobite, anyway, reflects a school of fly tying practiced by what I like to refer to as the imaginative angler. Like many tyers, especially those of us who tend to take existing patterns and turn them into flies for our own specific fish and waters, Peter rarely settles on precise recipes for any of his flies. Experimentation and improvisation serve him as much at the vise as they do on the water. He'll suggest—but he generally avoids making claims.

Asked about hooks for the Trilobite, Peter lists a number of different Gamakatsus. But then: "If I only had one hook to use, it would be a size 2 SC-15. That size seems to be a compromise that allows you to put enough material on the fly to make an impression in the water while still being small enough to fit inside a perch's mouth."

Likewise, each of the three essential components of the Trilobite—eyes, hair, and legs: "I have used," says Peter, "and will probably still feel free to use, whatever materials I come across that will give me the desired profile and action in the water."

What this means is that the Trilobite is not so much a pattern as it is an effective template that adapts to the wide variety of conditions one finds fishing in the surf. If you're paying attention, you've probably also made this connection: An adaptable template is how a class of animals can hang around for two or three hundred million years, give or take a few million either way.

"For hair," says Peter, "I've used bucktail, calf tail, squirrel tail, fox hair, and coyote hair." For the eyes he prefers black nickel dumbbell beads, but he's used black, chrome, and bronze plumbing chain, plus, he says, "those expensive Real Eyes, that I am not sure offer any advantage in 95 percent of the situations that I've fished, as well as those heavy painted-lead dumbbell eyes, which confer the compounding disadvantages of expense, chipping, and the tendency to knock me hard on the back of my head while casting."

Of the countless options for rubber-leg material, Peter likes the limp, square-cut strips with subtle markings or reflective flake, a preference based on nothing more, he says, than the way the material ties and how it looks. But he's under no illusions that any of these details will make or break the fly. "I'll tie the Trilobite sparse, I'll tie it dense," he says. "A single color or shade, or two colors—dark hair, bright legs. Red is a go-to color for perch, and I always have some in my box, but I am more likely to fish a drab or dark fly than anything bright."

After forty years, I don't have to ask Peter why. His preferences and hunches belong to a long career of patient observation in the ever-changing and shape-shifting environment of the surf. Nobody on the beach has any final answers. It's always been a game of long shots.

"I could go on and on how to fish the things," says Peter, rising from the vise. And for a moment he seems tempted to start. "Sinking shooting heads, six- to nine-foot leaders, put the fly down to where the fish are. It might not be that deep, maybe two or three feet, but often there isn't a lot of time for it to sink into the strike zone while the fish are there."

Still, there's too much to tell. Where to begin? A fly like the Trilobite would be a good bet. Plus a tide book. And learn how to read the water.

After forty years, you'll probably have some sound opinions, too.

TRILOBITE

(Note: The materials listed below were used for the perch flies I tied and photographed after seeing a selection of Peter Syka's own Trilobites. The tying instructions come directly from Peter.)

▓ **Hook:** #2 Gamakatsu SC-15
▓ **Thread:** Red Danville 140 Denier Waxed Flymaster, or similar
▓ **Eyes:** Red dumbbell lead eyes (small, ¹⁄₄₀ oz.)
▓ **Tail:** Olive Grizzly Barred Rubber Legs
▓ **Body:** Tying thread
▓ **Legs:** Olive Grizzly Barred Rubber Legs
▓ **Wing:** Red marabou

Tying the Trilobite

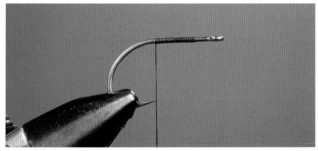

1. Secure the hook and wind on a thread base of whatever color your wing is going to be.

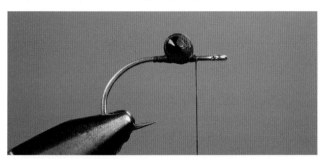

2. Tie in the dumbbell eyes. Give yourself plenty of room between the dumbbells and the eye of the hook. For shorter-shanked hooks like the SC-15, I'll put the eyes about midway along the hook shank. With larger, longer-shanked hooks, I'll put the eyes about one-third down the shank. You're going to need room to tie in bulky materials without covering the hook eye.

3. After the eyes are secure, fold a length of rubber leg in half and tie it in at the start of the hook bend.

Use thread wraps to even out and bulk up the body. Cover the body wraps and thread wraps holding the dumbbell eyes with a cyanoacrylate glue (Krazy Glue) or UV-activated epoxy.

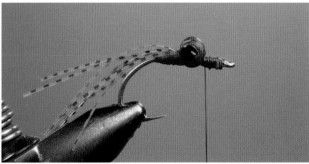

4. After the body wraps are dry, take a few wraps of thread in front of the eyes, then tie in the rubber legs. Most of the time it's three rubber legs, folded in half, with the bundle of midway loops tied in just ahead of the dumbbell eyes. Then pull the legs over the "handle" of the dumbbell and secure them with thread wraps behind the eyes. Trim the excess leg material at the tie-in point just aft of the hook eye. You can also trim the length of the legs so they extend in the neighborhood of the length of the tail. Bring the thread forward and even out the area between the dumbbell eyes and the hook eye. At this point it's a good idea to put a dab of Krazy Glue or UV epoxy on the rubber legs where they stretch across the midsection of the dumbbell. These flies are going to be spending a lot of time getting dragged across whatever bottom you're fishing on (notice I said *on* as opposed to *over*). That little dab of glue or epoxy will help the fly last a lot longer.

5. After the glue has dried, rotate the fly (flip it over, hook point up, if your vise is fixed) and tie in the wing on the underside of the hook. I like to have the thread match the color or shade of the wing. When the wing is secured, tidy up the head, whip-finish, and, yes, saturate the head with Krazy Glue or UV epoxy.

BULLADOR

Bullador, designed by Gary Bulla, with input from Shane Chung

(Note: Since an early draft of this essay was published years ago in *California Fly Fisher*, Shane Chung has left us, carried off at the age of forty-six by a brain aneurism. His sudden passing was felt deeply throughout the West Coast angling community.)

Shane Chung imagines it's all been caught on film. Somewhere in footage shot by security cameras peering into parking lots around LAX, he's sure he's shown handing over an unmarked packet to a mule, a perfect stranger willing to carry a quick shipment of goods aimed to satisfy a sudden demand in Baja. With the immunity of innocence, Chung delights in these deals; out of the chaos that surrounds the busy airport, suddenly there's a car model or color or some physical aspect of the stranger himself—a recognition that creates a connection between two anglers who, like so many of us, might otherwise pass like ships in the night.

Shane Chung ties flies. He contacted me this summer, hoping I could deliver a fresh batch of an as-yet unnamed pattern, a fly that had caused a stir among the panga fleet working out of Punta Arenas. I was happy to play along. When it comes to outlaw fantasies, I can do as well as the next guy. What is the sport of fly fishing if not an invitation or license to walk on the wild side?

The appeal of crossing borders armed with potions and secret talismans—a secret stash devised for the express purpose of an engagement with ritualized sport—is no different today from when my father first hauled me and my mother and sisters down to the beaches of northern Baja to pluck lobster from the rocks and kelp more than fifty years ago. *More than fifty years ago*—long enough, anyway, to gain some perspective on such adventure, as well as the notion that you had better show up in Baja with the Right Fly, one delivered by a dark stranger outside the departure terminals for international flights.

A fly pattern that *really* matters?

In blue waters off the Baja peninsula?

What a joke.

Of course, I've been wrong before.

Picture, if you will, a time when you were humbled on some blessed trout water. You know the score: fish up and feeding, good fish, not just feeding but *macking* on whatever insect it is that's hatching—whatever it is that you don't have matched with what's tied to your tippet, or that's there, indeed, but you fail again and again to present it in such a way to fool even one of these miserable dim-witted trout, beautiful as angels lighting up the stream.

Now imagine, if you can bear it, that the feeding fish are all as big as diving pelicans. Or springer spaniels. Better yet, if you're really imaginative, picture yourself *beneath* the water and these same dog-size fish crashing through the surface are falling from the sky. Imagine, anyway, a lot of commotion—yet none of it adds up to the one thing you want right now more than anything you've ever wanted in your life, a grab from one of these fish and that sudden, horrible, heart-wrenching pull on the end of your empty line.

Imagine all of that and maybe, then, you—like I did—can suddenly get interested in a new fly after all.

New flies are born out of necessity. Tyers tinker and tweak, and if it doesn't really matter, you end up with patterns as twisted and nonsensical as those from the nineteenth-century Atlantic salmon craze—or as simple as West Coast steelhead patterns when you could count on dozens of fish spotting your swinging fly on any given run. That was sort of the thinking during the early decades of offshore saltwater fly fishing. You find a school of pelagic fish hammering bait, who needs more than a tuft of feathers tied to a hook?

Only when fish are present and you don't catch them does serious thinking begin.

Nobody I know gets more chances to watch feeding fish in blue water off of Baja—and feeding fish that refuse to eat flies—than my old pal Gary Bulla. Both a guide and an outfitter, as well as a pioneer saltwater angler, Bulla is the first fly fisher I knew who began to field a lineup of patterns specific to the bait—or, if you'd like, *hatches*—found in Baja waters. Bulla gets busy—he's one of those guys who seems to operate just beyond the edge of chaos—and he turns to Shane Chung to keep himself stocked with flies he offers for sale to his clients. Sometimes he needs more flies than he planned for. Sometimes he needs them in a hurry.

Especially when a new pattern works better than he or anyone else expected.

One thing you can be sure of: Few if any anglers agree on when and where and how a pattern begins.

The way Bulla tells it, he was south of Isla Cerralvo at the end of his spring season, fishing with Ricky Hall and their panga captain, Valente Lucero. Things were pretty much wide open: yellowtail, big pargo mulattos, some of those teenage-size roosterfish that are really as much as any angler should ever ask for.

Then some big roosters showed up.

When Gary Bulla says big roosterfish, he is talking about fish in the forty- to fifty-pound range. I don't want to make too big a deal of it, but roosterfish this size have changed the face of West Coast fly fishing. Suddenly we're on the map again—the way we were when our steelhead were the envy and aim of fly fishers from all around the world.

But these ones wouldn't eat—at least not the standard roosterfish flies, the Papagallos and Tan Sardinas that Bulla and experienced Baja aficionados like Hall have come to rely on for these elusive giants. Valente suspected the roosters were into something other than the usual flathead herring. He mentioned the color blue, which surprised Bulla, as Valente, over the years, has usually removed any hint of blue or blue flash from flies. Bulla dug through his fly boxes and found a large Tuna Tux with a blue Mylar lateral line. He threw it. A big rooster ate it.

So it begins. The most prominent blue-colored bait in Baja is the flying fish—the *volador*. Bulla asked Chung to devise his own impression of a flying fish, something five to six inches long, with blue saddle hackle and deer hair and flash, and a light-colored belly. By the time I saw the fly in fall, when Chung was shipping them south by way of traveling anglers in order to replenish Bulla's rapidly diminishing supply, the dressing included Lady Amherst feathers dyed kingfisher blue for the gill plates, as well as badger saddle hackle dyed dark blue for the pectoral "wings."

Big and blue, the fly seemed at first glance little more to me than yet another variation on a two-tone minnow. I was sure, anyway, I'd be fine without it, that my own evolving Baja lineup would cover what came my way. After all, I'd caught my share of roosterfish.

Even a couple of big ones.

But come fall in Baja, roosterfish are no longer, in some years, part of the game.

I knew that, too. So when I heard from Chung about picking up flies on my way through LAX, and he told me that the new blue pattern was fooling the yellowfin tuna, I figured the important piece of the equation was that the tuna were there and I was headed that way—and beyond that I just needed to make sure my knots were sound, my reels oiled, and my back and arms strong enough to go to war with these terrible beasts.

When you first see yellowfin tuna, they are often completely out of the water, having rocketed a hundred feet or more straight up to the surface to claim a single herring tossed into the sea by your obliging *pangero*. Unable to stop its terrifying momentum, the yellowfin pierces the surface of the sea and tumbles headlong through the air, until it finally crashes again through the water and disappears beneath exactly the kind of disturbance you would expect to see if somebody dropped a fifteen- or twenty- or thirty-pound anvil into the sea.

This is the only kind of "rise" from fish I know of that doesn't just make me drool. I see a yellowfin tuna come out of the water like that and I think *uh-oh*. Sometimes, when a big one shows, not just thirty pounds but the kind of yellowfin that more or less makes a joke out of the whole notion of bluewater fly fishing, I think thoughts that I assume are on the order of those shared by the crew of the *Pequod* when they finally realized that *they*, not the whale, were the prey.

Of course, such thoughts have never stopped any angler or fisher or whaler of any sort from making a cast.

Which is probably what that whale of a novel is really about—regardless of what you heard in the last course you took in American lit.

The yellowfin tuna, anyway, had arrived, yet another pelagic species that I consider a sucker for virtually anything you toss their way once you find them and stir their interest to the surface with some well-placed chum. When I arrived in Baja and received the initial fish report, Bulla tried immediately to disabuse me of my cavalier attitude toward flies.

"At least half the tuna hooked last week were on the new fly," he said. "I think it's a real breakthrough."

"Make sure you get a couple," added Hall, joining us on a patio with a view of Isla Cerralvo. "I don't want to be out there spanking fish and have you crying because you don't have the right fly."

"Have I ever complained about not having the right fly?" I countered.

"Have you ever been surrounded by yellowfin popping up on the surface and refusing every fly you try?"

Despite appearances to the contrary, I sometimes listen to my experienced colleagues. Much as I hate buying anyone else's flies, I purchased a couple of Bulladors—and over the course of the week I bought a couple more each day, as my daily ration kept disappearing from the end of first twenty- and then twenty-five-pound tippet material. Without the Bullador on my line, I caught plenty of other fish—skipjack tuna, big dorado, little roosters. But yellowfin tuna? Sadly, all I can report is that there's a new fly they seem ready to eat. Your problem, then, is stopping them while, like a contraband-running mule, they set off to deliver the goods somewhere far, far away.

BULLADOR

- **Hook:** #2/0-4/0 Owner Aki
- **Thread:** White Danville 140 Denier Waxed Flymaster, or similar
- **Tail:** White Unique Hair or similar
- **Belly:** White Super Hair or similar
- **Lateral line:** Saddle hackle, dyed blue
- **Body:** Light blue Steve Farrar SF Blend
- **Back:** Blue Steve Farrar SF Blend
- **Gill plates:** Silver Doctor Blue guinea feathers
- **Eyes:** Yellow or chartreuse holographic eyes (9/32")
- **Head:** UV epoxy

Tying the Bullador

1. Secure your hook and start your thread. Starting aft of the middle of the hook shank, tie in a small tuft (about thirty to forty strands) of fairly stiff Unique Hair or similar synthetic product. Clip the butts at a sharp angle so that you don't create a severe step in the body as you work your way forward.

2. Invert the fly in the vise or rotate the vise jaws. With the fly upside down, tie in a short tuft of Super Hair or similar synthetic fiber, securing the material on the underside of the hook about midway up the hook shank. These fibers should extend well beyond the bend of the hook. Again, clip the butts at a sharp taper.

3. Reposition the fly upright again in the vise. Select two saddle hackles, preferably from opposite sides of a neck so that they curve in opposite directions. Strip the webby material and lowest fibers from each feather. Hold both feathers, tips aligned, so that the concave undersides are mated. Secure the stems of the feathers along the top of the fly, doing your best to keep them mated and aligned with the hook shank.

4. Ahead of the tie-in point for your saddle hackles, tie in a fairly substantial tuft of light blue SF flash blend. Allow some of the longest fibers to extend as far back, or farther, than the tail

5. Tie in another tuft of SF flash blend, this one a darker blue. Keep the fibers on top of the fly, and again allow some of the fibers to extend out toward the tips of the tail.

6. For the gill plates, select two dyed guinea feathers. Strip the fuzz from the lower stems and about a third or even half of the lowest, longest fibers. Secure each feather, good side out, along the side of the fly; after a couple of thread wraps, you can pull the feathers forward and get the fibers to squeeze in slightly tighter.

7. Now form a tidy head, whip-finish, and clip your thread. Position an eye on each side of the head and secure them with a bit of UV epoxy and a shot of light. Continue to build up the head until it fairs in with the edges of the eyes and the rest of the fly.

CLOUSER MINNOW

Clouser Minnow, designed by Bob Clouser

Of the handful of good decisions I've stumbled into during my fishing career, none seems sounder than a commitment I made nearly two decades ago to tie flies *after* fishing trips, not just before.

I'd been on the Deschutes a few days, going through a store of Wild Hares, my own version of the well-known Gold-Ribbed Hare's Ear, a fly I use more times than not as part of my two-fly nymphing rig. I knew I'd be headed to the Deschutes again soon. When I got home, I immediately sat down at the vise and tied a dozen more Wild Hares, loaded them into the appropriate box—and forgot about the anxiety I'd begun to feel, earlier that day, when yet another big redside took me to school, leaving my lineup of Wild Hares looking dangerously thin.

There was more going on, however, than simply replenishing depleted stocks. After time spent on the water, we all begin to view our flies—even flies of the same pattern—with sharper, more discerning eyes. Some of them, hopefully, look just right; others seem . . . well, second-rate. At the end of a trip, you usually know exactly what you're looking for when you open your box. Go home and tie those flies, and chances are you'll match what you're after in a way you never quite replicate come two or three or six months later.

That's an awfully strong argument as well for tying *during* a fishing trip, too.

Yet there was one other aspect to this on-return-home tying session, a way of going about it that I had already flirted with but still not committed to as part of my regular practice. This was the notion to tie those dozen Wild Hares at a single crack: size 16s, all of them the same, all tied one after the other.

Up until this point in my career, I had rarely been able to tie more than a couple of flies that looked moderately alike before I felt the need to try something different. I defended the approach on the grounds of creativity. Or artistic license. God forbid I tie flies like a robot. Even after reading A. K. Best's *Production Fly Tying*, now over twenty-five years old and counting, I couldn't bring myself to parse out materials for a single pattern and crank out the same fly, one after another.

It's still not my natural inclination. Is it anyone's? But those Wild Hares confirmed again that there is no more efficient way to fill a fly box than tying flies a dozen—or more—at a time. And nothing makes your flies look better than choosing a pattern you believe in, gathering together the appropriate materials, giving yourself an hour or two of uninterrupted time—and then settling in and finding your rhythm while visions of feeding fish dimple the surface of the less engaged portions of your tying mind.

Which is how, on starting home from a summer spent on Baja California's Magdalena Bay, I decide to tie *fifty* Clousers.

On my way north I stop in Santa Paula to visit Gary Bulla, home for a spell between stints in Baja hosting anglers hoping to test themselves against a lineup of the Sea of Cortez's most formidable fly-rod prey. Gary and I go back a ways; sadly, we can also go years without fishing together. This year Gary had to cancel his annual kayak trip to Magdalena Bay when Hurricane Blanca, spinning north out of the tropics, set her sights on the Pacific coast of Baja. Though much diminished by the time she made landfall, Blanca was still the earliest tropical storm of the season anyone could remember striking Magdalena Bay.

For once a wee bit envious of someone else's time in Baja, Gary asks how the fishing was in Mag Bay.

Where to start? After a dinner of Baja dorado and a bottle of what I call "Jim Harrison wine," the Côtes du Rhône so often favored by characters in the author's stories and novels, we retreat to the den of Gary and his wife Teresa's funky cedar-shingled bungalow perched in a grove of towering oaks alongside Santa Paula Creek, dry this summer like so many coastal streams from San Diego to Eureka. The creek-side oaks, points out Gary, have also fallen victim to the drought, losing limbs and dying at an alarming and even dangerous pace. I try to put into context a summer spent sailing and fishing on the largest unspoiled estuary on the North American continent. Would it succumb somehow, too, to the cascading effects of climate change?

Mag Bay fishing approaches more closely California inshore fisheries than it does the exotic pelagic sport found along the Sea of Cortez. Single-digit rods are the call; ten-pound fish are rare. It's intimate sport for the same sort of angler who enjoys back bays, streams, the surf. You poke around and find fish here and there: corvina, jacks, grouper, halibut, bonito, bass—all of which Gary and his hosted clients often catch out of a single Mag Bay estero, while I covered countless esteros and hundreds of miles of shoreline to replicate virtually the same bag.

"So what flies d'you use?" asks Gary, pouring us each a couple of fingers of the kind of good Scotch he seems always able to pull from his stash.

The list is short. Even when I got into bonefish, I didn't feel the need to switch from the conventional baitfish pattern I generally use, a drab tan or olive back above white saddle hackle, white bucktail, and a white fox fur belly—with 3-D hologram eyes embedded in a head of clear epoxy. Once I found fish, especially in the mangrove-lined esteros, I could rarely resist tying on a Crease Fly as a popper, if only because the opportunity to watch fish crush a surface pattern still seems like the whole point of picking up a fly rod in the first place.

And when I got serious, I tied on a Clouser.

"Three flies," says Gary, holding the bottle up to the light.

We've been here before; with any luck, we'll get there again.

"That's really about all you ever need."

The reputation of the Clouser Minnow is unassailable—and impossible to overstate. In the interest of casting this essay in a new light, I could have easily chosen other Clouser-type patterns, or swapped out materials and claim I've invented a pattern of my own. Ever since Bob Clouser created the fly in the late 1980s, and Lefty Kreh wrote about it—and named it—in an article for *Fly Fisherman*, tyers have been tweaking and renaming it like branded ball caps. But I fail to see the point. Clousers, especially for saltwater anglers, remain a basic ingredient in any coherent fly box, in much the same way that your Hare's Ear Nymphs—by whatever name you call them—are essential to a box of trout flies.

When I state I *got serious and tied on a Clouser*, I mean this: Many times this summer as I explored Magdalena Bay in *Madrina*, my home-built double-ended beach yawl, I found myself in need of fish to eat. Beans and rice and steel-cut oats can only take you so far. Usually I could just sort of pick a fish out of the catching and releasing—but now and then a couple of days passed without meat in the skillet, and I reached that point where the hunger began to feel real.

It's a healthy feeling, I think—especially when all you have is a fly rod at hand. We may all have a tendency to forget what it is we're really doing. You get out of practice. Twice I lost fish—fish I wanted to eat—during sloppy landings. Once I even put a bass on the stringer, dangled it over the side of *Madrina*, and two hours later when I went to clean the fish, it wiggled out of my hands and swam away.

Tie a Clouser on your line, however, and it's pretty clear what you're trying to make happen. Give yourself an outgoing tide after any one of the dozens of mangrove esteros in Mag Bay has flooded, and look for a channel where the current swings tight to shore. Clousers, of course, are sort of a jig with wings; pitch it across the current and close to the bank, and let it glide out of the shallows and dive into the trough about the same moment you began to strip and retrieve.

Get it right, you can begin to wonder how many good fish can possibly be stacked up feeding in a slot like that.

Get it wrong, you wonder how big *that one* was as you strip in your Clouser-less line.

Do this often enough and you promise yourself you'll bring *fifty* Clousers next time you head to Mag Bay. Driving north past the delta, I figure *Madrina* and enough Clousers could prove a pretty good equation elsewhere, too.

CLOUSER MINNOW

- **Hook:** #1 Mustad 34007, Gamakatsu SL12S, or similar
- **Thread:** White Danville 3/0 Waxed Monocord, 140-denier UTC Ultra Thread, or similar
- **Eyes:** Fluorescent chartreuse painted dumbbell eyes (medium)
- **Tail/belly:** White bucktail
- **Flash:** Pearl Krystal Flash
- **Body:** Bucktail, dyed chartreuse, lime green, or light olive
- **Topping (optional):** Peacock herl

Tying the Clouser Minnow

Clousers are a classic "guides' fly": few materials, quick to tie, and an easy pattern to customize for local fish or conditions—or when you find you've run out of an ingredient far from the nearest fly shop. If you ever get the chance, watch a guide or professional tyer fashion a Clouser—or any other standard pattern, as far as that goes. These Real Guys all have subtle tricks and techniques they employ to make tying go faster while maintaining the quality of their flies. Watch any one of them and you're bound to learn something new.

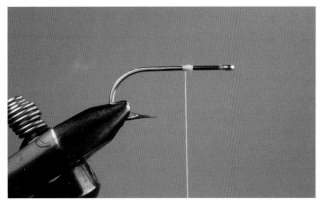

1. Secure the hook and start your thread about one-third of the way back from the hook eye. Create a small ball with thread wraps to help with positioning the dumbbell eyes in the next step.

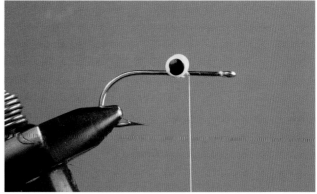

2. Set the dumbbell eyes on the hook shank and slide them forward until they sit tight to the ball of thread wraps. Anchor the eyes with thread wraps across the wrist of the dumbbell, forward and aft and aft and forward. Some tyers use glue or head cement to help hold their dumbbell eyes in place. I like to take wraps of thread below the eyes but above the hook shank, as if starting the post of a parachute fly, to help tighten the cross-wraps.

3. Clip a tuft of hair from a bucktail; the farther from the root of the tail, the softer the material, which makes it easier to keep aligned on a hook shank without splaying. Clean out any underfur or short hairs. I like to stack my bucktail to align the tips; others don't. Clip the butts of hair so that the hair length is about twice the length of the hook. Hold the butts of the hair at a downward angle between the dumbbell eyes and the eye of the hook. Starting with a couple of loose thread wraps, lash the butts to the hook shank, increasing tension on the wraps as you cover the clipped hair butts. Then draw the tuft of bucktail over the wrist of the dumbbell eyes. Wind your thread aft of the dumbbell eyes by taking a turn around the tuft of hair, securing it along the top of the hook shank. Continue your thread wraps toward the start of the hook bend, being careful not to tighten your wraps to the point that the bucktail splays. Return the thread forward of the dumbbell eyes to the spot you began lashing down the bucktail.

4. Spin your vise jaws or flip your fly; you are now working on the top of the fly. (The weighted eyes cause the fly to swim with the hook point up.) Just back from the hook eye, secure three or four full-length strands of Krystal Flash by folding them in half around the thread and then pulling the thread tight to the hook shank. You've now doubled the number of strands. Take several wraps of thread to help the strands lie in line with the axis of the fly. Clip the aft ends of the Krystal Flash to match the length of the white bucktail.

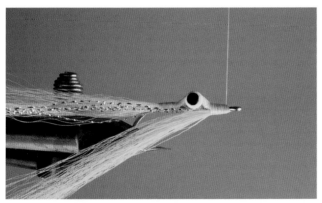

5. Opposite the tie-in point above the first tuft of white bucktail, tie in an equal amount of chartreuse bucktail hair. Follow the same procedure used when tying in the white bucktail: stack if you like, clip the butts, hold the tuft at an angle, and then cover the butts after securing them. A few extra light wraps of thread can also help keep the hair from extending obliquely from the hook axis.

6. Many Clousers end here. Sometimes I like to add a small dressing of darker bucktail to what is now the top of the fly. On top of that, I might also add a few strands of peacock herl, knowing full well it may not last more than a fish or two.

7. After your whip-finish, saturate the head with lacquer or your favorite head cement. Also saturate the bucktail where it passes over the wrist of the dumbbell eyes, as well as any thread wraps aft of the eyes. Some tyers will also use epoxy or a similar product to create a more pronounced head, one that fairs into the dumbbell eyes.

OLIVE HERRING

Olive Herring, adapted by author from various traditional saltwater baitfish patterns

Red Herring: something that distracts attention from the real issue.

—Merriam-Webster's

For a long time I didn't fish in the ocean. This is no place to go into that—other than to say that for someone who wrote a couple of books devoted to the subject, clearly I changed directions in my sporting life. Or—and this is another way to look at it—life *took* me in new directions, requiring I adjust to its unpredictable demands, until one day I stopped and looked around and discovered I hadn't thrown a fly in the surf or the sea for a long, long time.

But I like to think we all have more control over things than we choose to admit. "Everything in life," claimed Silly Mountain, the rough-hewn Ming Dynasty poet known elsewhere as Han Shan Te'-Ch'ing, "depends on the choices we make." Or, as Jim Harrison has reminded us, one way or another, throughout his long career, "We are all, in totality, what we wish to be."

Still, stuff happens. And if we're not careful, or we fail to pay attention to where we stand from one moment to the next, we can find ourselves floundering in mucky waters far from the elegant currents life has promised each one of us at one time in our lives or another. The problem, for most of us, begins when sport of any sort comes to seem like something other than what we do in our *real* lives—as if it doesn't count or matter as much as taking out the trash, cleaning the rain gutters, or earning our daily bread.

This is not an abstract point. Fly fishing comes freighted with a lot of metaphorical baggage, but the truth for most serious practitioners is that the enterprise really is a matter of catching fish—or trying to catch fish—with flies. I wouldn't go quite so far as to say that this is the sport's most profound secret—but I'm surprised how often I come across otherwise sensible individuals who believe fly fishing is actually about something else.

Then again, I'm often surprised by people who argue that our lives harbor metaphorical meaning as well—that what we're doing here is about something other than what we're doing here. I'm willing to concede the possibility that I might be proven wrong in all this. But considering the number of great minds that have looked at life and reached the same conclusion, I don't imagine I'm destined to figure out anything more than what matters is what we do—and what it all means is anybody's guess.

Or, as the poet William Stafford once wrote, "What the river says, that is what I say."

Now, where was I?

The longer I stayed away from fishing in the ocean, the more hesitant I grew to return, for fear the sport had passed me by. When I left the beaches of San Diego, corbina remained an incidental, maybe even *accidental*, catch for the isolated handfuls of fly anglers plying the Southern California surf. But it wasn't long before the region was awash with waves of corbina aficionados, including an incessant web presence detailing remarkable successes and the latest refinements in lines, flies, and theory—that peculiar blend of technical advice and sporting bombast that can make the outsider, even an experienced one, feel intimidated because of his or her paltry desire to merely show up and go fishing.

I recall my good pal Peter Syka reporting, following a day of surfing, that he had spotted a guide and client working the deep hole in front of the road down to Black's Beach. For the both of us, this seemed a profound shift, like tow-in surfing or, say, permission to use aluminum bats in the big leagues. It wasn't a question of someone needing or wanting to fish in the surf with a guide. Instead, what we both found extraordinary was that anyone felt he knew enough about catching fish in the surf on flies that he would accept money to stand there and point out to someone else how to do it.

Even more significant, however, were transformations taking place in the bluewater scene. Prior to my retreat, most of what was done in the way of offshore fly fishing—in California and Baja, at least—seemed a reckless and often misguided attempt to battle fish with equipment that was woefully overmatched by the demands of the sport, a kind of intoxicating lark that often resulted in wrecked gear and humbled egos. Later, through a sequence of happenstance, I pointed Peter in the direction of Gary Bulla, and after the two of them returned from a trip to Baja, Peter informed me that our surf rods, click-and-pawl reels, and shooting heads affixed to Amnesia running line were so far behind the times that he immediately went out and purchased the works, end to end, something neither of us had ever done in our frugal, do-it-yourself careers.

Finally, there was the matter of flies. By the time I tied a collection of personal favorites for *Angling Baja*, with its color plate of simple impressionistic patterns I had used in the surf, I was well aware that I was part of the rear guard. Instead of bucktail and saddle hackle dyed in a rainbow of grade-school colors, tyers were now employing brighter, bolder, and more exotic synthetic materials, with epoxies, plastic fibers, and prefabricated eyes that helped make flies that looked like they had just jumped or crawled out of an aquarium. Surrounded by trout and steelhead waters, I found myself trying to catch up with the centuries-old traditions of the sport—the techniques, materials, and entomology—while anglers tying for the Left Coast salt and surf seemed captivated by ideas inspired by the technological imagery shared by the recently salvaged Hubble space telescope.

Yet beyond my usual doubts and misgivings, one other peculiarity cropped up in my thinking to keep me away from surf and sunny seas. I had a hunch, way back when, that I was playing with fire, and if I didn't start showing a little caution, my favorite fishing just might end up killing me.

Rarely do my premonitions prove this accurate. Fair-skinned and pale-eyed, I felt certain that after nearly forty years of work and play beneath the Southern California sun, with seldom hat or sunglasses or protective ointments between me and our brilliant friend's ultraviolet rays, I was textbook material for the kind of damage that children now receive warnings about long before lectures concerning drugs, deviancy, saturated fats, or unprotected promiscuity. Growing up in the sixties, I was raised to believe that a radiant suntan was not only a sign of health and well-being, but a touchstone of success and material abundance—a line of reasoning that now seems as fraudulent as claims, a generation earlier, that cigarette smoking made you appear *cool*. In my own case, it wasn't so much that a suntan mattered, only that I never did anything to prevent one, especially on discovering that given enough "color," I could be outside from daybreak until dusk without so much as a shadow of protection on my sun-brightened hair and ruddy skin.

On the other hand, after gaining employment building and remodeling houses, I saw exactly what the sun did to wood, plastics, and paint, in addition to what I also saw it do to surfboards, monofilament, and fly lines. Did I think my pale, freckled skin was immune to this same abuse? Hardly. Which was why, when the chance came, I figured it might be a good idea I escape those sunny Southern California beaches for someplace grayer, darker, farther from the harsh Mediterranean glare.

A good idea, perhaps—but a little late. For though I shied away, finally, from ocean sport, the damage, apparently, was well under way. Plus, there was still the wee problem of summer trout streams, nearly all of which seem located in places known more for bristling sun than the cool embrace of soggy clouds or sodden fogs.

What's a poor guy to do?

Tonight, feeling the rash effects of a fresh dose of Carac, another treatment for the actinic keratoses that currently has my face and forehead looking like I just finished a make-out session with a vibrating palm sander, I might consider the possibility that ocean sport in general, and fly fishing specifically, have left me damaged beyond repair. In the past couple of years I've enjoyed countless occasions of cyrosurgery (liquid nitrogen), plus one excisional surgery (scalpel) for a classic example of squamous cell carcinoma, otherwise known as skin cancer, a spot right there on the back of my rod hand that has received more hours of direct sunlight than some readers of this story may have been alive. I should also mention, for the record, that I'm feeling the effects as well of a healthy shot of tequila in my evening coffee—which could explain why I'm feeling vulnerable to this sort of sentimental reflection in the first place.

My point? Simply this: In the face of an array of doubts and misgivings, of signs and warnings that suggested I might want to do otherwise, I decided, somewhere along the way, that I really do like casting flies in the ocean—and whatever reasons I might have for fishing elsewhere, none of them were good enough to outweigh this, the oldest of arguments of all: If I waited any longer, it might turn out to be too late.

───────●────────────●───────

Oddly enough, it was the flies, more than anything else, that hadn't much changed. There were plenty of new patterns, of course—and some, like the Crease Fly and Tres Generaciones, seemed genuinely different, so that you feel you have to find new materials and learn how to use them if you want to get up to speed. But for every unique fly developed, dozens of others appeared that look pretty much like what everyone else has been doing since day one—baitfish streamers that, depending on the size and color of the bait you're trying to imitate, resemble a Lefty's Deceiver, give or take the eyes and the latest and greatest synthetic flash you might add.

This isn't a rap on anyone's creativity or imagination. The point is, what else *should* you tie if you're casting in the ocean, where the food chain replicates fairly closely a kindergartner's impression of big fish eating smaller fish, link after link after link? Naturally, there's more to it than that, and variables like squid and crustaceans do come into play. But nothing in the diet of ocean gamefish seems quite so varied as that of a year-round menu served up to trout, and it seems to me you can go a long ways in bluewater fly fishing working from a single template rather than trying to reinvent patterns for every fish that swims in the sea.

More than searching for or trying to create new and improved patterns that might or might not catch more fish, I spend most of my saltwater tying efforts trying to create flies that will *last*. So different than, say, steelheading, where a fly that finally hooks a single fish seems to have accomplished as much as one might reasonably expect from a fly, a fly fished for schooling pelagic fish can stay tied or retied to the leader for an entire morning, fooling countless fish despite suffering the wear and tear of aggravated assault by toothy predators.

On my maiden return visit to Baja, an unplanned leap in response to a string of serendipitous offers, I showed up with a bunch of Clouser Minnows, tied in such haste that I hadn't even epoxied the heads. I figured, *What the heck—I never used the stuff on any of my old surf flies.* Days later, I could liken with accuracy the contents of the front pockets of my tropical-weight trousers with a pair of bird's nests, each a tangle of

hooks and painted dumbbell eyes woven together by broken and splayed bucktail in assorted prismatic colors. Come to think of it, what these balls of destroyed flies—saved for recycled parts—really looked like were something a pack rat builds, a collection of debris that should remind any of us of the eventual fate of our fleeting bodies.

Now, quick study that I am, I finish all my saltwater flies with epoxy. There's no better way to protect the heads and tying thread of your flies, and of course you'll nearly always employ eyes on these patterns, which require epoxy or some combination of adhesive and protective coating material to affix and hold them in place.

I also use a lot more synthetic hair than I ever thought I would, because the truth is, plastic is tougher than most natural fibers. On the other hand, there are qualities to animal hair—bucktail, calf tail, arctic fox— that nothing artificial seems able to reproduce, and though I use synthetic hair and flash freely, I return again and again to simple hair configurations, knowing full well they may shrink in size and volume as they get hammered and abused in the course of their violent, temporal lives.

Then there's the matter of hooks. I probably still don't know enough to weigh in on the subject with authority, other than to agree with what we've heard from the start: Buy the best hooks you can find. Or afford. For nine out of ten fish—or ninety-nine out of a hundred—it probably doesn't matter if you use anybody's model designed for salt water. Just keep it sharp—which gets to the heart of the matter. The very best hooks come sharp and *stay* sharp—even after penetrating the tough mouths of so many predaceous fish.

Good hooks are strong, too—which I find important *not* because hooks straighten (rare unless you use oversized tippet), but when twisting free a fly with pliers, a lousy hook can come away looking like the end of a corkscrew. Nobody pays me anything to endorse products, so when I say I love the Owner Aki hook, it's not because I get them any cheaper than you have to pay. But that's an example of a hell of a hook, the kind of tool you'll reach for more and more often the more you fish in the ocean.

If only skin came that tough.

On my tying bench I have an Olive Herring (or maybe it's an Olive Tuna Tux, or Richie's Ranchero—hard to tell the difference) that I fished for three days in Baja, hooking I don't know how many skipjack, dorado, and big jack crevalle. Dozens. Two nights in a row, under the scrutiny of some Real Guys, I had to replace eyes on the fly, and now there's so much epoxy built up around the thread between the bucktail and the eye of the hook that the head looks like the front of a bullet-head hopper or stonefly—an ugly, sun-yellowed glob. Yet it's one of those flies that matches perfectly the medium-size flathead herring you find sometimes in Baja, and ugly as it is, I'd fish it again in a heartbeat.

Funny thing is, now that I look at it more closely, the surface of that scabby epoxy looks sort of like the skin between *my* eyes and the start of *my* hair. Probably a message there. But I'll be damned if I can figure it out.

OLIVE HERRING

- **Hook:** #1/0 Ahrex SA280 Minnow
- **Thread:** White Danville 140-denier Waxed Flymaster, or similar
- **Tail:** White yak hair
- **Body:** White bucktail and olive yak hair
- **Belly:** White calf tail
- **Lateral line:** Silver Flashabou
- **Back:** Light olive bucktail
- **Topping:** Dark olive or "sculpin" olive bucktail
- **Eyes:** 3-D stick-on, silver or yellow with black pupil (³⁄₁₆″ or ¼″)

Tying the Olive Herring

1. Mount your hook and start your thread. For the tail, tie in a fairly sparse clump of yak hair. (Throughout this pattern, go lightly on materials. It's easy to overdress big flies.) For this, a medium-size bait pattern, the tail should extend about 2 inches beyond the bend of the hook.

2. Clean and stack a clump of white bucktail. Tie it in so that it extends just short of the tips of the tail.

3. Invert the fly and for the belly tie in a layer of calf tail that extends about a third of the length of the tail.

4. Return the fly to the upright position and tie in a sparse clump of olive yak hair.

5. For a lateral line, fold a length of Flashabou around the thread and secure the material to one side of the fly. Repeat for the other side.

6. Again, turn the fly upside down and tie another shorter layer of calf tail for the rest of the belly.

7. Return the fly to an upright position. Clip and stack a small tuft of light olive bucktail. Tie it in along the top of the fly.

8. Add one more bit of bucktail, this one dark or "sculpin" olive, along the top or back of the fly. Create a tidy head, whip-finish, and clip your thread.

9. Now, if you've come this far, here's some of the best practical information I've ever delivered: how to put eyes on a big saltwater streamer if you haven't invested in a UV-activated epoxy kit. Get a pair of cheap needle-nose pliers and put a rubber band around the handles. With the business end of the pliers, grip the fly at about the middle of the hook, flattening the hair while leaving enough space to position the eyes. The rubber band keeps the pliers closed on the fly. Now mix up a small batch of five-minute epoxy. (Obviously, if you're tying in earnest, you should have two or three flies ready to work on at this point, so get yourself a couple more pairs of pliers.) Cover the thread and front part of the fly. When the epoxy just starts to set up, put the eyes in place. Continue to adjust the eyes as the epoxy dries. Then mix up a second batch, and cover the eyes and again the thread and front of the fly. Watch for sagging epoxy or unsightly drips. Just spin or invert the fly if they begin to form.

And here's another tip worth the price of admission: The best way I know to store big saltwater flies is to slip them individually into 2 × 5" 4 mil polyethylene baggies. Buy them by the thousand from an industrial supply company like Uline.

SQUID ME

Squid Me, Fred Trujillo adaptation of design by Mark Mandell

The first time I went kayak fishing in the ocean I found myself thinking, *Boy, this is pretty easy.* You could do all kinds of clever things to send your fly down to where the fish were—but it wasn't long before I recognized that I got most of my strikes while paddling around with my line dangling in the distance behind me. Tom McGuane once described trailing a Mickey Finn behind a canoe as "about the minimum, fly-wise," yet the first time you hook into a tuna or other pelagic speedster and feel yourself getting dragged toward the middle of the sea, you can be forgiven for rehearsing lines to describe this epic battle while ignoring altogether the lowly means by which it began.

Of course, I also soon noticed that the experienced kayak fishers were hooking a lot more fish than I was—and usually bigger and better fish, too.

Fishing a mangrove estero in Magdalena Bay confirmed my suspicions that there's a lot more to kayak fishing than the beginner first sees. Attempting long, accurate casts while seated at water level will remind you once again of the ugly little secrets you try so hard to ignore in your loop and casting stroke. Add wind, strong tides, and the very necessary paddling licks to position yourself at an angle from which you can actually launch a cast—and suddenly you realize you not only need to be an accomplished fly fisher to succeed at

this, but could also use the cool head of a harbor pilot and the facility of a bow hunter just to get yourself in the game.

And I haven't even mentioned how to deal with that damn paddle.

So when my old pal Fred Trujillo said he was driving to Reno to pick up a Hobie fishing kayak he found on eBay, and then he started catching fish with a simple squid pattern he concocted that "even the salmon are going nuts over," I figured it was time to send him an invitation and sit him down at the Roost and see just what it is that's captured his imagination these days.

At the very least, we need to give Fred's squid a name.

⬤━━━━⬤

My own attempts—at creating squid patterns, not naming them—have been marginal at best. Yet ever since tying my very first Seaducer—a fly with as much story under its hackles as the Matuka streamer or Green Butt Skunk—I've kept an eye out for patterns that suggest something besides baitfish that swim in the surf and sea. No doubt, squid get *our* attention when they're left behind by the tide, looking like so many skinned Chihuahuas lying dead upon a beach—and if you worked hard enough at it, and employed enough rubber in the fly, you could end up with something resembling a Hoochie, a trolling lure known up and down the coast in all manner of conventional angling circles.

By way of context, I should also mention that squid claimed a spot in my personal angling history when, as a bait fisher, I used a chunk of it, freshly thawed, to hook the biggest sheepshead I've ever seen, anywhere—a beast I eventually lost at my feet while standing on a wave-swept rock, wondering if it's okay to eat these things.

It is.

And this: A long, long time ago—even before I lost that big sheepshead—the seawall in front of the raggedy beach break known as Lots between La Jolla Shores and Scripps Pier featured, for a spell, what seemed to me the slyest bit of graffiti—*Squid me*—which probably offers as much explanation as any for why I became a writer.

•————•

I'm a little nervous when Fred arrives. A professional tyer, he makes a habit of setting out the exact materials he needs and nothing more. Where my tying station, at the Roost or on a picnic table on the Deschutes, will soon look like a dog tore into my supplies of feathers and fur, Fred will still be working with the same bits and pieces he began with, turning out nearly identical examples of the pattern he's settled on.

That lesson right there is worth the price of a book.

But today Fred shows up with a toolbox full of materials. Don't tell me it's going to be one of those patterns. Like many tyers, I'm a minimalist—that is, I want to do the minimal amount and still end up with a fly that works. Guides are experts at this kind of tying. I'll tie a replica sea anemone—with moving parts—if I believe I need it to catch a fish. But I'd much rather tie an all-white baitfish streamer and go fishing, working on craft and presentation to get the job done.

While Fred piles up a menu's worth of plastic packets and other paraphernalia, he recounts some recent kayak fishing news. He's told me—hasn't he?—about getting spilled in that run we sometimes wade across to get to a couple of favorite steelhead holes. And over on the coast, a guy after rockfish got caught inside by a set wave and lost everything but his life. Of course I heard—didn't I?—the story about the guy in Hawaii who just had his leg bit off by a great white and bled to death before his rescuers could get him to a hospital.

So when am *I* going to get a kayak?

Turns out Fred's brought not only a well-stocked stash of materials to go with his motivational kayak tales, but also his full arsenal of squid flies. So enamored of late with their effectiveness while fishing for anything that swims in the sea, he's been creating an assortment of variations, all of which point back to Mark Mandell's original Calamarko Squid, a pattern that first showed up in Les Johnson's *Tube Flies* from 1995.

Fred likes tube flies as much as anybody—but he's started tying his squid pattern with a trailing "stinger"

hook, a practice employed by steelheaders who feel it increases their touch-to-hookup rate. I've seen a few online photos of the Calamarko Squid, and though Fred seems to have wandered some ways away from the original pattern, you can see again that here at the Roost, as elsewhere, we're nearly always dealing with derivatives, flies that belong to a lineage that stretches far beyond our own sudden, individual genius.

Still, Fred knows a few things—and it's a pleasure to watch him work. Despite his shaved head and wrestler's build, he's got the fine wrists and delicate touch of a jeweler, and he ties with an economy of effort that's similar to what you notice in a sound and practiced caster. An extra thread wrap is as senseless as an extra backcast. Enough is enough. One more is too many. Start there and you begin to notice a dozen different ways you waste time picking up tools and setting them down, fussing with materials that could have been prepared *before* you began tying, fiddlings and false starts that not only break your tying rhythm but leave you frustrated because of the extra effort required to wrangle a fly into shape.

Practice makes perfect—but like most everything in this kooky sport, if you don't practice smart, all you do is end up developing bad habits.

I ought to know.

•————•

Parasquid? Squidillo? Calamarillo? Try as we might, we're unable to come with a name that rings true. Squid Vicious, I'm sad to report, has already been claimed. Because squid patterns seem perfectly married to kayak fishing, I suggest we switch part of the fly to yak hair; that way we can use a play on words and call it—

Fred stops me with a look that says that's the dumbest way to go about designing a fly he's ever heard.

A fly, of course, is more than a name. And as I paw through Fred's lineup of squid patterns, I suspect that what he's tied this evening at the Roost is merely another stage in an evolution that still hasn't reached completion. When the pattern stops evolving, a name will come. Or vice versa.

Until then, squid me.

SQUID ME

- **Hook:** #2 Mustad 3407
- **Thread:** White Danville 140-denier Flymaster; at step 5, switch to fine Danville Monofilament
- **Stinger loop:** Black Intruder Trailer Hook Wire
- **Stinger hook:** #1 red Gamakatsu Octopus
- **Tail:** White saddle hackle
- **Topping 1:** White synthetic yak hair
- **Topping 2:** Fluorescent shrimp pink Iceabou
- **Sides:** Fluorescent shrimp pink Krystal Flash
- **Body:** Everglow Tubing (medium)
- **Eyes:** Hologram, red with black pupil (3/16")

Tying the Squid Me

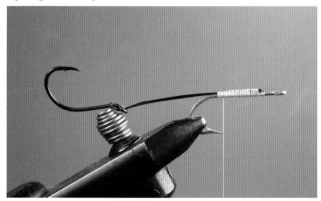

1. Secure your hook and start the thread. Run the trailer hook wire through your stinger hook and create your stinger loop approximately the same length as the forward hook. Stinger hook point up or stinger hook point down, hard to say which is better. For big-fish security, leave the front ends of the wire long, then fold them back along the hook shank and cover with thread.

2. Select two or three saddle hackles from each side of a neck. Clean off the stems so that you're left with feathers that extend an inch or so past the back of the stinger loop. Secure the feathers along both sides of the hook, as though you were tying a Lefty's Deceiver.

3. Lay a couple dozen fibers of synthetic yak hair or similar material along the top of the tails, extending about even with the tips. Secure the yak hair along the length of the top of the hook. Then fold the fibers back and, keeping them aligned with the others, wrap your thread back to the root of the tail. Clip the ends of the folded fibers to match the length of the others.

4. Follow the same procedure with the fluorescent shrimp pink Iceabou.

5. For the sides of the fly, start by aligning Krystal Flash along the side nearest you. Again, wrap the thread forward, fold the fibers, and now align them with the far side of the fly. Trim the tips of the Krystal Flash so that they are the same length on both sides of the fly, again about the same length as the original tail. Wrap your thread back to the bend of the hook, then advance it to just behind the hook eye, whip-finish, cut, and start your monofilament thread.

6. Take a moment now to *fair* the body of the fly. Fairing is a boatbuilding term that, in this case, means to even out the shape of an object. I like a long gradual taper, from the aft end of the hook to the hook eye. Now wind the monofilament thread back to the original tie-in point. Cut a length of Everglow Tubing about the length of the hook plus the stinger loop. Pull the packing material from inside the tubing. Using a bodkin or similar tool, unravel the back two-thirds of the tubing. Slide the tubing over the eye of the hook, so that the unraveled portions extend wildly around the other materials that extend past the bend of the hook. Wrap the monofilament over the intact tubing, then run your wraps forward and back over the length of the hook shank, again creating an even body. Whip-finish at the eye of the hook and cut your thread.

7. Position eyes at the back end of the body. Secure them with a bit of epoxy and keep them in place with a shot of UV light. Now cover the entire body with epoxy, hit with your light, and continue increasing the profile with additional epoxy layers until you have fair, clean head.

AMIGO

Amigo, designed by Guy Wright

On the approach of a recent birthday, I began to announce, to those who would listen, that I've lived longer than I'm going to live. This seemed a remarkable admission, and much as I hated to make it, it forced me to view life from a brand-new perspective: From this point forward, I have less time than I've had up to now.

Of course, I recognize the absurdity of this new outlook. Given my actual age, there's a very good chance I passed the halfway point in my life many years ago. Just because I can *behave* like a teenager offers little defense against the disturbing evidence revealed to me each glance in a mirror. *What the hell happened?* you wonder. *I feel like I was just getting warmed up.*

Not surprisingly, it was John Gierach who pointed out that nobody finds himself on his deathbed thinking he spent too much of his life fishing. Granted, there have been spells when I *imagined* I was spending a wee bit too much time on the water. But it seems safe to bet that such episodes are probably not going to come back and haunt me when I feel my ghost tugging free of this deteriorating body. Instead, I sense, as I gaze both forward and back from my newfound perch at the middle of my life, the only feeling I need fear is the regret that I wasted too much time doing things I

didn't want to do, not that I spent too much of my life doing what I loved.

———•————————•———

The gift arrived in a great wooden crate, solidly built, formidable in its dimensions. I needed one of my sons to help me carry it into our house. *What gets shipped anymore packaged like this?* I asked myself. When's the last time *anything* showed up in a box built better than most everything *inside* of packaging today?

It took a screw gun to free the lid—*with* a #2 square drive bit. Of course, I could have used a pry bar. But my son already had designs on the crate, picturing it as a piece of furniture in his humble student quarters.

The fact is, *I* had ideas for the crate as well, seeing as it was built better, and with finer materials, than all but a handful of items throughout my entire house.

Yet by now my attention had turned to the contents of the crate. I had a hunch—no, really, more than a hunch, a pretty good idea based on clues on the crate itself, plus an enigmatic note I had received from a close friend during the winter holidays.

I know only one person in Santa Paula, my old saltwater pal, Baja guide, and woodworker extraordinaire

Gary Bulla. And lately I'd been admiring one of his elegant fly-tying cabinets, very near the size of this crate, a cabinet situated in front of a bank of windows in the corner of a bedroom I'd been visiting overlooking a river we all love.

These . . . *friends*, I thought, admiring the panel of solid maple revealed inside the open crate. *You mean to tell me she got me one, too?* I wondered—while I eagerly had my son help me lift the cabinet out of the box.

I slid open the top drawer, and there resting on the green felt, neatly packaged in individual polyethylene sleeves, lay three flies that I've come to know well while fishing with Bulla in Baja: the Tuna Tux, Larry's Minnow, a Tan Tux with Tails. But what about that other pattern Gary likes so well? What about the . . . *Amigo*?

I pulled open the other drawers, releasing the fragrance of aromatic cedar used for the bottom of each. No Amigo? But when I slid out the top drawer again, drawing it all the way free of the cabinet, there it was, the fly I associate with a kind of fishing I've had in Baja and the California surf and no place else in my life.

Now, the reader may ask: *What's all this got to do with age, flies, or fly fishing?* Or even the themes, as Whitman said, that the Soul loves pondering best: "Night, sleep, death and stars."

It's a difficult lie I'm trying to cast to—a tough notion from which I'm trying to inspire a rise.

But let me give it a shot: Say what I might—and I've said plenty—about all of the wisdom and wonder available through fly fishing, I've reached some strange new territory in my life where I'm about to concede what so many have learned before me. That is, the best reason to indulge one's passions in this all-consuming silly game is the people one meets along the way, the friends one makes, the characters one discovers, the stories lived, told, and shared.

The argument might be made, of course, that this particular bit of wisdom, profound though it may be, is available to *everyone* who lives a conscious life, who pays attention to what is and isn't important in the brief light of our temporal existence.

Or, to phrase this last idea from a different angle, isn't it fair to ask: *Wouldn't you meet just as many good people and make just as many interesting friends if you spent your life racing sports cars, growing ferns, attending Anime conventions, playing bridge, or socializing on . . . Facebook?*

Fair to ask, yes. And a question to which I would answer *yes . . .* and *no.*

For it has seemed to me, ever since I sat at a table at Bob Marriot's fly shop signing books alongside the likes of Dave Whitlock, the late Gary LaFontaine, and Seth Norman, that there's a spirit of goodwill attached to the sport, one that extends so far beyond all expectations of courtesy, generosity, hope, and common decency that I can only assume the sport is blessed with more than its fair share of noble and angelic personages.

Either that or else everyone involved in the sport is having so much fun that he or she can't help but be nice to friend, family, neighbor, stranger, and foe alike.

Or, by some grace inherent in the sport itself, good men and good women are attracted to it, because angling has always been, as we know from Sir Henry Wotton, quoted in Walton's *Compleat Angler*, "a rest to the mind, a cheerer of spirits, a diversion of sadness, a calmer of unquiet thoughts, a moderator of passions, a procurer of contentedness, and it begots habits of peace and patience in those that profest and practic'd it."

Yet maybe my own generous attitude toward the people inhabiting my fly-fishing life is exactly what happens when you reach a certain age. Maybe this is what's *supposed to* happen when you begin to glimpse the end—and from here on out the whole point seems to be to share the wealth, protect the resources, and have more and more fun.

Or maybe I suddenly think this way because somebody's injecting something into the avocados I so heartily consume these days.

Or maybe, just maybe—are you ready?—maybe this is what finally happens to you if you fly-fish all your life.

●——————●

Like so many other flies we tie to the end of our tippets, the Amigo is a derivative pattern, not unique so much as it is a combination of good ideas assembled into one. It came to me through Gary Bulla, when I returned to Baja following a fifteen-year hiatus spent trying to hold a marriage together and then, afterward, recovering from these hapless efforts. The Amigo looks more or less like a Gremmie mated to a Clouser Minnow. Or mating *with* a Clouser . . . or at least suggestive of the two flies getting along a heck of a lot better than a husband and wife on the brink of a collapsed marriage.

Returning to Baja after my long exile, I felt slightly awed by the radical changes in flies and fly-tying materials since my withdrawal years before. I've recounted this passage elsewhere. Yet it's worth noting that when I stopped visiting Baja, Bob Clouser's Deep Minnow was a brand-new pattern, and the first Gremmie had not even been conceived. No wonder I'm old enough now that I'm sure I've lived at least half my life. One look at the Amigo, however, suggested that good sense and practical insight were still the guiding principles driving fly design along the saltwater reaches of Baja and Southern California, and I could see immediately why Bulla had made it a member of his very short lineup of must-have flies.

But there was something else about the Amigo—certain aspects about it that made it seem familiar to me, that spoke to the demands I knew so well of stalking fish inshore and in the surf. Tying the Amigo to my tippet reminded me of meeting someone who, for some strange reason, already seems like an old friend. I didn't have to make a single cast, I didn't have to catch even one fish, to know that I had a fly on my leader that, for all intents and purposes, I wouldn't need to change all day.

Funny how we know.

Or maybe not so funny—or even strange—at all.

Interested in the history of the Amigo, where it came from and how it came to be, I phoned Bulla. Of course, I also wanted to thank him for the new cabinet, a welcome addition to any living room that offers no degree of separation from the impressive tumult of the fitful, working, fly-tying station.

"Don't thank me," said Gary. "That friend of yours paid for it. Thank *her*."

I said I would do just that.

"And call Guy Wright," added Bulla. "He's the one who can tell you about the Amigo."

Which is where this fly tale begins to come full circle—how it ends, it seems, practically the same spot it began.

Guy Wright lives in Cleveland now—Cleveland, *Ohio*. But for most of his life he did that California thing, growing up with surf on his mind, backpacking in the Sierra, learning a trade that allowed him time for sport between cobbling together a living. Like a lot of the old crew, he kind of figured out the whole fly-fishing-in-the-surf game on his own, walking the Santa Barbara beaches in Tevas with a 9-weight rod, a good line, a cheap reel, a home-made stripping basket. He learned to cast that whole line, all the way down to the braided backing. And he also learned where the fish are, and where they aren't, and that the ones you want most—the halibut, the corbina, the white sea bass—are feeding predators aiming to make a meal out of your fly.

The Amigo, says Guy, "represents an image, an illusion, of live bait." Right away I could tell we speak the same language. He believes the Amigo should be tied sparsely, suggesting something that's "there but not there," thus triggering the predator to strike. If you read his tying instructions carefully, you'll also see that by leaving the butt ends of his clipped body materials, he creates both gill plates and side fins, a feature that causes a disturbance in the water as the fly is retrieved. Like all Clouser-style flies, the Amigo swims with the hook point on top, and the dumbbell eyes, set far back on the hook shank, give the fly that "jig" behavior that probably has as much to do with the pattern's efficacy as all its other attributes combined.

The more I talked to Guy Wright, the more impressed I was by the spirit of the angler *behind* the Amigo than by the fly he created for the southland surf. The more he said, the more I could tell that I was talking to yet another one of those rarely glimpsed fly rodders stalking the beaches way back when, a guy who certainly would have been a source of insight and information, if not also a friend, had our paths crossed while tracing, when young, the margins of the tides.

The Amigo *is* a simple, elegant fly, an indigenous pattern created by grafting local ideas onto proven rootstock from elsewhere. Yet for me, today, looking down the short slope of life, I see the Amigo as not so much an innovation, but testimony to the wisdom inspired by a kind of fishing that still seems closer to the heart of the sport than anything money can buy—standing at the edge of the ocean casting a fly, believing, like fools and heroes, that something wild is about to straighten your line.

AMIGO

- **Hook:** #1 standard saltwater
- **Thread:** Red or olive Danville 140-denier Flymaster, or similar,
- **Eyes:** Red dumbbell (small or medium)
- **Body:** White Supreme Hair or similar and white synthetic yak hair or similar
- **Gill plates:** Butt ends of body materials clipped to stand behind eyes
- **Gills:** Red marabou
- **Lateral lines (optional):** Peacock herl
- **Upper body/fins:** Layer of light olive Supreme Hair or similar, followed by another layer of darker olive Unique Hair or similar

Tying the Amigo

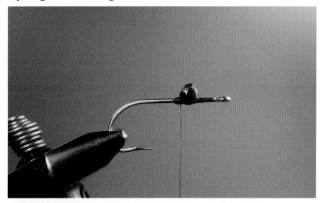

1. Start the Amigo much as you would a Clouser Minnow. Create a bump of thread wraps about one-third the length of the hook shank back from the hook eye. Hold the dumbbell eyes against the forward side of the bump and lash the eyes in place. A little glue or other saturating adhesive helps secure these thread wraps.

2. While the fly is upside down (opposite the way it will swim through the water), tie in the lower half or belly of the body beginning with a layer of white Supreme Hair that extends about two hook lengths past the bend of the hook. Using tight thread wraps, force the butts of the hair to stand up directly behind the dumbbell eyes.

3. Repeat with a layer of synthetic yak hair or similar crinkly material, again forcing the butt ends to stand up straight. Clip the butts of both belly materials so they stand about a quarter-inch proud of the dumbbell eyes. These butt ends create the impression of gill plates.

4. Clip a small tuft of marabou plume fibers from the middle of a feather. Clip the butts so that the length of the fibers will extend to the bend of the hook, with the butts standing up about even with the gill plates. Secure the marabou directly behind the dumbbell eyes, again using tight thread wraps to make the butt ends erect.

5. If you choose to create lateral lines, tie in the peacock herl now. I like them, knowing full well they may disappear after a fish or two. Since lateral lines are located somewhere in the middle of both sides of the body, position them along the lower edges of the material tied in so far.

6. Rotate the fly in the vise. Forward and opposite the dumbbell eyes, tie in a sparse tuft of light olive Supreme Hair, followed by a darker shade of Unique Hair. The aft tips of these two materials should extend about even with the material tied to the opposite side of the hook. Now create a tidy head with thread wraps, whip-finish, and saturate the head with lacquer, your favorite head cement, or a coating of UV-activated epoxy.

KOGA'S BONE

Koga's Bone, designed by Peter Koga

(Note: Peter Koga passed away in the spring of 2019. He shared this pattern with me years before at the Northwest Fly Tying Expo, held annually, pre-pandemic, in Albany, Oregon. A gracious tying instructor and upbeat storyteller, Koga always proved a welcome stop at these events as I wandered about, often a wee bit bleary-eyed, looking for a fly to tie or write about or maybe even fish.)

In a pinch I could claim this a surf fly, one that can reliably fool perch and croaker, maybe even a corbina now and then, and leave it at that. Anybody with any experience tying for the surf will recognize a host of proven attributes: small size, sparse body, inverted hook and weighted eyes, a wing that says nothing more than *I'm alive!* I wouldn't hesitate to pitch the fly anywhere fish are grubbing about the shore break. All the better if I could find a little trough or riptide, a deep spot or pinch of current that stirs up the bottom, exposing what all to fish feeding on the push of an incoming tide.

Or I could use it the next time I fish for carp.

But most readers will immediately recognize the fly for what it actually is, a version of a Crazy Charlie, perhaps the most successful template ever created for flies tied specifically for fooling bonefish. And from a goodly portion of this same erudite group, I can anticipate a uniform howl of dissent: *What the hell do I need with a bonefish fly?*

Funny you should ask.

For a long time now we've all heard reports of bonefish getting caught in San Diego Bay—not necessarily by fly rodders, but genuine Pacific bonefish (*Albula esuncula* or, more recently, *A. gilberti*) nonetheless. Now and then there are also claims made from Mission Bay, Dana Point Harbor, Newport Bay, Huntington Harbor, Alamitos Bay, and, in the opposite direction, from Estero Beach below Ensenada. All such reports share a hint of the fantastic; they're usually secondhand, at best, and the sense is that each is another case of a weird anomaly, like someone hooking striped bass off the Ventura river mouth or bluefin tuna just outside the La Jolla kelp beds.

Yet the seas are big and there's so much we still don't know. Plus, there's the odd tilt to the climate these days, such that nothing seems too far-fetched, even if we can't quite imagine bonefish ghosting the inshore wash, snatching sand crabs as if corbina haunting shadows beneath foamy lies.

Or so all things bonefish stood for me—until I began poking around in the surf outside Baja's Magdalena Bay.

●——————●

I didn't have to go far when I decided to look for a genuine bonefish pattern, something more specific than the Clousers and common baitfish flies I used to fool those first Baja bonefish. Why I thought I needed a pattern other than those perfectly effective surf flies probably has a lot to do with how I ended up writing a fly-tying book, yet might reflect as well some of the same interests—or compulsions—of readers of the same. If all I hoped to accomplish in this sport was catching fish, I'm sure I would have given it up long ago. What it is I'm actually after remains anybody's guess, but finding new fish in new waters, and then proceeding to the vise to tie flies designed for that specific species in those specific lies, goes a long ways still, effecting a sense of clarity in the face of so much else that seems fuzzy or caked in mud.

Now, where was I?

I had met Peter Koga the previous year. It was at one of those venues where tyers from five different states gather to demonstrate patterns and skills that most of the rest of us consider beyond the pale. Koga, however, was tying a little surf fly that seemed both doable and something that might actually catch fish. From Huntington Beach, Koga fished water I was familiar with—but as we got talking, I soon discovered the real target for this and many of his flies was the bonefish that haunt the flats sprinkled about the islands of Hawaii.

We don't need to hear about another distant bonefish destination, other than to say that Hawaii is the real deal, with big spooky bones that test every aspect of an angler's game. Peter Koga qualified as a genuine pioneer of Hawaiian bonefishing, and even though the islands' flats have far more in common with Caribbean or other tropical waters than they do with anything found in California or even Magdalena Bay, I recognized elements in Koga's flies that urged me to pay attention.

As luck would have it, Koga was tying another bonefish pattern when I ran into him the following spring at the same tyers' venue as the previous year. A precise, graceful tyer, Koga gave off an air of quiet confidence that I expect he carried to the water, although I'm sure he got as excited as the next guy when a bonefish ate. Only when pressed did he sheepishly offer possible names for the fly: Magic Charlie, Peter's Magic, Koga's Magic. It's a Crazy Charlie—but with the usual tweaks and subtle variants that work their way into patterns that eventually become our own.

I don't take careful enough notes to replicate anybody's pattern perfectly. Of course, there's also the challenge of locating specific materials, especially if the guy tying selects just the right hair from the whole tail of an animal that most suppliers sell patches of the size of a 99-cent chip brush. Which is only to say that the fly described *isn't* exactly Peter Koga's pattern—but it's close enough that he gets all the credit, unless the slight changes I've made screwed it up somehow so that it fails to fool even a lowly surfperch.

I don't think so. Besides the classic elements of a Crazy Charlie, what intrigues me most about the pattern is its color and segmented body. Has anyone done a better job of creating the impression of the ubiquitous ghost shrimp? If there's one thing California bonefishers agree on, it's the use of ghost shrimp as bait. Steelheaders employ orange in their General Practitioners and the like, but otherwise it's not a color I turn to with any frequency. But here Koga fashioned an orange that looks less like juice and more like the translucent tint of the youngest, tenderest *Noetrypaea californiensis*.

Does color matter? Does size, profile, or the precise difference between bead-chain and dumbbell eyes? When I emailed Koga after taking up so much of his time at the tying venue, he wrote back to say that I shouldn't get too excited about his fly. "You've been fishing long enough to know," he said, "that 80 percent of catching fish is presentation." Which is like telling a doctor that diet and exercise is the best prescription for health. *I* know the fly's not the answer. But the next time I find Pacific bonefish rafting like mullet in the inshore wash, I'll have one more thing to believe in as I try to make the cast.

KOGA'S BONE

- **Hook:** #4-6 Gamakatsu SL11-3H or similar
- **Thread:** Tan 8/0 Veevus
- **Eyes:** Gold bead chain ($\frac{5}{32}$")
- **Tail:** Two strands clear Flashabou and two strands yellow Krystal Flash
- **Body:** Amber D-Rib (medium), tied over tan Veevus Body Quill
- **Underwing:** Pink bonefish wing Ice Fur
- **Overwing:** Tan arctic fox

Tying Koga's Bone

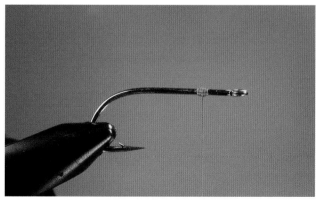

1. Secure the hook and start your thread. As I've suggested elsewhere, create a bump of thread wraps just forward of where you intend to position the eyes, in this case about one-quarter of the hook shank length back from the eye of the hook. This bump of thread helps to stabilize the eyes.

2. Position the eyes just aft of the thread bump. Because of the slender wrist between them, bead-chain eyes seem easier than dumbbell eyes to secure. Go across the wrist in one direction with a dozen or so wraps, then the other direction with a dozen or so more. Tighten the wraps by winding around them, staying above the hook shank and beneath the eyes, again using a dozen or so wraps. Repeat the entire process. Finally, add a drop or two of lacquer or head cement or UV-activated epoxy to the entire lashing.

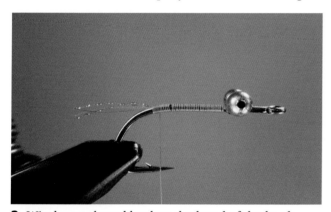

3. Wind your thread back to the bend of the hook. Double a length of Flashabou around the thread and secure it to the hook shank. Do the same with a length of Krystal Flash. With the tailing material secure and reasonably aligned, clip them evenly about ¾ inch long.

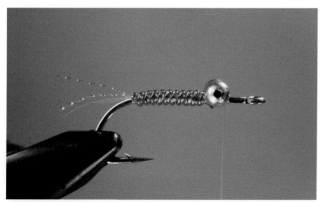

4. I'm ambivalent about adding an underbody other than thread wraps to this fly, but I'll include it because Peter Koga did something similar with his pattern. First attach a length of D-Rib, securing it at the root of the tail so that when wound forward the round side of the material will be away from the hook. Hold the D-Rib aside. Attach a length of body quill, also at the root of the tail. Advance your thread to just aft of the eyes. Wrap the hook shank with the body quill. Then cover the body quill with wraps of D-Rib set one against the other. Secure behind the eyes and clip excess.

5. Advance your thread just forward of the eyes. Turn the hook upside down by rotating your vise or removing and reinserting the hook in the jaws. For the underwing, use a slender tuft of Ice Fur and secure it just ahead of the eyes on what's now the top of the hook. Ice Fur is so easy to work with as a winging material that it's easy to overdress a fly. Don't—more is *not* better. Clip the Ice Fur so that the wing ends about even with the bend of the hook.

6. Koga tied the overwing of this fly with material clipped from a beautiful tail that he bought for twenty bucks from a guy at an East Coast fly show. You probably won't have that luxury. Instead, you'll be tying from a fluffy swatch that seems mostly underfur, rather than the actual hairs you really want. Do the best you can. Start with a big tuft, rake out as much of the underfur as you can, and hopefully you'll be left with enough hair to constitute a wing. You don't need too much. Pull out the longest hairs so that the tips are somewhat aligned. Tie in the wing so that it extends just past the bend of the hook. Clip excess. Fashion a smooth head. Whip-finish and saturate the head with lacquer or your favorite head cement.

ALL SYN MINNOW

All Syn Minnow, designed by author

We're going to have to get past the fact, right here at the start, that this pattern was triggered by the problem of fifty-fish days. Nothing repels a reader more quickly than a writer who dwells on his own remarkable success: Our gut feeling is that the fishing must just be easy; anybody could load up. Besides, don't you have something better to do?

I recall reading a story a guy from a local river asked me to critique, a piece in which he described, in passionate detail, how he caught one steelhead after another with a fly he touted, naturally, as the latest and greatest. And the truth is, for two seasons running I had seen this same guy absolutely hammer fish. There was a rock; he knew exactly where to stand; he had just the right amount of sink-tip on his line—and he could make that cast all day long, swimming his clever little pattern right where the steelhead lay.

In twenty years of serious steelheading, I've never seen anybody hook and land so many fish. Not even close. And when the guy wasn't there, I jumped right into his spot, mimicking his every move, right down to the fly he had shown me—and catching nothing more than had I swung a lawn chair downstream.

The guy's story? As a teacher, I've often failed to uphold my fundamental pedagogical tenet: *Do no harm*. Then again, you're asked for help.

"It's pretty good," I said, glancing away as the river behind us sighed. "But you probably don't need to use the word *whammo* so many times."

I get it. If I'm going to write about problems with flies holding up under the assault of fifty, or thirty, or even five fish, I need to be careful. And if I tell you this problem occurs while hooking all sorts of groovy fish from remote beaches where footprints other than my own rarely mar the pristine sand, I should expect a fair number of readers to quit the page as surely as if I began writing about politics, religion—or my most recent bout with skin cancer. Yet everyone out there, I suspect, has experienced the same felicitous problem—when the fishing heats up to the point that flies are singed into thin shadows of themselves. It happens. And though most of us would gladly accept a box full of trashed flies now and then for a shot of wide-open sport, others in the crowd might view these same ruined flies as a prodigal waste of time, money, or resources. Can't we do any better than that?

If nothing else, maybe we can agree on this: Who wants to stop and replace a winning fly when the fish are going bonkers?

●━━━━━●

Let's begin with the Brooklyn Bridge.

If you recall anything from the hundreds of hours you've spent watching Ken Burns's public television documentaries, you remember that the cables holding up this massive testimony to humankind's technological ingenuity are, in fact, surprisingly thin pieces of steel wire spun together to create cables of fabulous strength. Of course, the principle of this steel rope was nothing new; sailors and shipbuilders had been relying on fibers spun together for as long as somebody needed to stay connected to an object with a tool longer than a stick. Today, what's remarkable is how many items rely on this same Brooklyn Bridge technology—how many things we use that are made of thin fibers spun together to make material that's both flexible and strong.

Woven straps, belts, your backpack or luggage, maybe all of your sporting attire and a good deal of the camping gear that goes with it—most anything, as well, that you tie a knot in or use to secure things to your car or boat or pet—nearly all share the Brooklyn Bridge technology in which a bunch of fine fibers, by themselves thin and relatively weak, become tough, durable products capable of withstanding much more wear and tear than the individual fibers of feathers and hair that fly tyers historically rely on.

You can see where I'm going with this. But don't get me wrong: I'm a huge fan of natural materials, whether it's genuine wood (not *ply*wood) for boats, wool sweaters, hog bristle varnish brushes—or oiled leather for wherever two hard surfaces meet and rub. Also, it's not my intent here to sing the virtues of synthetic fly-tying materials for tying "better" flies; if I anticipate seeing a big roosterfish, I'll have feather and hair on the hook every time. I will argue, however, that synthetic materials hold up better to toothy fish. What's more, because these synthetic fibers are found virtually everywhere, you're never far from *something* you can use to create a pretty fair saltwater minnow or other baitfish fly.

How about the webbing from an old beach chair? I got the idea from an longtimer in Baja who made billfish jigs by lashing a strip of webbing to a hook and then combing out the individual fibers. Cool colors; tough as nails. I'm particularly proud of my own Paracord Minnow, an olive-over-white baitfish pattern tied from the soft crinkly fibers I discovered by using an awl and an eyebrow brush and carefully teasing apart both the inner and outer material that has the quiet colors and subtle contrasts that I look for in most of my saltwater flies. And there's good stuff in almost every tie-down strap you can find; I've combed out fibers that, I'm sorry, rival anything that shops and wholesale suppliers have to offer, material you can use as wings, dubbing, tails—or a twisted-floss segmented body that will make your Salmonflies the hit of the next *Pteronarcys* party.

This notion that we're surrounded by man-made products composed of fibers we can use for flies is nothing new. For many of us, an acceptance of synthetic material on our tying benches began with Antron. That's what you needed to tie Gary LaFontaine's Sparkle Pupa, a fly that formalized the more impressionistic effect most of us had learned to obtain with our traditional soft hackles. I will confess I never thought much about my use of Antron, whether or not it violated some sort of aesthetic or even moral principle, until Tom McGuane mentioned in an essay some flies made out of "carpet fibers"—a statement that had nearly the same effect on me as when he described, in passing, a guy showing up at a high-end camp with his rods carried in "sewage pipe"—the same stuff, I suspected, I had used for years for my own rod tubes.

Still, carpet fiber or not, Antron also worked well when used as wing (actually the *over*wing) material for LaFontaine's Diving or Spent Caddis, a fly I began to use at all depths and on all occasions caddis were anywhere near the river. Then it showed up as a trailing shuck on my emerging mayflies, as a wing for spent spinners, and, occasionally, twisted tight, as an intriguing ribbing material for the segmented abdomens of both nymphs and big dries.

Tying for salt water, both the surf and, later, bluewater panga fishing, I was easily seduced by all manner of synthetic materials. Over the course of my career, as attention to saltwater fly fishing grew dramatically, the range of materials for tying saltwater patterns kept pace, to the point that one faced a bewildering choice of things sparkly and bright, in colors often associated with certain recreational antics in the 1960s.

What many saltwater anglers soon discovered, however, was that in some situations (casting to those big roosterfish, especially), *flash* was a drawback; often synthetics ended up looking wrong in the water—*too* bright, the wrong color, sometimes just *weird.* Like others, I returned in large part to traditional hair and feather, not for aesthetic reasons, but only because it seemed empirically to reduce the number of painful occasions that a big, heart-stopping fish suddenly veered off, refusing the fly.

But the downside to natural materials, their limited durability, has grown more and more apparent to me as I've found better and better fishing along the Baja coast. Some of this, I believe, is what happens to hair when you dye it; it loses much of what can make it nice to touch, becoming brittle as straw—or uncooked pasta. And, really, if you wanted your favorite bucktail streamer to last, you could probably treat it with bear fat and linseed oil and extend its life through a few dozen more fish. Sun and salt water also grind away at our flies, although the damage to your natural materials may be no worse than what happens to plastic-based synthetics.

Still, short of rusting hooks, by far the most serious damage inflicted on your saltwater flies comes from the fish themselves. Each year I have to remind myself—usually after blood has already been spilled—to use pliers on *every* fish, no matter how small, that I bring to the beach. Fish in the ocean nearly all eat other fish; teeth, obviously, play a big role in the predator's game. There may be vegans out there; I'm not sure. But most fish that chase and eat a fly have weapons in their mouths that help them grab and latch on to things trying to get away. Also, in a pinch, to defend themselves—even against do-good anglers trying to return them safely to the water.

Don't get me wrong: I'm perfectly willing to tie one-fish flies—that is, flies I know won't last but have what I need to fool a single good fish. I trust I'm not alone. Nearly all flies, no matter how delicate, actually hold up better than we might imagine, and we've all had the experience of a tattered fly working better than when it was fresh out of the box. But believe me, I'd tie a fly out of the seed head of a dandelion if I thought it would trigger a rise from a dour steelhead.

Still, durability becomes a factor when you've found a bunch of fish willing to eat, whether they're surfperch or skipjack tuna. Or you've ventured off without your vise for all of the reasons that at home make perfect sense—until you find yourself faced with a depleted stash or the inside dope on a killer pattern that money can't buy, even if you could find a local supplier.

I won't go into judgments about recycling, sustainability, and the like, other than to mention that anything we can use and reuse again and again is generally a sound option—and in the case of the All Syn Minnow, the choices for creating a fly both effective and durable are all but endless.

Maybe even *too* many choices. I wrote out a list of materials I might use for an all-synthetic minnow or baitfish pattern, sticking to what's available at a couple of shops where I get tying supplies. I filled an entire sheet from an 8½ by 11 notepad. Narrow ruled. I'd be a liar—or a salesman—if I told you that one of these materials fools more fish than another. And you can bet if I claimed I'd discovered a new product that creates minnow patterns fish can't resist, something else—new and better—would come along soon.

In the meantime, this one—*whammo*—ought to hold up fine.

ALL SYN MINNOW

- **Hook:** #2-2/0 Mustad 34007 or similar
- **Thread:** Olive 70-denier UTC Ultra Thread
- **Tail:** White Super Hair
- **Body:** White EP Fibers
- **Underwing:** Olive Supreme Hair
- **Overwing:** Olive EP Fibers
- **Lateral line:** Chartreuse Sea Hair
- **Belly:** White Slinky Fiber
- **Topping:** Olive synthetic yak hair
- **Gills:** Red Krystal Flash
- **Eyes:** Yellow hologram eyes (¼")
- **Head:** Five-minute or UV-activated epoxy

Tying the All Syn Minnow

1. Secure the hook and start the thread. For the tail, tie in a fairly sparse tuft of Super Hair that extends about twice the shank length beyond the bend of the hook.

2. Clip a tuft of body fibers about twice the length of the tail. Forward the root of the tail, tie in the body fibers so that they extend just short of the tips of the tail. Then split in half the material forward the tie-in point, lay each half alongside the hook shank, and lash in place. At this point you can begin shaping the fly with judicious snips of your scissors.

3. Secure a sparse tuft of Supreme Hair along the top of the fly. The underwing should reach the shortest portion of the body material.

4. Secure on top of the underwing a tuft of the softer EP Fibers. Ideally, the wing material should be about twice the length of the underwing. Fold the material that's forward the tie-in point and lash it over the wing fibers already in place. This doubling over of both the body and wing materials creates an especially durable fly.

5. For lateral lines, I've grown fond of a few strands of fairly coarse Sea Hair rather than the more typical Krystal Flash. Lash in three or four strands along each side of the fly. The effect is subtle enough that it's hard to see in the accompanying photos, but to my eye the overall look of the fly appears more lifelike.

6. For the belly, turn the fly upside down and attach a short tuft of Slinky Fiber. The belly material should end up extending just beyond the bend of the hook and covering most of the thread wraps along the length of the hook shank.

7. For the wing topping, right the fly in the vise and tie in a tuft of synthetic yak hair. Is synthetic yak hair more durable than the real stuff? You decide.

8. For gills, again spin the fly upside down. Just forward the tie-in point of the belly, tie in a short tuft of red Krystal Flash.

9. Use your thread to fair the forward taper of the fly. Whip-finish and coat the thread wraps with lacquer or head cement or UV epoxy. To finish the fly, affix eyes; I find a hot glue gun helps with this sometimes aggravating step. Or position the eyes, drop a bit of UV epoxy where they touch the fly, and shine your light to hold the eyes in place. Finally, brush or drip more epoxy between the eyes to even out the head, and then activate with your UV light.

ED'S GRUB

Ed's Grub, designed by Ed Simpson

Just to put this in perspective, I should mention, right here at the start, that Ed Simpson is the only guy I know who has been fly fishing in the Southern and Baja California surf longer than I have. There are others, sure—but our paths haven't crossed. Or if they have, I wasn't aware of it—probably because it was some old fart, just like me, who you can't imagine as a young buck up to his waist in the shore break, double-hauling against the heavy bend of a thick-butted fiberglass rod.

I first met Ed while still throwing chrome lures with jigging rods with my buddy Peter Syka at Black's Beach in La Jolla. Two things immediately impressed us about Ed. One, like us, he was that rare surf angler who was using artificial lures at a time when the sport was, by definition, a static waiting game played with pyramid sinkers or sand-filled tobacco sacks, a bucket of sand crabs or mussels—and maybe even a sand spike. Ed had a lightweight spinning rod matched to a classic Mitchell 300 reel, and with a little lead-headed rubber jig he was working the edges of the deep hole that often formed in spring those years following the big winter swells out of the north.

Peter and I were far enough into the juju of artificials in the surf—and the sometimes miraculous sport these fresh techniques could conjure—that we could tell Ed was the real deal. And when Ed looked down the beach and saw us firing our Kastmasters and chrome Krocodiles far beyond the surf line with our light-tipped

jigging rods and conventional-wind reels, he had to have noticed, on occasion, the sparks jumping from the tips of our rods, too.

He called us the Iron Men.

The other thing about Ed that impressed us was that he had a key to the gate at Black's—in our eyes an all but royal privilege that allowed him to drive his VW Bug down the private road and park in the little lot right above the beach.

Only later did I discover that Ed was a refugee from the same sort of humble interior suburbia from which Peter and I had escaped. Hometown? San Bernardino. Husband and new father, I ran into Ed again at a nursery he turned out to own between Cardiff and Encinitas, a place that specialized in aquatic plants. I had a little brick-lined patio pond at my house in Oceanside. Since I'd last seen him fishing, Ed had become something of a local pond guru—while at the same time raising some of the loveliest water lilies found anywhere in San Diego County.

We hit it off. A sun-bright welterweight, Ed seemed possessed of some sort of manic zeal that made him as enthusiastic about healthy ponds and aquatic habitat as he was about fish and fishing—and utterly distractible from one moment to the next. A spring visit to Santa Fe Nursery to pick up a few oxygenating grasses would turn into an all-morning affair as Ed, talking to three customers at once, scampered from one pond to the next, stuffing plastic garbage sacks with dripping plant material. Then there were fish I needed, and snails, and then Ed would remember something he wanted to show me in the drafty A-frame, half greenhouse, half loft, that he shared with his wife and daughter—and off we would go to look for an essay or photo in an old garden or fishing book, or a snapshot from a recent trip to trout country a thousand miles away.

Or remnants of Baja travels. Ed knew the turf, some of the same sacred tracts that I haunted—and to equally alarming effect. For years Ed and his wife traveled in the inner circle of the intrepid Baja field biologist Dennis Bostic, who dropped dead at thirty-eight after walking away from a Jeep that he had just finished piling up into a tree. Around the same time, Ed got his first saltwater fish on a fly, a San Ignacio Lagoon corvina caught on a popper. Tragedy we understand, but nobody comes away from his first saltwater surface strike unchanged—more so, perhaps, back when only a handful of anglers had ever called up such spirits before.

It was Ed's stories, I should add, that inspired my first trip to San Ignacio. Ed gave me directions and a sophisticated boat compass to pass along to Francisco Mayoral, the official gatekeeper when the lagoon was designated a reserve to limit tourist access to this important nursery for breeding and nursing gray whales. Was it illegal to fish in the lagoon? Francisco took one look at Ed's gift and said go right ahead.

Ed was also the first person to mention to me that I might be interested in reading something by a writer named John Gierach.

We kept in touch. To this day Ed has never embraced the use of computers, and I welcome his handwritten notes and postcards, with misspelled and crossed-out words and often a handful of processed photos printed from honest-to-god film. For years Ed and his wife owned a plot of land in central Oregon, so it seemed somehow fitting that I should guide him into his first steelhead, back when a dozen such fish made for a good week rather than a whole season. Ed also had inside dope on some of the classiest trout water in the West: A buddy still rents the house next to the Nature Conservancy at Silver Creek; before dying, old John from Encinitas used to take Ed each fall to the reservation water on one of the best stretches of brown trout water in all of Wyoming.

And while all this and, of course, much more was happening, Ed and his wife were also slipping off to a reach of tidewater south of the border, a place Ed has asked me to "whitewash" if I ever mention it in writing so that readers don't show up and crowd him out on the tongue of the next flood. All I can say is that Ed's found himself a spot that's a textbook replica of everything enchanting about Southern California inshore fly fishing. As far as he's concerned, there's no place else he'd rather call home.

After thirty-five years, Ed has a right to lay at least partial claim to his little slice of paradise. Over time he's built a beachside cabaña, complete with kitchen cabinets fashioned from redwood salvaged out of an Encinitas greenhouse torn down to make way for North County gentrification. He fishes out of a thirteen-foot Boston Whaler with a two-stroke Yamaha 40. The tide goes in and the tide goes out—and Ed gets his share of bass, corbina, halibut, and a host of more exotic species that show up during El Niño years, all the while fishing almost exclusively with the simplest of flies tied to replicate the little rubber jig Peter and I saw him fishing with all those decades ago below the end of the road at Black's.

There's something refreshing about a fly tied to imitate nothing so much as a similar deception from another genre of the angling arts. Here we begin to approach the deepest roots of the sport, a form of alchemy we would be wise to regard when trying to design our next so-called lifelike imitation of, say, the anadromous phase of the California killifish *Fundulus parvipinnis*. What makes a fish strike? Why does it eat this fly and not another? Ed has pushed the limits of simplicity with his stripped-down grub—a rabbit-fur replica of the famous rubbery Kalin's Grub—but is there anything about it that suggests it needs any other element than what's already there?

Ed doesn't think so. What you have, in fact, is a remarkably *bold* fly, a single confident brushstroke that announces its unambiguous guile without retreat into hedged bets or affectation. Ed's Grub is as subtle as a nightstick. It makes a Clouser Minnow look as if it were created by Winslow Homer.

If it were a poem, it would be William Carlos Williams's red wheelbarrow.

Which is why we won't find Ed's Grub this year in anybody's catalogue—or on a list of "Must-Have Flies for Inshore Lunkers!" The concept's too simple. *I* could've thought of that. It's the sort of fly that actually irritates a certain school of fly angler—those who think there's something low or unsporting in a pattern without pretense of imitating any form of life found in the natural world.

Forty years ago, Ed didn't know any better. He just wanted to catch fish in the ocean on flies. He'd fished the rubber Kalin's Grub for ages; he fashioned a fly that looked like one. Until I started this essay, the fly never even had a name.

ED'S GRUB

- **Hook:** #2 Mustad 34007 or similar
- **Thread:** White or cream Danville 3/0 Waxed Monocord or similar
- **Eyes:** Plain, unpainted dumbbell eyes (small, medium, or large)
- **Body:** White or cream rabbit fur strip

Tying Ed's Grub

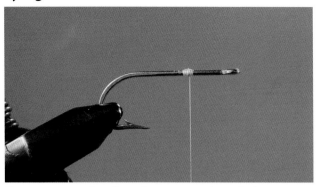

1. Secure your hook and start your thread about one-third to halfway back from the hook eye. Create a small lump of thread aft of where you will secure the eyes.

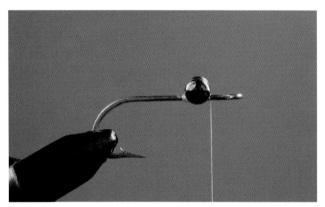

2. We've covered techniques for securing dumbbell eyes in other patterns. A few things to remember: First, position the wrist of the dumbbell tight to the forward edge of lump of thread. Then take five or six wraps in one direction, aft to forward, across the dumbbell wrist, then five or six, forward to aft, in the opposite direction. Square the eyes to the hook shank if necessary. Repeat the cross-wrist wraps. Now—and here's the most important step—bring your thread *above* the hook shank and begin winding the thread around the existing thread wraps, keeping your thread parallel to and above the hook shank, much as if you were tying the base of a wing post for a parachute fly. These wraps around the thread wraps and *between* the dumbbell eyes and the hook shank lash and tighten the forward and aft wraps, creating a grip you can't get no matter how many figure-eights you might use around both the shank and the dumbbell wrist. At this point I also saturate the thread wraps with the same lacquer I use for head cement. (Since the point of Ed's Grub is the efficacy of simplicity, I might as well add that I refill my head cement jar from the same gallon of high-gloss industrial lacquer that I bought at least fifteen years ago. When the viscosity of the stuff in the jar changes the least bit, I dump it and, using a plastic syringe, draw out another jarful from the gallon can where, after all this time, the lacquer remains as clear as Scotch and as runny as warm maple syrup.)

3. Cut a strip of rabbit fur about two or three times the length of the hook shank. Clip the fur from the forward ⅛ inch or so and then taper the remaining exposed skin. Secure the tapered piece forward of the eyes, at the same time creating a conical head with your wraps of thread. Wrap back to the eyes, pass behind them, and secure the rabbit strip with several more turns of thread.

4. When Ed ties his Grub, he whip-finishes and applies head cement after step 3. That's it. Done. An inveterate tinkerer, I've added another step—difficult to see in the image shown. After securing the rabbit strip behind the dumbbell eyes, I spiral the thread, back and forth, through small sections of fur, much like tying an old Matuka streamer. Now I begin to think I've got a fly that has something of a dorsal fin. Or more to the point, maybe the divided fur creates the impression of the segmented rubber body of a Kalin's Grub. I'll mail Ed a couple of examples and see what he thinks of these superfluous efforts.

MY MULLET

My Mullet, adaptation of design by Jeff deBrown

We had seen the mullet when we first walked up the beach, stalking a fringe of rolling shore break. A long sandbar extended perpendicular from shore; a confusion of chop and colliding currents, waves spasming this way and that, marked the boundary of the wide boca between two islands and what felt like beaches exposed to the open Pacific. The small school of mullet hovered in the deep hole on the windward edge of the sandbar; current and rips had carved out what was surely a sweet spot, an invitation to a long line hauled against a heavy head, launching the fly into the mystic.

Then they were gone. Joe and I scoured the hole with casts angled into the light midmorning wind; I tried wading out onto the sandbar until I was belly deep, tangled with the crisscrossed waves. Joe thought he might have seen the sparks of a small roosterfish. When nothing more showed, we ventured farther out along the open shore, searching for that rare confluence of waves and currents—and God knows what else—that translates into prime surf-fishing water.

The tide was dead low by the time we returned to the mullet hole. Joe passed the sandbar and continued along the bend of the beach that soon transformed into the edge of the boca, more of a tidal channel than the rough-and-tumble open shore. I hung back. I approached the hole a cast and two steps at a time,

much like the rhythm of steelheading, sliding closer and closer toward the wavy contours and emerald hollows at the heart of the hole, all the while thinking *Damn, this is good water.*

Then a fish was on and I was losing line. I hollered Joe's way. I suffered the backing knot rattling through the guides, a knot I certainly hadn't checked in a while. Then it was just between me and a heavy fish, the affirmation, once more, that life is good—despite what so many others claim.

The telling moment saw a foot-long mullet, fresh enough to swim, disgorged from a big halibut's toothy mouth. In the tussle for photos and weighing the beast, we watched two more full-size mullet, in decreasing degrees of freshness, expelled as well. With three of us in camp, and a panga arriving the next morning to ferry us back to where we could get ice, we chose to kill our catch—not an easy decision, ending the life of a big predator, top dog in a deep hole in the Baja surf.

⬤━━━━⬤

The challenge of flies tied to represent or suggest bait the size of mullet makes me hesitant to offer solutions. First, you have to figure out how to construct a giant fly, a particular challenge for traditional anglers practiced in tying flies to catch trout the size, on the average, of the bait they now want to imitate. Then you have to be able to cast the darn thing. Midwest muskie fly fishers deal with these issues, too. John Gierach shared some photos with me after he first got serious about muskie fishing, and I was startled to see what looked like somebody's hairpiece, dangling from the mouth of a fish held proudly for the camera.

Big flies, of course, catch big fish. The only evidence I've ever seen of a fly-caught halibut from the surf anywhere near the size of the recent mullet-belcher was a photo supplied some thirty years ago by my father, who claimed the fish went forty pounds. I still have the fly; it's a crude, double-hooked concoction, sophisticated as a bath toy. The real question is what possessed my father to try casting such a thing in the first place. For the record, my halibut bottomed out Joe's fifteen-kilo handheld scale. I've tried to compare the two fish from photos. Sometimes I give my father's fish the nod because of the dimensions of its outline—while at other times mine looks heavier because of the cross-sectional thickness, its mottled green and brown side raised as if an enormous loaf of freshly baked bread.

I got some fresh ideas about tying big flies for the surf from Jeff deBrown, the experienced guide out of the cape region of southern Baja. DeBrown chases, among other things, big roosterfish—another mullet lover—along the beaches near Los Barriles, the popular gringo fishing and windsport destination, little more than a place to launch a panga just twenty-five or thirty years ago. I ran into deBrown in Puerto López Mateos along Magdalena Bay; he was putting clients onto striped marlin, teasing them into casting range behind a dual-engine cat boat before his captain shifted into neutral, giving anglers repeated shots at what, for most of us, would be fish of a lifetime.

I had spent the afternoon tying flies at a table in the Whale's Tale Inn, Bob and Diana Hoyt's bar and recently opened hotel. I finished tidying up materials from my saltwater travel kit; deBrown walked in, a bundle of rods in hand. He asked to see what I'd been tying.

Later that evening, seated at the bar, I studied the contents of a yellow Pelican storm case—a box of deBrown's beach flies. As is usually the case, I was struck by how much more elaborate and refined the flies in a guide's stash are than the flies in mine. DeBrown showed off a current shrimp pattern that would not have spent but seconds in the water of Mag Bay's endless mangrove esteros without getting eaten. He had other flies that seemed models of efficiency and effect, fresh approaches to the problem of presenting bold baitfish profiles in the surf in ways I had never imagined.

But it was his big roosterfish flies that really grabbed my attention. He kept taking them out, one after the other, stroking back the extravagantly long fibers, aligning things just so—and then complaining, as he repositioned the fly in the box, that it was too small, that

each one was a third under size because it had been "chewed on."

How do you create a *big* fly? DeBrown mentioned "brushes." Really? I've described the use of spinning blocks and dubbing brushes elsewhere; readers also know I'm a big fan of using dubbing loops for effects I don't feel you can create with other dubbing techniques. But until I saw deBrown's big beach flies, I had never considered dubbing brushes for my own saltwater patterns.

That's another aspect to this tale—an old dog *can* learn a new trick. A bigger lesson, perhaps, is the intrigue and delight of tying new flies with the limited supplies you carry while traveling. It's not easy; you know you could do a better job if you just had this and that from your vast store of materials back home. But you don't. Some anglers find this problem so daunting that they simply don't attempt tying while on the road. I encourage you to reject this impulse. Very rarely is space so limited that you can't carry some sort of small tying kit: tools, hooks, a smattering of materials specific to the type of fly you may end up tying.

The real challenge is to get over our incessant need to create flies as good as the ones we tie at home. It's just not going to happen. Still, the constraints you face can prove the very thing that stimulates a fresh idea, a new way of using old materials, the invention of a technique you would have never tried with your arsenal of tools on your tying bench at home.

The dubbing brush for My Mullet, for example. The obvious way to create a dubbing brush is the use of some sort of block; you can find all sorts of groovy or even DIY dubbing blocks demonstrated online. But because I had never considered a dubbing brush for my saltwater flies, a dubbing block—or even a dubbing loop tool—was the last thing I thought to include in my minimalist saltwater travel kit.

Silly me.

Not next time.

MY MULTI

- **Hook:** #2/0-6/0 Owner Aki, Ahrex SA280 or SA220, or similar
- **Thread:** Salmon Danville 140-denier Flymaster or similar
- **Undertail:** White synthetic yak hair
- **Tail:** Cream synthetic yak hair
- **Tail topping:** Tan EP Fibers, topped with olive Steve Farrar SF Blend
- **Body:** Olive EP Fibers, spun into a brush, or chartreuse EP Foxy Brush (3")
- **Head:** Thread wraps saturated in several coats of lacquer or covered in UV-activated epoxy

Tying My Mullet

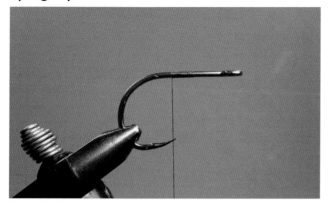

1. Secure the hook and start the thread. Once again, I can't recommend a hook more highly than the Owner Aki—forged, sharp, a multi-edged point. The fly photographed here was tied on an Ahrex SA280 minnow hook.

2. Just forward the bend of the hook, secure about a 4-inch tuft of white synthetic yak hair so that it extends about 2 inches beyond the hook bend. Then fold the butts back along the top of the hook, pull them directly in line with the hook shank, and secure the hair with tight thread wraps, making sure the folded fibers remain on top of the hook. This short undertail will help prevent the long tail fibers, tied in next, from fouling when the fly is cast.

3. Now tie in the actual tail. Use a sparse tuft of fibers about 8 to 10 inches in length—sparse, because you'll double the fibers when you fold them back over themselves. Again, tie in the fibers at their midpoint, just ahead of the undertail. Fold the fiber butts back over the tail and secure with tight thread wraps.

4. Using the same tie-in-and-fold technique, secure first a tuft of tan EP Fibers, followed by olive SF Flash Blend. These materials should extend about the same distance aft as the rest of the tail.

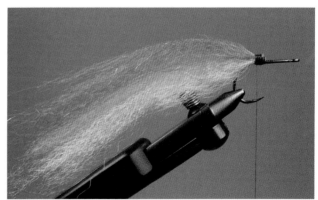

5. If you haven't already developed a taste for dubbing loops and dubbing brushes, now's your chance. Create your loop just forward the root of the tail; the loop itself should be 4 or 5 inches long. From the loop hang a dubbing loop tool or some other weighted device; traveling without all of my tools, I secure a long hook in a pair of needle-nose pliers, held shut with a rubber band, and hang the hook from the loop. Clip fibers about 1½ inch long for your dubbing brush. Separate the legs of the loop and between them begin sliding in a sparse layer of fibers, perpendicular to the legs, starting from the bottom of the loop and working your way up. It's easy to use too many fibers, which end up creating a bulky, hard-to-manipulate dubbing brush. Once the fibers are in place, spin the dubbing loop tool; this is where the weighted tool, even one improvised, works better than, say, just a pair of hackle pliers. As the loop spins, the legs twist, securing the fibers at a right angle to the twisted thread, creating the bottle brush effect you're after. Once your brush has formed, you can spend time teasing out fibers trapped in the rope-like core of the brush before wrapping the brush around the hook. (Or, closer to home, purchase premade brushes. Strip the fibers from one end of the brush and secure the tip just ahead of the root of the tail. As you wind the brush forward, stroke the fibers toward the tail of the fly, keeping them from twisting around the hook shank.)

6. Create a tidy yet substantial head with thread wraps. The purpose of the colored thread is to provide that splash of red or pink or orange that so many saltwater anglers like near the heads of their flies, something that suggests the colors seen in the gills of fish. I fish a saltwater fly with reddish tints near the head with more confidence, even though no fish yet has revealed to me if it really matters. Finish My Mullet by coating the thread wraps with lacquer or UV-activated or five-minute epoxy.

SURF SHRIMP

Surf Shrimp, variation of design by John Makim

I always hesitate before offering up ideas about surf flies. More than any other sort of fishing I do, more so even than steelheading, fly fishing in the surf inspires few anxieties about what to tie to the end of my leader. I'm not as bad as my buddy Ed Simpson, who's fished nothing but his white rabbit-fur grub for the past several decades, on the theory that fish in the surf can't possibly be too choosy, and there's no reason for them to reject anything that looks alive, good enough to eat.

The theory rests, of course, on the assumption that fish near shore or in the surf—or most anywhere, for that matter—are looking for food. Eating and spawning, that about covers any fish's life—besides doing its damnedest as well not to get eaten by something bigger or tougher than it is. Naturally, fish are on the lookout for food they normally see. But just as if I went into a restaurant, hungry, looking for a good burger, should it turn out that's not available, I'll readily take the pizza, the fish-and-chips—or even, God forbid, the fettuccine Alfredo.

That's the theory. I tend to agree. Corbina anglers will argue that you need a good sand crab or mole crab pattern, because that's what these spooky fish are looking for when they slide in over the sand with the inshore wash, a point I concede even though I've caught my fair share of corbina on baitfish patterns and Clousers. Most of my success in the surf, however, has little to do with fly patterns. Instead, I put my faith in reading the water, strong casts, and the willingness to put in the sort of time it takes to find fish moving with the tides.

Still, I understand as much as anyone that a profound and often overlooked appeal of the sport is getting fish to eat patterns we've created to look like bait, of whatever form, that the fish we're after typically feed on. This is the reason many of us moved on from marshmallows, Velveeta cheese, or Super Dupers—despite their efficacy in any number of angling circumstances. It really isn't just about catching fish. Nor, for that matter, is the point of the sport merely to hook and land fish with a fly rod, a fly reel, and a fly attached to a leader on the end of a fly line. Of course, that's what we all try to do. Yet as Ken Kesey said in *Sometimes a Great Notion* about reality, fly fishing, I'd suggest, is "greater than the sum of its parts, also a damn sight holier."

Now, where were we?

My own go-to lineup of surf flies consists of little more than a couple of baitfish patterns, some Clouser-like minnows with dumbbell eyes, a bunch of surface Crease Flies in various colors, and something I think mimics any of a variety of small crustaceans you might see gathered near shore. That's what the Surf Shrimp is all about.

Before a recent visit to San Diego, I tied up a half-dozen Holy Moleys, Al Quattrocchi's sand or mole crab pattern, but then I found myself fishing in an estuary without the sort of rolling wash that sand crabs inhabit. I've written elsewhere about the late Peter Koga's bonefish pattern Koga's Bone, a good little bay shrimp fly I've used with success in Baja's Magdalena Bay. But after seeing the size shrimp grow to by the end of summer and into fall, I've been looking for a more substantial pattern to toss into the troughs and slots found near the edges of surf.

The Surf Shrimp is a very minor variation on the Ultimate Shrimp, a fly tied by Jon Makim in Australia. I stumbled on the pattern while investigating the possibility of a visit to Western Australia, a wild coastline reminiscent of the Pacific reaches of the Baja peninsula before it was tamed by pavement and the heavy influx of gringos from the north. The drive from Perth to Carnarvon is almost exactly the same as San Diego to Mag Bay—same latitudes, only south of the equator. Same fish? Same baits? If my theories hold, what works Down Under should transfer nicely, thank you, into the range of waters we find along our own California beaches.

Like many saltwater patterns, however, especially those that attempt to imitate crustaceans, the Surf Shrimp feels more like something you *assemble* rather than actually tie. Dumbbells, prefab eyes, rubber legs, epoxy—it all reminds me of building model airplanes or model cars, something I was never good at as a kid because I wanted to be outside playing games that involved some sort of ball and a way to best an opponent. Admittedly, this sort of competitiveness still informs some of my efforts at the tying bench: I like nothing better than tying flies I know beyond doubt will fool fish if I can just find and hit the target. The big challenge in surf fishing is locating likely water that holds fish in the first place. Your fly—if you've chosen correctly—should vanish from your thoughts, so that you can bear down on what you need to do to catch fish.

Still, the question remains: How much do patterns really matter in the surf? I've advocated in the past for impressionistic shrimp patterns for steelheading (Ally's Shrimp, Badger Shrimp); is the Surf Shrimp, instead, just another example of a fly created to catch the attention of anglers, a pattern that looks good in their eyes but ends up failing to possess the appropriate juju that actually makes fish eat? No doubt there are plenty of those flies crowding out better, simpler, more provocative patterns in fly boxes carried to surf's edge. But like traditional, old-school soft hackles for trout, it's hard to sell most anglers on a fly like, say, Ed Simpson's grub, tied out of a single strip of rabbit fur.

I was with Ed, armed with my new Holy Moleys, when we failed to find sand crab and corbina water and ended up on the sand spit of a pretty estuary. Ed had tied on his white grub even though he was hoping to catch a bonefish, which are showing up more and more these days this far north, what with changing ocean conditions. I knotted on my version of Peter Koga's Crazy Charlie, Koga's Bone, caught nothing, and quickly switched to one of my standard unweighted baitfish patterns.

Had I already stumbled upon and tied a few Surf Shrimps, this would have been the moment to experiment. Who knows if it would have done the trick? Instead of those bonefish Ed was hoping for, we both caught a share of small halibut—proving, once again, little else but that you catch fish with the fly you keep in the water.

SURF SHRIMP

▦ **Hook:** #2 Gamakatsu SL12S or similar
▦ **Thread:** Clear Veevus Monofil, fine Danville Monofilament, or similar
▦ **Mouthparts/body/tail:** White Unique Hair, Fish Hair, or similar
▦ **Eyes:** Melted 100-lb. monofilament tips, EP Crab and Shrimp Eyes, or similar
▦ **Feelers:** UV orange Krystal Flash or similar
▦ **Legs:** Clear/pearl silver flake Sili Legs or similar
▦ **Head:** Orange or tan dubbing
▦ **Weight:** Black Dazl-Eyes (⁵⁄₃₂") or similar
▦ **Shell:** Five-minute epoxy, UV-cure fly finish, or similar

Tying the Surf Shrimp

1. Mount your hook and start the thread just back from the eye of the hook. If you haven't tied with fine monofilament before, this is your chance to get some and try it out. You'll like the see-through effects with epoxy; plus, it's a lot tougher when you accidentally catch it, while winding aft, on the point of the hook. Lay down a thread base over the entire hook shank and down into the bend. Now fiddle with a tuft of Unique Hair so the aft ends are tapered and then secure the tuft to the top of the hook bend. Secure the entire tuft along the top of the hook shank. Clip the forward ends, leaving about ⅜ inch in front of the eye. Later, you'll clip these forward ends—the "tail" of the fly—even shorter.

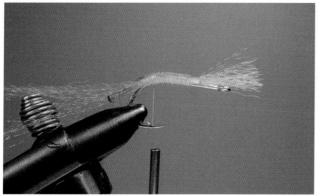

2. Now the eyes. Whether you use the prefabricated Enrico Puglisi variety or make your own eyes by melting the tips of heavy monofilament (for jumbo shrimp I've also used heavy line made for a garden trimmer), it's a good idea to flatten the stalk or stem of the eye with a pair of flat-jawed pliers. The flattened stalk is easier to hold in place along the sides of the hook shank while you cover them with thread wraps. After securing the eyes, trim the base of the stalks so that you have room for the dumbbell weight you'll eventually tie in just behind the hook eye.

3. For feelers, fold a single strand of Krystal Flash over the thread, secure it on top of the hook shank, and position the two halves so that they lie above the eyes and along the sides of the tapered Unique Hair. Frankly, I suspect these feelers are just the kind of thing that are included to catch the attention of anglers and are superfluous to the overall efficacy of the fly. But what do I know?

4. For the legs or skirt of the fly, use the full length of three Sili Legs. At the start of the bend of the hook, secure the legs at their midpoint along one side of the fly. Then fold the other half of the three legs over to the far side of the hook and secure them with more thread wraps, so that you end up with six legs hanging aft of the hook bend, three on each side. At this point, leave the legs, like the feelers, running long; you can come back to them later and trim them as you see fit for the size of shrimp you think the fish you're after feed on.

5. For the head of the fly, form a small dubbing noodle and cover the tie-in bulge left from the legs and feeler. The color of the dubbing—anything from orange to tan—can vary according to the shrimp you encounter in your own waters. After forming the head, clean any excess dubbing material from the thread and make a few more wraps over the dubbing head, tidying it up so that it will be easier to cover evenly, later, with epoxy. (Again, this is an attribute of clear monofilament thread.)

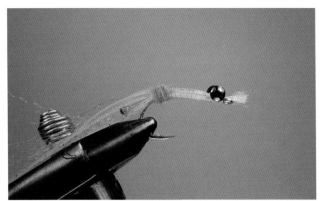

6. Secure the dumbbell weights (in this fly they aren't actually eyes) on top of the hook just behind the hook eye. As always, do whatever you can to keep the dumbbells from spinning or twisting once you're fishing; fortunately, in this case, you'll have plenty of epoxy to help out. At this point you can also do any fairing with thread wraps between the butts of the eye stalks and the dumbbells. Of course, all of this will be covered with epoxy as well.

7. After whip-finishing and cutting off your thread, create an epoxy body that covers the head, the entire hook shank, and the wrist of the dumbbells. Now, I also trim the Unique Hair so that it extends only about 3/16 inch past the hook eye, and I cut the feelers to about whatever length I cut or leave the legs. Although I can't speak highly enough about UV-cured epoxy, I used traditional two-part five-minute epoxy for the example shown here, which accounts for the less than perfectly transparent body. Who knows, but that opacity might actually be "truer to life."

INDEX